DATE DUE

DEMCO 38-296

POWER COMPETITION IN EAST ASIA

POWER COMPETITION IN EAST ASIA

From the Old Chinese World Order to
Post–Cold War Regional Multipolarity

SUISHENG ZHAO

ST. MARTIN'S PRESS
NEW YORK

POWER COMPETITION IN EAST ASIA
Copyright © 1997 by Suisheng Zhao
All rights reserved. Printed in the United States of America.
No part of this book may be used or reproduced in any manner
whatsoever without written permission except in the case of brief
quotations embodied in critical articles or reviews. For information,
address St. Martin's Press, Scholarly and Reference Division,
175 Fifth Avenue, New York, N.Y. 10010

ISBN 0–312–16258–8

Library of Congress Cataloging-in-Publication Data

Zhao, Suisheng, 1954–
    Power competition in East Asia: from the old Chinese world
order to post–cold war regional multipolarity / Suisheng Zhao.
        p. cm.
    Includes bibliographical references and index.
    ISBN 0–312–16258–8
    1. East Asia—Foreign relations.   I. Title.
DS515.Z45   1997
327.5–dc20
                                                    96–28351
                                                        CIP

Interior design by Harry Katz

First Edition: March 1997
10   9   8   7   6   5   4   3   2   1

To my wife, Ren Yi, whose faith in me
has sustained me in my quest for identity.

And to our beloved children
Lillian, Sandra, and Justinian.

Contents

Abbreviations

ADB	Asian Development Bank
ANZUS	Australia, New Zealand and the United States
APEC	Asia–Pacific Economic Cooperation
ARF	ASEAN Regional Forum
ASEAN	Association of Southeast Asian Nations
CCP	Chinese Communist Party
CEA	Chinese Economic Area
CMEA	Council for Mutual Economic Assistance
CPSU	Communist Party of the Soviet Union
DMZ	Demilitarized Zone
DPRK	Democratic People's Republic of Korea
EAEC	East Asian Economic Caucus
EAEG	East Asian Economic Group
EC	European Community
EEZ	Exclusive Economic Zone
EPG	Eminent Persons Group
ESCAP	Economic and Social Commission for Asia and Pacific (the United Nations)
EU	European Union
GATT	General Agreement on Tariffs and Trade
GNP	Gross National Product
IMF	International Monetary Fund
INF	Intermediate–Range Nuclear Force
LDP	Liberal Democratic Party
KMT	Kuomintang (Nationalist Party of China)
MFN	Most Favored Nation
NAFTA	North American Free Trade Agreement
NATO	North Atlantic Treaty Organization
NICs	Newly Industrialized Countries
NIEs	Newly Industrialized Economies
NLF	National Liberation Front
NSC	National Security Council
ODA	Official Development Assistance
OECD	Organization for Economic Cooperation and Development
PECC	Pacific Economic Cooperation Council
PLA	People's Liberation Army
PRC	People's Republic of China
R&D	Research and Development
ROC	Republic of China
ROK	Republic of Korea
SDF	Self–Defense Forces
SCAP	Supreme Commander of Allied Powers
SEATO	Southeast Asia Treaty Organization
SEZ	Special Economic Zone
START	Strategic Arms Reduction Treaty
TRA	Taiwan Relations Acts
UNDP	United Nations Development Program
ZOPFAN	Zone of Peace, Freedom, and Neutrality

The significant difference between the twenty-first century and the preceding centuries is that there will be three centers of world power (Europe, North America, and East Asia) as opposed to two in the twentieth (Europe and North America) and one before that (Europe).

—KRISHORE MAHBUBANI,
Permanent Secretary of Singapore's
Ministry of Foreign Affairs

America is a Pacific nation, and our stake in the region is enormous. No region is more important to the United States and its future than Asia and the Pacific.

—WARREN CHRISTOPHER,
U.S. Secretary of State
in the Clinton administration

East Asia

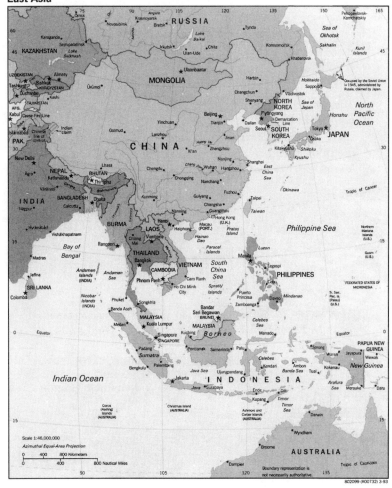

802099 (R00732) 3-93

Preface

The great power competition in East Asia has been in many respects the most critical in respect to determining the basic international trend of our times. Tensions and conflicts in this region have been frequently transmitted to that of the global system. As a 1995 U.S. Defense Department report indicates, "Asian tensions have the potential to erupt in conflict, with dire consequences for global security."[1] The Russo–Japanese War, the Pacific War, the Korean War, and the Vietnam War provided classical examples. The Great Powers have drawn East Asia into their rivalries, because this region is where the geographic reaches of the United States, Russia (the former Soviet Union), Japan, and China come into contact, and it is where the Great Powers have vital political, economic, and military interests. The importance of East Asia in the international arena was further enhanced during the last few decades when it experienced a dramatic political transformation and led the world in rapid industrialization and commercial expansion. Some people even predict the arrival of a Pacific century in which the center of the global distribution of power will move from the Atlantic region to the Pacific region, where East Asia holds a position of central importance.[2]

Nevertheless, there have been remarkably few attempts to systematically analyze the dynamics of power competition in this critical region, although many fine studies of the East Asian political economy have been published in recent years.[3] The reasons behind this ignorance may be twofold. First, in recent decades, East Asia has been the site of rapid economic growth and intensified industrialization that has attracted worldwide attention and emulation. The East Asian economies in 1960 comprised 14 percent of the world's GNP. By 1991 this number rose to 25 percent (roughly equal to that of the United States). By the year 2020, they are projected by Singapore's former prime minister, Lee Kuan Yew, to account for 40 percent of the world's total GNP, as compared to North America's 18 percent and the European Union's (EU) 15 percent.[4] In 1993, seven leading East Asian economies had 41 percent of global bank reserves, up from 17 percent in 1980. According to World Bank's estimates, Asia will account for half of the global GNP growth and half of the global trade growth in the decade from 1990 to 2000.[5] Due to the dramatic economic dynamism, most scholarly attention on East Asia concentrated on models of economic development rather than patterns of strategic interactions among the great powers. In other words, the geopolitical power competition has been overshadowed by unrivaled economic dynamism in the region.[6] The field of East Asian international relations still, at this very late date, lacks comprehensive works covering the whole period from the early nineteenth century to the present, except a few classics published in the 1950s and 1960s that have served as standard texts.[7]

Second, since the contemporary international system acquired its present shape and definition with the emergence of a nation–state system in Europe, contemporary international relations theory has taken its shape primarily by the study of European interstate politics and is essentially European–centered. It has been customary to assume that East Asian nations, including China and Japan, were absorbed into the international systems dominated by European countries and the United States, and that the vital issues of war and peace in East Asia were largely decided by great power competitions in other regions or on a global scale.[8] This assumption certainly contains partial truth. Europe and North America have held the world's concentration of wealth and been at the center of global power competition in the past several centuries. Nevertheless, global wealth and power distribution has been changing as the twentieth century approaches.[9] As Kishore Mahbubani, Permanent Secretary of Ministry of Foreign Affairs in Singapore, indicates, "the significant difference between the twenty first century and the preceding centuries is that there will be three centers of world power (Europe, North America, and East Asia) as opposed to two in the twentieth (Europe and North America) and one before that (Europe)."[10] In view of the dramatic change in global power distribution, we must reconfirm if the knowledge of international relations that is extrapolated from European and North American cases is adequate to understand other parts of the world, in particular East Asia.[11] As a newly emerging center of the competition for world power, it is time for scholars to integrate East Asia into the mainstream study of international relations.

This book is an attempt to provide a comprehensive analysis of the power competition in East Asia, a region that was once so weak that western powers, while intensively involved politically and economically, felt little need to seriously understand or accommodate it.[12] East Asia has recently witnessed such profound and powerful economic and political development that a systematic survey of international relations in the region is an urgent need. This book grew out of years of frustration developing reading lists for my students in order to provide a theoretical perspective to identify general trends in East Asian international relations based on the analysis of important historical events. Its aim is to offer a systematic resource, historically comprehensive and theoretically coherent, for those who are interested in the evolution of power competition in East Asia. It attempts to apply the traditional realist theory of international relations to the case study of East Asia in a historical sweep covering the period from the decay of the Chinese world order in the nineteenth century to the vanishing of superpower rivalry and emergence of a regional multipolarity in the post–Cold War era.

With this objective, this book does not intend to develop a completely new theoretical perspective or a distinctive conceptual framework of international relations. Rather, it is a synthesis and enrichment of many perspectives scattered across much of the latter–day monographic literature. It seeks to incorporate East Asian power competition into the mainstream studies of international relations. This book is not a monograph rooted in primary sources. It relies largely on the best and most recent books and articles found in major libraries, although some primary sources such as personal memoirs, government documents, and newly available Chinese publications on diplomatic history, wherever possible, are included. As a theoretical survey of East Asian power competition, it does not seek to cover all historical events and every country in the region. The scope of this book is largely confined to the boundary of Northeast Asia and concentrates on major events involving China and Japan, the two most important regional powers. The western powers and the events that took place in Southeast Asia are discussed largely in the context of Northeast Asian international relations.[13]

The book is composed of eleven chapters. Chapter 1 is an introduction to the theoretical approach utilized in this book. Chapter 2 provides a background survey of the Chinese world order and its decline in confrontation with the western powers. Chapters 3 through 7 present an analytical history of power competition in East Asia from the late nineteenth century to the end of the Cold War in the late 1980s and serves as a basis for understanding the evolution of the post–Cold War era. Specifically, chapter 3 examines the rise of Japan and the fall of China in a comparative perspective and explores the origins of the Sino–Japanese War in 1895 and the Russo–Japanese War in 1905. Chapter 4 examines the multilateral efforts of Washington Conference System in maintaining peace in the 1920s and explains the Pacific War largely as a result of Japan's attempts to secure its economic and security needs unilaterally after the failure of multilateralism in the 1930s. Chapter 5 analyzes the origins of the Cold War bipolar competition in East Asia with an emphasis on the impacts of Communist victory in China and the outbreak of the Korean War. Chapter 6 investigates the deterioration of the bipolar system in terms of the Sino–Soviet dispute and Japan's reemergence as an economic giant. It also examines the Vietnam War and its legacies. Chapter 7 examines the dynamics of the strategic triangular relationship among the United States, the Soviet Union, and China during the last stage of the Cold War.

Chapters 8 through 10 discuss the recent developments in the post–Cold War era. Chapter 8 investigates the changes of power competition in nonmilitary dimensions. Chapter 9 deals with the difficult regional cooperation efforts when growing economic interdependence poses a regional approach toward power competition. Chapter 10 examines the emerging regional multipolarity and the movement from the Cold War alliance to the post–Cold War alignment relationship. Although the United States does not geographically belong to East Asia, it has been involved culturally, militarily, and economically in the region since the eighteenth century. A brief exploration of U.S.–East Asian relations with respect to policy objectives concludes the book. For those who wish to pursue additional reading on the subject, a selected bibliography on the existing literature is provided.

I began to structure the book when I taught a course on East Asian International Relations for the first time in the Department of Political Science at the University of California, San Diego (UCSD), in the spring of 1993. I have continued my research and taught on the subject since I came to Colby College in the fall of 1993. During the past four years of teaching and writing the book, I have profited from my colleagues and students at both UCSD and Colby. In particular, I am thankful for the intellectually encouraging and supportive environment at Colby College. I learned a lot from my distinguished colleagues in the Government Department, especially Tony Corrado, Kenneth Rodman, Calvin Mackenzie, Sandy Maisel, and Guilain Denoeux, who demonstrate that one can be an excellent teacher and, at the same time, a distinguished scholar in a fine liberal arts college. I would also like to thank my students. The Colby campus, located in the most northeast corner of the nation, has drawn increasing interest from students of East Asia and a group of individuals who are respectful of my hard work. Just as glorious, sun-filled afternoons in the spring remind me why I endured the brutal winter of Maine, the rich time of sharing my knowledge with students rewards me for the struggles and makes the rough spells worthwhile. The college has also provided generous support and facilities for faculty research. My research trips to China in the summers of 1994 and 1995 were partially funded by Colby Social Science Research Grants. The librarians, particularly Chuck Lakin, at the Miller Library, have been extremely helpful. Colby Faculty Manuscript Service staff proofread my manuscript. Daniel Beaudin and Ying Lin served as my research assistants.

I benefitted from comments and criticisms from colleagues in other institutions at professional conferences where portions of the book were presented. Part of chapter 7 was presented at the American Political Science Association Annual Convention in Chicago in September 1995, and part of chapter 9 was presented at the International Studies Association Annual Convention in San Diego in April 1996. I would like to thank Walter Mattli, Nanette S. Levinson, Mark Selden, June Tuefel Dreyer, and Jay Parker for their constructive comments. Also, the final revision of the book was guided by concrete comments and suggestions from a number of anonymous referees at several presses who read the entire book manuscript although I was able to publish this book only with one of these presses. Michael J. Flamini, Senior Editor at St. Martin's Press, impressed me greatly with his quick action and effective work style at the manuscript reviewing stage. As always, the author is solely responsible for the accuracy of facts and views expressed in the book.

This book is dedicated to my wife and children. In particular, it is for my wife, Ren Yi. I owe an enormous debt to her. As a chemist graduating from Qinghua University in Beijing, one of China's elite universities, she had a prominent career in one of Beijing's research institutes under the Ministry of Civil Affairs before joining me in the United States on Christmas of 1985. Since then, like wives of many Chinese students pursuing academic degrees in the United States, she has sacrificed her own career to struggle together with me in a country where she still has difficulties with language and culture. To her, I am deeply grateful.

INTRODUCTION

SCOPE AND DIVERSITY OF THE REGION

The importance of East Asia as a region is buttressed by its sheer size and remarkable dynamism, which imply considerable regional diversity and complexity. This makes efforts to understand the region's evolving international relations a very challenging task.

Among the major cultural and geographical realms of the world, the East Asia mainland, especially the heartland of China, has the longest continuous advanced civilization.[1] With well over a billion people, the East Asia mainland is the home of more than one-quarter of the world's population. It is isolated from the rest of the world by the high plateaus and mountains of Asia and by the broad expanses of the Pacific Ocean. From Europe it was indeed the "Far East," in spite of the fact that, with the advent of modern ocean shipping and aviation, the isolation has been largely penetrated. Although the Chinese imperial writ extended from time to time far into Tibet and Central Asia, the heartland of China along the Yellow River was protected by the mountains and plateaus of Asia before the Europeans came to the region. Occasionally conquerors came into China; for example, the Mongols invaded China from the west in 1279, but were quickly absorbed and Sinicized, as were the Manchu conquerors after 1644.

The forests and cold expanses of Siberia protect East Asia from the north. The abruptly rising mountains, deep valleys, and tropical vegetation along the southern boundaries cut off China and Northeast Asia from easy access to South and Southeast Asia. The Pacific Ocean with its vastness, its currents, and its storms further isolate East Asia from the rest of the world. The festoons of islands and peninsulas that border its mainland area have historically faced inward toward the continent rather than outward toward the Pacific Ocean. Maritime activities were confined largely to short internal movements within East Asia, tying the maritime periphery to the continental core area. In the last century, however, with the opening of world trade and communications, this peripheral maritime area, particularly Japan, Taiwan, and the Southeast Asian countries, has faced outward to a greater extent and become newly industrialized centers.

Though East Asia has a uniqueness among the large cultural, economic, and political realms of the world, it has within it great geographical diversity. This diversity has developed as a consequence of variations in the physical character of the land, of the varying diffusion of ethnic and cultural traits, and of the contrasting economic, social, and political developments that have taken place. As a scholar of East Asian geopolitics indicates, "because of this geographical diversity, East Asia has significant internal contrasts in its patterns of lands and peoples."[2] A variety of ethnic groups, cultural traditions, economic systems, and political ideologies has existed in East Asia. If countries are grouped, as Samuel Huntington did in his 1993 controversial article, in terms of their culture and civilization, East Asia would be a fascinating and critical region to test the "clash of civilization" thesis, for this area includes at least five of Huntington's seven distinct groups of major civilizations.[3] The countries of Northeast Asia tend to share a common cultural legacy from its source in China. Japan, Korea, Taiwan, Hong Kong, and Singapore are deeply influenced by Confucianism. The Southeast Asian countries are a rather heterogeneous group. This is because they are geographically located at the intersection of Indian, Chinese, Middle Eastern, and Western cultural influences. Thus, for example, there are a variety of religions practiced throughout the region. It can be found that Islam is practiced in Indonesia and Malaysia, Buddhism in Thailand and Cambodia, and Catholicism in the Philippines. As a result of earlier immigration, some countries such as Singapore and Malaysia also feature considerable ethnic diversity.

The impact of modernization and Westernization has been of great consequence in the changing political and economic face of the lands in East Asia. New political, economic, and social patterns developed after the decline of the relatively benevolent Chinese World Order of the nineteenth century. The China-centered East Asian world order, though weakened from time to time, stood through centuries. But it was not able to withstand the impact of Western ideology concerning sovereign nation-states.[4] Today the modern nation-states of Japan, the Republic of Korea (ROK), the Democratic People's Republic of Korea (DPRK), the People's Republic of China (PRC), the Republic of China (ROC) in Taiwan, the British colony of Hong Kong and Portuguese province of Macao, as well as the Republic of Singapore and other ASEAN countries, Vietnam and other Indochinese countries, are in rivalry and contention, jealous of their national sovereignty and territory. The forms of government and the political systems in each of these nation-states contrast greatly with each other. At the wake of the post–Cold War era, East Asia contains three distinctive types of political and economic systems. First, Japan is a highly industrialized society that has had democratic institutions since the end of World War II. Second, South Korea, Taiwan, Singapore, Thailand, the Philippines, and Hong Kong have capitalist economies based on the principles of market competition. They have in recent years liberalized their political system to allow more personal freedom and electoral contest. Third, North Korea, Vietnam, and China have the Leninist version of socialism, where the government instead of the market assumes the primary role of determining the supply and the price of goods, and political dissent is still not tolerated. Although China and Vietnam have been in recent years successfully reforming their economies toward a market system, the political control remains.

Economically, East Asia embraces a large number of nations at very different levels of development. Their populations range from the world's largest, China, with 1.2 billion, to one of the smallest, Brunei, with less than half a million. The levels of their development range from the world's wealthiest, Japan, with a per capita GNP of more than $31,000, to those such as China and Indonesia with less than $1,000; and to the East Asian Newly Industrialized Countries (NICs) clustering at $5,000 to $15,000.[5]

In addition to the great diversity in ethnic and cultural traits, political systems, and economies, there are a number of persistent local security theaters in the region.[6] At the core of each theater there is often an adversarial relationship: on one side is the power or powers in possession of the disputed value—the so-called have or status quo powers—and on the other is the power or powers that want to obtain it—the so-called have-not or anti-status quo powers. A selected list would include the Taiwan Strait where China and Taiwan jockey for control of Taiwan; the Sea of Japan where Japan and Russia are in dispute over the ownership of the islands to the north of Hokkaido; the Korean peninsula, where North Korea and South Korea are locked in a struggle at least for survival and at most for peninsular control; the Sino-Russia border where China, Mongolia, and Russia still have forces arrayed in a confrontational posture; the South China border where Chinese forces eye those of Burma, Laos, and Vietnam; Indochina where peace and stability still depend upon the cooperative efforts of Vietnam, Cambodia, China, and the ASEAN states; and the South China Sea where ownership of the Spratly and Paracel islands is hotly disputed by China, Taiwan, Vietnam, the Philippines, and Malaysia.[7] All these local theaters are linked together or overlap in what may be termed larger subregional theaters. For example, the Taiwan Strait, the Sea of Okhotsk, the Korean Peninsula, and the Sino-Soviet border local theaters are linked together in the Northeast Asian subregional theater, in which the power balance among the United States, China, Russia, and Japan make up a system that affects the outcomes throughout the subregion. Similarly, one may identify a Southeast Asian subregional theater, where the balance is among the locally limited powers of the ASEAN and Indochinese states and the locally available power of China and the United States.

In the last episode of the Cold War era, three of the participating powers —the United States, the Soviet Union, and China—were key players and formed a strategic triangular relationship in most local and in the two subregional theaters. In the post–Cold War era Russia has played a less important role while Japan's influence has increased. Many small and mid-sized powers are vitally concerned with the balance of power among the Big Four (China, Japan, America, and Russia). Beyond this region, of course, are other regions where some East Asian states are engaged. Most important for all states is the overarching global theater engaged in only by those nations that are interested in and capable of countering threats globally as they occur. Obviously, East Asia is only a part of that vast theater, but it is an important part. Thus, although the security map of East Asia of the West Pacific may seem more complex than that of most other regions of the world—especially Europe of the Atlantic region—the complexity does not arise because of irrationality or because it is constructed from generically different material. What distinguishes East Asia from other parts of the world in this regard is the multiplicity of its theaters and the diversity of emphasis given them by participating states.

Due to the diversity in economic, political, cultural, and security issues, tensions and conflicts have been frequent in East Asia. Although the passing of the Cold War has somewhat lessened military and ideological tension, it has not removed most of the potential sources of conflict left by history and nor has it prevented new causes of conflict from appearing. For example, China and Korea have remained as the only two divided nations in the post–Cold War world after the reunification of Germany in 1990. The Korean peninsula is still a hot spot of potential conflict. The future shape of Korea and the manner in which it is decided will be matters of intense concern to the United States, China, Japan, and Russia, to say nothing of the Korean people themselves. Potential conflicts in East Asia exist also between mainland China and Taiwan. It is still uncertain if the division across the Taiwan Straits will be resolved through the use of force.[8] In addition, some historical legacies, especially the rivalries between Japan and other East Asian countries, have not been completely removed. In the meantime, new sources of conflict are arising. There has been mounting economic friction between countries on opposite sides of the Pacific Ocean. The East Asian trading nations have been very successful in penetrating the consumer markets of North America and have amassed large surpluses in trade with the United States. This has aroused strong sentiments of protectionism in the latter. The United States has had the largest trade deficit with Japan for many years, running about $40 billion annually. The United States also incurred a deficit in its trade with China every year since 1983. Although initially trivial in size, the deficit grew rapidly after 1985 and was $22 billion in 1993.[9] In 1990, China recorded the third largest deficit with the United States. Beginning in 1991, China's deficit became the second largest, exceeded only by Japan.[10] The large and growing trade deficits have underlined many contentious issues in the relationship between the United States and many East Asian countries.

While the diversity in East Asia may create tensions and conflict, it does not necessarily prevent nation-states in the region from cooperating on economic and security issues. The growing intraregional trade and capital flows have dramatically increased economic interdependence among East Asian nations, which, in turn, has led to the emergence of "growth clusters," that is, economic networks forming without regard to, and often despite national borders, based on geographic proximity and history linkages as well as on comparative advantage, especially in labor costs. Until very recently, East Asia has been largely devoid of regional cooperative and integrative institutions. Nevertheless, the recent institution-building efforts of the Asia-Pacific Economic Cooperation (APEC) has forced East Asian nations to rethink their neighbor relationships. As a region East Asia is now in the midst of significant structural and institutional change, which may eventually lead to substantial reorganization of power competition.

THREE DIMENSIONS OF POWER COMPETITION

Power is a crucial factor in the international politics of East Asia just as in other part of the world. Some realists argue that power is the single most important element in determining the course of international competition.

Other scholars would reject this view as an overstatement, but few would deny the importance of power. The realist theory of international relations characterizes international politics as "a struggle for power not only because of the inherent logic of a competitive realm such as world politics, but also because of the limitless character of the lust for power which reveals a general quality of the human mind."[11] International political process commences "when any state seeks through various acts or signals to change or sustain the behavior (for instance, the acts, images, and policies) of other states."[12] Power is thus defined by realists as the general capacity of a state to influence the behavior of others or as the ability to get others to do what they otherwise would not do. In a similar fashion, Akira Iriye, an international cultural historian of East Asia, states that power in international relations is the way in which states "respect, defend, or infringe upon each other's sovereignty and independence."[13]

Theoretically speaking, power in the international sphere may be divided into three dimensions: military, economic, and cultural. In reality, these dimensions are closely interdependent and it is difficult to imagine a country possessing one kind of power in isolation from other for any length of time. Nevertheless, it has taken a long period in recent history for East Asian countries to realize that "power is an indivisible whole,"[14] and includes all three dimensions.

In comparison to their European counterparts, East Asian countries came to realize the importance of military power relatively late, not until the mid-nineteenth century when European gunboats opened the Chinese and Japanese seaports. Military power then became the most important dimension in East Asian international relations because, ever since, each has had to justify its existence by its ability to defend itself. Defensive or offensive, the ability entailed military power, actual or potential, exercised unilaterally or in combination with the power of other countries. For many decades between then and the end of World War II, military power competition dominated East Asian international relations. Newly emerged nation-states saw the mighty nations of the West primarily as "military powers, with strong arms, a powerful class of military leaders, and overseas bases, colonies, and spheres of influence."[15] Potential war was thus a dominant factor in East Asian international politics, and military strength became a recognized standard of political values. In this region, just as in most other regions of the world during that time, powers were graded according to the quality and the supposed efficiency of the military equipment at their disposal. Such equipment included manpower. An authoritative scholar, Edward H. Carr, stated in his description of Europe, "recognition as a Great

Power" was normally "the reward of fighting a successful large-scale war."[16] Realizing the importance of military power, the East Asian great powers, China and Japan, had determined to transform their nations into military strongholds. The power framework of East Asian international relations defined nations fundamentally as military powers. Power was not construed solely as armed forces but included demography, natural resources, productivity, technology, and similar things that could enhance military force. States were seen as greater or lesser powers depending on the size, extent, and effectiveness of their armed forces. East Asian international relations, in short, were defined as military power competitions.

However, states may pursue power not only through the acquisition of military power and the use of force but also through economic power. Economic strength has always been a pragmatic instrument of political power although its effectiveness was recognized primarily through its association with the military instrument for some time in human history. In recent decades, many nations have sought influence via economic activities, such as trade, shipping, investment, and migration. A group of East Asian Newly Industrialized Economies (NIEs), most successfully Japan and the four small tigers (Taiwan, Hong Kong, South Korea, and Singapore), have been known as "the trading states"—nations that expand their resources through economic development and foreign trade. From the Sino-Japanese War in 1895 to the end of the Pacific War in 1945, Japan launched repeated campaigns of military conquest in an attempt to establish its regional hegemony. These military actions turned out to be an utter disaster. Nevertheless, through trade and economic development, Japan, a defeated nation in the Pacific War, became the third largest industrial nation in the world before the end of the Cold War and is the second largest after the collapse of the Soviet Union. Thirty years after its military defeat, Japan obtained the international status and influence that it was not able to gain by military force. As Richard Rosecrance points out, this development demonstrates "the advantages of economic approaches to world power and global influence."[17] In light of the growing importance of economic power, Japan and East Asian NIEs, now including China and several other Southeast Asian nations, have vigorously pursued their economic power and successfully turned their economic strength into political clout in the post—Cold War world. Japan and China are surely contenders for hegemonial patrimony in the post—Cold War East Asia. From these experiences, East Asian nations have gradually learned that military capacity and economic activities are both vehicles of power. They bring prosperity and preeminence on the world stage.

In addition to military and economic dimensions of power, culture can also be a vehicle to influence the behavior of other nations. Here culture is defined anthropologically as a system of symbols or structures of meaning that provides order for a given set of individuals. In a sense, military force and economic activities may comprise the "hard" core of power whereas cultural pursuits and interactions may belong to the realm of "soft" power.[18] The cultural dimension of power in this contest is different from what Edward Hallett Carr called "power over opinion," which emphasized "propaganda as a distinctively modern weapon" in the annals of statesmanship.[19] Cultural power in the context of East Asia is not simply an "art of persuasion." It is, in David D. Laitin's words, "hegemonic." It provides a "framework of values" that each country "either adapts itself to or loses its ability to guide action outside of its functional domain."[20] In his study of Asian political culture, Lucian Pye argues that, in East Asia, "political power is extraordinarily sensitive to cultural nuances . . . Asian cultures have historically had a rich variety of concepts of power." According to Pye, Asian countries shared "the common denominator of idealizing benevolent, paternalistic leadership and of legitimizing dependency. Thus, although Europe did succeed in imposing on Asia its legalistic concept of the nation-state, the Asian response has been a new, and powerful, form of nationalism based on paternalistic authority."[21]

Indeed, before the arriving of Europeans, the China-centered East Asian order was maintained not merely by the military and economic forces but also by the superior Chinese culture and the virtue of the benevolent Chinese emperor. The cultural dimension of power was downgraded for some time during the late nineteenth and most of the twentieth century. In the last a few decades, certainly in the post–Cold War era, however, there has been a growing re-awareness of cultural dimension of international relations in East Asia as well as in other part of the world. As Samuel P. Huntington suggests, "with the end of the Cold War, international politics moves out of its Western phase, and its centerpiece becomes the interactions between the West and non-Western civilizations and among non-Western civilizations."[22] The East Asians believe that Westerners had difficulties in understanding East Asian civilizations and often misunderstood the non-Western societies. The overconcern over the issue of human rights reflects a cultural misunderstanding between the East and the West. Therefore there is a need for "a fusion of Western and East Asian cultures."[23] This gave rise to "cultural diplomacy" as a means to promote national interests and enhance power positions in East Asia. It was over the long road of power competition during the last one and a half centuries that East Asian nations gradually realized the importance and interdependence of all three dimensions of power competition.

A NEOREALIST APPROACH

Since its advent as a discipline, international relations has defined the boundaries of theoretical debate by the discourse between the realist and liberal visions.[24] The historical evolution and, particularly, the unfolding three dimensions of power competition in East Asia may be studied in the context of the realism-liberalism debate.

Realism perceives the world as an anarchy in which there is an absence of a common sovereign and each state must look out for its own survival. For the realist, the central problem of international relations is war and the use of force. Classical realism focuses on human nature while neorealism emphasizes structural attributes of international system in explaining the causes of international conflict and war. On crucial issues—the meaning of international anarchy, its effects on states, and the problem of cooperation—neorealists are very much in accord with classical realists.[25] Neorealists believe that war happens because there is nothing in the anarchical system to prevent it when countries would rather defend conflicting claims than relinquish them. Without any supranational enforcer, each state must be vitally concerned about the level and effectiveness of its military power vis-à-vis its adversaries. Military power determines whose claims prevail, so peace must flow from a balance of power that convinces states that the costs of enforcing or resisting claims exceed the gains. According to the balance of power theory, states balance military power to preserve their independence and security and the balance of power behavior has preserved the anarchic system of separate states. The state is under imperatives to increase, decrease, maintain, use or abandon military power, depending, first, on whether it sees itself as a status quo or anti-status quo power, that is, whether it does or doesn't have the international values it desires; and second, on whether it views the trend in the international balance of power, that is, in its own strength vis-à-vis its adversaries, as favorable or unfavorable. "These imperatives are simple ones, not essentially different from those felt by schoolboys on their first day in the schoolyard; but they are powerful ones, felt by all states in every region of the world."[26] In the neorealist image of international relations, the distribution of power is the most important concern of nation-states.[27] Neorealists describe an international system where there is one preponderant power as unipolar. In a bipolar system, two major centers of power, either two large countries or two tightly knit alliance systems, dominate international politics. A multipolar system has three or more centers of power. The concept of the distribution of power helps make predictions about certain aspects of states' behavior and their propensity toward war and peace.[28] Unipolar systems tend to erode as states try to preserve their independence by balancing against the hegemony or a rising anti–status quo state eventually challenges the leader. In multipolar systems, states tend to form alliances to balance power, but alliances can be flexible. Wars may occur, but they can be relatively limited. In bipolar systems, alliances become more rigid, which in turn contributes to the probability of a large conflict, perhaps a global war.[29]

Since its outset, the realist paradigm has been faced with a major challenge mounted from diverse perspectives grounded in the liberal—or its subset, the so-called idealist—theoretical orientation.[30] Liberal theorists have cast doubt on the "power of power politics."[31] Classical liberalists believe that power politics and the balance of power system are morally unacceptable and need to be replaced by more humane global structures. They also believe that global cohesion can be strengthened through increased functional interdependence. During the last half of the nineteenth century, British liberalists, for example, advocated "peace through trade" in the belief that unregulated international commerce would promote peaceful international relations. In recent years, liberalism has been expressed increasingly through a modified version known as neoliberal institutionalism. According to neoliberalists, although nation-states continue to be important international actors, they possess a declining ability to control their own destinies. In the context of trade across borders, communication between peoples, and the creation of international institutions, the realist view of pure anarchy is insufficient. The agenda of problems confronting states has vastly expanded. A liberal critique of realism is that realism cannot account meaningfully for the new issues and cleavages that define today's global agenda. In the wake of the Cold War conflict, the critic views a window open to expose a view of international relations that realism largely ignores. "The problem . . . today . . . is not new challengers for hegemony; it is the new challenge of transnational interdependence,"[32] and it appears probable that "welfare, not warfare, will shape the rules and global threats as ozone holes and pollution will dictate the agenda."[33] Attention to military power is by no means misdirected, but concerns for welfare, modernization, environment, and the like are today no less potent sources of motivation and action. Many liberals therefore define power in terms that are broader than the geomilitary spheres. Some neoliberalists even believe that the emerging transnational problems will produce new nonterritorial loyalties that will change the state system and make non-state actors and international organizations as important as state actors.[34]

The historical context and recent conduct of East Asian power competition for military, economic, and cultural strength coincide more with the vision of realism than liberalism. Military power has always been the central concern in the region since the nineteenth century. East Asian countries have demonstrated a strong territoriality and the unilateral use of military means to defend national boundaries even after the end of the Cold War. These actions persist despite their evident economic success and their dependence on the international economy. The "trading state" is tilted toward concern for territorial acquisition and military capacities rather than national goals of economic welfare and cultural hegemony. Therefore, while the liberal view may become more applicable in the future, the realist approach is the most appropriate for the study of East Asian international relations in the twentieth century.

Since the downfall of the China-centered tributary system, the nation-state system has exhibited intrasystemic variations consonant with the tenants of neorealism, particularly with the balance of power. Prior to the arrival of the Western powers in the mid-nineteenth century, China was a proud and strong country that overshadowed other Asian nations and maintained ethnocentric foreign relations for centuries. There were no concepts such as nation-states, let alone interactions based on the principle of state sovereignty. It was distinctly an age before international relations. Only after China was defeated by Britain in the Opium War of the nineteenth century, was the Chinese hierarchical world order replaced by an anarchic nation-state system. The Western notions of sovereignty and modern diplomacy were then introduced into East Asia, and international relations were transformed into one of military power competition. As seen through realist theory, since then, East Asian nations, just like their counterparts in other parts of the world, have been taking actions to increase or decrease their military capacities in response to their perceptions of the balance of power. For example, China, as a status quo power in the late nineteenth and the early twentieth centuries, had to increase its military power because it perceived the balance of power to be unfavorable to its security, whereas Japan, as an anti-status quo power in the same period, saw imperatives to increase military power at any situation. After the decisive defeat in the Pacific War, Japan became a status quo power and was forced to decrease its military forces.[35]

Ever since the decline of the Chinese empire and the emergence of the anarchic nation-state system in East Asia, military capacity has become the most important source of security for all nations and access to dominant positions by the great powers. War was irrevocably fought between or among nation-states for national security and military dominance. Thus, all East Asian states, just like their counterparts in other parts of the world, were caught by a security dilemma that is an essential characteristic of anarchic international system. Under anarchy, independent action taken by one state to increase its security may make other states more insecure. The others, seeing the first getting stronger, may build their strength to protect themselves from the first. The result is that the independent efforts of each to build its own strength and security makes every state more insecure. "It is an ironic result, yet neither has acted irrationally."[36] These states act not from anger or pride, but from fear caused by the perceived threat of growth in others. After all, building defenses is a rational response to a perceived threat. The causes of most major wars in East Asia, namely, the Sino-Japanese War in 1894-95, the Russo-Japanese War in 1904-05, and the Pacific War in 1941-45, can be traced to the security dilemma. Even Japan's initial interest in continental East Asia was defensive, rather than an expansionist attempt. Key-hiuk Kim, a Korean scholar, noted that Japan's concern was primarily "how to defend Japan from Russian aggression."[37] The origins of two major wars fought in the region during the Cold War era, namely, the Korean War in 1950-53 and the Vietnam War in 1968-75, were also caught in the security dilemma. The ideological division between communism and capitalism only intensified the conflicts.

From the early twentieth century to the late 1980s, the power distribution in East Asia experienced several changes, ranging from the abortive Japanese dominated unipolar system, known as the Greater East Asia Co-Prosperity Sphere in the 1930s, to the early Cold War bipolar alliance system, to the loosing quadrilateral system, to the strategic triangle in the 1970s and the early 1980s. These systemic variations had not taken place beyond the decentralized, self-helping nation-state system—one in which power and responsibility remained in the hands of the constituent states. The key to the system was the ability of one state or a coalition to balance the power of another state or another coalition so that it could not gobble up smaller units and create a universal empire. In other words, the balance of power was the most important concern of East Asian power competition.

The historical development of East Asian international relations, especially the military centered power competition, conforms largely with the realist image of international politics. After the end of the Cold War, states in East Asia have not rid themselves of the security dilemma that pertains to the realist tradition. In the neorealist fashion of power competition,[38] self-interested nation-states continued their competition for territorial integrity and military capacity while recognizing economic interdependence and devising cooperative regional economic and security forums and institutions. With the collapse of the Soviet Union and the drawdown of U.S. forces, there has been increasing competition between the regional powers. Many countries in East Asia have determined to enhance their "defense self-reliance" in order to handle regional contingencies out of their own resources.[39] After the rivalry of the superpower vanished and with increasing resources available due to the economic growth, East Asia has been "rushing to arm itself as never before."[40] It is ironic that in spite of the evident success of East Asian economies internally and internationally, very few East Asian countries have really reduced their military expenses. Japan, often cited as the paragon of the new trading state, has increased its military spending significantly during the late 1980s although it remains a conventional, not a nuclear, power.[41] China has also steadily increased its military expenditures in recent years.[42] Figures for other East Asian countries vary but are also significant.[43]

Some scholars predict that Japan will become a world power with commensurate political and military interests and China will become a regional military hegemony after its successful economic modernization. Indeed, there is the possibility that trading states will be assimilated into the military-political realm. Although it would be very unlikely for Japan or China to follow the United States or the former Soviet Union to become the world's leading naval or military power in the foreseeable future, the very possibility brought about by the economic success in these two countries has made many of its East Asian neighbors nervous and forced them to turn their wealth into arms. Here the issue is not that posed by Rosecrance that the American model would ultimately be followed by Japan or the Japanese model might be ultimately followed by America.[44] Rather, we are witnessing an interaction of economic and military power competition in post–Cold War East Asia where trading states not only depend upon open trade and commercial routes to produce their goods but also seek military guarantees to their domestic stability and external market. Thus, a parallel development of power competition has emerged in post–Cold War East Asia. On one hand, the success of economic development has induced many East Asian countries to redefine national security to include nonmilitary dimensions and facilitate regional cooperation efforts. On the other hand, they have continued a hundred-year-long effort to strengthen their military capabilities. The dispute between China, Vietnam, and the Philippines over the Spratly islands, the tension between China and Japan over the Senkaku (diaoyu in Chinese) island group, and the clash between mainland China and Taiwan over the sovereignty of Taiwan island after the end of the Cold War have made clear that old-fashioned territorial disputes persist in the new age of economic interdependence.

One important new development in the post–Cold War era has been the regionalization of power competition in East Asia. During the period of the Cold War, superpower competition first between the United States and the Soviet Union and then the China-America-Russia strategic triangularity overshadowed the attributes of the distribution of power in the region. The end of the Cold War facilitated the rise of regional (local) powers such as China and Japan while reducing the role of global (outside) powers such as the United States in the region. Regionalized strategic interactions became dominant. Under these circumstances, the global dimension of strategic competition becomes less relevant to regional power competition and the worldwide distribution of power no longer governs the regional distribution of power. In strategic terms, the vanished triangle or bipolarity has given way, not to unipolarity, but to an uncertain regional multipolarity. It is still subject to dispute whether movement toward a new multipolarity is prone to instability as predicted by the "back to the future" argument.[45] One thing for sure is that the regional (local) powers play a more and more important role, along with the outside powers, in shaping peace and war in the region.

·2·

THE DECLINE OF THE CHINESE WORLD ORDER

The contemporary international system began to acquire its present shape and definition more than three centuries ago with the emergence of a nation-state system in Europe following the Thirty Years' War.[1] Correspondingly, the traditional image of world order in the West has been the Westphalian model, which derived from the Peace of Westphalia after the Thirty Years' War in 1648. "World order" is used descriptively by scholars as "an aggregate conception of dominant values, norms, and structures as well as of established patterns of actors' behavior that give shape and substance to international society at any given time."[2] The Westphalian model of world order constitutes a traditional approach to regulating a highly decentralized world of sovereign states in the West.[3] It emerged following the system transition from the unipolar/papal hierarchical conception of medieval society, dominated by the Eurocentric Christian commonwealth, to a multipolar horizontal conception of world order based on the coexistence and coordination of sovereign states. The Peace of Westphalia was the starting point for the development of new norms applicable to sovereigns, providing the main normative basis for the state-centric international order. Territorial states became the sole legitimate actors in the international system and the sole subject of international law. International politics has since been defined as politics in the absence of a common sovereign. The principle of state sovereignty has provided the general framework from which evolved specific state practices on war, peace, commerce, and political competition.[4]

World order meant very different things to East Asian countries prior to the coming of the Western powers in the mid-nineteenth century. A China-centered hierarchical world order existed there for thousands of years. Before the Europeans opened China's door in the nineteenth century, China was an Asian empire with one of the longest continuous civilizations in the world. It was a proud and strong continental power overshadowing other nations in the region. It had not only an advanced civilization, but also a self-sufficient agricultural economy and a workable bureaucracy. As a result, China held a different world outlook from the West, maintaining ethnocentric foreign relations for centuries. There were no concepts such as nation-states, let alone interactions based on the principle of state sovereignty. It was distinctly an age before international relations. This chapter will explore the nature of the Chinese world order that, in John Fairbank's words, "handled the interstate relations of a large part of mankind through most of recorded history,"[5] and its collapse after confronting the challenge of Western powers in the nineteenth century.

SINOCENTRISM AND THE CHINESE WORLD ORDER

With a recorded history of nearly 4,000 years, Chinese civilization is one of the oldest in the world in spite of the fact that China throughout history was often in disunion or under foreign invasion. Prior to the Qin Dynasty (245-210 B.C.), which established key precedents for the first Chinese empire, China was divided into many small warring kingdoms fighting wars and balancing power.[6] After the establishment of the first Chinese dynasty by the Qin emperor, the geographical scope and military power of China expanded greatly. Its bureaucratic organization grew stronger; the Chinese language spread in usage; and Confucianism, along with other philosophies, gained prominence and influence. With the advent of the Tang Dynasty (618-907 C.E.), China came to exert a powerful influence, politically and culturally, throughout most of East Asia. Even though some countries, such as Japan, never fell under China's political domination, they could not escape from the strong influence of Chinese culture. China's contact with the distant Mediterranean world was modest but influential over the following centuries, fluctuating according to the openness of the Silk Road and maritime routes. East Asia was not a static and unchanging world when Europeans began arriving in large numbers in the sixteenth century. During Europe's medieval period, East Asia boasted several cities of great size and wealth. The average living standard and scale of commerce in China was well above that in Europe.

After the establishment of the first Chinese empire, there existed a Chinese world order that was described by scholars as "a Sinocentric hierarchy."[7] The "international" relations of China with surrounding areas, and with non-Chinese peoples generally, were colored by the concept of Sinocentrism and an assumption of Chinese superiority. Sinocentrism and the Chinese world order was a set of ideas and practices developed and perpetuated by the rulers of China over many centuries. In an abbreviated and somewhat oversimplified form, Sinocentrism and the traditional Chinese world order were portrayed in Chinese classics by a framework of the following four dimensions.

First, the Chinese world system was a closed system with a limited understanding of China's place in the world. In his Prolegomena to *The Ch'un Ts'ew with the Tso Chun* published in 1872, James Legge bitterly criticized China's ministers and people for their failure to "realize the fact that China is only one of many independent nations in the world."[8] For example, Chinese maps were wholly ignorant of the wider Pacific. While some third-century maps understood India and seventh-century ones had a detailed sense of the Southeast Asian islands, the Chinese orient was blank. Eleventh-century Chinese maps depicted Hainan Island but not Taiwan. Fourteenth-century maps showed the coast of Africa but not of Australia.[9] The Chinese knew the earth was spherical, but never sent out eastward voyages of discovery except the short-lived Zheng He fleet expedition in the fifteenth century.[10] Of course, China did trade with the outside world, even with far-off Rome along the silk route, or by hugging the Eurasian coast in sea trade through middlemen. Michael H. Hunt, an American historian, even described an "extroverted pattern of the Han (206 B.C.-220 A.D.) and Tang (618-907 A.D.)" aside from the tribute system model "with its unshakable Sinocentrism."[11] But while Chinese exports were coveted in the Mediterranean world, in return China only collected such curiosities as jugglers, acrobats, and giraffes. China's self-sufficiency and imperial position was never seriously challenged from the outside world. Until modern times the Chinese empire was able to maintain the Chinese ethnocentric worldview and did not care whether people outside the Sinitic world knew about China.

Second, the Chinese world order was hierarchical and anti-egalitarian. It was hierarchical in the sense of "China being internal, large, and high and the barbarians being external, small, and low."[12] In China-centered East Asia, nations were hierarchically ranked around China in three main zones. In the inner, there was a Sinitic zone, including "core China," and the most nearby and culturally similar tributaries, Korea and Annam (modern-day Vietnam), parts of which had in ancient times been ruled by the Chinese empires, and also the Ryukyu Islands (today's Okinawa of Japan). In the next zone there was inner Asia, usually including Tibet and Central Asia. In the outer zone there were *wai-i* (outer barbarians), at a further distance over land or sea, eventually including Indochina and

Southeast Asia.[13] All states were supposed to pay tribute to the Chinese court. In the Chinese world, the concept of legal equality or sovereignty of the individual political units did not exist. All political units arranged themselves hierarchically. There was a centrally recognized authority: the Chinese emperor known as *tianzhi* (the Son of Heaven). China's authority was institutionalized in the tributary system. All forms of international intercourse, including political, cultural, and economic relations, took place within the framework of the tributary system, as will be discussed in detail later in this chapter.

Third, China's centrality in the world order was a function of her civilization and virtue, particularly the virtue of China's ruler, although military means were used constantly to defend as well as to expand the Chinese empire. Lucian Pye's study of Asian power indicates that "the Chinese, with their Confucianism, created an elaborate intellectual structure of an ethical order which all enlightened peoples were expected to acknowledge and respect."[14] The Chinese world order, therefore, was as much an ethical as a political phenomenon. Harmony internationally as well as domestically was the product of the emperor's virtue. If he committed unvirtuous acts, the rivers would flood, the mountains shake, the people revolt. By extension, the world order would crumble if the barbarians invaded China's frontier. The mandate of heaven extended to international society through China's primacy in the tributary system. Thus, the Chinese world order was sustained by a heavy stress on ideological orthodoxy, especially on the idea that adherence to the correct teachings would be manifested in virtuous conduct and would enhance one's authority and influence. Right conduct according to the proper norms was believed to move others by its example. According to this mystique, proper ceremonial forms influenced the beholder and confirmed in his mind the authority of a ruler, official, or superior man. Thus, the Chinese emperor's superior position exhibited through proper conduct, including ceremonies, gave one prestige among others and power over them. In the Chinese world order, a hierarchical power relationship, therefore, was by definition more "moral" than in the West.[15]

And finally, international society was the extension of internal society. As John K. Fairbank put it, "The Chinese tended to think of their foreign relations as giving expression externally to the same principles of social and political order that were manifested internally within the Chinese state and society."[16] There were no nation-states, and concepts such as international and interstate are inappropriate to describe the Chinese world order. Clear legal boundaries of jurisdiction and power simply did not exist. The most important boundary was cultural. The Great Wall demarcated the boundary between China's sedentary agricultural bureaucratic Confucian society and the barbarian's nomadic steppe societies. The ocean could not prevent Korea, the Ryukyus, and the Southeast Asian kingdoms from coming to China to learn Chinese culture. Therefore China's power, despite her continental orientation, extended culturally and sometimes politically to maritime nations as well.[17] The hegemonic nature of Chinese culture in the region gave rise to a false security among the Chinese emperors that the world hierarchy was universal. There were no other hierarchies and no other sources of power on the international scene. All countries within the tributary system were subservient to China, and those countries that were geographically too distant to participate simply lived in a kind of limbo or international political vacuum. In modern parlance, one might say that all states were "satellites" of China. Within the satellites, a great deal of "self-determination" existed, but opposition to China was considered rebellion against the established order and the traditional values, and should be dealt with accordingly.

Such Sinocentrism and the Chinese world order were unusual and maintained for centuries by the strength of the Chinese civilization as well as by military force. Sinocentrism was an evolution of traditional political theory and longtime practice. In theory, the Middle Kingdom regarded itself as the center of the world, with a civilization superior to other nations. Its rulers were designated with the mandate of heaven, governing the land from dynasty to dynasty. In practice, surrounded by culturally and often militarily inferior peoples, the Middle Kingdom was condescending toward the uncivilized barbarians.

Most of the societies in East Asia, especially in Northeast Asia, stemmed from ancient China and developed within Chinese cultural boundaries. They were strongly influenced by the civilization of ancient China, for example, by the Chinese ideographic writing system, the Confucian classical teachings about family and social order, the official examination system, and the imperial Chinese monarchy and bureaucracy. The influence of Chinese political and cultural institutions was especially strong in Korea, Japan, and Vietnam. For instance, Japan, although not a tributary state, adopted its current character-based writing system from China during the period from the fourth to the sixth century A.D.; knowledge of the Buddhist religion reached Japan from China, through Korea. Vietnam was a Chinese tributary state, like Korea and the Ryukyus, participating in the East Asian world order on the basis of its own Confucian heritage, the product of long centuries of direct Chinese control and indirect political and cultural influence. Its state structure and literature were patterned on China's, and its written language and its spoken tongue were strongly influenced by the Chinese. Confucianism, along with its characteristic examination system, dominated the country's political and intellectual life. The degree to which the Vietnamese kings, themselves, accepted the Confucian view of the world order is apparent in the *Khamdinh Viet-su Thong-giam Cuong-muc* (The Complete Mirror of Vietnamese History, Text and Documentary), compiled by the Vietnamese imperial court in 1884 and published in 1885. The text was intended for Vietnamese edification. This nineteenth-century document describes many events that took place in China. It clearly illustrates "Vietnam's full acceptance of Confucian institutions on their own terms."[18] The strength of the Chinese civilization made China "*zhongguo,*" (the Middle Kingdom) and "the natural center of this East Asian world."[19] Geography kept East Asia separate from the other centers of civilization and made it the most distinctive of all great cultural areas. Chinese civilization was so powerful in this region that even the "barbarians," such as the Mongols and the Manchus who conquered the "Middle Kingdom" occasionally, had to utilize the Chinese tradition in governing China and to a large extent in conducting their foreign relations.

Sinocentrism and the Chinese world order also derived from China's military strength in East Asia.[20] Warfare was a constant in the Chinese world order, albeit Confucian pretensions of harmonious rule through the civilizing power stated the contrary. For example, China's ruler during the Yuan dynasty, Kublai Khan (the successor to legendary Genghis Khan), expanded the empire by military expedition, stretching across Central Asia, Burma, and Vietnam. In 1263, Kublai Khan made Korea his vassal and aspired to the conquest of Japan. His fleets twice reached the shores of Japan in 1274 and 1281 but were shipwrecked by typhoons, which were to become legendary in Japan as the *kamikaze,* or "divine wind."[21] The last Chinese dynasty, Qing, nearly doubled in size—through military means—from the previous Ming dynasty. Unlike the Mediterranean or European world where several sovereign countries with relatively equal capabilities were constantly competing for power, China was a "world empire" without rivals in East Asia for many centuries. This position easily bred a sense of superiority. China claimed suzerainty over its smaller neighbors, which paid tribute to the Chinese emperor as a sign of submission. Although the Chinese empire was not shy about military conquest when tribute was not given, the Chinese empire was able to sustain both the illusion and sometimes the reality of great power status and self-sufficiency as a result of rarely facing serious or durable rivals. When troubles did occur occasionally in China's frontiers, the Chinese emperors usually could use either militarism or pacifism (coercion or virtue) to suppress them.[22] The absence of serious and durable rivals helped develop the ethnocentrist Chinese approach to its neighbors that was disdainful when it could afford to be and cautious when it needed to appease external threats. In this historical background, it was only natural that the Chinese empire had no initial desire to establish equal relations with barbarous foreigners.

THE TRIBUTARY SYSTEM AS AN INSTITUTION OF "INTERNATIONAL" RELATIONS

In China-centered East Asia, China had a superior-inferior, overlord-vassal relationship with its neighbors. It was manifested in a highly sophisticated tributary system that was, in effect, the only institution for traditional "international" relations in the region before the intrusion of Western powers.[23]

The concept of the tributary system was a "Western invention for descriptive purposes."[24] The Confucian scholar-bureaucrats did not conceive of a tributary system as an institutional complex complete within itself or distinct from the other institutions of Confucian society.[25] The tributary system institutionalized the hierarchical relationship between the Middle Kingdom, China, and its barbarian neighbors through the presentation of tribute to the emperor by tributary states with a set of rituals and ceremonies. On the plane of social philosophy, the tributary relationship was conceived of as extending the social structure of civilization into realms beyond the immediate power of the emperor. Presentation of tribute to the emperor was the ritual that acknowledged the Chinese world order.

The tributary system was most developed in the Ming and Qing periods when the Chinese world order achieved its classic form.[26] Korea, the Ryukyus, Annam, Burma, Laos, and Nepal sent tributary missions regularly to China, although in the unending machinations of kingdoms and principalities in the maritime periphery of Southeast Asia, the tributary system had only marginal relevance.[27] Japan could not accept the consumption of the tributary system and found a way to participate in it on its own terms.

During the Ming dynasty, tributary relations were supervised by the Board of Rites Reception Department. Relations with certain tribes of aborigines along China's cultural frontiers were managed by a department of the Board of War. After the Manchus' entrance into China and the establishment of the Qing dynasty in 1644, *Li-fan Yuan* (barbarous affairs department) became an integral part of the tributary system, and it used the rites and forms of the traditional Confucian Chinese system to conduct relations with the "barbarians." Tribute in the outer zone merely meant recognition of the greatness of Chinese civilization. In financial terms China paid out far more than it received. The tributary relationship was always bilateral, never multilateral: one partner was always the ruler of China. According to one classic study, the tributary system during the Qing dynasty operated in a very ceremonial way. The Chinese government, in most cases, paid for all the expenses of the tributary missions from their arrival in China to their departure. The tributaries bore tribute with them and were escorted to court by the Qing officials. After performing appropriate ceremonies at the Qing court, notably the *kowtow* (three kneeling and nine prostrating), they presented tribute memorials and a symbolic tribute of their precious native products. Then they were granted tributary status and given an official seal and imperial gifts in return. Usually they were also granted certain privileges of trade. Most used the Qing calendar to date their communications with China, and some (like Vietnam) used the Chinese lunar calendar as their calendar. Finally, Chinese missions were sent to visit in return.[28]

Although it sometimes embarrassed the tributary states and bore a heavy cost to China, the tributary system was valuable for both the tributary states and the tribute receiver. Economically, the presentation of tribute enabled the tributary to trade with China through the legalization of controlled trade along the frontiers. This was important for small countries. For example, through the imperial bestowal and legal trade Korea could get certain luxuries and necessary medicines.[29] The Ryukyus' tributary missions received the privilege of carrying trade goods duty-free to China's southeast coast and missions stayed in China at the expense of the Chinese government.[30] Politically, the tributary often received validation for his political power in his own environment from the Chinese emperor, in the form of patents of office and investiture. This was a valuable technique for the establishment of legitimacy by local native rulers. China, the tribute receiver, also benefited from the system. The surrounding tributary barbarians recognized that, to participate in the benefits of China's civilization, they had to recognize the existence of China's power and, consequently, the inviolability of China's frontiers. China, at the same time, was able to trade with the barbarians for items necessary to her economy without admitting her dependence for these items of trade with barbarians.[31] For instance, the Central Asian nomads were "permitted" to present horses in tribute and to trade horses for Chinese products at frontier markets as a gracious boon granted by the emperor. China, needing horses for her armies, actually depended on the nomads for this important item. In this way, "the myth of China's self-sufficiency was preserved."[32]

Within the framework of the tributary system, the Chinese empire exercised its Sinocentric policies of persuasion and coercion through various forms. The foreigners were brought under peaceful control to secure their allegiance by explaining the system with just reasons and by treating them with honors and materials. When it was necessary, the Chinese empire could use one barbarian against another through the art of diplomacy. It could also award those who were obedient and chastise those who were defiant. Such practices worked successfully when China was unified and strong. When China was weak and divided, however, the foreigners demanded China's tribute, and at worst, they conquered the Middle Kingdom. Indeed, China was occasionally invaded by nomadic tribesmen from the north. These invasions brought about the rule of the Mongols and the Manchus during the Yuan (1237-1368) and the Qing (1644-1911) dynasties respectively. However, despite these military setbacks, the Chinese felt secure in their sense of superiority, for their culture and society had always been able to absorb and assimilate alien forces. The Mongols and Manchus had to rely on Chinese bureaucracy and Confucian ideology to maintain their rule and the tributary system remained the institution that dealt with barbarians.

The effects of the long practice of the tributary system were of great and far-reaching significance. Politically, China's power yielded to no one except stronger foreign military forces that invaded China occasionally in history. National prestige was high. But political domination was often accompanied by political isolation. This was one of the most significant characteristics of China's foreign relations for centuries. Culturally, the system reinforced the preeminence of Confucian culture, which precluded the Chinese from accepting other cultures to an appreciable extent. It built up an attitude of superiority to Chinese that not only made it intellectually difficult for the Chinese to adjust themselves to new and different systems, but also psychologically left them unprepared to meet new challenges. That was why many Western scholars were "overwhelmingly impressed by the stubborn persistence" of the Sinocentric perception during the late nineteenth century when the Chinese state faced the new and unprecedented challenge of a Western international system with its own absolutistic claims.[33]

THE GUANGZHOU (CANTON) SYSTEM

The process through which East Asia was forcibly drawn into the world-wide European-dominated international system was through the demise of Sinocentrism and the Chinese world order. The collapse of Sinocentrism in the development of world politics was also a process of "China's struggle to resist aggressive European expansion, to adjust itself to the changing international realities, to meet its problems without totally abandoning its imperial tradition, and finally to accept slowly and gradually, though sometimes reluctantly, some of the European standards, institutions, rules and values."[34] This process took several centuries. China was relatively successful in resisting incorporation into the expanding European system of states through trade and missionary contacts prior to the outbreak of the Opium War in 1840.

The riches and the grandeur of the fabulous Far East fascinated Europeans for ages. Chinese goods, especially tea, silk, and porcelain, which were carried over the legendary silk routes winding through central Asia, were in great demand even as far back as the time of the Roman Empire. With the fall of Constantinople to the Turks in 1453, the rise of the Ottoman Empire in the Middle East threatened to cut off traditional caravan routes connecting Europe to Asia. The Europeans felt this loss sorely, for "without an alternative trade route to the East, they faced the high costs of a series of commercial intermediaries."[35] Following the "geographical revolution" led by Prince Henry of Portugal, whose sponsorship of exploration and research provided Vasco da Gama and his successors with the information, navigational tools, and sailing technology they needed to reach the Indian Ocean by sea via the Cape of Good Hope, Christopher Columbus was able to convince the Spanish crown to provide him with a small fleet to look for a sea route to China. His journey of 1492 gave him credit for discovering the New World. However, when he first contacted the American continent, he mistook it for India, which he believed to lie midway between Europe and China. The Portuguese were the first to establish a presence in Asia (Goa in India, Macao in China). They were followed by the Dutch (in Taiwan and Japan) and the Spaniards (in the Philippines). By the sixteenth century, the Europeans had successfully circumnavigated the globe and set up provisioning stations and trading posts in different parts of the world, including East Asia. Thus the groundwork for a global system of international relations was laid down.[36]

Until the nineteenth century, China was relatively successful in holding European traders and missionaries at bay. Chinese imperial bureaucrats perceived Westerners as no different from their East Asian neighbors. Westerners were "barbarians" who "should observe the rules of the tributary system and fit themselves into the civilized Sinocentric world order in their pursuit of foreign trade."[37] Early European traders and missionaries were often rebuffed by the rulers of China and were usually restricted to a small enclave in order to control their contact with the native people. The Chinese court assumed an aloof and patronizing attitude toward Westerners, keeping them confined to the southern port cities of Macao and later Guangzhou (Canton). China's rulers, supremely confident in their own tradition, professed little need for Western goods and ideas. This pattern of trade relationship was known as the Guangzhou system, which "was built on a central theme of contempt for foreigners and disdain for merchants."[38]

Running under the Guangzhou system, Westerners were confined to a dozen buildings called factories outside the walls of Guangzhou city. These buildings were the property of Chinese Hang merchants and were leased to the foreigners, who were forbidden to trade outside these factories and were not allowed to enter the city of Guangzhou. They could not even reside permanently in these buildings, as they had to leave China at the end of the trading season.[39]

The old Guangzhou trade in its heyday (1760-1840) was carried on under a working compromise between the Chinese tributary system and European mercantilism. During the Napoleonic wars, one of the great survivors of the mercantilist era, the British East India Company beat out its continental competitors and brought the growing tea exports of Guangzhou into a profitable triangular trade between England, India, and China. Fleets of the East India voyaged annually from London to Guangzhou, where the company by its charter monopolized all British trade and dealt with a comparable monopoly on the Chinese side—a licensed guild of about a dozen firms. At the heart of the trade was Chinese tea. At the opening of the nineteenth century, the English was consuming 20 million pounds and by the late 1820s almost 30 million pounds tea. The British shipped cargo of woolens and lead from England, raw cotton from Bombay, tin rattans from the Straits of Malacca in exchange for the Chinese tea. [40] Although the British East India Company had the monopoly over the trade, under the Guangzhou system, the foreigners were restricted by various regulations. Thus, by mutual agreement during most of the nineteenth century, "the old Canton (Guangzhou) system proved mutually profitable within the limits imposed by two, Chinese and foreign, systems of trade regulation."[41]

THE ROAD TO THE OPIUM WAR

European expansion, and free trade in particular, disrupted the Guangzhou system after the East India Company lost its monopoly over Britain's China trade in 1833. As long as the Company maintained control over the China trade, the British accepted the rules imposed on them by the Qing court, and, from a Chinese perspective, acquiesced to the notion that the Chinese Emperor held a status superior to that of the British crown.[42] The deregulation of the British trade brought about a flood of new merchants to attempt entry into the Chinese market. Unfortunately for the repute of private enterprise in the Orient, it reached the China coast at this time chiefly in the form of the opium trade conducted by private traders. This historical circumstance poisoned Sino-European relations.

The opium trade was the solution the British found to deal with the difficulty of having goods China would buy from the West. They wanted to exchange goods with China rather than pay silver for its tea and porcelain. Nevertheless, as the quantity of teas taken by the British went up, lead, rattans, and cotton fell further short of covering the cost, and the gap in the balance of trade grew wider. The obvious way out of this balance of payment difficulty was to fill the gap with silver; "for years a very high proportion of its cargoes to China, sometimes almost the whole of them, consisted of silver."[43] But silver was hard to get, and, in the early nineteenth century, when the mercantilist option began to dissolve, the precious metal grew scarcer than ever. The British were eager to find a new commodity to replace silver. "Fortunately a new commodity did appear. It was, of course, opium."[44] For the British, it did not matter if the trade was in opium, cotton, sewing needles, or any other product, for they did not view opium as a nefarious, addictive drug. In addition, they needed to solve the balance of payment problem as well as access more ports than Guangzhou.

By the late eighteenth century, as Britain came to dominate world commerce, the trade constraints under the Guangzhou system were intolerable: foreign traders had no direct access to markets; they could not inquire about prices but had to accept without objection the prices offered by Chinese merchants.[45] The answer, from the British standpoint, was to promote a flourishing trade in opium with China in the name of free trade. This had devastating consequences for China's society and national wealth. As the trade balance began to turn in favor of Britain and the Chinese court became aware of the danger of opium, political tensions between the British and the imperial court in Beijing mounted.

Ever since the opium trade started, there had been debate among the Qing government officials: one group advocated thorough suppression, the other legalization. Those in the first group "demanded that both opium dealers and addicts should be dealt with severely," and those who favored legalization held that, in the face of the constant silver outflow, "it would be wiser just to put a tax on opium to relieve the treasury's problem."[46] The debate in the upper echelons of the Qing court took place at a time when large-scale opium imports had become a menace to the regime. When the spread of opium addiction and its consequent drain on the country's silver supply reached alarming proportions by the late 1830s, a genuinely uncorrupted official, Lin Zexu (Lin Tse-hsu), was appointed as the commissioner to oversee the Guangzhou trade in 1839. Lin Zexu took firm actions to break up the network of Chinese importers and suppliers. Then he destroyed the opium stock of European merchants without compensation. Lin's draconian measures to stop the drug trade were successful, forcing the British to surrender vast stores of their opium stocks. Paradoxically, his actions played into British hands: the office of the Crown in Guangzhou took responsibility for the loss on behalf of the British government, thus laying claim to an indemnity from China.[47] The Beijing court refused this demand. Both countries were willing to back their positions with force. After retreating from Guangzhou to Macao where they held a more defensible position, the British began a series of naval assaults on China.

The pretext for British attack arose from a drunken brawl in Guangzhou. When none of the British and American sailors responsible for the disturbance were handed over for justice, Lin Zexu ordered that supplies be withheld from all foreign shipping. A clash occurred at Kowloon, where several British vessels tried to obtain food illegally from local villagers. As a result of casualties sustained on both sides, the British were excluded from Chinese waters. In retaliation an expeditionary force of 20 ships arrived off Macao with 4,000 British and Indian troops. China's resistance to the opium trade and the British expansion in Asia resulted in the Opium War in 1840-42. The Chinese had little appreciation of their relative military weakness at this time. This is suggested by their initial action in sending a fleet of war junks against two British naval ships at Hong Kong. The British easily destroyed four of the Chinese vessels and went on to blockade Guangzhou in 1840, bombarding it and other coastal cities in 1841.[48] By 1842, the southern capital of Nanjing lay at the mercy of the British fleet, and China was forced to sign what became known as the Treaty of Nanjing and other "unequal" treaties that signaled a turning point in China's fortune. The Treaty of Nanjing stipulated that China cede Hong Kong to the British as its colony.[49] In addition, five Chinese ports (Shanghai, Ningbo, Canton, Xiamen, and Fouzhou) were to be opened to foreign trade. The Chinese government could not regulate this trade, nor could it impose its own tariffs. Furthermore, it did not have any authority over British subjects residing in the foreign "concessions" on Chinese soil in accordance with the concept of extraterritoriality, which meant that foreign rather than Chinese laws would apply to foreigners living in China. Thus, China lost its national autonomy in trade, customs, and legal jurisdiction. Finally, to add injury to insult, China was required to pay Britain 21 million taels (a traditional Chinese unit of weight) of silver as compensation for the opium destroyed by Chinese officials.[50]

THE COLLAPSE OF THE CHINESE WORLD ORDER

The Opium War, which signified the first violent encounter between China and a Western nation, came as a terrible shock to the Chinese. As an American scholar observed, "there was no room for this phenomenon in the Chinese universe."[51] It was as if the world was suddenly turned upside down. Strange and inferior people suddenly assaulted them out of nowhere and broke their ramparts with superior firepower. Shortly after the Treaty of Nanjing was signed, a Chinese edict to the British stated: "Except for your ships being solid, your gunfire fierce, and your rockets powerful, what other abilities have you?"[52]

In any case, the outcome of the Opium War was a heavy blow to the Chinese sense of superiority. "It signaled that China was besieged, and an easy target for any industrial power bent on war."[53] The blow to its prestige was to reverberate and expand throughout the rest of the nineteenth century, exacerbated by a variety of other internal factors. The dynastic weakness that made China vulnerable to foreign assault decreased the empire's resistance to internal rebellion, which reached its climax in the 1851 Taiping uprising.[54] The domestic rebellion and foreign humiliation created a revolutionary crisis, cumulating in 1911 in the fall of the Qing dynasty and revolutionary change.[55] Most importantly for the subject of this book, it led to the collapse of Sinocentrism and the disintegration of the Chinese world order. In the 60 years after its humiliating defeat in the Opium War, the Qing government was forced to sign numerous treaties with foreign powers. This began a transition from the old tributary system to a treaty system. The Chinese empire was forced to enter into "the Eurocentric family of nations."[56] The new treaty system affirmed the principle of diplomatic equality between China and its treaty partners, shattering the fictive remnants of the ancient tributary system. Former tributary states became European colonies. Foreign representatives were established in Beijing on an equal footing with Chinese officials. European diplomatic institutions had to be adopted to combat the West. The Middle Kingdom no longer held preeminence in the East Asian world.

China's official recognition of legal equality with other states was for the first time found in an imperial edict issued by Emperor Xian Feng after the joint Anglo-French Expedition in 1860 that invaded Beijing and forced the emperor to flee. In an edict sanctioning the signing of the Treaty of Tianjin in 1861, the emperor reluctantly decreed, "England is an independent sovereign state, let it have equal status (with China)."[57] China's recognition of the equal status of other states was followed and partially borne out by two institutional changes in the 1860s in the traditional Chinese system and statecraft: the compulsory acceptance of diplomatic representation of Western powers in Beijing and the initiation of *Zongli Yamen,* a government office to handle aspects of relations with Western powers.[58] According to one scholarly study, the establishment of *Zongli Yamen,* the prototype of a foreign office, signaled the end of the traditional tributary system based on unequal relations and the acceptance of foreign relations defined by European international society.[59] "Barbarian affairs" became foreign affairs, which eventually brought East Asian international relations into line with that of the European states.

The death knell of the Sinocentric East Asian world order was sounded by the Empire's loss of its tributary vassal-states to Western imperialist powers. One of the significant consequences of the Opium War was the establishment of a global colonial trade system in which China and its former tributary states were part of. Under the treaty system, China was initially forced to open five and eventually more than eight ports to trade with European powers. By the early 1860s, nearly all East Asian countries had been opened to Western trade and diplomacy and some became their colonies. The expansion of European imperialism and later Japanese imperial expansion reached every corner of the old Chinese-dominated East Asia. The chief British possessions in East Asia included Hong Kong, Singapore, and Malaysia. France had claimed Indochina, whereas the Netherlands had taken over Indonesia. Russia had pacified Central Asia, colonized Siberia, and appeared to have acquired a major influence in outer Mongolia and northern Manchuria. The Ryukyus went under the protection of, and in the 1870s was annexed by, Japan. At the same time, the United States' territorial limits had reached beyond the West Coast. In 1898 the Hawaiian Islands were annexed by Washington. In the same year, despite its avowed anticolonial heritage, the United States took over the Philippines as booty of the Spanish-American War. A global network of economic, cultural, and military outposts that was critical to Western domination of Asia in the subsequent century was thus completed. Whereas East Asia had previously existed in relative isolation from the rest of the world, now it was being integrated into one international colonial trade system and thereby tied to a global system of economic exchange. In this way, China and its former tributary nations were brought together in a single commercial and production system dominated by the West.[60]

In this new international system, as a Chinese scholar indicated, "China was not at the center as arbiter but at the center as target of European imperialist power politics in East Asia."[61] By the end of the nineteenth century, all major imperial powers had established their spheres of influence in Chinese territory. Britain carved out a sphere of influence in the Yangtze Valley, France in the Bay of Guangzhou, Germany in Shandong, Japan in southern Manchuria, and Russia in northern Manchuria and outer Mongolia. The United States, as a newly arrived imperial power, demanded equal treatment. In September 1899, John Hay, secretary of state in the William McKinley administration, dispatched the Open Door notes to Germany, Russia, England, Japan, Italy, and France, requesting formal assurances that they would refrain from interfering with any treaty port, vested interest, or Chinese treaty tariff within their spheres of interest and that they would grant traders of all countries equal of treatment with respect to harbor dues and railroad charges.[62] In July 1900, during the Boxer Rebellion, he sent a circular to great powers, informing them that "The policy of the Government of the United States is to seek a solution which may bring about permanent safety and peace to China, preserve China's territorial and administrative entity, protect all rights guaranteed to friendly powers by treaty and international law, and safeguard for the world the principle of equal and impartial trade with all parts of the Chinese Empire."[63]

As a consequence of the famous U.S. Open Door Notes submitted by John Hay to the Great Powers during 1899-1900, a legal provision, known as the most-favored-nation clause, was inserted into every treaty signed by China. Concessions granted to one foreign country by Beijing would automatically be extended to the others.[64]

The first decade of the twentieth century was the end of a transition from the Chinese world order to a modern nation-state system under the impact of the Western powers. China no longer constituted a world unto itself, but was part of the greater world, a unit in the anarchical international system. After the long and sustained resistance of Sinocentrism, the Chinese world order collapsed, giving way to an international order defined by Europeans. In the confrontation between the East and the West, the Middle Kingdom was defeated. By adapting to Western diplomatic practices and ceding its tributary states, China finally was brought into the framework of the expanding European international system.

·3·

THE RISE OF MODERN JAPAN AND ITS
WARS AGAINST CHINA AND RUSSIA

As a result of new waves of European expansion, the nineteenth century saw profound disturbances in East Asia, which led to the collapse of the Chinese world order. The change in the region, however, cannot be ascribed to Western action alone. The rise of Meiji Japan presented an immediate challenge to the Chinese world order. As one Korean scholar suggested, "the subsequent disintegration and ultimate demise of the traditional world order in East Asia was as much a result of an emerging rivalry between China and Japan as of the broad cultural conflict between the East and the West."[1] The challenges of Western expansion encouraged the rise of nationalism and the formation of the modern nation-state of Japan. The process of nation-buildinzg in Japan, however, was different from the emergence of national consciousness in most other East Asian countries. For one thing, Japan escaped the fate of colonization by Western powers, and Japanese nationalism was not associated with a struggle for national independence. As the first self-modernized non-Western country, Japan became an aggressive challenger to the status quo defined at first by China and later by the Western powers. After the Meiji Restoration, Japan sought to assert its dominance in the entire region by launching wars against China in 1895 and against Russia in 1905.

Japan could challenge the status quo by its economic and military prowess because the emerging world order in East Asia was close to Kenneth Waltz's concept of "international anarchy," where imperial powers and newly emerged nation-states pursued their own interests, however defined, in ways they judged best. Force became the major means of achieving the ends of states and each nation sought to maximize its power position through strengthening military capability. Since each state acted upon its own interpretation of its requirements for security, interest, and well-being, the end justified the means and military victory was the sole legitimization of its act. War was irrevocably utilized by Great Powers and fought between or among them for national security and military dominance.

THE MEIJI RESTORATION

Rutherford Alcock, a British diplomat writing in 1863 after spending three years in Japan, described Japan in terms of Europe's medieval ages. Feudalism, he said, was found in Japan "with sufficient identity and analogy in all its leading features to make the coincidence striking."[2] W. G. Beaslay, an American historian, indicated that "in 1850, members of Japan's ruling class, the lords and their samurai, remained bound to each other by ties of vassalage and for the most part exacted from the peasantry a portion of the crop as feudal dues."[3] The largest feudal lord was the Tokugawa House, also known as the shogun. The shogun was nominally the emperor's military deputy, but held by de facto rulers of Japan for more than two centuries (from 1603 to 1868). In 1868 a group of samurai reformers seized control of the country from the toppling Tokugawa shogunate. They wanted their regime to be known as the "Meiji Restoration," which purportedly "restored " the imperial family to its proper role after centuries of de facto rule by the shoguns. The emperor at that time was the 15-year-old Mutsuhito, known as the Meiji emperor. A system emerged after the Meiji Restoration that was shaped for one overriding national purpose: "creating modern industries and armaments as quickly as possible, to keep the foreigners at bay."[4]

The Meiji Restoration was the starting point for the rise of modern Japan. Geasley's study suggests that "the Restoration has something of the significance that the English Revolution has for England or the French Revolution for France."[5] Indeed, the political and economic changes that were instituted in the 21 years from the Meiji Restoration in 1868 to the promulgation of the Meiji Constitution in 1889 were truly revolutionary in their scope and magnitude. In the 1860s the country still was divided politically into numerous feudal domains under the ebbing authority of the Tokugawa shogun in Edo (Tokyo). But in 1900 imperial Japan became the only modern state in East Asia, having abolished feudalism and imported from the West the institutions, finance, and technology necessary for the establishment of an industrialized economy.[6]

The revolutionary set of Meiji reforms started with political centralization, which resulted in the abolition of feudal domains, the division of the country into prefectures, and the end of administrative localism. "A single monolithic bureaucracy stretched downward from a handful of decision makers with authoritarian powers, through ministers headed by samurai ministers, to prefectures with appointed governors, and then to the districts and villages or cities and wards."[7] To set up a strong and stable financial base, Meiji leaders settled a new agrarian system by establishing a uniform land tax. It was only through the establishment of an absolutist and centralized state that "the tremendous task of modernization could be accomplished without the risk of social upheaval which might attend the attempts to extend the democratic method in a nation which had emerged so suddenly and so tardily from feudal isolation."[8]

The most significant reform that made Japan a military power was the establishment of a centrally commanded conscript army and the abolition of the samurai as a class. The Meiji government, at first, continued to rely on the old-style army of various samurai units. In late 1870, when the Meiji government was ready to clean up the final remnants of opposition, this force proved unsatisfactory because samurai soldiers would not submit to modern military discipline. This resulted in the adoption in 1873 of a conscript army, drawing on both samurai and commoner alike.[9] The establishment of a conscript army was an attack on the old samurai class that lacked functionality and also was very expensive. In 1873, for example, the government spent as much on payments to the samurai as it did on all administrative expenses. This could not continue and, in that year, the government decided to tax the stipends it paid to the samurai and offered to transform the annual pensions paid to samurai into interest-bearing government bonds, hoping that the samurai would use these bonds as capital to invest in land and industry. In 1876, the government forbid samurai to wear the two swords that for centuries had set samurai apart from the commoners. Thus the abolition of the samurai as a class was complete.[10] The effects of the abolition were mixed. On the one hand, it did result in the impoverishment of many samurai families, since rising prices reduced the value of the government bonds. On the other hand, many samurai were now forced to make their way in the world without the benefit of a guaranteed income. Some went into business; others became policeman, teachers, military officers, and so on.[11]

The ultimate Meiji goals of "rich country, strong army" were reached when the Meiji leaders managed to begin the industrialization process by a series of government initiatives. The Meiji leaders saw economic development in nationalist terms just as the present Japanese government does.[12] "It made the best of the shock effect by harnessing all of the national virtues toward the great single goal of accepting the challenge and overtaking the most advanced Western countries."[13] During the early Meiji era, to build industry was beyond the resources and imagination of the old merchant class. Private capital was too weak, too timid, and too inexperienced to undertake industrial efforts. Profits were still high in traditional enterprises, and the old merchant class did not have the motivation to get involved in anything as risky as new industrial operations. For example, in 1869 the government worked through the house of Mitsui, trying to get local merchants to invest in a new railroad line, with a guarantee of high returns on their investment. But the merchants refused. Thus, the government had to take matters into its own hands and began a policy of state capitalism, by which the government served as the principal though not sole entrepreneur, manager, and financier of modern industry. The government took a number of pilot plant operations, buying whole factories overseas, assembling them in Japan, and bringing in foreign technicians and workmen to get them started. Many of these state enterprises were strategic industries (shipyards, arsenals, and mines) directly related to military needs. Others were meant to supply the government's needs without relying on foreign goods such as cement, glass, and wool. There was a gradual change in personnel in these enterprises. At first they relied heavily on foreigners. But once native Japanese mastered managerial and technical skills, foreigners were released and Japanese workers became the nucleus of a new technocracy that spread their new skills throughout the country.[14]

The result of the Meiji Restoration was impressive. By the end of the nineteenth century, Japan had emerged as the first industrialized Asian country with a strong military, challenging China's supremacy and competing with Western powers for dominance of the region. At the beginning of the sixteenth century, China possessed an economy larger than that of European countries and a technology at least as advanced as theirs. However, it lagged behind Europe as well as Japan in capitalist industrialization in the nineteenth century. One interesting question is why Meiji Japan succeeded in meeting the Western challenge and managed to rise as a modern state whereas China declined facing the same Western challenge? Answers to this important question may be found by a comparative study of their distinctive external and internal conditions in the nineteenth century.

OPPORTUNITIES AND THREATS

In his study of Japanese relations with the West, Theodore Friend wrote that "the intrusion of Western power into East Asia . . . shattered the

Chinese idea of a world order based on the Middle Kingdom . . . Only Japanese power kept native initiative in Asia."[15] The arrival of Western powers meant both opportunities and threats to East Asian countries. Westerners provided them with political and technical models to follow and adapt. In the meantime, they posed a severe challenge to these countries' independence. Taking the opportunity, Japan caught up, kept its independence, and became a strong nation. Facing the threats, China became weak, torn apart, and dominated by the imperialists. The different outcomes resulted partly from the nature of the foreign impact itself. For one thing, Western interest and presence in Japan was not so great as to put Japan in danger of losing its territorial integrity and to stop the Japanese from reorganizing their society as they saw fit. The reasons were simple: first, Japan's importance as a market for Western goods did not seem that great; second, Japan had few natural resources to exploit; and third, Japan was mainly of interest to the West as a way station to China. After a global system of economic production and exchange was formulated in the sixteenth century, lured by the prospects of huge profits or mass converts, Westerners had been knocking insistently on China's door. Luckily for Japan, because Western attention was deflected toward the bigger prize it was afforded a critical breathing space to undertake its self-strengthening programs.

Indeed, as a less-tempting target, Japan was able to make "a certain psychological preparation for the onslaught from the outside."[16] Its seclusion in the Tokugawa era worked well for about two centuries because Westerners had as little interest in getting into Japan as the Japanese had in letting them in. For a while, Japan remained outside the imagination of most Westerners, "a little-known country with no exotic appeal and hardly any practical significance."[17] It was only in the last decade of the eighteenth century that the expanding horizons of the Western world began to converge on Japan. English trading ships were snooping up from the south, and Russian missions were coming from the north. By 1825, the shogun's government, or *bakufu,* issued sweeping orders to repel foreign intruders.[18] Until the mid-nineteenth century, Japan rebuffed attempts by Britain, Russia, and the United States to open the islands to foreign trade. The United States was particularly interested in opening Japan in the mid-nineteenth century. America at that time had the world's largest whaling fleet, and the oceans around Japan were particularly rich in that animal. The Americans wanted to be able to go ashore to get fresh water and buy pine trunks to replace broken masts. In 1853, Commodore Matthew Perry steamed into Edo Harbor with his squadron of "black ships." Perry treated the Tokukawa *bakufu* officials to a mixture of moral lecture and open-ended threat. The moral uplift lay in the "better life" and "higher civilization" Japan would attain through trade with the West. The threat was an unspecified "or else," implicit in the big, armored steamships that Perry took fearlessly into Japanese harbors.[19] Perry then sailed away for a season to give the Japanese time to think about his offers. Any easy confidence that the Westerners might be put off by force was already rudely shaken in the 1840s by news of the Opium War in China. The defeat of the Chinese by British naval and military forces was a tremendous shock. It not only shattered the image of Chinese centrality and strength, but also "raised the question of whether a similar fate might be in store for Japan."[20] Thus, the Japanese were able to see what the British had done to China and knew that Japan was not going to be able to keep the foreigners out forever.[21] They yielded to the inevitable, and, when Perry returned, agreed in principle to a commercial treaty with the United States.[22]

In comparison, the Chinese imperial system and Confucian ideology, which had preserved social order and political stability for more than 2,000 years, gave Chinese officials an unwarranted sense of self-confidence and self-satisfaction. Chinese elite were understandably loath to abandon this orthodoxy in exchange for Western values and ideas. The Japanese leaders, however, were not saddled with illusions about Confucianism or reluctance to adopt foreign ways. Having imported different aspects of traditional Chinese culture at earlier times, they were ready and eager to learn from the West. When the opening came, they knew that, without change, Japan would be powerless in the face of superior Western technology. There was an explosion of Japanese learning from the outside world during the Meiji era. In 1866, Yukichi Fukuzawa, who later founded Keio University and was to become one of Japan's great reformers (and whose portrait now graces the 10,000-yen bill), published a book called *Seiyo Jijo* (the Situation in the Western World), based on his discoveries during travel outside Japan. The title page showed a drawing of the globe begirdled by telegraph wires and with Western trains roaring past. The characters on the cover helpfully informed readers: "Steam Ferries People. Electricity Carries Messages."[23] Americans were present as missionaries, athletic coaches, and advisers on building a university system. The public school curriculum was standardized around the country and school uniforms were based on those of Prussian cadets. Japanese learning from the West was not a general, unplanned import of Western culture and technology. As a Japanese historian said, the Meiji government followed "a careful analysis of their potential contribution to the economy and defense of the nation."[24] The systematic attempt to master foreign techniques and apply them rapidly within the country distinguished Japan from China and the rest of Asia in the late nineteenth century.

As a result of stubbornness and shortsightedness, China deteriorated to a point where it was beaten in war and thoroughly humiliated by the Europeans. In contrast, "Japan demonstrated its ability to adapt to its own use the material and mechanical elements of Western civilization."[25] Japan resisted the West as long as it could. When the struggle proved to be hopeless, it surrendered as gracefully as possible and proceeded to make an all-out effort to graft whatever seemed of value onto its ancient way of life. Japan suffered losses of sovereignty due to "unequal" treaties only for a short period, and it was never in danger of losing either its independence or territorial integrity. In this context, part of the answer to the question why Japan handled the Western challenge more successful than China is very simple: "Japan had a longer time to prepare for the challenge, and could profit from China's (bad) example."[26] Whereas China was not able to undertake modernization relatively free of foreign interference and control, Japan could do so. Timing was critical. The Westerners did not pay much attention to Japan before the 1850s while, in contrast, they concentrated on dividing China. Japan was successful in building a strong army and economy during the entire nineteenth century. By the mid-1880s Japan had developed sufficient military and economic strength to discourage Western invasion. This interim period gave Japan the vital breathing space to catch up, an opportunity that China did not have.

THE INTERNAL ENVIRONMENT FOR INDUSTRIALIZATION

In addition to their different relations with the external world, their distinctive domestic social structures are important in explaining the results of modernization in Japan and China. The contrast could be seen by a comparative study of the following four domestic conditions in relation to industrialization.

First, entrepreneurship was encouraged more in traditional Japan than in imperial China. The Confucian orthodoxy that prevailed in both traditional China and Japan denigrated the merchant class. However, social mobility for the merchant class was different in China and Japan, which brought about different outcomes for the development of entrepreneurs. Upward social mobility was not possible for ordinary Japanese merchants. A study of the Japanese society conducted at the wake of the twentieth century found that "the individual of every class above the lowest must continue to be at once coercer and coerced. Like an atom within a solid body, he can vibrate, but the orbit of his vibration is fixed."[27] The status of samurai was hereditary and for commoners, unless they were adopted, such status was beyond reach. Thus Japanese merchants were forced to concentrate on business pursuits.[28] In imperial China, successful merchants could convert their wealth into social respectability. They could purchase land and thereby join the rural gentry class. They could also invest in their sons' education in the hope that the latter would successfully pass the imperial examination and become officials. Finally, they could buy official titles and literary degrees from the government. Given the mobility in China's social system, Chinese merchant families sought to enter officialdom and the rural landlord class instead of plowing their profits back into business ventures. The drain of business capital for status consumption was exacerbated by the fact that most Chinese titles for status could not be inherited. Thus, we encounter "the paradox of a rigid and closed social structure (in Japan) helping to promote entrepreneurship and economic development and of a fluid and open social structure (in China) having the opposite effect."[29]

Second, capitalist development was enhanced in Japan by a system of primogeniture—the custom according to which the eldest son inherits all his father's property—and was hampered in traditional China by its absence. In traditional China all sons were entitled to a share of their father's property. This practice, eminently fair by contemporary standards, had several significant effects. One was the fragmentation of the family's financial resources. The Chinese inheritance practice dissipated family wealth, so that even the richest families would have their wealth greatly diminished as a result of the successive division of the patrimony over several generations. Thus Chinese peasants had very small and scattered plots, a situation hardly conducive to agricultural mechanization. Another effect was early marriage and large families. Inheritance shares provided the financial means for the male descendants to start their own families early and indirectly resulted in excessive population growth in rural China. The explosion of the Chinese population in the nineteenth century was one cause of the declining standard of living and of the widespread social disorder and economic hardship that followed in its wake.[30] Unlike China but like England, in traditional Japan, "the principle of primogeniture governed the succession to the position of family head."[31] This custom tended to preserve family fortunes and promote capital accumulation essential for economic modernization. It pushed younger sons to undertake social and economic pursuits unconnected with their fathers' occupation. Moreover, it delayed marriages and tempered population growth because, deprived of a share of the family inheritance, younger sons had to establish an independent financial basis before considering marriage (especially if the bride's family demanded a dowry as a condition for marriage). "Thus, the existence of primogeniture facilitated social and economic modernization in Japan, and its absence in China had the reverse effect."[32]

Third, the commercialization that developed in Japanese society along with the arrival of Westerners encouraged a revolution from above and discouraged the mass rebellions from below that occurred in China. There were two major currents of opposition to the Tokugawa social order in the nineteenth century. One was the opposition from above—the coalition of low-ranking samurai, rich peasants, and rural merchants. The second was opposition from below, peasants resisting exploitation through high rents, high taxes, and an increasing gap between rich and poor. The peasants movement was weakened and eventually defused by the effect of trade on their income. Japan's relations with the West after Perry's visit in 1853 resulted in an expansion of trade that, in turn, resulted in a boom and inflation. With rising prices and demand for goods such as tea, silkworm eggs, silk, and other goods, peasant producers and urban merchants began to do well, while the samurai who were on fixed incomes did poorly.[33] In addition, the coming of Westerners increased the power of the daimyos relative to the shogun. As soon as the shogun had signed treaties with the West, it came under strong criticism from the daimyo for failing to throw out the Westerners. The shogun was forced to make concessions to the opposition, allowing some into the government and promising to cancel the treaties and push the Westerners into the sea in a few years.[34] Most important, the shogun eliminated the *sankin kotai* system that required the daimyo to establish residence in the shogun's territory and be supervised by the shogun.[35] The major reason for this was to encourage the daimyo to return to their domain and to prepare for Japan's expulsion of Westerners into the sea. But many of the daimyo did not go home, instead they went to the imperial court at Kyoto where they participated in opposition to the shogun. Thus, commercialization in society encouraged a revolution from above, a revolution led by samurai that started the industrialization and met the challenge from the West. In contrast, the opposition to the old regime from the low classes in China never was defused and eventually combined with the discontent of intellectuals to create a revolution from below. This delayed China's industrialization for nearly a century.[36]

Finally, a strong state was necessary in meeting the challenge from the West in the nineteenth century. China, the Middle Kingdom without rival in Asia for centuries, did not face the pressure for constant military preparation and the consequent stimulus to develop a strong state. Although China had a long coastline, it did not send naval expeditions or trade missions abroad, except for a short period during the Ming dynasty. Unlike imperial China, traditional Japan was divided into many fiefs, each of them ruled by a feudal lord or daimyo. Even the most powerful daimyo, Lord Tokugawa, whose administration, or shogunate, ruled in the name of the Japanese emperor, controlled only 60 percent of the country's domains. Some 260 domains governed by the daimyo and their bureaucracies were in effect small "countries" whose autonomy remained intact so long as it did no violence to the shogun's nationwide responsibilities and concerns. Thus the shogun had to guard constantly against disloyalty by the daimyo. Consequently, the situation in Tokugawa Japan resembled more the armed rivalry of Europe than the imperial peace of China. The Tokugawa's military victory over daimyos in 1600 "laid the foundation of a modern centralized state." The Meiji Restoration, by abolishing the daimyo "completed the process" and produced a strong state, which started rapid economic development.[37]

JAPANESE NATIONALISM AND CONTINENTAL EXPANSIONISM

The Meiji Restoration made Japan the first and most successful self-modernized non-Western country. The Meiji Restoration not only set Japan totally apart from the old East Asian system, but also embodied Japanese nationalism in response to the Western powers. As a Japanese political commentator, Tokutomi Soho, put it, "A threat from abroad immediately directs the nation's thoughts outwards. This leads immediately to the rise of a spirit of nationalism."[38] Nationalism in Japan was somehow different from nationalism in China. Chinese nationalism was stimulated by the humiliating setbacks suffered at the hands of Western imperialists. Western gunboat diplomacy, the looting and sacking of the Imperial Palace, and the institutions of extraterritoriality and foreign concessions provided the historical background for China's subsequent struggle for independence and national liberation. In contrast, because Japan escaped the fate of colonization by the Western powers, its nationalism was inextricably connected to the issue of Western learning, including the emulation of Western powers in European-style imperialism, and the creation of Japan's own empire in East Asia. Japanese nationalism made it an imperialist power and "led eventually to confrontation, not only with the West, but also with the other Asian nations over which Japan sought to assert economic and political domination."[39]

As an island nation, Japan's fundamental predicament is that it is vulnerable to powerful foreigners who might overtly or subtly force their ways on Japan. James Fallows found that "in attempting to solve its problem of vulnerability, Japan has had two basic choices. One is to try to wall itself off from the outside world. The other choice is to attempt to control the surrounding environment so it will not be capable of springing surprises on the Japanese."[40] After the failed attempt by the great Japanese warlord Hideyoshi to conquer the Korean Peninsula in 1592, the Tokugawa shogun insulated the nation from outside disturbances for over two centuries. After the success of the Meiji Restoration, Japan turned to the second alternative again. Thus, Meiji Japan underwent a radical transformation not only from handicrafts to modern industry but also from reclusive feudalism to expansionism. "In my opinion," wrote Japanese Foreign Minister Inoue Kaoru in 1885, "What we must do is to transform our empire and our people . . . To put it differently, we have to establish a new, European-style empire on the edge of Asia."[41] For Japanese leaders like Inoue, imperial expansion was part of the process of imitating and learning from the great European powers. Japan, they believed, would be able to win the respect of nations like Britain and France only when it too had demonstrated its ability to acquire overseas territories through conquest and diplomacy. In addition, overseas expansion into the neighboring countries of continental Asia would provide a "buffer, protecting Japan from potential rivals such as the Russian Empire."[42] Indeed, Japan's initial interest in continental East Asia in the late eighteenth century was "defensive rather than expansionist in nature, concerned chiefly with the strategic problem of how to defend Japan from Russian aggression."[43] It was after the Meiji restoration that Japan's active interest in continental Asia "took the form of an aggressive call for continental expansion."[44]

Japan's military expansion to neighboring countries began with an expedition against Taiwan in 1874. When some shipwrecked fishermen from the Ryukyu Islands to the south were killed by aborigines on Taiwan, Japan turned their misfortune into a diplomatic incident. Assuming the role of Ryukyu's protector, Japan responded by sending a punitive expedition against Taiwan. Alert leadership in Beijing would have protested but the Chinese were preoccupied with rebellions in Central Asia and agreed to pay Japan an indemnity of 500,000 taels silver by way of settlement.[45] In the logic of the newly emerged nation-state system in East Asia, Japan thus established recognizable sovereignty over the Ryukyus.

The priority for the Meiji leaders was not the Ryukyus, however, but Korea, China's long-standing tributary state and Japan's springboard to continental Asia. "Japan thought that it would be in her interest if Korea could be brought within the treaty system."[46] In the competition over Korea, China insisted "on a tributary relationship and Japan on modern treaties."[47] The antagonism and confrontation between the two powers thus took on increasingly grave overtones in Korea, "regarded as a vassal by China on the one hand, and championed as an independent state by Japan on the other."[48] To the Japanese, "the Western idea of sovereign statehood was a convenient tool with which to start the process of breaking the bonds uniting Korea and China."[49] The Meiji leaders desperately wanted to find a way to open Korea as much as Commodore Perry had opened their own country. The reasons for this geographical focus were partly strategic because of Korea's proximity to Japan as well as Japan's striving to secure strategic advantage over Russia and diplomatic advantage over China in Korea; and partly ideological, that is, to transform the "corrupt" regime of its neighbor; and partly economic, in order to "secure additional food supplies and a market for Japan's nascent industries."[50]

Korea imposed isolation on itself, watching with growing horror the depredations of the West in China. The Taewongun,[51] Korea's conservative regent, declared the country off-limits to all foreigners except Korea's ancient benefactor, China. The official isolationism of the Korean court was powerfully reinforced by the preachments of a new creed, called *Tonghak* (Eastern learning) founded by a wandering aristocrat named Ch'oe Che'u in 1860. It seemed a bulwark against the encroachments of *Sohak* (Western learning), as Roman Catholicism was called at the time because it threatened the traditional Korean social order and national identity.[52] In spite of official isolationism, the Korean court was faced with increasing efforts by foreign powers to open Korea to international trade. The ships of various Western nations appeared repeatedly off the coasts of Korea, but Korea refused to open her doors to foreigners, strengthened her border defenses, and redoubled her efforts in persecution of Christians. In 1866, about 30,000 believers were executed, and an American ship, the *General Sherman,* sailing up the Taedong River seeking trade was attacked and destroyed by fire rafts.[53] In the face of Korea's determined opposition and refusal to open her doors, Westerners withdrew. This was in sharp contrast to the early opening of China. But this was not due solely to Korea's strong stand and military defense. Western powers were in search of trade and not motivated to conquer Korea by force, for "the foreign powers, at that time, had more important problems on their hands."[54]

While the Western powers were distracted from immediate advances on Korea, a new and vigorous Japan now appeared on the scene and persevered in opening Korea. The Japanese had sought to open Korea as early as 1868 when they sent a mission to announce the reorganization of their government, in the expectation of a congratulatory mission in return. But the Taewongun refused to have anything to do with the envoys, and subsequent missions in 1869 and 1871 received the same curt treatment.[55] The Japanese waited for a more definite pretext to secure its interest in Korea. This occurred in September 1875, when a small boat lowered from the Japanese gunboat *Unyokan* violated the territorial waters of Korea at a strategic location near the mouth of the Han River and drew fire from the shore batteries. The Japanese retaliated by storming the fort, destroying both the bastion and its defenders.[56] Amid a popular clamor for war, the Japanese government decided to use this incident as a means to force Korea into a treaty relationship. In 1876 the Koreans were sufficiently intimidated by Japan for it displayed superior naval power, and signed the Treaty of Kanghwa, opening two ports to Japanese trade.[57] Japan thus succeeded in negotiating the first treaty with Korea based on the Western idea of sovereign statehood.

THE SINO-JAPANESE WAR (1894–1895)

The Japanese success in the opening of Korea had two consequences. First, the Korean government was divided into two principal factions: one advocating the pro-Chinese conservatism and the other advocating pro-Japanese progressivism. The second consequence was that "the conclusion of the Treaty of Kanghwa, by which the Japanese specifically recognized the independence of Korea from China, marked the beginning of a rivalry between China and Japan for control of Korea."[58] By recognizing Korea as an independent state, the Kangwha Treaty ignored China's exclusive claim to suzerainty and abrogated China's long-standing dominance over Korea.[59] Other colonial powers, stirred by Japan's success, moved rapidly to make their own treaties with Korea. They were encouraged and assisted in their efforts by the Chinese government, who saw the need to introduce counterbalancing forces against Japan in a country that the authorities in Beijing still deemed as China's fiefdom.[60]

In any case, after the Kanghwa Treaty of 1876, Japanese influence greatly increased in Korea. Japan not only succeeded in monopolizing the

Korean market, but also established an influential position in the Korean court. Japan forced the Korean king to employ a Japanese special training commander and to organize the Korean military academy on the Japanese model. A Korean scholar has noted that "this was part of Japan's plan to gain control over Korea."[61] Favoritism to Japan infuriated traditional soldiers. Nearly 10,000 of them mutinied in Seoul and attacked Min officials and the Japanese on July 23, 1882. This military insurrection, known as the Im-O Soldiers' Mutiny, started as a revolt against the government's discriminatory treatment of traditional soldiers, but the wrath of the soldiers soon turned into a spontaneous political revolt of anti-Japanese, anti-corruption, and anti-pro-Chinese Min faction.[62] The Queen Min and her pro-Chinese clique barely escaped the rioting army and asked China to send troops to help suppress the revolt. Looking for an opportunity to block the rapidly growing Japanese influence and reinstate Chinese control in Korea, the Beijing court responded by sending four warships and 5,000 troops to Korea in August.[63]

In the same month, the Japanese minister Hanabusa, who had managed to escape to Japan, returned to Seoul with 1,500 Japanese troops. He could not recover Japan's influential position in the Korean court because the Korean king was already influenced by the Chinese. As soon as the Chinese forces suppressed the rebellion and restored the pro-Chinese regime, China proceeded to assert its suzerain status with renewed vigor by signing a new Sino-Korean agreement and by reorganizing and training the Korean troops in Chinese fashion while the Japanese-trained forces were disbanded. The strength of the Chinese forces under General Wei Chang-qing that stayed on in Korea "in order to keep the Japanese in check" was impressive.[64] China, by taking advantage of the Korean soldiers' mutiny, restored its position in Korea.

For a time, the Japanese hoped to outmaneuver China by fomenting an internal uprising in Seoul and establishing a pro-Japanese government led by Kim Ok-Kyun, a reform-minded scholar who studied under Fukuzawa Yukichi in Japan.[65] On the night of December 4, 1884, during a festive dinner party, Kim and his followers launched a coup and seized control of the royal palace. The coup was engineered by the "progressive Koreans," with the "encouragement and assistance of the Japanese . . . to sweep away in one blow" the ruling conservative government.[66] The aim of the progressives was to wipe out "the conservative pro-China faction" then in power, and to terminate all connections with China—"Meiji Japan was their model, and Fukuzawa Yukichi their mentor."[67] Immediately after the coup, Kim Ok-Kyun called in the local garrison of 200 Japanese troops for protection, and quickly announced a new political program for national independence by abolishing Korea's tributary relations with China. However, this new government lasted only three days for "at the suggestion of the Chinese, anti-coup Korean officials submitted a formal request for Chinese aid."[68] Chinese troops of more than 1,000 men counterattacked and moved into the royal palace by force, overwhelming the Korean rebels and their Japanese defenders. After a brief but lively exchange of fire between the hopelessly outnumbered Japanese defenders and the Chinese attackers, the king was brought under the protection of the Chinese.

After the failure of the pro-Japanese coup, which became known as the Kapsin coup (after the year name), Japan steadily lost influence in Korea, while China further strengthened its traditional suzerainty. The failure marked a tactical turning point in Japan's relations with Korea. Abandoning all hope of "reform" in Korea and thereby of controlling it from within, Japan reverted to bold, strong-arm tactics,[69] and looked for opportunity to recover its political interests and establish Japanese power in Korea. When the *Tonghak* mass rebellion occurred in 1894, it provided a welcome opportunity to Japan. The rebellion, staged by military leader Chon Pyong-jun in February 1894, was essentially a political and social protest against corrupt ruling elites, ineffectual Korean government, and foreign infiltration. When the *Tonghak* forces marched toward Seoul, the Korean government asked for Chinese military aid to suppress the *Tonghak* rebellion. On June 6, 1894, China sent 1,500 troops, with 725 to follow, to Korea, ensuring that "the Middle Kingdom was merely following the traditional practice of protecting its tributary states."[70] In response to China's action, Japan, without Korea's request, sent six times as many troops as China to Korea. Japan justified its decision on the grounds that it had never recognized Korea's tributary position to China, and it dispatched troops under the treaty of 1882, whereby Japanese guards were sent for the protection of Japanese legation, residents, and properties.[71] The underlying Japanese intention was to act decisively to end Chinese supremacy in Korea.

The stage for the Sino-Japanese War was set. The war represented the two countries' struggle for political, strategic, and economic interests in Korea. For Japan, it was a war to establish hegemony over Korea; for China, the last effort to preserve its traditional position in East Asia. Most Western military experts predicted that China would be the victor if war broke out. The United States took a stand of neutrality, while European nations, particularly Great Britain, urged the United States to intervene in a joint diplomatic venture to restore peace in East Asia.[72] The action of the war quickly demonstrated how far the balance had turned in Japan's favor.

On July 25, 1894, without a declaration of war, Japanese warships intercepted and destroyed the Chinese fleet off Asan Bay in the Yellow Sea.[73] The Japanese land forces, meanwhile, scored a series of decisive victories at Sonhwan and Asan, inflicting crippling blows on the enemy in subsequent battles. After a series of swift victories, the Japanese drove the Chinese forces north out of Korea. The strategic naval base of Port Arthur (Lüda) was captured, as well as Taiwan. As it became apparent to China that "the tide of war was irreversible, the Chinese sued for peace, affixing after prolonged negotiations its signature to the Treaty of Shimonoseki" on April 7, 1895.[74] China's defeat in this contest was formalized by this treaty.[75] According to its terms China was forced to recognize Korea's independence and Japan's paramount interest in Korea, to pay an indemnity of 200 million taels, to cede to Japan Formosa (Taiwan), the Pesadores (Penghu) Islands, and the Liaodong Peninsula, to open up a specified section of the Yangtze River to Japanese commerce and the ports of Shasi, Chongqing, Suzhou, and Hankou to Japanese trade, and to grant most-favored-nation status to Japan.[76]

Japan's military victory over China was not incidental. The outcome was partially attributable to the divergent paths used by the Japanese and Chinese to obtain military power. Facing the Western challenge in the nineteenth century, both Japanese and Chinese elites shared a common determination to transform their countries into militarily strong ones, and saw "the mighty nations of the West primarily as military power, with strong arms, a powerful class of military leaders, and overseas bases, colonies, and spheres of influences."[77] Both China and Japan began to build modern military capabilities at about the same period of the 1860s. But the provincial nature of new armed units remained in China. It is important to recall that the Huai army led by Li Hungzhang was first organized by scholar-gentry as a provincial force to combat the Taipings. It later gained official recognition as the armed power of the country and went on to constitute the core fighting force against the Japanese army in 1894.[78] Like the Huai army, the Xiang army led by Zeng Guofan (Tseng Kou-fan) and several other provincial forces were national military forces only in the sense that the Qing court gave it official endorsement.[79] The recruitment and training of their officers was done at the provincial level, and their units were commanded by men who were closely related to one another. These leaders were "a band of provincial dignitaries."[80] A Western scholar wrote in the 1930s that "to the present . . . no effective national army—to the exclusion of local armies under provincial war lords—has ever been formed."[81] To make things worse, the Chinese elite who led the military strengthening of their country were misguided because they put their emphasis only on armed forces and ignored other aspects of modern nationhood such as industrialization or political reform. Their immediate objective was "a build-up in military power; and its ultimate aim was to preserve and strengthen the traditional way of life."[82] For these leaders, the adoption of Western arms could be justified only on the ground of "utility and practicality as a means of defending China and preserving Chinese civilization."[83]

The Meiji leaders, unlike their Chinese scholar-gentry counterparts, came from the warrior (samurai) background. They knew what was entailed in their efforts and recognized the need for centralization of military power. Starting with the abolition of the *han* (feudal domains) in 1871, intensive attempts were made to create a centralized national army during the Meiji era. In January 1873, the Meiji government promulgated a universal conscription law that required "every male regardless of social rank to spend three years on active service followed by four in the reserves."[84] Despite the resentment from some local military leaders (samurai), who opposed the military plan because it would deprive them of their traditional function, the new army, which was designed after the Prussian model, became an established institution. By 1883 all the men in the army were conscript soldiers.[85] It is worth noting that the core of the new Japanese army was primarily men from Choshu, Tosa, and Satsuma Han, those who had played major roles in bringing down the Tokugawa regime. This situation was not very different from the emergence of provincial armies in China during the 1860s. However, the two countries' armies soon began to differ, as the Meiji leaders launched a systematic campaign to establish a strong central army and the officers from local domains were transformed into the leaders of the national army.

The result of the Sino-Japanese War reveals that in the military sphere China failed to develop as a modern army, whereas Japan succeeded.[86] But behind this success is a great historical irony in that Japan's military triumphs came at the expense of China and Korea, its immediate continental neighbors and countries that had influenced Japan so much. The Japanese learned from China's disastrous wars with the European nations, made war on China in turn, and established their own country as a colonial power by snatching territory away from China. An interesting question in this context would be the extent to which Japan's success was achieved at the expense of China's failure. According to a Japanese scholar, Akira Iriye, much of Japan's economic gain came about because China offered it reparations, territory rich in resources, and easily accessible markets for trade and investment. The reparation payment of 200 million taels, about 360 million yen, that China paid to Japan in 1895, not only paid for Japan's costs of the war—which were estimated to have amounted to 247 million yen—but also provided funds for the construction of the Yawata Iron Works, the first modern factory built during the Meiji era.[87] Without the reparations of 1895, without the cession of Taiwan and the lease of the Liaodong Peninsula, and without the treaties Japan forced upon China that kept import duties low and protected foreign merchants and industrialists from Chinese jurisdiction, Japanese industrialization would have been much slower than it actually was. In this sense, Iriye asserts that "China unwillingly assisted Japan's economic modernization."[88]

THE TRIPLE INTERVENTION AND THE ANGLO-JAPANESE ALLIANCE

During the Sino-Japanese War, Russia and the other Western powers had generally remained neutral. However, Russia felt threatened by Japan's acquisition of the Liaodong Peninsula, which was a strategically important foothold on the Asian mainland. Russia was a continental power and never possessed a strong navy to establish scattered colonies overseas as England and other European powers. Instead, the Russian expansion was overland from west to east. In 1865 Japan and Russia had negotiated the Treaty of Shimoda, which partitioned the Kurile Islands, with the northern half to Russia and the southern half to Japan. In 1875 by the Sakhalin-Kurile Islands Exchange Treaty, the entire Kurile archipelago was recognized as belonging to Japan and the entire island of Sakhalin to Russia.[89] Having reached Vladivostok and the Pacific, Russia showed its greater interest in a search for ice-free ports on the Korean peninsula. In particular, the decision in 1885 to construct a trans-Siberia railway from St. Petersburg marked a turning point in Russian foreign policy and signaled its intention to partially divert diplomacy from Europe and carry on an extensive drive toward the Far East. The rationale was revealed by a Russian diplomat when he said that

> In Europe we were hangers-on and slaves, whereas we shall go to Asia as masters. In Europe we were Asiatics, whereas in Asia, too, Europeans . . . When we turn to Asia, with our new vision of her, in Russia there may occur something akin to what happened in Europe when America was discovered. Since, in truth, to us Asia is like the then undiscovered America. With our aspiration for Asia, our spirit and force will be regenerated.[90]

The Russian diplomat believed that "in our future destinies Asia is, perhaps, our main outlet."[91]

In fact, the Russians had anxiously searched for the ice-free ports of Dalian and Port Author at Liaodong for years and decided to seek preservation of the status quo ante bellum after the Sino-Japanese War. On the initiative of Russia on April 23, 1895, six days after the signature of the Shimonoseki Treaty, Germany, France, and Russia sent a joint memorandum to Tokyo "advising" the restoration of Liaodong to China on the ground that Japanese possession of that territory would menace China's capital, Beijing; render Korean independence an illusive phase; and constitute a permanent obstacle in the way of peace in the Far East.[92] This became the event known as the Triple Intervention.

To cope with this situation, an urgent conference was convened in the presence of the emperor in Hiroshima on April 24, 1895, a day after Japan received the three-power notification. The Premier Ito Hirobumi presented to the conference three alternative responses that Japan would have to adopt: one, reject the three powers' demands at the risk of inviting their enmity; two, refer the issue to an international conference; or three, accept the demands and restore the territory in question to China.[93] It was doubtful whether the three powers could fight Japan on land in the short run; but they could cut off Japan's land armies in Manchuria by assembling their combined naval strength. Japan, "already over-stretched as the result of her war efforts over six months, did not dare to risk challenging any joint move which was in contemplation."[94] Failure to receive a favorable answer from the British to the request for international support,[95] Japan had no choice by to comply with the request of the Triple Intervention. Realizing that Japan was militarily too weak and diplomatically too isolated, the Japanese leaders decided to follow a conciliatory policy and looked for a modus vivendi with the Russians. There followed a long period of negotiation that lasted six months and was supposed to be confined to Japanese and Chinese delegates. However, the Russians and their partners were breathing down the necks of the Chinese plenipotentiaries throughout the talks, so determined were they to secure an advantageous settlement over the return of Liaodong. Eventually the supplementary convention was signed on November 8, 1895, whereby within three months of China paying a supplementary indemnity of 30 million taels the Japanese troops would evacuate Liaodong.[96]

The Triple Intervention threatening to deprive Japan of the fruits of her hard-won victory aroused an intense feeling of national indignation among the Japanese people. The intervention brought to the surface the basic conflict in the objectives that Japan and Russia were trying to achieve in continental Asia. In addition, it intensified the widespread anti-Russian feeling among the Japanese public because Russia was perceived as the initiator of the affair. Shocked and outraged by this Triple Intervention, the Japanese public supported an all-out military buildup to prevent any such future humiliation. By 1897 military spending had increased to 55 percent of the national budget.[97]

After the Triple Intervention, Russia established a strong friendship with China by helping the return of Liaodong to China and by offering loans to pay Japanese indemnity.[98] Russia's influence was further increased by the conclusion of a secret treaty of alliance in 1896, known as the Li-Lobanov Agreement: China and Russia agreed to defend each other against Japanese aggression in China, in Russian territory in the Far East Asia or in Korea; and China consented to the construction of a railway across Manchuria towards Vladivostok in order to facilitate the access of Russian land troops in the event of war.[99] Two years later, by the Treaty of St. Petersburg in March 1898, Russia gained the right to lease Port Arthur and Dalian for 25 years. Thus Russia pushed its advance further, occupying the whole South Manchuria as a specially Russian sphere of interest.

Expanding in China, Russia's influence in Korea was also increasing. After the end of the Sino-Japanese War, the Russians took the place of the Chinese in Korea. The struggle between the pro-Japanese party and the pro-Russian party became intense and erupted in the murder of Queen Min in her own palace by Japanese intruders in October 1895. Her death was followed by the assassination of Premier Kim Hong-jip, leader of the pro-Japanese party, and the subsequent flight of the Korean King Kojong into the Russian legation to seek political asylum and organize a new cabinet that included pro-Russian ministers. This symbolized Russia's increasing political role in Korea.[100] Having sensed Russia's mounting interest in Korea, Japan designed a policy to block Russian expansion by proposing a division of Korea along the 38th parallel—the Russian sphere of influence in the north and the Japanese in the south. When the Russians were in a more influential position than the Japanese, the Russians rejected the proposal on the ground that it would contradict their recognition of the independence of Korea. In 1898, Japan again proposed that if Russia would recognize Japan's predominance in Korea, Japan would consider, in return, Manchuria being outside of Japan's sphere of influence. But Russia firmly refused to be excluded from Korea.[101]

The Japanese suspected that Russia would attempt to seize Korea after Manchuria because of its policy to acquire an ice-free port on the Pacific coast. With Russia now her chief rival for dominance in Asia, Japan sought to find a counterweight. The obvious choice was Great Britain, the czar's ubiquitous competitor. At that time, the United States and Britain had already begun to wonder how the Russian drive toward the Pacific could be halted when the Russian government searched for a lease for a Russian coal station on Masan near the port of Pusan, a strategically and militarily important area. Such a lease could extend the Russian naval defense line from Vladivostok to Pusan and from Pusan to Port Arthur. This naval line could easily block or restrict Japanese sea power and also make Russia an influential Pacific power. Russia's advance in the Far East caused Great Britain to draw closer to Japan. On January 30, 1902, the British agreed to a formal Anglo-Japanese Alliance, the first military alliance between an Asian nation and a European power: "It was to maintain the balance of power in East Asia and to protect her vital interests that Britain endeavored to make the best use of victorious Japan."[102]

It was not easy for the Japanese to enter into alliance with the British. There was much "bitter feeling toward London" during the Sino-Japanese War and the British advice to yield to the Triple Intervention after the war.[103] However, Marshal Yamagata Aritomo, a major architect of an aggressive Japanese foreign policy, believed that a war with Russia would be inevitable in the long run and that Japan needed to strengthen its military forces and diplomatic defense by signing the Anglo-Japanese Alliance.[104] The Anglo-Japanese Alliance was a logical outcome of British concern over the encroachment of Russia and other European countries, such as Germany and France, in the British sphere of interest in China proper and of Japanese fear of the Russian menace directed against Korea. The Anglo-Japanese treaty recognized Britain's special interests in China and Japan's in Korea.[105]

To the Japanese mind, the primary purpose of the Anglo-Japanese Alliance was to keep Russian out of Korea and to act together in defense of their interests in China. In Japan, the psychological effects of the alliance were far-reaching. It signaled that Japan had become an equal in the eyes of the West. With Britain on its side, Japan adopted a more belligerent attitude toward Russia. This was evidenced in a memo to the British King written by Lord Lansdowne, who, more than any others, was responsible for the alliance on the British side. He recognized that "The Anglo-Japanese Alliance, although not intended to encourage the Japanese Government to resort to extremities, had, and was sure to have, the effect of making Japan feel that she might try conclusions with her great rival in the Far East—free from all risk of an European coalition such as that which had on a previous occasion deprived her of the fruit of victory (the Triple Intervention)."[106] The stage for the Russo-Japanese War was now set.

THE RUSSO-JAPANESE WAR (1904–1905)

The conclusion of the Anglo-Japanese alliance seemed to check the Russian advance toward East Asia. In an agreement with the Chinese government in April 1902, the Russians pledged to evacuate their forces from Manchuria within two years in three successive withdrawals to occur at six-month intervals. However, in April 1903, when the time limit for the second evacuation came, the Russians not only failed to carry out the terms of the Russo-Chinese agreement but also entered upon a new venture in north Korea by obtaining lumber concessions and putting forces along the Russian-Korean border.[107] During this period, pressures for war against Russia were building within Japan. In May 1903 a group called the Kogetsukai, organized by middle-ranking army and navy officers and officials of the foreign ministry, met to exert pressure on the decision-makers to take up arms. On June 22 General Oyama Iwao, chief of the General Staff, presented a memorandum to the emperor stating that "Japan should realize an early solution of the Korean question; it now has the advantage from a strategic point of view and a few years' delay would place Russia in a superior position."[108]

Observing the development of the Anglo-Japanese alliance and the increasing pressure in support of a strong Russian policy in Japan, the Russian government proposed in 1903 to provide the 38th parallel as the southern boundary of a neutral zone as originally envisioned by the Japanese, but "Japan turned down the proposal."[109] By the end of December 1903, Japanese decision-makers had decided to resort to arms to resolve the Russian issue. Japan launched a surprise attack on the Russian fleet at Port Arthur, sinking virtually the entire Russian squadron at anchor on February 8, 1904. Two days afterward, Tokyo issued an official declaration of war.

Great Britain, while fully supporting the position of the Japanese government, had no intention of encouraging Japan either to enter into war with Russia, or to recommend that Japan compromise with Russia. When Japan made her momentous decision to enter into a state of war with Russia, "it did so without any expectation of military assistance from Great Britain."[110] On the other hand, Japan did request economic and financial assistance, which her European ally willingly provided. Britain was to abide faithfully by the provisions of the alliance and to extend to

Japan the maximum assistance possible through her obligations. The U.S. government, too, extended economic assistance to Japan. This foreign aid constituted a very important part of the Japanese government's resources in defraying the cost of war.[111]

The Russo-Japanese War was an event of the first magnitude for Japan, a veritable life-and-death struggle for the small island nation pitted against a European power. However, Japan had the advantage of fighting close to its main sources of supply. With control of the sea, the Japanese quickly landed troops on Port Arthur. There Japanese generals threw wave after wave of troops against entrenched machine gun positions in a lesson that seemingly went unnoticed by generals on the European continent until a decade later. After spectacular losses, Japanese forces prevailed. Later on, Shenyang (Mukden) fell in a collision of armies numbering 300,000 on each side. In the meantime, Russia's Baltic fleet was making its way painfully around the world after having its use of the Suez Canal denied by Japan's new ally, Great Britain. Immediately on its arrival in the Tsushima Straits, which separate Japan from Korea, the Russians found Japan's warships lying in wait. The Russian fleet was utterly demolished.[112]

Despite military success, Japan responded favorably to the initiative taken by President Theodore Roosevelt of the United States to act as a peacemaker. The United States, while officially neutral during the war, was in reality a spiritual ally of Japan. Theodore Roosevelt was particularly fearful that Russian possession of Manchuria would be the beginning of a systematic effort to limit American commercial enterprise in northeast Asia. When the United States asked China to open three Manchurian cities—Tatongkou, Shenyang (Mukden), and Harbin—to foreign trade and to block Russia's exclusive privilege there, China under Russian pressure refused. Americans interpreted the Russian policy as a violation of the principle of the Open Door policy. Thus President Roosevelt thought that Japan was "playing our game" in the war against Russia. On the other hand, the president also realized that Japan might cause trouble to American possession in the Pacific and the Far East.[113] Therefore, upon receiving Russian willingness to conclude a treaty of peace with Japan, and, in the meantime, receiving Japanese assurance that Japan would abide by the Open Door doctrine in Manchuria, would recognize Chinese sovereignty in the returned area, and would not harbor any aggressive design on the Philippines, President Roosevelt was able to bring the two warring nations around the conference table in Portsmouth in August 1905.[114] With the Treaty of Portsmouth mediated by the United States on September 5, 1905, Japan obtained from Russia recognition of its paramount economic, political, and military interest in Korea, and special interests in Manchuria by possession of the Changchun-Dalian portion of the Russian-controlled Chinese Eastern Railway and the transfer from Russia of the Liaodong Peninsula. In order to protect these newly acquired rights, a Kanto (East Manchuria) army was created, which became the symbol of Japan's continental imperialism.[115]

Japan's emergence as an expansionist power was an unbroken chain of events stretching from the Japanese opening of Korea in 1874 to the Sino-Japanese War in 1895 to the Russo-Japanese War in 1905. The victory over Russia had special historical significance because it was the first victory of an Asian nation over a major European power. It established Japan as the peer of the other Western Great Powers. If the Sino-Japanese War was a turning point that acquired for Japan its first overseas colonial possession (Taiwan), the Russo-Japanese War marked "the takeoff point of Japanese imperialism" due to "the establishment of a sphere of influence recognized by the other powers."[116] The Russo-Japanese War established Japan's undisputed position among the foremost powers in East Asia. The result of the war diminished Russia's influence and opened a new chapter in world history. By demonstrating her national strength, Japan ushered in a new age of equal relations with the Western powers and secured formal recognition of its new sphere of influence by a series of bilateral agreements with Russia, Great Britain, the United States, and France. "Western assent to the new Japanese position on the Asian mainland reflected a mixture of self-interest, indifference, and helplessness."[117]

POWER COMPETITION AT THE WAKE OF THE POST–CHINESE ORDER

The power competition immediately after the decline of Chinese world order was centered around the struggle of Japan, a late-coming industrializing state, for security and power status in East Asia. This power competition displayed a number of distinctive characteristics that were not found in the old Chinese system.

First, power competition was carried out under a decentralized, anarchical system. The emerging international order in East Asia was dominated by a small number of militarily strong sovereign nations. There was no supranational authority at the apex of the system to keep the Great Powers in line, to regulate their quarrels, to ensure that these quarrels would not erupt into war. Any power could pose legitimate challenge to the status quo by force if necessary for its national security if it was capable of doing so. Japan was eligible to become the newest member of the Great Powers because it had the essential prerequisites for membership: armaments, successful military campaigns, and colonies. China, on the other hand, did not quite fit into the emerging system. Although some countries, notably the United States, spoke of upholding its territorial and administrative integrity, there was something antithetical to this anarchical system to admit a nation whose sovereignty depended upon foreign goodwill. The different fates of China and Japan were ultimately determined by military power. Japan was able to do what China could not because it succeeded in building up modern armed forces. Japan came to be recognized as one of the major military powers, whereas China did not. To a great extent, the underlying causes of the Sino-Japanese War was that Japan wished to cultivate its security and Great Power position in East Asia by attempting to eliminate China's influence from Korea; and China, in the meantime, tried to maintain its traditional position in Korea. The Korean soldiers' mutiny and the *Tonghak* movement were essentially sociopolitical protests against corrupt Korean officials and widespread foreign influence. Ironically, they gave rise to Chinese military interventions that led eventually to the Sino-Japanese War. By means of the Sino-Japanese War, Japan successfully replaced China and achieved its influential position in Korean affairs. The Japanese government achieved "one of the major goals it had set for itself under its diplomatic reform program, launched in 1871: diplomatic and commercial parity with Western powers in dealing with East Asian countries."[118] In acquiring Taiwan and the Pesadores Islands in the south and Korea in the north, the Japanese secured a solid base for future advances in East Asia and a convenient strategic springboard to Manchuria. Japan's victory in the Sino-Japanese War paved the way for its challenge to Russia in 1904 and its rise to Great Power status.

Second, in the anarchical system of power competition, the balance of power consideration became one important factor overshadowing the actions of the Great Powers. The major challenge to the Great Powers was to preserve the balance, which was seen as the principal means for discouraging anti-status quo power from dominance. Therefore, power competition in East Asia was characterized by the constantly changing process of balancing and counterbalancing actions. Considerable flexibility in making alliances and shifting partners was necessary. From this perspective, the Russo-Japanese War was caused both by the challenge from an anti-status quo power, Japan and the balance of power behavior of other Great Powers. After the Triple Intervention took place, most of the Great Powers, alarmed by Russia's expansion policies, leaned toward a policy of checking Russian ambition in East Asia. The Anglo-Japanese alliance was a result of British concern over Russia's southward advance. Without the alliance, it would be much more difficult for Japan to declare war on Russia. The involvement of U.S. President Roosevelt to mediate the Treaty of Portsmouth was also to keep a balance of power. As Roosevelt himself stated, "the best situation for the Open Door and American interests in the Far East would be a balance of power between Russia and Japan, not a triumph that would make Japan supreme in East Asia."[119] For the Great Powers in the region, the balance of power, rather than a bandwagon, was considered the only effective mechanism to promote their respective national interests, to safeguard their security, and to maintain relative peace and order in East Asia.

Third, small or weak nations were typically victims in this Great Power competition. A number of small nations were unable to influence, resist, or change the status quo imposed by the outcome of power competition. The Great Powers attempted to conquer a small nation if possible; to partition it if it was unable to conquer; and to trade their interest in, if it was secondary, with other Great Powers whose interests were primary. For example, Japan, through the Sino-Japanese war, the Russo-Japanese war, and through diplomatic approval of Japanese special interest in Korea by the United States and England, established the ascendancy of Japan and her paramount political, military, and economic interests in Korea. In 1896 and 1904 Japan and Russia separately proposed that Korea be divided into Russian and Japanese spheres of influence. These proposals were unsuccessful because each contender wanted supremacy when it felt sufficiently strong in its power position. After the Russo-Japanese War, the United States recognized Japanese suzerainty over Korea, and Japan, in turn, guaranteed the America's special interests in the Philippines. In such a situation, Korea, while a small nation, easily became a victim of Great Power rivalry. China, a declining weak power, could also fall, in spite of the fact that China was able to maintain its statehood, whereas Korea completely lost its statehood. The fact that China could maintain its statehood was due to one of the major "rules" of the balance of power politics. That is, China as one of the Great Powers, although declining into a passive object of the power competition, had to remain in the balance-of-power system. The integration of China into any of the Great Powers would result in an imbalance in the system. Thus the rival powers assisted the constrained China to remain as a regular but weak member in the emerging nation-state system. However, the situation of Korea was completely different. During the years from 1882 to 1904, Korea tried to maintain its independence by manipulating one imperial power against another. However, such efforts were vain. The weakness of Korea was first of all responsible for its fate. However, "the systemic factor of the balance of power in East Asia was a crucial determinant of the fate of Korea."[120] The Great Powers such as Japan and, to a lesser extent, China and Russia, competed for hegemony over Korea. The Sino-Japanese War and the Russo-Japanese War were fought to deny rival powers' political, economic, and military penetration in the peripheral area of Korea. As a small nation, the annexation of Korea to a Great Power was not necessarily a violation of the balance of power that jeopardized the overall East Asian equilibrium. Rather, countries such as the United States and Great Britain whose interests in Korea were secondary feared the growth of Russian expansion and influence in East Asia. For them, the Japanese annexation of Korea was acceptable as a contribution to the containment of Russian expansion and the maintenance of the balance of power.

+4+

FAILED MULTILATERALISM
IN THE AGE OF IMPERIALISM

After victory in wars against China and Russia, Japan began to redefine its position in the international system in general and in East Asia in particular, with an attempt to establish a Japanese-centered East Asian empire, known as the Greater East Asian Co-prosperity Sphere. In order to constrain the Japanese expansion, Western powers made a multilateral effort embodied in the Washington Conference system in the 1920s. After this multilateralism failed, a passive policy to the Japanese aggression rather than active balance of power characterized the behavior pattern of the Great Powers in the 1930s. The failure of multilateralism largely resulted from the distractions that the Great Powers experienced during this period. The old European imperialist powers were preoccupied by the problems of the two world wars back in Europe and were forced to turn their back on Japanese expansion into their Asian colonies. Russia, once an ambitious Pacific power, spent most of the period engrossed in domestic revolution and European affairs. The United States, the region's premier power, took the policy of self-imposed isolation and defined its interests mostly in trade and investment. It tended to accept Japanese dominance in the Far East as long as America's security and economic interests in the region were not disturbed. China, the sick man of Asia, was recuperating from abortive revolutions and was a ripe target for Japanese expansionism.

This situation left Japan involved in empire-making for the entire period in East Asia from the mid-1930s to the early 1940s. Japan tried to secure its economic and security needs unilaterally after multilateral efforts failed. Japanese expansion and its effort to establish a new East Asian world order under Japanese dominance occupied the central stage of East Asian international relations. Step by step, Japan moved toward its superior position in the regional system either through diplomatic maneuvers or through military conquest. The failure of multilateralism and Japan's unilateral attempts tilted the balance of power toward Japanese advantage. As the first modernized non-white empire in the Pacific, Japan attempted to reorder East Asian politics in its own image. The result was the invasion in China in the early 1930s and a southward movement that entered Indochina and Southeast Asian countries in the late 1930s. Confronted by the incoherence of the United States and the other Great Powers' policies, Japan successfully pursued aggressive expansionism and looked for a new status quo that granted it greater recognition. When its invasion in East Asia eventually encountered resistance from the United States, Japan struck a preemptive attack on Pearl Harbor, which led to the outbreak of the Pacific War. Japan's attempts to establish its regional dominance ended in catastrophe when it was defeated in the Pacific War in 1945.

THE DIPLOMACY OF IMPERIALISM

International relations in East Asia during the early twentieth century were characterized by a "diplomacy of imperialism," a term used by Akira Iriye to refer to "a distinctive era in the history of international affairs."[1] Myung H. Cho, a Korean scholar, elaborated the "diplomacy of imperialism" to mean that "major powers, through diplomatic negotiations, acted to preserve and enlarge their powers and national interests, and maintain the status quo or balance, at the expense of small or weak nations."[2] The diplomacy of imperialism was a new comprehensive framework for international relations in East Asia. The imperialist powers safeguarded their economic and political interests by partitioning the region into colonies or by defining the limits of their spheres of interest through a series of agreements and ententes among the imperialist countries. Under this system, small and weak countries became the objects of the Great Powers' diplomatic agreements. Even China, an old Great Power in decline, was forced to make territorial concessions to the rising Great Powers, to grant unequal treaties and extraterritorial rights, and to place its economic interests under foreign control. In contrast, the aggressive and expansionist ambition of Japan was facilitated by the system because of its vast military and economic superiority as well as its skillful diplomatic maneuvers.

After the Russo-Japanese War, Japan was recognized as a major player in the East Asian power competition and became a member of the world imperialist club. Its expansion in East Asia thereafter was accomplished by military conquest as well as imperialist diplomacy. Through a cautious diplomatic offensive, the Japanese government successfully consolidated its battlefield victories soon after the Russo-Japanese War. It carefully reassured the vested interests of other imperialist powers, particularly Great Britain and the United States, which had done much to help finance the war. In 1906, when both countries complained that Japanese military forces in Manchuria were restricting the activities of their businessmen, the Japanese government agreed to a troop withdrawal, establishing instead a colonial administration on the southern Manchuria and the Liaodong Peninsula. At the same time, through a series of bilateral diplomatic agreements, the Japanese secured recognition of her rights there from the British, American, and French, and in 1907 concluded a secret agreement with the Russians to divide southern and northern Manchuria into separate spheres of influence. In southern Manchuria, without China's agreement, Japan began to create a powerful military and economic base. Taking advantage elsewhere of "equal opportunities," Japan became active in the Yangtze Valley.[3] All these moves committed Japan more and more deeply to the "diplomacy of imperialism," by which "Europeans and Americans attempted to reduce the possibility of conflict among themselves over East Asian problems."[4]

In East Asian power politics, China became the focal point of imperialist diplomacy, especially for the Japanese expansion. Japan badly needed new territories and new markets because of a rapid increase in the Japanese population and accelerating industrialization. America's discriminatory restrictions against Japanese immigration barred any relief of Japan's population problem in that direction.[5] In view of its needs and difficulties in other parts of the world, Japan pursued the expansion of its power in China and began to plan the construction of a Japanese empire in Manchuria. Japanese high officials thought that the Japanese position in Manchuria was a "foundation of national expansion" and, moreover, that Korea, Manchuria, China, and the South Seas were most suitable for Japanese colonization since they were close to Japan.[6] On the eve of World War I, direct Japanese capital investment in China amounted to $192.5 million, and 68.9 percent of that was in Manchuria. Japanese investment in Manchuria allotted approximately 55 percent to the South Manchurian Railroad Company, created in 1906 using Russian railroad property. The port of Dalien expanded. The Fuchun coal mines and various other auxiliary enterprises sprang up.[7]

In October 1911, a republican revolution overthrew the Qing dynasty in China. The upheaval incited Japanese anxiety. As long as Qing had been in power, Japanese interests on the mainland seemed relative secure. The Manchus had guaranteed the Japanese a foothold in Manchuria and they remained militarily weak, unable to challenge a foreign presence.

Republican revolutionaries were ardent nationalists, who were determined to build a strong and modern "new China" capable of ending the shameful Chinese subjugation to the imperialist powers, but they proved inept as nation-builders. Far from rescuing China from her plight, the revolution plunged the country into even graver political chaos.[8] In spite of anxiety about China, the Japanese government's initial response followed a path of caution, waiting to see how the other imperialist powers would react. It soon became clear that the powers, Great Britain in particular, did not care who ruled China as long as it was ruled by a stable regime willing to recognize imperialist privileges granted by the Qing government. The most likely leader for such a regime was Yuan Shi-kai, the man who commanded the only modern fighting force in China and became the president of the republic in 1912. An international consortium in 1913 offered financial assistance in the form of a "Reorganization Loan" of 25 million pounds to Yuan's government. Japan joined the consortium with a contribution of funds.[9]

The eruption of World War I in Europe gave Japan an opportunity to move against a weak and decentralized China and expand its sphere of influence in East Asia. The decision to enter the war on the side of the Allies against Germany in 1914 enabled Japan to root out German bases in China and certain Pacific Islands and extended its power into those areas (that is, the Liaodong Peninsula and the German-controlled islands in the Pacific, such as the Marianas, the Carolines, and Marshalls) after the war. Since the Europeans were wrapped up in problems of their own, the war also provided opportunities for Japan to steal a march in consolidating its position in China. One year after Japan entered World War I (January 1915), the Japanese government submitted to China the famous "Twenty-one Demands," a draft treaty providing for an overall settlement of many issues pending between the two countries. It consisted of 14 "demands" and seven "wishes," outlined in five groups, in which Japan demanded, among other things, the extension of the 25-year lease of Guandong (South Manchuria) and of the South Manchuria Railway to 99 years, the recognition of Japanese control of German bases in Shandong province, and the transformation of the Hanyeping Company, which was supplying iron ore to Japan, into a Sino-Japanese joint enterprise.[10] The primary objective of the Twenty-one Demands was to establish Japanese hegemony in China and Manchuria by controlling Chinese political, military, and diplomatic affairs. They were tantamount to making China a Japanese protectorate. Japan would thus have established a preponderant position on the East Asian mainland.

With the signing of the armistice on November 11, 1918, World War I ended with the defeat of Germany. The formal Peace Conference of Versailles began on May 7 and the Treaty of Peace was signed on June 28, 1919. Under the terms of that treaty, earlier Japanese demands and basic interests were generally assured, including the disposition of the German territory in Shandong province. Suspicion about Japanese colonial intentions toward China and anger at imperialist diplomacy, especially among the new generation of educated Chinese, fed a rising tide of anti-Japanese sentiment. It finally exploded on May 4, 1919, when thousands of Chinese students, merchants, and workers staged demonstrations all over China in protest against the Twenty-one Demands and the decision of the Versailles Peace Conference to leave Japan in control of the Shandong territories.[11]

THE WASHINGTON CONFERENCE SYSTEM

Japan was not completely unchecked in the pursuit of its aggressive continental expansionism. It took no special insight to see that after World War I, Japan was the most active challenger to what passed for a balance of power in East Asia. Japan's unilateral policy of playing the lone wolf on the continent invited Western suspicion and Chinese hostility. Japanese policy after 1914 seemed to confirm fears of Japanese domination in Asia. Although the United States never challenged Japanese expansion in Korea, it was not willing to give up its interest in Manchuria and China proper and hence protested the Twenty-one Demands on the ground that they contradicted the principles of equal opportunity and the Open Door policy, threatening Chinese sovereignty. An American official wrote during the Twenty-one Demands episode of 1915 that the demands "would make China politically and in a military sense a protectorate of Japan and establish a Japanese monopoly in the commercial resources of China most requisite for military purposes."[12] If Japan controlled China, echoed E. T. William, head of the Far Eastern division of the U.S. State Department, Japan "could become a greater menace than ever to the U.S." because it is not "restrained by the scruples of the West and . . . declines to enter into peace pacts."[13]

Unlike the United States, Great Britain took a passive attitude toward Japanese expansion in East Asia, seeing Germany as the most dangerous challenger to British supremacy in various parts of the world and as an ally of Japan. Sir Edward Greay, Minister of Foreign Affairs, spoke well of Japan's moderate demands in his memoirs, claiming that "Japan's demands toward China were moderate when compared with those of the

Western powers. If a powerful European nation had been similarly placed, the demands would have been more aggressive."[14]

Taking advantage of the expiration of the Anglo-Japanese Alliance in 1921, the United States took the initiative in summoning a historic conference, known as the Washington Conference. It became a multilateral effort of the Great Powers, excluding the USSR and Germany, aimed at redefining relations between the Great Powers and re-establishing order and stability in East Asia. The Washington Conference that met from November 11, 1921, until February 1922 was intended to satisfy American and other Western nations' desire to control Japanese power, while not having to engage in a costly arms race. To gain some leverage against the United States, prior to the conference, the Japanese government had evinced a desire to renew the Anglo-Japanese Alliance. Great Britain raised no objection. Primarily due to American insistence, the Anglo-Japanese Alliance was finally abrogated.[15]

In place of this alliance there emerged a multilateralism embodied in the Four Power Treaty entered into by Japan, Great Britain, the United States, and France for the maintenance of the status quo in the Asia Pacific. The Four Power Treaty was followed by the Nine Power Treaty of February 1922, which enunciated a series of principles of Sino-foreign relations to replace the existing particularistic arrangements.[16] Charles Evans Hughes, the U.S. Secretary of State, presented a draft resolution to apply more effectively the principle of the Open Door policy and equal opportunity for trade and industry for all nations in China. Consequently, the words "equal opportunity" in matters concerning China were written into the Nine Power Treaty.[17] The signatories of the Nine Power Treaty were Japan, Great Britain, the United States, France, China, Italy, Belgium, the Netherlands, and Portugal.

Another agreement reached at the Washington Conference, the Naval Limitation Treaty of February 1922, known as the Five Power Treaty, "provided for the maintenance of the status quo in fortifications and naval bases in the Pacific."[18] The treaty established the maximum capital ship tonnage at the ratio of 5, 5, 3, 1.75, 1.75, respectively for Great Britain, the United States, Japan, France, and Italy. Japan felt cornered into accepting an inferior military status with the naval ratio lower than that of the United States and Britain. The Japanese navy had to give up its cherished plans for eight new battleships. A Japanese historian said, "this was taken by the Japanese as a move by America and Britain to keep them down."[19] As a compromise, the Americans and the British agreed to build no new fortifications west of Pearl Harbor in the Pacific, or east of Singapore. Since the

Japanese fleet would be equal in size to the combined Pacific fleets of the Anglo-American powers in the western Pacific, and hence strong enough to defend her home islands and colonial possessions, Japan accepted the inferior ratio.[20] Vital for Japan, no new naval fortifications could be built in the western Pacific, thereby ensuring Japanese hegemony.[21] On the Japanese side, although it saw a great need to control wider parts of the Asia Pacific for markets and resources, it also saw the benefits of a formal agreement with the United States and Britain in order to allay the suspicions of other powers about the aims of Japanese imperialism. Thus during the course of the Washington Conference Japan decided to avoid conflict with the United States, and, to this end, it was willing to embrace the principles of the new diplomacy, as embodied in multilateralism.

It was generally felt in the West that the Washington Conference, by demolishing the old structure of imperial power diplomacy, was an attempt to redefine the politics of the Asian Pacific region through a new concert of powers in a multilateral fashion. In reality, as Gerald Segal points out, "the mutual interest in avoiding an arms race and the mutual recognition of Japan's predominance in the Western Pacific meant that the treaty merely ratified the status quo."[22] The Washington Conference recognized and guaranteed Japanese naval hegemony in the western Pacific, as well as Japan's extensive rights and privileges on the mainland. It was for this reason that it was possible, for the first time, "to base Japan's diplomatic and military policies on the principle of cooperation with the Anglo-American nations."[23]

Indeed, after the Washington Conference, Japanese leadership and national opinion emphasized "the cardinal importance of establishing Japan as a respected member of the community of advanced powers."[24] During this period, the reins of Japan's policy toward China were firm in the hands of Kijuro Shidehara, minister of Foreign Affairs in the years 1924-29. He faithfully guided the destiny of Japan's foreign policy toward China in line with the conference agreements. Popularly known as Shidehara Diplomacy, the four principles as enunciated in the Diet by Baron Shidehara on January 18, 1927, may be summarized as follows: one, to respect the sovereignty and territorial integrity of China, and scrupulously avoid all interference in her domestic strife; two, to promote solidarity and economic rapprochement between the two nations; three, to entertain sympathetically and helpfully the just efforts for the realization of such rapprochement; and four, to maintain an attitude of patience and tolerance in the present situation of China, and, at the same time, protect Japan's legitimate and essential rights and interests by all reasonable means at the disposal of the Japanese government.[25]

However, Shidehara diplomacy soon collapsed. It turned out that it was not as if "the diplomatic settlement achieved at Washington determined the political status of Asia and the Pacific for a decade."[26] The Washington Conference system was challenged and undermined soon by China and the Soviet Union. With the lapse of the Anglo-Japanese Alliance and the consequent weakening of Japan's international bonds, China began to exhibit an increasingly aggressive attitude by openly boycotting Japanese goods and insisting on recovery of its Manchurian interests.[27] In the eyes of the Chinese, the Washington formula was a new cooperative economic method of exploitation of China, as the conference failed to restore to China full sovereignty. The Nationalist Northern Expedition of 1926 represented a Chinese effort to define order of its own choosing on the East Asian continent.[28] The Soviet Union was also a challenger to the Washington Conference system. Because the Soviet Union was not included in the Washington Conference, the conference represented an isolation imposed by imperialist powers of the world. The anti-imperialist initiative undertaken by the Soviet Union was given a tremendous boost when the Chinese Nationalist Party, Kuomintang (KMT), decided to join forces with the Chinese Communist Party (CCP) and the Comintern. The Soviet anti-imperialist policy scored a triumph in constructing the KMT and the CCP alliance in 1924. Following a Chinese workers' strike against Japanese imperialists on May 30, 1925, a nationwide movement of protest against foreign penetration and exploitation was developed and Soviet influence grew rapidly in China.[29]

The growing Soviet influence in China and emerging Chinese nationalism aroused concern in Japanese military leaders regarding their interests in China. A unified China under the nationalist regime in 1928 seriously threatened the Japanese position in Manchuria.[30] The Washington Conference system was thereafter resented in Japan, where many military leaders believed that it was ratified by civilian leaders who did not understand the imperatives of imperial defense. Senior army leaders began to take foreign policy into their own hands. The Jinan Incident (April 28, 1928), the assassination of a prominent Manchurian warlord Zhang Zuolin (June 4, 1928), and the Mukden Incident (September 18, 1931) were a series of events exploited or planned by the Japanese militarists to provide a pretext for military actions in order to counteract emerging Chinese nationalism and the rising influence of Sino-Soviet rapprochement.[31] As the scope of the incidents widened, the growing influence of the military clique in the government of Japan could no longer be held in check. The extreme elements among the Japanese militarists, especially in the Kanto army in

Manchuria, took up an inflexible position against Shidehara diplomacy, culminating in Japan's withdrawal from the Washington Conference system
as well as from the League of Nations. Under these circumstances, the multilateralism of the Washington treaty became useless in controlling
Japanese expansion in the Asia Pacific. From this perspective, Gerald Segal
suggested that the Washington system was not a "new form of diplomacy,
but rather the addition of the 'diplomacy of confusion' to the already anarchical phase of 'the diplomacy of imperialism.'"[32]

"THE GREATER EAST ASIAN CO-PROSPERITY SPHERE"

The Washington system of 1922 proved to be unsuccessful and Western
powers, hit by the Great Depression, were too involved in their domestic
problems to block Japanese aggression in the early 1930s. Japanese strategists put forth a slogan of "Greater East Asian Co-Prosperity Sphere,"
attempting to form a gigantic Asian bloc under Japanese leadership. The
"Greater East Asian Co-Prosperity" was in essence an anti-European colo-
nialist policy based on an idea of Pan-Asianism. Being racially different
from the other Great Powers of the world, Japan felt it was unjustly denied
its rightful place. The covenant of the League of Nations adopted in 1919
rejected the provision of racial equality for which Japan so forcefully cam-
paigned.[33] In addition, as a latecomer to the Great Power politics and to
colonial competition, when Japan "was ready to join the game of imperialist aggrandizement, the world had been pretty much carved up already.
Instead of a far-flung empire, Japan had to settle for small territories
nearby."[34] Although Japan was relatively successful at expanding its colonial possessions beyond Korea and Taiwan, it run into opposition from the
West. The British and Americans were concerned about Japan's dominance in China. The Americans promoted the idea of an Open Door as a
means of checking a rising Japanese influence. In his "outline of state policy for national defense" in mid-summer 1936, Ishiwara Kanji, a Japanese
military historian, strategist, and Pan-Asianist, presented a staged plan for
the expulsion of the white races from East Asia in order that the continent
might be free to develop under the leadership of Japan. He believed that
Japanese expansion in China and Asia was to "liberate Asia."[35] Just before
the outbreak of the Pacific War, Emperor Hirohito issued an imperial
rescript to outline the country's war aims. A book of commentaries on the
rescript sold more than three million copies during the war. It said that
"The various races of East Asia look upon the British and Americans as
superior to the Nippon race ... Therefore we must show our real strength

before all our fellow races of East Asia. We must show them an object lesson. It is not a lesson in words. It should be a lesson in facts. In other
words, before we can expel the Anglo-Saxons and make them removed all
their traces from East Asia, we must annihilate them."[36]

A large-scale invasion of China was Japan's most important first step
in establishing the Greater East Asian Co-Prosperity Sphere. On the night
of September 18, 1931, Japanese Kanto army leaders created an incident,
known as the Mukden Incident. They initiated a plot to seize control of
China's three northeastern provinces (Manchuria) on the pretext that a
detachment of Chinese soldiers dynamited a section of the South
Manchurian Railroad of Mukden.[37] Acting without direct approval of military authorities in Tokyo, and certainly counter to the wishes of civilian
leadership of Japan, the instigators directed the Kanto forces from the
Japanese-leased territory of the Liaodong Peninsula and from bases along
the Japanese-controlled South Manchurian railway. Within hours, the
major cities of southern Manchuria—Shenyang (Mukden), Yingkou,
Antong, and Changchun—fell under Japanese control. Within days, most
of the Liaodong Peninsula and Jilin province were brought inside the
Kanto army's orbit; and within weeks, the Japanese military established
a puppet government over the entire northeast. The last emperor of the
Qing dynasty, Puyi, who was deposed as a small child, was resurrected to
serve as "emperor" of the puppet state "Manzhouguo" (Manchukuo). The
independent action of the Kanto army brought down the civilian government and started a military dominance in Japan. Assassinations of ex-
ministers in early 1932 underscored the loss of civilian authority in a
country gripped by ultra-nationalism. Nothing that the Kanto army did in
China thereafter was considered wrong.[38]

After the Mukden Incident, Japanese forces spread out easily across
Manchuria, with the larger Chinese forces putting up little that could be
dignified with the name resistance. The Chinese government under
Chiang Kai-shek was not eager to clash with the Japanese military
machine. Chiang felt that his own army was inferior to Japan's and that
war between the two nations would be disastrous both for China and for
himself.[39] Domestic considerations also loomed larger in Chiang's concerns. His priority was to defeat domestic enemies—both regional militarists and Chinese Communists—and to cement control of China under
his central authority.[40] Chiang therefore sought to avoid or delay war with
Japan, adopting a policy of conciliation with Tokyo. He proclaimed a formula of "first internal pacification, then external resistance."[41] Domestic
enemies, most notably the Communists, had to be eliminated, he argued,

before China would be sufficiently united to resist the Japanese. When Japan attacked Manchuria, he telegraphed Zhang Xueliang, military commander of the northeast, instructing him not to provoke the Japanese and to rely on an appeal to the League of Nations.[42]

However, the League of Nations was powerless to intervene. The Western powers' policy toward the Japanese invasion was mostly passive, if not preaching appeasement. In December, the League of Nations agreed to send a committee under Britain's Lord Lytton to investigate the events in Manchuria. But the committee did not issue a report until one year later, and the League of Nations did not adopt the report until February 1933, almost a year and a half after the Japanese invasion. Although the report rejected Japan's pretext as an unjustified intervention, it did not call for applying Article 16 sanctions against Japan. When the report was adopted, the Japanese delegation walked out and announced that Japan was resigning from the League.[43] Under these circumstances, while the League of Nations temporized and then "investigated" the causes of the invasion, the Japanese aggression was not punished and the League of Nations failed to implement collective security against the aggressor. Consolidating its control over Manchuria, Japan extended its invasion to Shanghai in January 1932. From their ringside seats in still-protected enclaves in Shanghai, Western powers watched as Japan leveled the Chinese section of what many called the greatest city in the Pacific. The cowardly response of Western powers to Japan's attack on China was largely a result of particularly complex limits of their foreign policies. Although the Western powers were more critical of Japan, having been exasperated by Japan's long series of unilateral acts, and more willing to take Japan to task for its violation of the Nine Power Treaty, this did not mean that "there was an anti-Japanese coalition forming in the world that would support China's struggle against Japan."[44] The Western powers would not go beyond criticizing Japan and endorsing the recommendations of the Lytton commission. Both the United States and Great Britain were satisfied with these steps and not prepared to employ anti-Japanese sanctions to help China.[45]

The United States could have led Western countries to stop Japan at this stage. However, the focus of American leaders in the 1932 presidential election was domestic recovery and, as far as foreign policy was concerned, the issues of European debts and disarmament. Actually, during the campaign, little was said about Asian affairs. While the United States morally denounced Japanese expansion in China, its isolationism kept it passive: "Washington often lacked either the intention or the power to back up its protestations, and it frequently compromised with unpleasant reality at China's expense."[46] America's stake in China was perceived as small. From that view, it naturally followed that if the United States concerned itself with China's integrity it was nothing less than "quixotic." Under these circumstances, there was a large gap between rhetoric and action in American policy. As Akira Iriye suggests, the American policy was characterized by a "mixture of moral globalism and fear of military involvement in Asia."[47] The United States reiterated its support for China's territorial integrity, but it also recognized that "territorial contiguity created special relations" between countries. The (Robert) Lansing-Ishii (Kikujiro) agreement in 1917 accepted "territorial propinquity," which justified Japan's claim that it had "special interests in China."[48] As Iriye indicates, "East Asia was essentially beyond the American zone of vital interests." So long as America's security and vital economic interests remained unaffected, as appeared to be the case, it saw "no reason why the U.S. should assume the responsibility of publicly castigating Japan and run the risk of war. . . . War with Japan on the question of Manchuria was unthinkable."[49]

In China, although Chiang's government attempted to avoid war with Japan, Chinese opinion became more and more adamantly anti-Japanese. An incidence took place in December 1936 when forces loyal to the former Manchurian warlord, Zhang Xueliang, placed Chiang Kai-shek under detention in the vicinity of the ancient capital of Xian. Chiang had been engaged in a campaign against the Communists who had recently completed their Long March out of their southeastern stronghold. The Communists were calling for an end to the civil war and the establishment of a united front against Japanese aggression. The Manchurian general had fallen under their influence. They demanded Chiang to stop fighting the Communists and released Chiang only after he pledged to accept the united front strategy.[50] After Chiang returned to Nanjing, his government and press began reflecting his pledge, while the Communists responded by incorporating their military units into the Nationalist Army.

Such developments forced some Japanese leaders to reconsider their policy objectives. At the beginning of 1937 some civilian and military officials in Tokyo were willing to stop encouraging separatist movements in north China because it could only strengthen Chinese nationalism. It would not be possible for Japan to prevent nationalist reunification of China proper unless it were prepared for war. The General Staff judged that a war should be avoided. However, this policy reorientation never had a chance to succeed and alarmed those in the army, especially in the Kanto army, who were convinced that the reorientation would merely play into

China's hands and weaken Japan's position on the continent.[51] From their point of view, there was every reason for Japan to continue its aggressive course in China and East Asia. After taking over Manchuria in 1932, they had been brought to battle readiness and awaited only a suitable provocation. On the night of July 7-8, 1937, Japanese soldiers of the Kanto army were engaged in night maneuvers near Luguoqiao (the Marco Polo bridge), located between Tianjin and Beijing. Their operations were part of general war games by the Japanese forces and included the use of blank ammunition. At some point in the darkness, unknown persons fired on the Japanese and a subsequent roll call revealed that one soldier was missing. Although the absent man returned within 20 minutes, Japanese commanders were unaware of this and demanded the right to search a nearby town, Wanping. When Chinese troops refused to allow the search, Japanese artillery began to shell Wanping and a battle broke out.[52]

The incident that occurred in Luguoqiao gave Japan a pretext to move supplementary military contingents into northern China. Twenty days later, on July 27, Japanese armies began a broad invasion that signaled the beginning of the undeclared but full-fledged Sino-Japanese War that continued for eight years. Taking advantage of concessions made by the Chiang Kai-shek government and by the United States and England, which still hoped to localize Japanese aggression, Japanese armies took Shanghai in November. By the end of 1937 they controlled China's capital, Nanjing, as the Japanese navy blocked the seacoast. After its capture, the Japanese army launched a massacre for six weeks in Nanjing. According to the records of several welfare organizations that buried the dead bodies after the massacre, around 300,000 people, mostly civilians and POWs, were brutally slaughtered. More than 20,000 cases of rape were reported. Many of the victims were gang-raped and then killed. This figure does not include those captives who were sent to army brothels (the so-called comfort stations).[53] Early success did not blind the Japanese to the difficulties that awaited them. The taking of Shanghai, Tianjin, and other cities threatened to cause a clash with the United States and England too soon. Therefore Japanese diplomacy continued to veil Japan's real aims, trying to "deny its territorial ambitions in central and southern China and insisting that Japan would respect the rights and interests of foreign powers in China."[54]

The Japanese invasion of China in July 1937 was part of its design of East Asian international politics under an initiative, the so-called Greater East Asian Co-Prosperity Sphere. Japan's economic and strategic plan included the former German Islands, French Indochina and Pacific Islands, Thailand, British Malaya, British Borneo, Dutch East Indies,

Burma, Australia, New Zealand, India, as well as other territories, with Japan, Manchuria, and China as the backbone.[55] In the summer of 1940, just before Japanese troops occupied Indochina, Japan's foreign minister, Matsuoka Yosuke, explained Japan's strategy: "The immediate aim of our foreign policy at present is to establish in accordance with the lofty spirit of the *kodo* (imperial way), a great East Asian chain of common prosperity with the Japanese-Manchukuo-China group as one of the links. We shall thus be able to demonstrate the *kodo* in the most effective manner, and pave the way toward the establishment of an equitable world peace."[56]

Japan saw its role in East Asia as "civilizing" and vital for the legitimate defense of its interests against the plundering Europeans.[57] The stress on one race led Japan to try to wipe out national differences and, at least culturally, to have its colonies support Japanese goals.[58] In spite of the liberationist rhetoric, East Asians soon choked on it, for the Japanese wasted little time in demonstrating how vicious conquest and colonial control could really be. Just like the European colonialists, the Japanese were quick to see the advantage of resources, trade, and investment that colonies provided. Japan's aim was to extract minerals and labor resources from Korea and Manchuria and rice and sugar from Taiwan and transfer them to the home islands. The Japanese colonialism created an enduring East Asian legacy of suspicion and outright hatred toward the Japanese. Nevertheless, Japanese colonialism was somehow different from the European colonialism. It resulted in a different pattern of control than that exercised by European powers. Japan eventually came to stress economic self-sufficiency, education, and central bureaucracies. The Japanese developed a strong bureaucratic apparatus to enforce political order and economic extraction in Taiwan, Korea, and Manchuria. For the purpose of more efficient exploitation of the colonies' resources, the Japanese introduced the necessary socioeconomic infrastructure. Roads and ports were built, schools were opened, surveys and registration of landed properties were undertaken, and tax codes were developed. Moreover, unlike the European colonialists, Japan brought some industries to its colonies when it appeared that these colonies could assume an intermediate role in processing the raw materials of China and Southeast Asia.[59]

THE OUTBREAK OF THE PACIFIC WAR

Japan's call for a Greater East Asian Co-prosperity Sphere did not meet any serious challenges as long as it concentrated on China. After 1937, the direction of Japanese aggression was expanded toward the Pacific, which was seen as "a Japanese lake" by Japanese leaders. This confronted the United States and other major powers and created a genuinely Pacific-wide war. To prepare for the Pacific War, Japan worked hard to develop its naval strength. The Washington Naval Conference had left considerable loopholes. Japan was not only able to maintain its superiority in the western Pacific but also set about compensating for restrictions on her battle-ship-building by announcing increases in its cruiser, destroyer, and submarine strength. This concerned the Americans and British who called for the Geneva Naval Conference in 1927 and the London Naval Conference in 1930 to extend some form of restriction to the category of auxiliary vessels and especially cruisers. However, the Geneva Conference "petered out" in a "flood of mutual recrimination," while the London Conference reached a compromise that allowed Japan to build more than the ratio of overall vessels set at the Washington Conference.[60]

Walking out of the latest naval arms-control conference, Japan fired the starting-gun for a race in naval and air-force equipment, as well as military fortifications across the Pacific. From 1935 Britain had turned its back on the Pacific to concentrate on the gathering clouds of war in Europe. The United States was able to confront Japan more directly, but was unwilling to take on Japan by itself.[61] Americans calculated that China was the key to stopping Japan. But China seemed incapable of an effective response. In the face of the Japanese assault, the Chinese nationalist government withdrew to the interior. The Communist guerrilla forces were able to gain military experience and political popularity in the anti-Japanese war.[62]

Without real resistance from the United States and the other Great Powers, the idea of a move southward gained currency among Japanese military leaders after the outbreak of war in Europe in the late 1930s. The early victories of Germany, culminating in the fall of France in June 1940, opened new and intoxicating perspectives for the military. With France and Holland under Nazi control and England besieged by the German air force, an Axis victory in Europe seemed imminent. The European colonies in South and Southeast Asia lay weak and unprotected. The power vacuum tempted the Japanese. In late July 1940 the Japanese government believed that the time had come to strengthen ties with the Axis in preparation for establishing military bases in French Indochina and securing access to the rich natural resources of the European colonies. A foothold in Southeast Asia would enable the Japanese to cut off Chiang's supply routes from the south, obtain a staging area for new campaigns in south China, and control rubber, tin, and oil resources essential for achieving military victory against China. Japan hoped to secure these ends by diplomatic means. Accordingly, in September 1940, after receiving the assent of the pro-Nazi Vichy government in France, Japanese troops moved into northern Indochina. A few days later the government signed a Tripartite Mutual Defense Pact with Germany and Italy (September 27, 1940), aimed at deterring United States intervention in either the European war or the Sino-Japanese conflict. Japan's diplomatic offensive reached a new height when a Soviet-Japanese Neutrality Treaty was signed in Moscow on April 13, 1941. It seemed that Japan could now successfully carry out its southward strategy.[63]

American interests in the Pacific were under threat when Japan made the policy of southward expansion. The British ambassador in Washington, Lord Lothian, urged in November 1939 that the United States enter the war if the Japanese expanded south.[64] Indeed, the new turn of events set Japan on a collision course with America, which no longer tolerated Japanese predominance. While Japanese leaders had begun to tout Japan's role as liberator of Asia, the American president, Roosevelt, spoke of the need to stop an "epidemic of world lawlessness" and was convinced that Japan's Pan-Asianist new order was the antithesis of American policy in the Pacific and Asia.[65] Commenting on the Japanese southward expansion, President Roosevelt said that "we are faced with the danger of Japan's continuing her expansion in the Far East especially toward the south. . . . If Japan, moving further southward, should gain possession of the region of the Netherlands' East Indies and the Malay Peninsula, would not the chances of Germany's defeat in Great Britain be increased and the chances of England's winning be decreased thereby?"[66]

Faced with a Japanese southward expansion, the Americans and British began to draw plans for a common front of resistance in the Pacific, feeling that U.S. and British security were interdependent. However, Britain was unable to protect its threatened colonies because all its ships and planes were needed in the Atlantic and Mediterranean. Thus the United States became involved in East Asian conflict because the survival of Britain both in Europe and in Asia was considered vital to America's own security and to the maintenance of a general balance of power in East Asia. The Americans were resolved to build a two ocean fleet. Although the United States tried to insist on limiting Japan's naval-building and on preserving a margin, beset by isolation and economic problems, the United States had not expanded the limits it had secured for itself. The Americans resolved to catch up. The "fundamental decision was taken in response to the European crisis, it affected the situation in Asia."[67] As early as the summer of 1938, Washington had placed an embargo on shipments of aircraft, arms, and other war materials to Japan. In July 1939 it abrogated its commercial treaty with Japan so that it could legally expand its economic warfare; and in the fall of 1940 the president terminated the export of scrap iron and steel to Japan. With the Japanese attack on Indochina in July 1941, the United States froze Japanese assets and imposed an embargo on the export of oil to Japan. At U.S. prompting, Great Britain, the British Commonwealth nations, and the government of the Dutch East Indies followed suit, cutting 90 percent of Japan's oil import. This sudden escalation of economic warfare was intended to deter Japan from further rashness, but it had precisely the opposite effect. Without oil imports Japan's whole war machine would have to come to a halt everywhere, including China, within a matter of months. Under these circumstances, Japan, as a trading nation, was fundamentally vulnerable in the case of a protracted, large-scale war.

The Japanese government was now forced to choose between abandoning military gains of the past decade or waging a war against the United States. Even before the embargo, the Japanese military leadership already considered war between America and Japan inevitable. An extraordinary document drafted by the military leadership said that as Japan's power expanded, America's resistance would naturally grow. The United States "will sooner or later, as part of its Asian policy, provoke a conflict with the empire."[68] The likelihood of a victory in a conflict with the United States seemed problematical to many leaders, but the alternative of submitting to the demands of the "white imperialists" was equally hard to accept. The inevitable conflict finally came, in the prevailing Japanese view, with the formation of the dreaded "ABCD line" (American, Britain, China, and Dutch or Holland) to choke off Japan's crucial shipments of raw materials and fuel.[69] The Japanese felt that if they did not go to war, they would eventually suffer defeat. With 90 percent of their oil imported, the Japanese government felt that it could not last for even a year if its supply was cut. They concluded that it was better to go to war than to be slowly strangled. As one scholar indicates, the oil embargo pushed the Japanese government inexorably toward a decision for war.[70] The navy high command, which had tended to urge caution and restraint in dealing with the Americans, concluded that if war was unavoidable it had better begin before Japan's precious oil reserves were exhausted and it was best to strike a preemptive blow before the United States could organize its defense. The Japanese military leaders understood that they might lose, but defeat was better than humiliation and submission. "Japan entered the war," wrote a prince of the imperial family, "with a tragic determination and in desperate self-abandonment." If Japan lost, "there will be nothing to regret because she is doomed to collapse even without war."[71]

Once the ABCD line was drawn, from the Japanese perspective, war really did become inevitable. If the Japanese did not strike first, at Pearl Harbor, they might lose their chance to fight at all as the Japanese navy used up its scarce remaining oil. Counting on the element of surprise, after concluding the Tripartite Pact between Germany, Italy, and Japan and the Soviet-Japanese Neutrality Treaty, Japan launched a preemptive attack on Pearl Harbor on Sunday, December 7, 1941. The Japanese plans aimed at forcing the larger and stronger America to the negotiating table before it could mobilize its full strength. A series of lightning-fast amphibious operations were to establish a defense perimeter stretching south and westward from the Marshall Islands in the Central Pacific down through Southeast Asia to Indochina. Once secured, this perimeter was to be held against American counterattack while German armies completed the conquest of Europe. Japanese planners expected that the United States, when finally faced with the overwhelming strength of the Axis powers in both Europe and Asia, would finally be forced to negotiate a peace settlement that would leave Japan in control of the Greater East Asia Co-Prosperity Sphere, an economic and military geopolitical bloc under Japanese hegemony.

Indeed, the United States was not prepared to enter a war with Japan. Although America had an economic stake in China and was bound by sentiment to China, the China problem alone would not have provoked war between the United States and Japan.[72] It is true that, were China to be incorporated in a Japanese-led Pan-Asianist sphere, America's economic and cultural role there would have been severely compromised, and perhaps even ended. One of the premises of Pan-Asianism was, after all, the elimination of the remnants of Western imperialism and the inroads of Western culture and values. However, as one American historian indicates, "too many Americans felt China was not worth it [a war with Japan]; too many Americans opposed war at all, in any form; too many Americans sensed that Chinese nationalists were themselves so anti-foreign that American interests in China would be endangered whoever should win."[73] What eventually stirred American diplomacy was not the fate of China but rather the European connection: the relationship perceived between the war in Asia and the war in Europe. Both Secretary Hull and President Roosevelt now believed that peace depended upon the credibility of the international community's commitment to collective security. Failure to respond effectively to aggression in Asia would encourage outbreaks of violence elsewhere. The linkage of American security interests in Asia and

Europe, and the Japanese striking southward to seize the mineral resources of the European empires in Southeast Asia, promoted Roosevelt to put an embargo on oil shipment to Japan in 1941. This action was at the urging of British Primer Minister Winston Churchill that the United States do something to protect British Malaya and the Netherlands East Indies (with their tin, rubber, bauxite, and oil). When the Americans tried to deter the Japanese from striking south by putting an embargo on oil shipments to Japan, they did not expect this would provoke Japan to attack the United States. Assistant Secretary of State Dean Acheson was quoted at the time that this would not lead to war because "no rational Japanese could believe that an attack on us could result in anything but disaster for his country."[74]

In this case, the Americans were caught by surprise on December 7, 1941, when the Japanese launched the attack on Pearl Harbor. The American army and navy leadership on Oahu, Hawaii, like American politicians in Washington, were unaware of Japan's specific aggressive intent toward the fleet in their care. They "deemed it suicide for Japan to initiate hostilities against a power with five times Japan's gross national product."[75] Shocked by the surprising attack and the heavy losses of the Pacific fleet at Pearl Harbor, the United States quickly mobilized its potential to fight back. Six hours after Pearl Harbor, Admiral Harold R. Stark, chief of naval operations, issued a terse order to the fleet, "execute unrestricted air and submarine warfare against Japan."[76] This eight-word command contained the formula by which the U.S. navy rounded on Japan and made possible its destruction as a military power.

American industrial potential outstripped Japan's in every essential war material and the Japanese industry lacked the productive capacities to support their far-flung forces in a war of attrition. Until Pearl Harbor, the Pacific War was really an East Asian war. Although Europeans were involved in the first phase by virtue of having their colonies invaded, the wider war reached the doors of Australia and out to Hawaii. The Pacific War was the first to be fought across the expanse of the Pacific. The final result of the war was determined primarily by the ability of the American economy to support a protracted naval strategy at long distance. As events were to prove, "Japan was economically outstripped to begin with, and steadily lost ground thereafter. Japanese war production expanded at a much slower rate than that of the United States, and her military technology began to lag behind as the Americans developed and refined new tools of war such as radar and long-range bombers."[77] The Japanese government surrendered unconditionally to the allies in 1945 after the United States dropped atomic bombs on Hiroshima and Nagasaki.

THE CAUSES OF THE PACIFIC WAR

The Pacific War was fought between Japan, who attempted to redefine the East Asian international order in its own terms, and the United States, who eventually decided to deter Japanese expansion in the Pacific and Asia. The war broke out unexpectedly but the seeds of war were sown decades earlier. Besides the aggressive nature of Japanese militarism, the failure of the multilateralism adopted by the Great Powers in the 1920s, and the thereafter passive policy toward aggression, were also responsible for the Pacific War. When the multilateral Washington Conference system was established in the early 1920s, Japan earnestly and vigorously participated. Only after the multilateralism was challenged by China and the Soviet Union and undermined by world depression, did Japan define its security and welfare unilaterally, with an attempt to establish its regional dominant position. After the collapse of the Washington Conference system, passivity emerged as a major theme of international affairs in East Asia just as appeasement did in Europe. Indeed, as indicated by Joseph Nye, "appeasement is not bad per se; it is a classic tool of diplomacy."[78] It was used successfully on several occasions in Western diplomatic history to preserve peace and stability. The examples include events such as the way the victorious powers appeased France in 1815 and Britain appeased the rising United States in the 1890s. However, appeasement was the wrong approach toward Japan and other aggressive powers in the 1930s. Although Japan's policy of imperialist expansion in East Asia became widely popular, Japan's desire to seek the predominant position in the Asian Pacific was never met with serious challenge until America's embargo actions in 1939. Without strong rivalries in the region, Japan's desires developed into the creation of regional hegemony, a call for a new East Asian international order, that is, the Greater East Asian Co-prosperity Sphere, which was carried out first in China, and then in Southeast Asia. Faced with Japanese aggression, the Chiang Kai-shek government in China was weak and could not resist the invasion. The United States and other Western powers were also hesitant to show their military firmness in maintaining the balance of power in the Asia Pacific. Militarists in Japan were thus able to carry out their attempts for a predominant position in East Asia in the 1930s.

From this perspective, Japan held center stage in the power competition for East Asia. This was largely due to the tolerance of status quo powers to the aggression of the anti-status quo power. While the balance of power was the major behavior pattern of power competition in the late nineteenth century, failed multilateralism and passive policy toward Japanese expansion characterized East Asian international relations in the early twentieth century. The Pacific War broke out when the United States began to shift its policy from passivity to active resistance. The shift in the American policy was largely because Japan became a serious threat to the interests of the United States and other Western powers when Japanese expansion extended to American and European colonies in Indochina and Southeast Asia. The new policy was adopted by the United States in the form of economic warfare. The basic objectives of the American decision was to stop the Japanese southward aggression and restore the status quo before 1931 by means of embargo. Economic warfare failed because the Japanese felt cornered in a situation where the alternative of peace (surrender) looked worse than losing a war, and because the United States was not prepared to fight a war in the Pacific while it adopted an economic embargo. The economic embargo was not backed up with sufficient military means. In the words of Tang Tsou, American policy toward Japan before outbreak of the Pacific War was an "imbalance between end and means." This imbalance took "the form of an unwillingness and, at times, an inability to use military power purposefully to achieve political objectives."[79]

From the Japanese perspective, the war with the United States was not chosen but was rather forced by the more terrible alternative of losing status or abandoning the national objective of imperialism. Japan wanted to use diplomacy to achieve its objectives if it were possible. In fact, before the strike on Pearl Harbor, as a last gamble of diplomatic effort, the Japanese government sent Washington a proposal to withdraw from Indochina if the United States agreed to end the oil embargo, help Japan get oil supplies from the Indies, and help Japan achieve a diplomatic end to hostilities in China. In November 1941 the Roosevelt administration indicated that it would accept nothing less than a return to the pre-1931 status quo, the withdrawal of Japanese troops from China, Manchuria, and Indochina, and Japanese recognition of the Chiang Kai-shek government.[80] The irresistible force had met an immovable object. Faced with diplomatic stalemate, the Japanese government decided to break off formal diplomatic talks with the Americans, took advantage of U.S. unpreparedness, and made a preemptive strike against American forces in the Pacific.

·5·

THE ORIGINS OF THE BIPOLAR
COLD WAR COMPETITION

The end of the Pacific War brought sweeping changes to East Asian international relations. As a defeated nation, Japan lost its Great Power position and became a subordinate state occupied by the allied powers. The United States established itself as a superpower whose interests were complicated and interwoven in every region of the world. It became a predominant East Asian power. The Soviet Union successfully regained its major power status by exploiting its participation in the Pacific War against Japan, by reestablishing its special rights in Manchuria, by occupying northern Korea, and by holding a controlling hand in the civil contest in China. At the Yalta Conference for the postwar order, China was expected to become a major actor as soon as Chiang Kai-shek unified China. However, the defeat of the Nationalists by the Communists in 1949 became a cause of grave concern to Americans who hoped to see China restored to the status of an independent power able to play a principal stabilizing role in East Asia. The emerging Sino-Soviet alliance seemed to give the Communists control of the Eurasian landmass stretching from the Baltic Sea to the South China Sea. In responding to North Korea's attack on the South in a bid to reunify Korea under the Communist regime, the United States intervened militarily in the Korean civil war and sent the Seventh Fleet to "neutralize" the Taiwan Strait—that is, to prevent an impending Chinese Communist takeover of Taiwan. After the Korean War, the United States began to elevate Japan to the role of a junior partner in the struggle against communism. In these circumstances, power competition in East Asia became the epitome of the Cold War global bipolar system.

The Cold War is a term that characterizes the hostile relationship that developed first in Europe and then in Asia and other parts of the world as a result of the intensified struggle between the United States and the Soviet Union in the latter half of the 1940s.[1] While loosely employed, "the term had an exceedingly important connotation: it called attention to the fact that, however acute their rivalry and conflict, the two sides were pursuing it by means short of another war and that, it was hoped, they would continue to do so."[2]

The power distribution in the Cold War era was characterized by a bipolar structure that did not become clear until 1947. As one scholar put it, "it did not seem likely that the United States, unraveled by war and the only possessor of nuclear weapons, could be effectively challenged by the Soviet Union for some time at least."[3] However, with surprising speed to the West, the Soviets successfully built an atomic device in August of 1949, which brooked America's nuclear monopoly. The Soviet Union became a genuine power contender confronting the United States in every region of the world. Without attempting to apportion the blame for starting the Cold War, the Cold War bipolar world may be regarded as a sparring match between the two nuclear superpowers in "a succession of moves and countermoves."[4] The process of involvement was gradual. The acute conflict between the United States and the Soviet Union was first confined to Europe but gradually spread to other continents, including East Asia. Eventually, the Soviet Union and the United States were not only threatening each other with nuclear extinction but were confronting each other all over the globe. Any change in any part of the world could affect the delicate balance between them. The East Asia power competition during this period was part of the Cold War bipolar confrontation.

THE YALTA SYSTEM FOR EAST ASIAN ORDER

The post–World War II East Asian order was originally shaped at the Yalta Conference in February 1945. The Big Three leaders—Churchill, Roosevelt, and Stalin—convened at Yalta in the Crimea and made a number of crucial agreements for the establishment of peace and order in the post–World War II world. The Yalta agreements covered practically every region of the world.[5] The disposition of territory in East Asia was one important issue in the Far Eastern agreement of the Big Three. Stalin pledged to enter the Pacific War within three months of Germany's surrender. In exchange for Russia's entry into the war against Japan, Stalin was to regain concessions lost by czarist Russia at the end of the Russo-Japanese War. These included control of the Kurile Islands, southern Sakhalin, and the lease of the naval base at Port Arthur. In addition, while Port Arthur and the Liaodong Peninsula would be international ports, Russia's preeminent interests in Manchuria were once again to be acknowledged. The agreement provided for joint Sino-Soviet management of the Chinese Eastern and South Manchurian railroads. Finally, the Soviet Union was also to receive recognition of its special interests in Mongolia.[6] Tang Tsou's study indicates that the Yalta agreement was "a price paid by the United States to insure Soviet entry into the Pacific War at such a moment as to save American lives . . . with or without American agreement the Soviet Union could have, in one way or another, acquired greater gains than those conceded her at Yalta."[7] As for Korea, Roosevelt and Stalin agreed that there should be a line of demarcation separating U.S. and U.S.S.R. air and sea operations. Their agreement was made for the purpose of accepting Japanese surrender and taking occupation of the country. Roosevelt presented the idea of a trusteeship for Korea at Yalta, and Stalin later agreed to a four-power joint trusteeship under Great Britain, the United States, the Soviet Union, and China.[8] The Yalta conference also agreed that the European colonies in Indochina and Southeast Asia would be part of the trusteeship system only if the colonial power consented.[9]

Taken together, the Far Eastern agreements offered the most comprehensive blueprint of the Big Three's postwar plans for East Asia. The economic and security interests of each of the Allied powers were given ample consideration. In effect, the Yalta agreement simply awarded to each of the Big Three what each already controlled or was on the point of controlling. President Roosevelt and most of his advisors were very optimistic that friendly relations and mutual cooperation that had emerged during the war would continue and that a common outlook and purposes would guarantee an enduring peace in the postwar era. They believed that their diplomatic efforts at Yalta had laid the foundation for a firm peace.[10]

Unfortunately, American optimism and high expectations were soon shattered in the aftermath of the war. The Yalta system deteriorated in the face of incipient distrust and friction between the two dominant superpowers in almost every region of the world. The Yalta definition of postwar world order proved to be unworkable, principally because neither power accepted the other's terms for peace based upon a realistic calculation of national interests and national security as traditionally defined in the balance of power. The Yalta accords reflected only momentarily and incompletely the interests of the United States and the Soviet Union and actually foreshadowed a new balance of power struggle in the postwar world. The East Asian order agreed upon among the Great Powers at Yalta was based on the following fleeting assumptions: one, wartime cooperation between the United States and the Soviet Union would continue; two, the Soviet Union would be a stabilizing force, as a partner in the new era of postwar international order, rather than a rival; three, the building of a strong, unified, and independent China under the Nationalists was feasible; and four, China would function as a provider of stability and order in East Asia. These Yalta assumptions were soon completely negated.

The United States' optimistic expectations that U.S.-Soviet wartime cooperation would continue and that the Soviet Union would function as a co-stabilizer in the postwar world was an illusion. The Soviet Union began to systematically despoil areas of Germany that the Russian army controlled and convert East European countries such as Poland, Hungary, Romania, Bulgaria, Yugoslavia, and Czechoslovakia, into Communist satellites. The Red Army became the arbiter of politics in Eastern Europe. In response to the Soviets' aggressive activities, American policymakers self-consciously made a rapid transition from collaboration to containment as the mode of Soviet-American relations. This policy was heavily influenced by the thoughts of senior state department analyst George Kennan, who coined the term containment in his famous article in *Foreign Affairs* published under the pseudonym of X in 1947. Kennan's central thesis was that Soviet expansionism could be contained by the "adroit and vigilant application of counterforce." In effect, the United States should use its military, economic, and political resources to stop the expansion of Soviet influence.[11] Accordingly, a series of American policies were adopted to contain the expansion of Soviet power. On March 12, 1947, the administration pushed through Congress the $400 million Truman Doctrine and made an open-ended pledge to protect friendly nations from subversion and aggression by the Soviet Union. A few months later Secretary of State George Marshall proposed a massive program of economic assistance to Europe, which was later incorporated into the $12 billion Marshall Plan (June 5, 1947).[12] When Harry S Truman was re-elected president in 1948, U.S. policymaking was grounded in the context of Soviet-American hostility.[13]

Initially, the Cold War rivalry was muted in Asia. Stalin did not make East Asia an immediate center of Soviet expansion beyond extending Communist control over North Korea, facilitating the extension of Chinese Communist control over Manchuria, and protesting the U.S. monopoly of control of Japan.[14] He in fact preferred that Chinese Communists have limited control and act as a buffer, remaining dependent on the Soviet Union, and Chiang's regime remained the government of a weak China as a buffer against American power.[15] The United States did not make East Asia a central concern of containment policy either. The Americans at Yalta expected an independent and democratic government in China to play a stabilizing role in cooperation with the United States to preserve peace and freedom in East Asia. The U.S. State Department defined its policy toward China in the following terms: "The principle and immediate objectives of the United States Government are to keep China in the war against Japan and to mobilize China's full military and economic strength in the vigorous prosecution of the war. The American government's long range policy with respect to China is based on the belief that the need for China to be a principal stabilizing factor in the Far East is a fundamental requirement for peace and security in that region."[16]

For a few years after the Yalta Conference, the situation in China remained ambiguous with the Nationalist government in control of South and Central China and the Communist entrenched in North China and the hinterland. However, whatever American and Soviet intentions were in regard to China, they were soon upset by the Communist victory of Mao over Chiang in 1949. The triumph of communism in China and its apparent entry into the Soviet orbit introduced a totally new factor in power distribution, jeopardized the Yalta framework of equilibrium, and identified a Soviet threat to the security of East Asia. Thus, the Cold War rivalry manifested itself in East Asia. Each superpower tried to consolidate its control wherever the power of its armies gave it the ability to do so—the Soviets in Manchuria and North Korea, the Americans in Japan and South Korea.

The Yalta system was replaced by the bipolar superpower confrontation and Yalta itself became a "foundation for what later developed as the Cold War."[17] The incipient competitiveness of Soviet and American policies after the Yalta Conference was most clearly evident in their treatment of China and Korea.

THE COMMUNIST VICTORY IN CHINA

Development in China in the late 1940s was of crucial importance for the sequence of events that shaped the East Asian bipolar Cold War structure of the 1950s. Although both the United States and the Soviet Union in the Yalta accords agreed to assist China in establishing a strong, unified, and democratic government under Chiang Kai-shek's leadership, this outcome soon proved unlikely because of a confrontation between them over growing ideological and national interests and because of the intensified civil war between the KMT and the CCP. The Communist triumph and the consequent Moscow-Beijing axis marked the virtual collapse of the Yalta system.

The seeds of Communist victory were sown before the Japanese surrender. By late 1944, events within China were increasingly favorable to the CCP. Communist forces were expanding rapidly. The Communist movement was dynamic and increasingly seemed to represent the hope of the nation. The KMT regime, on the other hand, was confronted with mounting corruption, demoralization, and catastrophic military defeat before renewed Japanese offensives. The surrender of Japan in 1945 brought additional benefits to the CCP. Communist forces were positioned to disarm many Japanese units, thereby substantially augmenting their own arsenals. They also seized cities and regions evacuated by Japanese forces. This situation presented greater opportunities for the CCP.[18]

After the Japanese surrender, in order to forestall a Communist seizure, about 50,000 American marines helped the Nationalists secure the surrender of the majority of Japanese troops in major cities. Without American assistance it would have been impossible for the Nationalists to successfully assert their authority as extensively as they did. But American policy as laid down in President Truman's instruction to General Marshall in December 1945, was to seek to mediate between the two parties and not to become involved militarily in China. The Truman administration continued to pursue Roosevelt's policy of working for a strong, unified, and democratic China as envisioned at the Yalta conference. As President Truman told General Marshall in his letter of instructions, "Secretary Byrnes and I are both anxious that unification of China by peaceful, democratic methods be achieved as soon as possible."[19] General Marshall was instructed "to persuade the Chinese government to call a national defense conference of representatives of the major political elements to bring about the unification of China and, concurrently, to effect a cessation of hostility."[20]

The traditional American attitude toward China had been one of sympathy for the sufferings and aspirations of the Chinese people but without any profound understanding of the forces at work in China.[21] The United States hoped for a coalition government in China, including both the KMT and the CCP, with Western-style democratic institutions. However, the American desire to introduce Western institutions to China failed from the very beginning. Tang Tsou's study points out three reasons for the failure: "first, that these Western institutions might have no application at all in China, at least for some time to come; second, that the intended effects of an institutional change might easily be nullified by adroit political maneuvers and other factors; and third, that an institutional change, desirable in itself, might have the consequence of weakening the groups which the United States intended to help."[22] Under these circumstances, while General Marshall devoted much time, between December 1945 and January 1947, in futile attempts to bring the KMT and the CCP together in a democratic type of a National Consultant Conference, the rivalry between the KMT and CCP made the achievement almost impossible. The failure of his mission led to an American policy resting on "letting the dust settle" and seeing what emerged from the civil war between 1947 and 1949.[23] The Truman administration was principally interested in Europe where the constructive aspects of American policy were advanced by Truman and Marshall. The most that the Truman administration felt able to do was to extend to Chiang economic and military aid while pressing him to form a coalition government with the CCP in the hope that stability of some sort might emerge: "There was little faith in the prospects of the KMT but equally little anticipation that Chiang Kai-shek's power would decline at such a catastrophic pace in 1949."[24]

In 1946-47 the KMT had seemed to be reasonably well placed in the sense that military defeat did not appear to be imminent. However, the economic problems facing the Nanjing government were rapidly worsening as wartime inflation continued to gather momentum. During 1947-48 the situation changed drastically. Chiang Kai-shek erred in attempting to regain Manchuria, then controlled by the Communists with the assistance of the Soviet Union, in the wake of the Soviet withdrawal in March 1946. Heavy fighting broke out between the KMT and CCP and Manchuria became the main theater of a civil war. The morale of KMT forces was poor, officers were frequently corrupt, and ordinary soldiers were treated with sickening brutality.

At this time the American stake in China was not clearly perceived. Truman felt constrained by public opinion from intervening in a civil war or calling up additional American troops for service in China. The Americans were not ready to participate in the Chinese civil war. Furthermore, the Truman administration was sufficiently skeptical of the KMT regime, not wanting to risk entering a hopeless struggle on the losing side. American officials felt that too many of Chiang's appointees were incompetent, untrustworthy, or corrupt. For example, an American military mission's study reported that 75 percent of American equipment furnished to Nationalist forces during and after the war fell into the Communist hands.[25] Moreover, the Chiang government not only failed to gain the support of the Chinese masses but also aroused resentment among them. The Truman administration was thus reluctant to launch a massive assistance program for the Chiang regime. Such aid, it was felt, would probably not alter the civil war and would serve to weaken the European program. As John Spanier found, aiding Chiang seemed to be "pouring money down the drain," and, in contrast, American economic aid to

Europe, which the administration considered the area most vital to American security, had a "good chance of achieving its objective." It would have been unwise in such circumstances to divert limited dollar funds "to attempt to restore a government that had lost the confidence of its own people."[26] Nothing better illustrated the tendency to view the Communist victory as a legitimate expression of popular demand than the noted *State Department White Paper* published in August 1949. In his letter of transmittal, which prefaced the *White Paper,* Secretary of State Dean Acheson assigned the responsibility for the Nationalist collapse to the failure of that regime. "The Nationalist armies," wrote Acheson, "did not have to be defeated; they disintegrated." The United States could have saved Chiang only by a "full-scale intervention in behalf of a government which had lost the confidence of its own troops and its own people."[27]

While the Truman administration maintained a policy of noninvolvement, with limited assistance to Chiang, the Soviet Union followed a cautious approach to expand its influence in China. When the Soviet Union declared war against Japan on August 8, 1945, 70 Soviet troop divisions entered Manchuria. They swiftly dismantled Manchuria's industry, which had provided important support for Japan's war efforts, and transported much of it back to the Soviet Union to help restore its badly destroyed industry. Soviet policy aimed at destroying the productive capacities of Manchuria and keeping the region weak and underdeveloped so that Manchuria would no longer serve as a base for attack on Soviet Far Eastern territories. The Soviet Union also wished to expand its sphere of influence to Manchuria. With respect to the Chinese Communists, Stalin had very complicated feelings. On the one hand, he cooperated with the CCP to increase its influence by allowing it to take large stockpiles of weapons and ammunitions surrounded by the Japanese in Manchuria, in spite of Stalin's pledge at Yalta to support a unified and democratic China.[28] On the other hand, Stalin remained apprehensive about an all-out CCP drive to seize power because he had considerable doubt about the character of the CCP and the prospects for the CCP taking power throughout China. Stalin was well aware of the independent spirit within the CCP encouraged by Mao Zedong. He did not want a strong and unified China that might serve to contain the Soviet expansion. For this very reason he did not want a Communist China either. Historical, geographical, and cultural reasons would render it difficult or impossible for the Soviets to dictate to Mao. Anticipating the decline of the KMT, balanced by the growth of the CCP, Stalin shrewdly employed a policy of "divide and rule," with the region north of the Yangtze dominated by the CCP and the area south by the KMT.[29] The Soviet strategy was based on the assumption that a weak and divided China under Nationalist control might serve as a better buffer against U.S. intervention while not becoming or posing a threat to the USSR. The Soviet Union thought that neither the Nationalists nor the Communists were strong enough to unify China, and it was happy to see a stalemate continued into an indefinite future. Stalin cabled Mao twice in late August 1945, warning the Chinese Communists not to risk civil war with the KMT, and in early 1949, Stalin advised Mao not to cross the Yangtze River in order to avert triggering a direct Soviet-American confrontation.[30]

In spite of the reservations of the Soviet Union, Mao's troops conquered Manchuria and pushed on into China proper in 1947. In January 1949, the Communists took over Beijing. At midnight, April 20, 1949, the People's Liberation Army (PLA) staged a dramatic crossing of the Yangtze River. The KMT government fled south to Guangzhou in humiliation. Within days, Nanjing, the capital of the KMT regime, fell to the Communists. Shanghai followed in May and the PLA then swept southward. Finally, Chiang abandoned the mainland and fled to the island of Taiwan. Americans were astounded. The United States adopted a policy of "nonrecognition" and took steps to convince the governments of major non-Communist powers to adopt "a common ground in this regard."[31]

The establishment of the PRC on October 1, 1949 had a great impact on the global balance of power. For the first time since 1911, all of China (except for Taiwan and Hong Kong) was united under a single authority that was able to mobilize the resources of the entire country to achieve national objectives. China was also the first major country to come under Communist rule since Russia in 1917. It would represent an addition to the Socialist camp as significant as the Soviet conquest of Eastern Europe in 1944 and 1945, if Communist China aligned with the Soviet bloc. Such an alliance would not be easy because Moscow's attitude toward Mao's CCP in the past had been one of suspicion, indifference, and passivity. However, Stalin changed his attitude when he met with the Chinese delegation of five top leaders led by Liu Shaoqi in May 1949. Stalin expressed his apology to his Chinese comrades by stating that the Soviet Union had not offered as much help to the Chinese Communists as it should have and had even hampered Chinese revolution to some extent because it did not know China's situation very well. He told Chinese comrades that "the victors should not be blamed."[32] The Sino-Soviet alliance officially occurred when Mao Zedong made a historical announcement on foreign policy, on the eve of the party's twenty-eighth anniversary (June 30, 1949), that China would "lean to one side" in the struggle between imperialism and socialism.[33] To make his position absolutely clear, he wrote, China must ally itself "with the Soviet Union, with every New Democratic country, and with the proletariat and broad masses in all other countries."[34] In December 1949, Mao left China for the first time in his life to travel to Moscow to negotiate a treaty of alliance with the Soviet Union.[35] These developments were unquestionably an abrupt tilting of the balance of power in East Asia and also meant defeat for the United States, which had vainly hoped to see a friendly regime in China.

THE KOREAN WAR AND BIPOLAR POLITICS

The fall of Nationalist China and the Moscow-Beijing alliance established Soviet ascendance in East Asia and put pressure on the United States to take counteroffensive measures. The locus of the American-Soviet rivalry was Korea at this time. At the end of World War II, the United States and the Soviet Union occupied Korea separated by the 38th parallel, the Americans in the south and the Soviets in the north. The original purpose of demarcating the Soviet and American zones of occupation was to accept the surrender of Japanese troops and to assist the formation of a unified, independent, and democratic Korean government. The decision to divide Korea at the 38th parallel originated in Washington, in recognition of the speedy Russian advance onto Korean soil two days after Japan surrendered. The nearest American troops at the time were in Okinawa, 600 miles away, and in the Philippines, 1,500 to 2,000 miles away.[36] The United States would be dependent on Soviet goodwill at first, since American forces were not immediately available to occupy south Korea. The Soviet Union accepted the 38th parallel demarcation line without question because Stalin wished to maintain satisfactory relations with the United States if possible and, perhaps, "he felt that sooner or later Korea would fall into the Soviet sphere in any case."[37] For the Americans, the decision to divide Korea at 38th parallel was a purely ad hoc military action. The line was intended to be temporary and only to fix responsibility between the United States and the Soviet Union for carrying out the Japanese surrender.[38]

However, the 38th parallel was soon turned into a permanent political line dividing Korea into two states, one under Soviet influence and the other under American. Once the Occupation was established, the United States and the Soviet Union competitively set up two rival governments as a mirror reflection of their determination to assert their respective influence: one under Kim Il Sung in the north and one under Syngman Rhee in the south. In this situation, the international trusteeship established at Yalta and to be administered by four big powers proved to be a failure because it was left to the uncertainty of unpredictable military decisions by the occupied forces. Under the separate military occupation, each occupying power acted differently in absence of any community of interest. Each was interested in establishing its friendly government—pro-Soviet and pro-American: "No cooperation or complementary in policy was possible between the American and the Soviet zones of responsibility."[39]

In many aspect, the Americans were firmly committed to South Korea, although it appeared more ambiguous than the Soviet relationship with the North. The initial American decision to station troops in Korea represented a deliberate denial of Far Eastern territory to the Soviet Union whose troops originally intended to occupy the whole of Korea. However "the extent of the American commitment to the new Republic of Korea (ROK) government was extremely unclear."[40] For example, the U.S. Defense Department accorded "little strategic significance to Korea in the event of another world war."[41] Forty-five thousand American troops withdrew from Korea on June 29, 1949, leaving an advisory group of about 500 officers. In January 1950, a bill providing U.S. military and economic aid to South Korea was defeated in the House of Representatives. This added to the impression that U.S. commitment to Korea did not have congressional support.[42] According to a Korean scholar, the U.S. failure to show a clear commitment to South Korea resulted from four misperceptions and miscalculations. First, North Korea was seen as completely under Kremlin control, and an aggressive move by North Korea against the South would be considered a Soviet move and a high-risk strategy. Therefore, American policymakers believed the Soviet Union would not chance a full-scale war for which they were not prepared. Second, American officials underestimated the strength of the Soviet-equipped and -trained North Korean Army and overestimated the South Korean Army's defense capacity. Third, American military strategists underestimated the Soviet's fundamental strategic concern with Korea and its desire to strive for hegemony in Northeast Asia. And fourth, the United States tried to avoid a drain of men and material on the peninsula that would weaken American capabilities elsewhere, especially in Europe.[43]

Against this background, Kim Il Sung visited Moscow twice in March and April 1949 to discuss a military-aid program and to gain Stalin's support for a takeover of the South. According to Khrushchev's memoir, Stalin doubted the sagacity of this action, but Kim convinced him that the war could be won quickly, before the United States had time to become involved. Mao Zedong, who was in Moscow during the winter of 1949-50, approved Kim's plans, saying that the Americans would not intervene since the war was an internal matter that the Korean people would decide for themselves.[44] Stalin agreed to furnish equipment and arms for six new infantry divisions. Military power in the two halves of Korea was unbalanced by the withdrawal of American troops from the South and the massive Soviet military assistance program in the North.[45] With the impression that the United States was highly unlikely to commit itself to the defense of South Korea, North Korea launched a massive attack on South on June 25, 1950.[46] They were superior in number, well-trained, and well-equipped with Russian-made tanks and artillery, advancing rapidly southward without much resistance from South Korean forces. Within six weeks, North Korean troops occupied most of the Korean Peninsula.

The United States was forced by the outbreak of the Korean civil war to redefine its security interests in Korea vis-à-vis the Soviet Union. A noted National Security Council study stated that abandonment of the American commitment in Korea "would be a major victory for Communism which would adversely affect the worldwide position of the United States. The security interest of the United States would be seriously jeopardized by the decision."[47] American officials both in South Korea and Washington perceived the North Korean move across the border as a Soviet-sponsored and Soviet-controlled attack against free world interests in Asia and elsewhere. In their mind the invasion was a test of American resolve to resist Communist expansion that would have serious consequences throughout East Asia. The elimination of South Korea would influence both Soviet and Chinese moves in Indochina, Taiwan, Malaysia, and Burma.[48] It was obvious that the United States' decision to oppose the North Korean invasion was not motivated by a sudden discovery that Korea's strategic importance to the American military security was greater than had been estimated earlier or by the fact that the survival of the Republic of Korea was at stake. Rather, American intervention was politically motivated by the expected damage to American interests from allowing the Soviet-sponsored North Koreans to take over the South.

Truman immediately committed American military forces to the defense of South Korea two days after the North Korean troops crossed the 38th parallel, although he thought it would be better to support the Korean War through international action by the United Nations rather than through a unilateral act. On U.S. initiative, the UN Security Council adopted two resolutions on June 25 and June 27, 1950, recommending members of the United Nations to restore international peace and security in Korea. In accordance with the resolutions, 16 nations contributed to the UN forces. The United States was the major contributor: 50 percent of the ground forces, 85 percent of the naval forces, and 93.4 percent of the air forces. On June 27, General MacArthur was authorized to use American naval and air forces to prevent the Inchon-Kimpo-Seoul area from falling into unfriendly hands. On June 30, Truman accepted MacArthur's recommendation to employ American ground forces in Korea. The commitment of American ground forces on a large scale in Korea constituted not only a reversal of the strategic plan symbolized by the withdrawal of American forces from South Korea in 1949. It also represented a departure from one of the strongly held views of General Marshall to the effect that "American ground forces should not be used on the continent of Asia—a view which contributed to his refusal to intervene in the Chinese civil war."[49] On September 15, 1950, MacArthur's successful amphibious landing of marines at Inchon altered the entire course of the Korean War. Seoul was recaptured and the UN forces approached the 38th parallel. On October 20, American forces captured Pyongyang, the capital city of North Korea. A week later the first American troops reached the Yalu River, which formed the border between Korea and China. General MacArthur's "home by Christmas" offensive seemed likely to be successful.

Nevertheless, MacArthur's dream was shattered by a massive Chinese intervention in November.[50] General MacArthur could put approximately 110,000 men in the field against an estimated 256,000 Chinese and 10,000 Northern Koreans.[51] MacArthur, believing that he was faced with 40,000 instead of 256,000 Chinese soldiers, advanced northward for the "final offensive."[52] However, during the two days of November 30 and December 1, UN casualties exceeded 11,000. Pyongyang was recaptured by Chinese troops on December 4, 1950, and Seoul fell again on January 5, 1951. In March 1951, UN forces retook Seoul. Thereafter, a stalemate ensued in which neither side achieved a military victory. General MacArthur urged an increase in military action against North Korea and Communist China to end the stalemate and to win military victory. But the Truman administration was much more concerned than MacArthur over a clash with the Chinese Communists.[53] Neither the Truman administration nor the United Nations could support MacArthur's plan because they thought it would bring a general war. Chairman of the Joint Chiefs of Staff, General Omar Bradley, opposed MacArthur's proposal by making the famous statement that the United States would be involved "in the wrong war, at the wrong place, at the wrong time, and with the wrong enemy."[54] The Korean conflict thus became a "limited war," which, according to Kissinger, "is fought for political objectives" and "to strive for specific goals." It was "not for complete annihilation."[55] Military victory was unthinkable unless the United States intended to fight a general war with China and the Soviet Union.

America's allies tended to blame the United States for provoking the Chinese. Washington's officials publicly blamed themselves for not realizing the depths of Chinese "deviousness" and privately blamed MacArthur's intelligence facilities. The general took "credit" for exposing Chinese perfidiousness through his "reconnaissance in force" but he blamed Washington for not allowing him to use America's full military arsenal against the Chinese. The Truman administration's explanation of China's actions emphasized Beijing's alliance with Moscow.[56] Indeed, Chinese and Soviet leaders discussed possible Chinese-Soviet cooperation in Korea when the Inchon landing took place in September 1950. Following the spirit of the Sino-Soviet alliance treaty, the Soviets agreed that if the Chinese troops entered the Korean War, the Soviet Union would provide the Chinese with air support. The Soviets also agreed to supply the Chinese with military equipment and war materiel.[57] However, the promised air umbrella from the Soviet Union was not provided after China joined the fighting.

China's decision to enter the Korean War was formally made on October 4, 1950, when Mao called an urgent CCP Politburo meeting to discuss sending Chinese troops to rescue the North Koreans. Present at the meeting was Peng Dehuai, soon to be the commander and political commissar of the Chinese People's Volunteers, who stated that "American occupation of Korea, separated from China by only a river, would threaten Northeast China." If this happened, he thought, the United States "could find a pretext at any time to launch a war of aggression against China." He found this prospect intolerable and argued that "without going into a test of strength with American imperialism, it would be difficult for us to build socialism."[58] The Politburo meeting reached the conclusion that "If we don't enter the war and let the enemy reach to the bank of Yalu River, domestic and international reactionary (fandongpai) would be swollen with arrogance, which would be a disadvantage to all of us, especially to northeast China. The entire northeast defense army would be trapped and the south Manchurian electric supply would be controlled . . . Overall, we are convinced that we should and must enter the war. Entering the war would be extremely beneficial and not entering the war would be extremely harmful."[59]

On October 8, 1950, Mao Zedong, as the Chairman of the Central Military Commission, ordered the Chinese People's Volunteers "to support the Korean people's war of liberation and to resist the attacks of American imperialism," or as the Chinese press later put it, "to keep the wolf from the door."[60]

However, Stalin changed his position when China decided to enter the war. Chinese sources now available indicate that when Premier Zhou Enlai flew to Moscow to finalize details of Chinese-Soviet military cooperation in Korea on October 10, 1950, Stalin told Zhou that the Soviet Union was not in a position to send troops to Korea because a direct confrontation between the Soviet Union and the United States would follow if he sent troops there.[61] This sudden change angered Chinese leaders. After receiving a telegram from Zhou in Moscow, Mao put the movement of Chinese troops temporarily on hold. The CCP Politburo held an emergency meeting on the afternoon of October 13 to discuss intervention without direct Soviet air support. After weighing the pros and cons, especially having evaluated the serious consequences of China's failure to send troops to Korea, participants reached a consensus that even without direct Soviet air support, the Chinese were still in a position to fight the Americans in Korea. They would now depend more on Mao's principles of self-reliance, emphasizing that an army with higher morale could beat an enemy with superior equipment.[62]

In light of these circumstances, Beijing's decision to enter the Korean War was based upon a calculation of its own national interests rather than the Sino-Soviet alliance. Beijing considered the American intervention and MacArthur's advance northward a serious threat to Chinese security.[63] The Chinese entered the Korean War when North Korea's armies had virtually collapsed and UN troops were closing in on the Sino-Korean border. Chinese leaders clearly remembered that Japanese imperialists had first annexed Korea, then penetrated and occupied China's northeast, and thus began a war of aggression.[64]

After the Chinese intervention, the Korean War became an entirely new war. With the danger of general war heightened while the military stalemated, the United States inclined to settle the war in Korea by political means. The Soviet and Chinese governments seemed to seek a peace solution too. The Soviet government did not want to see increased Chinese influence in Korea. Beijing needed peace because China's economy was exhausted by lengthy internal warfare and by its involvement in the conflict in Korea. In July 1951, armistice talks started between the United Nations and Communist representatives at Kaesong.[65] On July 27, 1953, an armistice agreement was signed by General Mark Clark, Commander-in-Chief of the UN command, Peng Dehuai, Commander of the Chinese People's Volunteers, and Kim Il Sung, Supreme Commander of the Korean

People's Army. The armistice agreement was a purely military agreement between two opposing rivals. It was to restabilize the Korean situation by restoring the status quo. No one won. The Korean War was an international war in which both Koreas were proxies and in which the United States and the Soviet Union attempted to protect and promote their respective security and strategic interests. As the result of East Asian bipolar politics, Korea remained divided after the war.

THE END OF OCCUPATION IN JAPAN AND THE SAN FRANCISCO SYSTEM

The immediate consequence of the Korean War was the American policy adjustment to end the Occupation in Japan so as to constitute Japan as a suitable bastion of American influence and as a long-term ally and military base in East Asia. Having observed the Cold War erupt into a hot war on the Korean Peninsula, the Americans could not help redefining the balance of power by strengthening its own position in the region. American policymakers came to the conclusion that Japan was essential to defend the Far East. A new awareness of the vital strategic importance of Japan to the American security interest in East Asia contributed to the start of a complete reversal in American policy toward Japan.

The reversal was not very difficult to accomplish. Unlike that of Germany, the Occupation of Japan was a wholly American enterprise. The Soviet Union objected to General Douglas MacArthur's high-handed manner in carrying it out and Moscow desired another system of four-power control and occupation in order to balance U.S. predominance in Japan. Nevertheless, because of the frustrating experience in the early months of the German occupation, Americans were determined to avoid a similar experience in Japan. MacArthur was directed only by orders from the American president. He was the supreme ruler and the most influential decision maker regarding Occupation policy.[66] In response to the transfer of U.S. troops from Japan to Korea after the outbreak of the Korean War, General MacArthur and Japanese Prime Minister Yoshida authorized the formation of a U.S.-equipped 75,000-man National Policy Reserve Force, which became the prototype of Japan's Self-Defense Forces (SDF).[67] In addition to the placement of the UN Command Headquarters for Korea in Tokyo and the designation of Supreme Commander of Allies Powers (SCAP) as UN commander in Korea, Japanese territory and facilities were used for the training, staging, logistic and material support, and medical care for the American troops.

The war demonstrated the indispensability of American troops and bases in Japan and Okinawa to U.S. regional security objectives. The U.S. government began to appreciate the disadvantages that prolonged Occupation rule might cause for future American-Japanese relations. At this point, the United States became willing to consider an eventual termination of the Occupation, to restore Japanese sovereignty, and to accept Japan as a new member of the Western community. But it was far from easy to devise a peace treaty that would "secure American objectives in Japan, retain Tokyo's goodwill and gain the necessary consent of Washington's allies."[68] The State Department supported an early conclusion of a peace treaty with Japan and held the view that the indefinite prolongation of the Occupation would be counterproductive politically and would encounter growing resentment from the Japanese people. However, the Defense Department opposed the early conclusion of a peace treaty because of basic uncertainties over Japan's position at the end of the Occupation: "Opinion in the Pentagon was that Japan was assuming more importance in global terms and that Japan must remain within the American sphere."[69] It was only after John Foster Dulles was appointed special ambassador for the peace issue that these divergent positions were reconciled. Dulles skillfully secured a compromise between the positions of the State Department and Defense Department by proposing to make the peace settlement conditional on a bilateral security treaty with Japan and to urge Japan's substantial rearmament at a level of 350,000 troops.[70]

The shift in American policy was made public by President Truman's press conference on May 18, 1950, during which he hoped that peace with Japan would be possible before too long and announced the appointment of Dulles as advisor to the State Department.[71] In September 1950, Dulles began preparing a peace treaty, and, in September 1951, a peace conference was held in San Francisco. On the morning of September 8, Japanese Primer Minister Yoshida signed the peace treaty with the United States and 47 other countries, but not with the Soviet Union, Poland, and Czechoslovakia. That same afternoon, he signed a bilateral, mutual security treaty secretly negotiated with the United States. The security treaty was designed to protect an independent but weak Japan and to present a countervailing force to the Sino-Soviet alliance.[72] Although Yoshida earlier indicated his preference for a "two China" approach in Japan's diplomatic and economic policies, he was compelled to sign a bilateral peace treaty with the Republic of China in Taiwan on the same day that the San Francisco treaties came into effect in 1952.[73]

Thus the structure of the two rival military coalitions in East Asia was formalized. The arrangements were known as "the San Francisco system."[74] Although it was not as systematically developed or regionally as integrated as the North Atlantic Treaty Organization (NATO), the San Francisco system established a framework for Cold War bipolar confrontation in East Asia. The San Francisco Conference and its adjunct, the Tokyo-Taipei peace treaty, constrained the development of security arrangements and diplomatic relations involving the major East Asian powers, namely, the United States, Japan, and China, over the next two decades.

The San Francisco system ended the Occupation of Japan and reintegrated it into the community of nations by becoming a UN member in 1956. In the meantime, the United States began assisting Japan in establishing itself as an independent, self-reliant country, capable of contributing to the security and stability of East Asia as a member of the American security system. Through the peace treaty and the Japanese-American mutual security pacts of the San Francisco conference, Japan had its sovereignty restored and its status changed from conquered enemy to friendly ally of the United States. Japan regained status as an independent state, in spite of the fact that in relation to the United States, Japan remained a deferent partner and played only a peripheral role.[75]

During the 1950s, Japan relatively enjoyed its deferent partner status by receiving a large amount of American economic aid and grants that helped it make remarkable economic progress. The massive aid and economic recovery effort represented a complete reversal of American policy toward Japan. The original purpose of American occupation was to uproot and destroy what remained of Japanese military and economic power and to frustrate the resurgence of Japanese imperialism and militarism.[76] During the early Occupation period from 1945 to 1947, the United States intended to reduce Japan's economy to the level of the years of 1930-34, before its major conquests, by eliminating munitions plants and the aircraft industry, as well as reducing steel, shipbuilding, and synthetic oil industries. However, after the San Francisco Conference, American policy objectives were drastically transformed into the idea of economic recovery, independence, and sovereignty for Japan in order to avoid a nationalist reaction against the Occupation and to use Japan as an anchor against further Communist expansion.[77] Very soon, Japan emerged as a principal economic beneficiary of the Korean War thanks to special procurement arrangements and service contracts concluded with the United States. The value of American procurement contracts during the three-year war was well above the value of total American aid from 1945 to

1951.[78] This created the so-called Korean War boom in Japan, which raised industrial production far above its prewar level and set the country on the road to economic self-sufficiency.

AMERICAN CONTAINMENT POLICY IN EAST ASIA

The San Francisco system, derived from the outbreak of the Korean War, symbolized the beginning of American containment policy in Asia. Before the Korean War, the interactions of the United States and the Soviet Union in East Asia were akin to classical diplomacy and involved few military means in the balance of power game. After the Korean War, communism in Asia was considered as dangerous as it was in Europe. The bitter debate over "who lost China," together with a stalemated Korean War, were key factors in President Dwight Eisenhower's 1952 election victory.[79] The Eisenhowever administration extended the containment policy from Europe to Asia, with the ideological goal of preventing the spread of communism by military involvement. It was taken for granted that Moscow and its minions—most importantly China—sought the destruction of the United States and the free world. Washington was determined to defend its global interests by war and nuclear war if necessary. It was determined to honor commitments to a growing list of associated and client states around the rim of Eurasia, "even if these commitments might eventuate in war."[80]

Traditionally, American foreign policy looked to Europe. Europe was seen as America's first line of defense and Asia was deemed marginal and not vitally related to the interest of America's national security. Until the North Korean invasion of South Korea, American policymakers had underestimated Asia's strategic importance and had largely pursued its economic and commercial interests in the region without direct military involvement. The Korean War showed American willingness to engage in limited military conflict in East Asia. Few Americans had expected the Communists to resort to open warfare as they did in Korea, and therefore thought "the best policy was to draw the lines as clearly as possible to deter further Communist military moves."[81] Thus, the containment strategy was based upon security links with the major non-Communist countries in the region. In contrast to NATO, the Asian containment system created by the United States was essentially a series of bilateral treaties with no unified command structure, but American leaders regarded it as the best that could be arranged since East Asian countries had differing perceptions of the most serious threats they faced.[82]

The San Francisco system constituted an important element in the American containment linkage in the Asia Pacific region. Unlike the NATO accord and other treaties that the United States signed with Asian Pacific countries later, whose signatories were bound by the principle of reciprocal obligation, the American-Japanese security treaty stipulated Japan's unilateral and unconditional dependency upon American military protection and was "not a mutual security treaty but a unilateral American agreement."[83] Nevertheless, it was one link in the chain of bilateral treaties that the United States signed with countries in the region to contain communism: the American-Philippines security treaty in August 1951, the United States-South Korean Mutual Defense Treaty in October 1953, and the United States-Taiwan Mutual Defense Treaty in December 1954. Besides these three bilateral treaties, the United States also entered into two multilateral regional pacts in this period. The United States completed the tripartite security treaty with Australia and New Zealand (ANZUS) in July 1951, and took the lead in organization of a new collective security system, the Southeast Asia Treaty Organization (SEATO), by the Malina Pact in September 1954. It was modeled after the NATO alliance for the purpose of protecting nations in Southeast Asia from external Communist aggression and subversion. SEATO, linking the United States, the United Kingdom, France, the Philippines, Thailand, and Pakistan, established a system of collective security to defend the status quo in Indochina, while the ANZUS brought Australia and New Zealand into the American containment arrangements in the Pacific. By signing these bilateral treaties and multilateral pacts, the United States extended its defense perimeter through an integral link in the American regional security chain and pledged to contain communism in the entire Asia-Pacific region.[84]

The containment system represented a recognition that Asia was of strategic importance to the United States not only because of its resources, geography, and the political and military force that it could generate, but also because of the demonstrated threat of the North Korean and Chinese military forces to American interests. American policymakers believed that the Soviet Union intended to bring the mainland of East Asia, Japan, and other principal islands of the West Pacific under Soviet control. This would present an unacceptable threat to the security of the United States.[85] According to a National Security Council report (NSC 48/5) in May 1951, the long-range containment objectives of the United States with respect to Asia were twofold. The first was to develop stable, independent, friendly non-Communist governments and the second was to eliminate the power and influence of the Soviet Union. In view of the threat to the American security interests resulting from Communist aggression, the immediate objectives of the containment policy were as follows: first, to detach China as an effective ally of the Soviet Union and support the development of an independent China; second, to maintain a security defense in the Western Pacific, to deny Taiwan to any Chinese Communist-aligned regime and to forestall Communist aggression in South and Southeast Asia; third, to prevent South Korea from being over-run militarily and to develop as rapidly as possible dependable South Korean military units of sufficient strength to assume the major part of the burden of the UN forces there; and fourth, to assist Japan to become an independent, economically self-supporting nation, friendly to the United States, capable of producing goods and services important to the United States, and capable of contributing to the security and stability of the Far East.

THE TAIWAN STRAIT CRISES

In the 1950s and 1960s, China was the major target of the American containment policy in East Asia. Through its intervention in the Korean War, China successfully demonstrated its ability to resist strong American military power and made its debut as a regional power: a debut that to the minds of American and its Asian allies constituted a constant menace to their security in the region. As Tang Tsou indicates, "The battle in North Korea was the first great victory won by Chinese forces over a major power which had a lasting effect on the outcome of an international war since the Opium War opened the modern era in China."[86] After the Korean War the balance of power in East Asia rested on a confrontation between the ground forces of the Communist bloc on the Asiatic mainland and the air and naval power of the United States based on the island perimeter. Taiwan thus became a focal point of the political-military struggle between the two blocs.

One of the first decisions made by the Truman administration after the North Korean attack on the South was the dispatch of the Seventh Fleet to neutralize the Taiwan Strait. Even before the Korean attack, there was continued pressure on the administration to provide military protection for Taiwan. When Secretary of Defense, Louis Johnson, and General Bradley came back from a ten-day tour of East Asia just before the North Korean aggression, they brought back with them a memorandum on Taiwan prepared by MacArthur stressing the strategic interest of the United States in denying Taiwan to the Communists.[87] Beijing reacted forcefully to America's dispatch of the Seventh Fleet to the Taiwan Strait. In a formal statement on June 28, 1950, Foreign Minister Zhou Enlai declared: "The fact that Taiwan is part of China will remain unchanged forever. This is not only a historical fact but has been affirmed by the Cairo Declaration, the Potsdam Declaration, and the existing conditions after Japan's surrender . . . The Chinese people . . . will surely be victorious in driving off American aggressors and in recovering Taiwan."[88]

To "liberate Taiwan and its offshore islands of Penghu, Jinmen (Quemoy), and Mazu (Matsu)" was the established national policy of the newly founded People's Republic, designed to preserve its right of sovereignty and territorial integrity. In October 1949, a PLA unit launched an offensive to take over Jinmen but did not succeed. After the Korean War erupted in 1950, the U.S. Seventh Fleet began to patrol the waters of the Taiwan Straits, which forced Beijing to delay its offensive campaign to recover the offshore islands.[89] After the cease-fire agreement in Korea in 1953 and the Geneva Accord for Indochina in 1954 were reached, Chinese leaders renewed their military campaign to recover China's offshore islands and, at the same time, were determined to take back Taiwan. On July 23, 1954, *Remin Ribao* published an editorial entitled "We must Liberate Taiwan," followed shortly by a speech given by PLA Commander-in-Chief Zhu De and by Zhou Enlai's "Government Work Report" to the National People's Congress. Beijing stressed that since a cease-fire had been reached in Korea and Vietnam, the Taiwan Straits appeared to be the next trouble spot. The Chinese people would not tolerate any separation of Taiwan from the mainland.[90]

The bombardment of Jinmen occurred on September 3 and lasted for 12 days. Its objective was to focus world attention on the Taiwan issue. In the meantime, the PLA launched an attack on the Dazhen Islands, the northernmost of the KMT occupied islands. They were the weakest point on the KMT defense line, and also a direct threat to Zhejiang—one of the most economically developed provinces in southeast China. When the Dazhens were liberated by the PLA, Beijing halted military activities at the end of January 1955. Chinese leaders expected the situation in the Taiwan Strait to calm down once the PLA stopped its military campaign. This, however, did not happen. Without lines of communication and little mutual understanding between China and the United States, the atmosphere of hostility between the two increased as a result of the Taiwan Strait crisis.

The focus of American hostility was directed toward China following a series of campaigns aimed at the liberation of Taiwan during the period of 1954-58 when China attacked Taiwan and the offshore islands.

President Eisenhower believed that Chinese actions would "seemingly carry the country to the edge of war, thus constituting one of the most serious problems of the first eighteen months of my administration."[91] In January 1955, the president submitted the Formosa (Taiwan) Resolution to Congress, which gave the president the right to order military aid for the defense of Jinmen and Mazu. In the many press conferences that followed, Eisenhower gave clear hints that the administration was seriously considering a nuclear strike against China.[92] This heightened tensions in the Taiwan Strait.

To reduce the tension, Zhou Enlai made a public statement at the Bandung Conference of Afro-Asian nations on April 23, 1955, explaining China's position. He said, "The Chinese people do not want to have a war with the United States of America. The Chinese government is willing to sit down to discuss the question of relaxing tension in the Far East, and especially the question of relaxing tension in the Taiwan area."[93]

After Zhou's reconciliation statement, Washington proposed diplomatic talks. On August 1, 1955, Chinese and American representatives started a series of ambassadorial-level talks in Geneva. The crisis in the Taiwan Straits began to ease.

The Sino-American ambassadorial talks continued for more than two years, through 73 meetings. The primary item on America's agenda was to get back American POWs being held in China and to persuade the Chinese government to renounce military force in its policy toward Taiwan. The Chinese hoped to resolve essential problems in Sino-American relations, including the long-standing Taiwan issue. However, no agreement was reached at Geneva and talks were officially terminated on December 12, 1957. The termination gravely disappointed the Chinese leaders, who grew increasingly distrustful of American government intentions. In Beijing's view, America's goal was to delay resolution of the Taiwan Straits issue until world opinion could be brought to bear on Chinese leaders, forcing them to accept the existence of Taiwan as an independent entity whose existence Beijing could not challenge. In the end, this American hidden agenda would have resulted in a situation similar to those that emerged in the post–World War II divided nations of Germany, Korea, and Vietnam.[94]

The Chinese decision to bombard Jinmen and Mazu for a second time in the summer of 1958 reflected anxiety and signaled the end of a three-year period of diplomatic negotiation with the United States. The bombardment began on August 23. Its initial objective was to recover the offshore islands. In response, President Eisenhower made public a statement on

August 27, implying that he would exercise the power entrusted to him under the 1955 Formosa Resolution to assist Taiwan in the defense of Jinmen and Mazu. On August 29, he instructed U.S. naval forces to implement the convoy-escort plan. By mid-September, the United States had amassed in the Taiwan Straits the largest single concentration of nuclear support forces in history.[95] However, Mao Zedong's assessment of the situation was that American policy toward China was primarily defensive rather than offensive in nature. Mao asserted that both China and America were afraid of war, but the United States were "more afraid than we are." Hence, war was unlikely to break out. Mao believed that the Americans would have to abandon the islands if war was really imminent.

Indeed, as the military tension in the Jinmen-Mazu area escalated, a polarization of opinion within the United States was occurring in regard to America's commitment to the offshore islands. There were many who were dubious about supporting Taiwan. Even the chairman of the Joint Chiefs of Staff warned that Chiang Kai-shek was interested in enlarging the crisis in order to drag America into his war with China for recovery of the mainland. He now recommended to the president that American forces should be withdrawn from Jinmen and Mazu.[96] In this situation, Mao Zedong decided to postpone implementation of the plan to "liberate" Jinmen and Mazu. On October 6, in the name of Peng Dehuai, the Minister of Defense, *Remin Ribao* published "A Message to our Taiwan Compatriots," drafted by Mao, which announced a unilateral seven-day cease-fire.[97] Subsequently, the Chinese government announced that bombardment of the offshore islands would occur only on even days. The new policy viewed Jinmen and Mazu as an integral part of the Taiwan reunification strategy and decided to temporarily keep these islands in KMT hands as a means of affirming Taiwan's ties with the mainland. From this point on, tensions began to diminish in the second Taiwan Straits crisis.

During the Taiwan Straits period, the main focus of America's hostility was deflected from the Soviet Union to Communist China. China was in direct confrontation with the United States in East Asia while the Soviet Union was involved indirectly. Chinese support of the Ho Chi Minh regime with arms and increased influence in Indochina took on a new significance for American foreign policy.[98] In effect, the U.S. containment line, erected through bilateral and multilateral alliances with strategically located powers along the fringes of east and southeast Asia, was primarily aimed at blocking China's expansion. As the major target of American containment policy, China's leadership was never at ease with their lack of security. Perceiving an external threat of American armed intervention, they acted accordingly and prepared a military counterthreat. These actions "gradually but surely caused the other side to respond in the same way and, perhaps, even more vigorously."[99] This chain of action and reaction (or security dilemma) laid out the battleground for the containment policy of the United States in East Asia.

POWER COMPETITION IN THE BIPOLAR COLD WAR SYSTEM

The Cold War in East Asia started when the Yalta assumptions of the American-Soviet collaboration in East Asia were completely negated by the development of rivalry, distrust, and hostility between the United States and the Soviet Union in the early 1950s. A bipolar Cold War system emerged out of the two bloc competition. The United States held the leadership of one pole, in which, Japan, as a junior partner, played the peripheral role of supplying war material and services to the United States, especially during the Korean War. Korea, Taiwan, the Philippines, and several southeast Asian countries were dependent partners, too. On the other pole, the Soviet Union played the dominant role, with China as a junior partner and North Korea and North Vietnam as dependent partners. The bipolar system was characterized by incessant confrontation and recurrent crises. However, within the Cold War system, crises were well controlled and limited to avoid escalating into a general war with nuclear-armed superpowers capable to annihilating mankind and civilization. Three distinctive patterns of power competition characterized the bipolar Cold War system in East Asia.

The first was that the East Asia bipolar Cold War system was a form of sensitive response to the global confrontation between democracy and communism. Both sides were governed by ideologies that rendered them intolerant in international relations: the expansive ambitions of communism were confronted by determined U.S. imperialism. The suddenly revealed ideological confrontation in the postwar world blinded political leaders of both superpowers to other aspects of reality and convinced them that eventually the whole world would be divided into two antagonistic blocs facing each other. Due to increased emphasis on the ideological division between the two antagonistic blocs, the bipolar system became tight and eventually formed "rigid" alliances or blocs. Because of the tightness in the competition, even the smallest loss of territory was inadmissible to either bloc. A gain of power by one bloc was seen as a loss of power by the other. The interests of the two superpowers tended to prevail because they were identified as common interests of their bloc members and, in the meantime, the superpowers tended to provide some compensation to satisfy some interests of their dependent partners in order to continue to have the fullest possible cooperation of their allies.

Second, although the balance of power was the most important approach for the superpowers to preserve peace in a bipolar competition, the balance was different from that in earlier periods when Great Powers pursued imperial and colonial types of domination and the balance of power was based on the interplay among a number of individual powers. In bipolar politics, the balance between two military alliances or rival blocs, rather than among individual imperial powers, became the most important objective of power competition. Either of the superpowers who threatened to assume a position of preponderance would be opposed and contained by the other superpower and its partners. With the possession of nuclear weapons by the two superpowers, the balance eventually resolved into a zero-sum game of uneasy equilibrium. For a short while in the 1950s, the bipolar "trend seemed more or less inexorable."[100] The spread of U.S. and Russian influences after the Yalta Peace Conference reflected dyadic interactions of the two dominant power centers to safeguard their respective interests and to maintain the balance of power between the two blocs. The Soviet Union, controlling unified China and attempting to control the entire Korean Peninsula by using North Korea as a "proxy" in the Korean War, strove to establish Soviet ascendancy in East Asia. In reaction to this Soviet move, the United States quickly sent its troops to the Korean Peninsula and adjusted to the situation by formulating the policy of containment against communism and restoring the East Asian equilibrium. Drawing lines between the two rival blocs and searching for alliances, the two superpowers tried to increase their military capacities and maintain the balance of power to stabilize the territorial status quo. U.S. efforts to resurrect Japan as a power and consolidate it in the American security system were a reaction to the Korean War and a growing Chinese power that significantly tipped the scale in favor of the Communist bloc. The two superpowers competed to increase their capabilities, to prevent the rival bloc from attaining a preponderant position, and to maintain the bipolar balance by extending the membership of their bloc and by consolidating alliances. Thus, the maintenance of the balance of power between the two blocs was at the heart of the bipolar politics.

The third important characteristic of the East Asian bipolar politics was that the functional role of each state as an actor in the region was conditioned by supranational actors (that is, security alliances). Even a minor crisis had to be settled at the bloc level with the involvement of the super-powers. Under these circumstances, superpowers negotiated rather than fought, or fought a limited war rather than a major war to pursue their interests. In a narrow sense, the Korean War might be viewed as a civil war in which the two conflicting Korean political groups fought to succeed to legitimacy as the sole government of Korea. However, according to the logic of the bipolar system, the Korean War was understood as a Soviet attempt to expand its strategic interests and to control the entire peninsula. Thus the United States revised its previous noncommitment policy and began a policy of defending the frontlines in Korea in response to the Soviet-sponsored North Korean attack. The Korean problem was no longer considered a domestic problem for the Koreans themselves, but an inter-national problem in which the interests of two large rival blocs were entangled. Kim's control of all of Korea was inadmissible to Washington; Rhee's unification of the northern half was unacceptable to the Soviet bloc. The fate of Korea became a function of the East Asian bipolar power competition. By the same token, the Taiwan Strait crises were no longer domestic crises. They involved not only the CCP regime on the mainland and the KMT regime on the Taiwan islands, but international crises that involved the United States and the Soviet Union. The Chinese leaders believed that the U.S. government had no right to interfere in China's domestic affairs (for example, liberation of Taiwan), nor had it any right to deny the Chinese the use of force.[101] However, neither the United States nor the Soviet Union perceived Beijing's military attack on Taiwan and off-shore islands as a domestic issue in the bipolar politics. Throughout the Taiwan Strait crises ideological and strategic pressures were mounted on both sides to repel each other and marked the rigidity of the bipolar situa-tion in the whole region. The two nuclear powers maintained the delicate "balance of terror" in a tight bipolar system. Neither North Korea and Beijing nor South Korea and Taipei could achieve territorial gains by force without risking the danger of a general war involving the two superpowers.

THE DETERIORATION OF THE BIPOLAR SYSTEM

During the 1960s, the distribution of power in East Asia began to experience a very subtle but important change due to the breakup of the rigid bipolar Cold War system. There were several key factors that contributed to this deterioration. The first was the Sino-Soviet dispute in the early 1960s. The Sino-Soviet dispute was misleadingly clad in an ideological garb but was in fact fundamentally an assertion of Chinese nationalist ambitions against Soviet tutelage. Growing Chinese consciousness under Mao's leadership created friction and conflict contrary to the policies and interests of Moscow. The dispute indicated that the Soviets would not be able to fully consolidate their empire, and that consequently there was no prospect that such an empire and its counterparts would swallow up the whole region. Out of the split, China emerged as an independent regional power from its early status as the junior partner of the Soviet Union.

The second factor that contributed to the deterioration of the bipolar system was the reemergence of Japan from a peripheral position dependent on the United States to a relatively independent economic giant. Through its economic success, Japan became an influential regional power and was ready to play a more and more active political and economic role in East Asia. This readiness was bolstered by the 1972 "Nixon shock," the sudden amazement of Nixon's visit to Beijing, which was a heavy blow to the U.S.-Japan partnership and forced Japan to move quickly and independently in the normalization of its diplomatic relations with China.

The third factor that contributed to the dismantling of the bipolar system was the failure of the U.S. intervention in Vietnam and the subsequent emergence of American neo-isolationism. The United States was forced to cooperate with China in resolving the Vietnam issue in the early 1970s. To avoid another Vietnam, the United States restrained its overextended military containment policy. The Nixon Doctrine and his de-commitment policy encouraged Japan to assume an active role as a regional power and to accept the PRC as a legitimate partner in the power competition.

Due to the failure of the bipolar system, the American-Soviet relationship became a less dominant axis of East Asian international politics. The maintenance of peace and order in the region was, to a certain extent, beyond the joint capacity of the two superpowers. It was, rather, dependent upon the quadrilateral Asian power balance. Nixon's détente policy with Beijing and Moscow and the Sino-Japanese rapprochement were the landmarks of the quadrilateral power competition, in which the "most important is the interest of each of the four powers in preventing any of the others from gaining hegemony over the region."[1]

THE ORIGINS OF THE SINO-SOVIET SPLIT

The Sino-Soviet split was the most important event leading to the deterioration of the bipolar power competition in East Asia. Despite the plethora of scholarly works on the split, it continues to be difficult to present a definitive analysis of the many forces that led to this pivotal rupture.[2] During the first few years after the signature of the Sino-Soviet Friendship and Mutual Alliance Treaty in 1950, the Chinese-Soviet relationship maintained a "remarkable degree of harmony."[3] The first serious evidence of the Sino-Soviet conflict emerged at the Twentieth Congress of the Communist Party of the Soviet Union (CPSU) in February 1956. The Twentieth Congress launched a two-pronged program, the policy of de-Stalinization and peaceful coexistence. When the congress opened its door, Zhou Enlai, the Chinese Premier, read a message from Mao Zedong that praised the CPSU, "created by Lenin and reared by Stalin."[4] Ten days later, however, Khrushchev denounced his predecessor and master, the man who had "reared" the party. Not only was Moscow's apparent lack of previous consultation with Mao most embarrassing to the Chinese delegation, Beijing also feared that Moscow's attempt at self-purification would irretrievably sully revolutionary socialism. More important, Khrushchev's bitter denunciation of Stalin's cult of personality exasperated Mao whose rule in China had many features in common with that of Stalin's.[5]

The situation reached crisis proportions in July 1958 when the Soviets leaders proposed a joint navy that would use the harbors on the Chinese coast and be commanded by a Russian admiral. When the Soviet Ambassador to Beijing, Yudin, conveyed the proposal to Mao Zedong, Mao asked Yudin to repeat his message to be certain he had heard accurately. Then he said, "We know Russia doesn't have any warm water ports; that is what Russia has wanted since the time of Peter the Great. Now it appears that we should give you control of all the ports we have. OK. After that I will go up into the mountains and lead our guerrillas against you."[6] Yudin's report to Moscow alarmed Khrushchev, who asked permission from Beijing to meet Mao, who agreed. At the Beijing airport, Khrushchev explained to the Chinese leaders that the affair was simply a mistake and the Soviets weren't talking about a joint navy but long-range wireless stations in China to communicate with their fleet and particularly with their submarines in the Pacific dealing with the America's Seventh Fleet because the situation in the Taiwan Strait was becoming increasingly tense. Chinese leaders told Khrushchev that China had no objection to long-distance wireless communications for the Soviet fleet, but they must be China-built, China-operated, and China-controlled. Otherwise the Russians were demanding "military bases on Chinese soil."[7]

At this critical juncture, Beijing wanted Moscow to support its effort to liberate Taiwan and take a tough response to the West during the Taiwan Strait crises, but, in contrast to China's wishes, the Soviet Union played "a vital off-stage role, avoiding direct involvement in the crises."[8] According to newly available Chinese sources, in the face of a nuclear threat from the United States following China's shelling of Jinmen island on August 23, 1958, Khrushchev was very upset and sent Foreign Minister Andrei Gromyko to Beijing to show a film about the devastation of nuclear weapons to Mao and CCP's Politburo members. Khrushchev refused the Chinese request for nuclear protection and warned the Chinese leaders about the dangers of a war with the United States.[9]

Mao was angry at the Soviets and decided to switch China's economic development strategy from an emphasis on heavy industry and dependence on Soviet aid to mass mobilization of the Great Leap Forward and the commune programs. Thus the rupture in Sino-Soviet relations increased and at times was quite explosive. In June 1959, the Soviet Union abruptly abrogated the 1957 agreement by which the Soviets had pledged to assist China in developing nuclear weapons.[10] In July and August 1960, the Soviet Union terminated its economic and military assistance by withdrawing its 1,300 economic and military advisors from China. Moreover, during the Sino-Indian border dispute (1959-62), the USSR sided with India and helped the Indian army buildup—instead of supporting its ally, the PRC.[11] Khrushchev's policy for "peaceful coexistence" further upset Chinese expectations.[12] His meeting with U.S. President Eisenhower in September 1959 and President Kennedy in 1961, the withdrawal of Cuban missiles at America's behest, and the Russo-American agreement on the

Nuclear Test Ban Treaty in August 1963 deepened Beijing's suspicion that the détente between the Soviets and the West might foster the encirclement of China.[13]

The unity of the two Communist giants began to deteriorate in the late 1950s, but the outside world did not see the Sino-Soviet tension until the outbreak of an ideological polemic during 1960-1963, which was reminiscent of medieval theological disputes. Each of the two powers looked upon the opposing side as an arch-heretic. An article published by the CCP's organ in 1960 was the first in a series that was to play a major role in the unfolding Sino-Soviet dispute. The major thrust of the article was a criticism of modern revisionism. The CCP asserted itself as the true heir of Lenin's legacy while the CPSU was held as betraying it.[14] In the spring of 1963, Beijing battered Moscow with the dispatch of three letters of protest against the Soviet agreement to sign the Nuclear Test Ban Treaty with the West. The Chinese warned that a one-sided reduction of the general line of the international Communist movement to peaceful coexistence and a peaceful transition to socialism betrayed the revolutionary principle.[15] In response to Beijing's criticism, *Pravda,* on July 14, 1963, published Moscow's reply to the letters of CCP and launched a sharp attack on those who gave no thought to the consequences of modern war, those who underestimated or simply dismissed the deadliness of nuclear weapons. In Moscow's view, at the center of the dispute were questions involving the vital interests of the people, namely, the question of war and peace, the cult of the individual, and the CCP was the leftist bugaboo, representing the heresy of "sectarianism and dogmatism."[16] The Sino-Soviet dispute had run the gamut from indirect and esoteric criticism to an all out and overt split along political, organizational, and ideological lines, and even actual confrontation along the border.

The 1964 coup that removed Khrushchev silenced briefly the contending parties in Moscow and Beijing. The personal antagonism between Mao and Khrushchev was an important element in the dispute.[17] Chinese leaders believed that "it was the endless peremptory actions of Khrushchev that brought the Sino-Soviet relations to the brink of collapse. The down of Khrushchev should bring an opportunity to improve the relationship."[18] Taking this opportunity, Chinese leaders sent warm congratulatory telegrams to the new Soviet leaders on October 16. Beijing held an unusually well-publicized rally to celebrate the forty-seventh anniversary of the October Revolution in November 1964. In the meantime, Premier Zhou Enlai led a high-level delegation from Beijing to Moscow on November 5 to find the "political reasons" behind Khrushchev's resignation and to explore the possibility of resuming a friendly relationship with Brezhnev and the other new Soviet leaders. But the Zhou-Brezhnev negotiations did not reach any agreement, and Zhou's mission failed. It soon became evident that, although both Zhou and Brezhnev displayed great diplomatic circumspection and tactical restraint, neither side was willing to yield on the substance of policy.[19] When the Cultural Revolution began to unfold in 1966, the anti-Soviet course of China intensified. A vigorous, unrelenting campaign against the Soviet Union followed noisy demonstrations before the wall of the Soviet Embassy in Beijing. The rhetorical tone of the period was evident in a headline of a *Remin Ribao* editorial, "Hit Back Hard at the Rabid Provocation of the Filthy Soviet Revisionist Swine."[20] In 1968, the Soviet Union interfered in Czechoslovakia and afterward produced a Brezhnev Doctrine, which aimed at the justification of Soviet intervention anywhere in East Europe for the alleged purpose of defending socialism. Beijing called these actions the new czarism.[21]

How to explain the Sino-Soviet split? Obviously, it can only be partially explained by ideological differences between the two Communist parties. The split was rooted in long-term tension over the relationship between the two Communist parties. The essence of the dispute was antagonistic nationalism. Because of historical discord and conflicting national interests, both sides were deeply convinced of the implacable hostility of the other. Each side was suspicious of the other's moves, especially of attempts to improve relations with the imperialist arch-enemy—the United States. Each side viewed any attempt at rapprochement as a collusion with capitalism and imperialism and as a military encirclement. Both sides were convinced that they were involved in a struggle that might last for decades and end in war.

Viewed in a historic context, the dispute started after the founding of the CCP in 1921 but remained hidden until it surfaced in the 1960s. During this early period, the Soviet government's two-pronged policy of assisting the formation of an unified KMT and army, and at the same time pressing its "United Front" tactics on the CCP, was evidence of the limits of Soviet support to Chinese Communist leaders. This two-pronged policy continued until the last phase of the Chinese civil war in the late 1940s. Contrary to a belief in a worldwide Communist conspiracy, which then and for years to come dominated Western public opinion and political thinking, the Soviet Union and the Chinese Communists were by no means working hand in glove. The Soviet Union gave full support neither to the Chinese Nationalists nor to the Communists, but "pursued a contradictory policy which left most by-standees puzzled."[22] In May 1948, just as Chinese Communist armies were moving out of Manchuria for the northern China and Yangtze basin, Soviet Deputy Prime Minister Anastas Mikoyan traveled clandestinely to China and advised the CCP to halt their offensive and forgo the liberation of southern China.[23] This policy was not only because of Russia's lack of knowledge of China or underestimation of Mao, but also because Stalin feared Communist China's independent stance and future competition with the Soviet Union.[24] The CCP ignored Soviet advice and crossed the Yangtze River. When the Communists entered Beijing on February 3, 1949, no Soviet weapons were seen when the Communist troops paraded through the city.[25]

The Korean War was another historical issue. Stalin broke his promise of air coverage, which was made before China entered the war. Although the Chinese received Soviet economic and military aid during the war, they had to pay it back with interest. The Chinese resented their disproportionate share of this burden.[26]

The Sino-Soviet disputes were, in essence, struggles between Soviet and Chinese nationalism. These disputes figured prominently in historical animosities over border regions. The two countries are geographical neighbors, along the longest boundary in the world. China often made ill-defined but persistent territorial demands, which were rooted in historical claims. The Chinese asserted that the present Sino-Soviet boundary was defined in "unequal" treaties that were imposed by czarist Russia on China. The treaties marked the seizure of more than 1.5 million square kilometers of Chinese territory. Specifically, the disputed areas were north of the Amur River, east of the Ussuri River on China's northeast border, and the part of the Ili Valley on China's northwest Xinjiang region. The Chinese claimed that 12,700 square miles of Chinese territory north of the Amur River were ceded to czarist Russia under pressure in 1860. The Ili Valley was taken by Russian troops in 1867 when the Muslims in Xinjiang rebelled against Chinese rule.[27] When the first Sino-Soviet boundary negotiation began in 1964, the Chinese government claimed land in the Ili Valley in the Pamir mountain range that borders China and Afghanistan. In refuting the claim, the Soviet Union argued that the boundary of the Pamir in the Ili Valley was established in a series of diplomatic notes in 1894.[28] The Chinese countered this by introducing documents to prove that the disputed Pamir boundary remained unsettled and that both governments had agreed to maintain a temporary status quo.[29] Western scholars believed that the Chinese were making a moral and propaganda case rather than seriously and suicidally pressing for the return of large territories.[30] But Soviet leaders took the Chinese claim to Soviet territory with deadly seriousness and they clearly thought of China's future menace.

The split of national minorities in their border regions further deepened their mutual antagonism. Both Great Russians and Han Chinese had chauvinistic and imperial tendencies. Khrushchev thought that Mao's words during his first visit to Moscow expressed his belief in the superiority of the Chinese race. The Soviet delegation had to sit through Mao's long-winded lectures on Chinese history, nationalism, superior culture, and Beijing's historical mission, which shocked the Soviet leaders.[31] In the meantime, Chinese leader Deng Xiaoping also criticized the CPSU for "acting like a patriarchal party" and the Soviet Union for "displaying great-power chauvinism."[32]

On border minority issues, both the Soviet Union and China were opposed to genuine self-determination and to secession of their border minorities and desired their cultural assimilation to the dominant nationality. Their ultimate aim was a complete assimilation of the national minorities and the creation of one nation-state rather than preserving the contemporary multinational state. Of the border nationalities, the largest Turkic nationality in China was the Uighurs of Xinjiang and only a few Uighurs lived in the Soviet Union. On the other hand, the three Soviet republics of Kazakhstan, Kirgizstan, and Tadzhikistan had substantial numbers of Kazakhs and Kirghizs, while on the Chinese side of the border these people were minority nationalities who had relatively few cultural ties with the Chinese and resented their suppression by China before and after the Communist seizure of power.

In 1954 when Mao attempted to reopen to Khrushchev the issue of separating Outer-Mongolia from China, Khrushchev reminded Mao that the majority of the Kazakh people lived in the USSR, while only some Kazakhs and Kirghizs resided in China, and that the Soviet Union was in favor of self-determination and wanted disputed issues to be settled on this basis.[33] This was obviously an ominous threat to China's territorial integrity. China always had difficulties in Xinjiang due to the aspirations of some of the national minorities who challenged Chinese sovereignty in the region. On April 22, 1962, about 60,000 Nomadic Kazakhs, Kirghiz, and Uighurs in Xinjiang crossed the border into the Soviet Union. The Chinese leaders labeled this incident as "Ili Counter-revolutionary Riot" and blamed the Soviet KGB for its role of agitation.[34]

The border dispute between China and the Soviet Union surfaced from March to September 1963 when a spate of Chinese editorials and open letters raised the question of the unsettled frontier north of the Ili Valley in Xinjiang.[35] In the fall of 1963, the Soviet Union responded by presenting an account of Chinese violations of the border from 1960 to 1963, including smuggling and other illegal entries. In 1964, amidst charges and countercharges, negotiations were begun to demarcate the border and to fix navigation lines on the boundary rivers of Amur and Ussuri. While these negotiations made little progress toward a mutual agreement on the disputed border, there were no serious flare-ups along the frontier. However, for a two-week period from March 2 to March 15, 1969, Chinese and Soviet troops clashed over the ownership of an island called Zhenbao Island by the Chinese and Mamansky by the Soviets. These clashes, or deliberated ambushes of each other's border patrols, resulted in some casualties on both side.[36] The immediate consequence of these border clashes was the intensified fortification of military installations on both sides of the frontier.[37] This led to further tension in Sino-Soviet relations.

THE EMERGENCE OF CHINA
AS AN INDEPENDENT POWER

The most significant consequence of the Sino-Soviet dispute was the emergence of China as an independent power. This was one of the most important factors that led to the deterioration of the rigid bipolar system in East Asia.

In the economic hierarchy, China was neither a superpower nor a regional power. In view of socioeconomic indicators, China was a huge underdeveloped country, lacking the corresponding well-developed economic and industrial capacity to be a major power. Nevertheless, through open dispute and the consequent split with the Soviet Union, China was able to establish a strategically independent position as a regional power with global influence. This independent position was enhanced further by the following developments in the 1960s: China's rivalry with the Soviet Union for the leadership of the Communist movement and the Third World national liberation movement; China's denotation of its first nuclear device; and China's diversification of diplomatic relations with non-Communist industrial countries.

After the split, China and the Soviet Union became rivals, competing not only for the leadership of the international Communist movement, but also for the leadership of the national liberation movement in the Third World. In 1956, Beijing and Moscow worked in tandem organizing the First Afro-Asian Conference in Bandung, Indonesia. At a preparatory meeting in Djakarta for the second Afro-Asian conference which was going to be held in March 1965, the Chinese Foreign Minister, Chen Yi, bluntly asserted that the Soviet Union, an allegedly non-Asian power, had no business at the forthcoming conference. The Soviets, in support of their right to participate, focused on the tangible service that the Soviet Union had rendered in the past and could offer to the national liberation movement in the future.[38] China also competed with the Soviet Union over aid to North Vietnam in its war against the South and the United States. The Chinese accused the Soviets that their aid was neither in quality nor quantity commensurate with their country's strength. The Soviets accused Beijing of needing a long conflict in Vietnam in order to keep up the international tension and portray China as a besieged fortress.[39] Chinese determination to compete with the Soviet Union enhanced China's international prestige and influence. China strove to lead the cause of the Third World in their "just struggle to achieve or safeguard national independence," against imperialism, neocolonialism, and the big power monopoly over the handling of international affairs.[40]

Without Soviet assistance, China detonated its first nuclear weapon on October 16, 1964, coincidentally the day that Khrushchev resigned from his office. Independent nuclear deterrence was "essential for China to guarantee its security,"[41] and consequently strengthened its independent power status. The official statement announcing the explosion called the event a "major achievement," and said that China had become "a nuclear weapon state after a decade of struggle to strengthen its defense."[42] This statement indicated China's intent and ability to be an independent actor in power competition. Indeed, China, with the third largest territory in the world, the world's largest population, its rich natural resources, its growing industrial capacity, its sizable conventional armed forces, as well as a modest nuclear capacity, and especially with its newly gained independent position from the Soviet Union in the divided world, was certainly an independent regional power in the 1960s.

From the time when the Soviet Union ceased to give its economic and technical assistance, China endeavored to diversify its economic and diplomatic relationship with non-Communist countries. This new policy grew out of Mao Zedong's understanding of the Cold War. Mao believed that the Soviet Union and the United States were separated by two "intermediate zones." The first "intermediate zone" was composed of colonial and semi-colonial developing countries in Asia, Africa, and Latin America, and the "second intermediate zone" was composed of European capitalist countries, Japan, Australia, and New Zealand. China worked mostly with the countries in the first intermediate zone during the 1950s and began to pay serious attention to the second intermediate zone in the early 1960s. In his meeting with the colorful, wiry British field marshal Bernard Montgomery in 1960, Mao said, "We don't feel any threat from Britain and France and hope you become stronger." He also told visiting French parliament members in Beijing, "Let's be good friends. You are not in communist party and I am not in your party. But we have two things in common: the first is that we don't allow any superpower to control us; and the second is that we want to strengthen our economic and cultural exchanges."[43] In light of this policy adjustment, 45 percent of China's trade was with non-Communist industrial countries by 1968. Japan, West Germany, Britain, Australia, Italy, and Canada were among Beijing's top ten trading partners.[44]

Following the establishment of France-China diplomatic relations in 1964, China won admission to the UN and became a permanent member of the Security Council in October 1971. These events marked the recognition of China as a legitimate state in the international community. China's influence reached the level of global significance when U.S. President Nixon visited Beijing in February 1972 and Japanese Prime Minister Tanaka visited Beijing in September of that same year. These visits were signs of their acceptance of the PRC as a legitimate partner in maintaining or reshaping the future international system. As a power independent of the Soviet bloc, Beijing was particularly happy for Nixon's vision that "there had emerged in the world five centers of power—the United States, Western Europe, the Soviet Union, China, and Japan."[45]

It was indeed unfortunate that it took nearly a decade before the United States and China acted upon the change that resulted from the Sino-Soviet split. Although NSC 48/5 called for every effort to take advantage of such a split whenever it emerged, the United States did not consciously seek to take advantage of the Sino-Soviet rift until the early 1970s. During preparations for the Vienna summit in 1961, President Kennedy's advisors recommended that he exploit Sino-Soviet tensions and seek a common understanding with Khrushchev about China. But Kennedy misperceived at Vienna that "the Soviets . . . were not ready to reject their former partner and enter into a marriage of convenience with the United States."[46] There were signs, however, that outside the narrow circle of policymakers, ideas for change were gaining currency in America's orientation in dealing with the Communist nations in the middle 1960s. Polycentrism became as familiar a word in the discussion of foreign affairs as "containment."[47] The idea connoted the image of a world divided, not between two poles but among groups of nations, with power centers no longer located only in Moscow and Washington. Opinion differed as to how the United States should chart its course in a polycentric world. No matter how serious China and Russia disagreed, their differences did not divide them in their opposition to the United States. Consequently, the Sino-Soviet dispute was not necessarily a welcome phenomenon. In fact, the loss of Soviet control over Chinese policy incurred more intransigence on the part of the Chinese. Others argued that diversity itself was to be welcomed since it might undermine the myth of a Communist monolith.[48]

Regardless of American views, China established its independent regional power status after the Sino-Soviet split. This brought a new condition that other nations had to reckon with in shaping the course of power competition. Chinese independent power created a variety of diplomatic options that the United States would have formerly considered in dealing with Beijing and Moscow. China was compelled by its perception of the Soviet threat to seek détente, or a new alignment with former adversaries such as the United States and Japan.

THE RISE OF JAPAN AS AN ECONOMIC GIANT

During the Sino-Soviet split, the United States continued to assist Japan's economic development, which, to an extent, helped the resurgence of Japan as an economic giant with regional political leverage. The rise of Japan became another key factor that contributed to the deterioration of the rigid bipolar system in East Asia.[49]

Japan's economic success within two decades of its defeat in World War II was certainly a miracle. Chalmers Johnson's classic study lists four competing explanations for the "Japanese miracle." The first focuses on national character; namely, Japan has a natural advantage as a homogeneous society whose members have a unique, culturally derived capacity to cooperate with one another. The second explanation looks at the unique structural features and holds that Japanese industry has three special advantages or "three sacred treasures:" a lifetime employment system, an efficient seniority-based wage system, and passive, company-dominated labor unions. The third explanation stresses the unique role of the developmental state in economic development. The fourth explanation sees Japan as a free rider who exploited its alliance with the United States through its low defense expenditures, cheap access to key technologies developed in the United States, and easy access to huge U.S. markets.[50]

Regardless of the controversy among these competing explanations, the Japanese government indeed played a decisive role in taking advantage of favorable postwar international conditions, which led to the resurgence of the Japanese economy. The Communist victory in China helped the speedy recovery of the Japanese economy. Japan benefited from the

Korean War and the Vietnam War because they provided great opportunities to expand its economy. Under America's military protection and nuclear umbrella, Japan spent less than 1 percent of GNP in defense expenditures and was able to concentrate its efforts on economic development. At the end of the 1950s, a self-confident Japanese government, headed by Prime Minister Ikeda Hayato, unveiled an "income doubling" plan that envisioned, on the basis of an average growth rate of 7.2 percent, a doubling of the GNP every ten years. As a coordinated national effort, Japanese GNP almost doubled in the five years from 1955 to 1960. It more than doubled in the following five years (1960-1965) and then rose another 2.5 times in five years (1965-1970). In this last period, the annual rate of growth (in real terms) averaged 12.1 percent.[51] In the 1960s, Japan emerged as an economic giant and in the 1970s appeared to be a regional power with economic leverage.

Japan's aspiration to promote its international status by means of economic strength was fulfilled for the first time in 1964 when Japan was both accepted into the Organization for Economic Cooperation and Development (OECD), the so-called rich nations' club, and granted Article 8 status by the International Monetary Fund (IMF).[52] This was an acknowledgment of Japan's growing economic power—sixth in the world in terms of GNP at the time. This move, together with Tokyo's hosting of the Olympic Games in the same year, contributed significantly to Japanese perception of finally belonging to the better part of the world community. Japan's economic status rose rapidly thereafter. In terms of total GNP, Japan overtook Italy in 1966, Britain in 1967, France in 1968, and finally West Germany in 1969.[53] By 1971, Japan had the world's third largest GNP, after the United States and the Soviet Union.[54] In 1975 Japan's critical role in international economic affairs was evident in its participation in the first summit of the G-5 nations.

In East Asia, the government of Sato Eisaku, who had succeeded Ikeda as prime minister in 1964, achieved its first diplomatic success by opening up relations with South Korea in the shape of the Korea-Japan Treaty in 1965. This achievement was due to the political change in both Japan and South Korea. The Sato government, which derived its support from right-center factions in the Liberal Democratic Party (LDP), was more sympathetic toward South Korea than the previous administration had been. In South Korea a strongly anti-Japanese president, Syngman Rhee, had been replaced by a more pragmatic Park Chung-hee, who believed that Japan could help in his country's economic development. Changes on both sides enabled the establishment of diplomatic relations. Japan pledged $500 million in economic assistance (in lieu of reparations), and South Korean fishing restrictions were lifted.[55]

In light of the "Asian Marshall Plan" put forward by Prime Minister Yoshida in the 1950s, Japan began to be actively involved in Southeast Asia in the 1960s. Trade relations were initially stimulated by the reparations payments that Japan made to a number of Southeast Asian nations that had been victims of Japanese aggression in World War II.[56] These payments usually took the form of capital goods. This helped Japan regain access to Asian markets and resources as well as political influence. Prime Minister Ikeda, after his visit to Jakarta in 1963, offered to mediate in the Malaysian-Indonesian confrontation. A three-country summit meeting—President Sukarno from Indonesia, Prime Minister Tunku Abdul Rahman from Malaysia, and President Diosdado Macapagal from the Philippines—was held in Tokyo in June 1964. Although this meeting ended without agreement, Japan continued to take an interest in the dispute, and during 1965-66, by offering conditional aid, was able to moderate Indonesia's militant stance toward Malaysia and to reduce dependence on China. This was the first important postwar political initiative that Japan made in Asia.[57]

In April 1966, at Japan's suggestion, a nine-nation Ministerial Conference for the Economic Development of Southeast Asia was held in Tokyo. South Vietnam, Laos, and Cambodia joined the five future members of ASEAN in accepting the Japanese invitation to discuss prospects and policies for agricultural development and industrialization in the region. Japan agreed to increase its economic aid to the region in what was seen at the time as a sign of a new positiveness in its Asian politics. At the same time, Japan became involved as one of the leading advocates of the Asian Development Bank (ADB), which began operation in December 1966. Japan and the United States were the two main donors. Although headquarters were set up in Manila rather than Tokyo, the governors of the ADB have always been Japanese, and it is one intergovernmental organization where Japan maintains a high visibility. Japan began to give economic aid to the developing countries in the 1960s.[58] Fifty-six percent of the total flow of Japanese aid went to Asia and 99 percent of the total Official Development Assistance (ODA) was directed toward Asia in 1963, with Southeast Asia claiming half of this amount. Official Japanese figures for the cumulative totals of Japanese economic assistance up to 1975 showed that 78 percent of this went to six East Asian countries: South Korea, Burma, Malaysia, Indonesia, the Philippines, and Thailand.[59]

In terms of the Japan-U.S. link, the Japanese government never broke with the United States on any important strategic issues before Nixon's visit to China in 1972. However, huge demonstrations and riots against the ratification of the U.S.-Japan Mutual Security Treaty in 1960 and the eventual resignation of Prime Minister Kishi revealed deep divisions in Japan over the desirability of a close relationship with United States and the international interests that it embodied.[60] Although massive demonstrations before the treaty ratification in 1960 and again before its renewal in 1970 were unsuccessful in severing Japan's link with the United States, Japan was treated more equitably in the newer treaty than in the 1951 treaty. The nature of "a unilateral U.S. agreement" of the 1951 Treaty "convinced the Japanese government that the Treaty needed to be revised as soon as it was signed."[61] Articles 5, 6, and 10 of the 1960 treaty embody the "formal, explicit guarantee and the mutuality sought by the Japanese government."[62] Articles 4 and 6 of the new treaty incorporate a system of prior consultation on certain matters dealing with major changes in the deployment of U.S. troops or equipment, and use of bases for the purpose of military combat.[63]

In this situation, although Japan did not have the independent power status that China obtained in the 1960s with its broad industrial base and technology, and, in particular, with its more or less equal status in relation with the United States, Japan began to assume a more active role in shaping and maintaining peace and order in East Asia.

THE VIETNAM WAR AND ITS LEGACIES

The Vietnam War was the last major war that the United States has fought in Asia during the twentieth century. American involvement in the war was based on a rigid, anti-Communist Cold War ideology. It was designed primarily to contain Chinese communism but, ironically, resulted in a Sino-US détente. American withdrawal and, ultimately, the humiliating defeat of its Vietnam policy in 1975 marked the beginning of the relative decline of U.S. influence, which contributed further to the deterioration of the rigid bipolar system.

American involvement in Vietnam could be clearly divided into four stages. At the first stage, the United States supported the French colonial regime by providing the French with economic and military assistance. When France was forced to withdraw, American involvement entered the second stage by sponsoring a non-Communist regime in South Vietnam. The third stage involved the Americanization of the war in Vietnam. In the fourth stage, the United States designed a Vietnamization policy, which was followed by the final withdrawal of American troops from Vietnam.

Vietnam, like other Indochinese countries, was a colony of the European powers for more than a century. During World War II, Japanese conquest of these countries shattered the aura of invincibility that European powers had enjoyed as colonial masters. After the war, Europe's former subjects no longer held their rulers in awe and would not tolerate foreign rule indefinitely. The Europeans found that they could either grant independence to their colonies voluntarily or be driven out militarily. Some, like the British in Malaysia, provided a peaceful transition to independence,[64] but others, like the French in Vietnam, delayed serious consideration of independence until it was too late to do so without bloodshed. From 1946 to 1954, the French battled Vietnamese insurgents in a vain attempt to stay in Indochina. In 1949, the French sponsored the establishment of a non-Communist regime in Saigon under the leadership of former emperor Bao Dai. After the Korean War broke out in 1950, the Chinese and the Soviet Union recognized Ho Chi Minh's Democratic Republic in the North and provided the Vietminh with material support, while America and Britain recognized the French regime in the South and sometime later began supplying aid to the French military effort against the Vietminh.[65] The Truman and Eisenhower administrations supported the French in Vietnam because they seemed to be fighting the spread of Asian communism: "In the dramatically altered strategic context of 1950s, support for France in Indochina was considered essential for the security of Western Europe."[66] Nevertheless, in a decisive battle between the French and the Vietminh in a small village named Dien Bien Phu, the French were forced to surrender to the Vietminh commander, General Nguyen Giap, on May 7, 1954, after 55 days of heroic fighting.[67]

The fall of Dien Bien Phu led to an international conference in Geneva to settle the independence of Indochinese countries. Representatives from the United States, France, China, North and South Vietnam, and Britain were present in the conference. The resultant Geneva Accords, signed on July 27, 1954, pledged to respect the independence and sovereignty of Vietnam, Laos, and Cambodia; temporarily accept the seventeenth parallel as a dividing line between North and South Vietnam; prohibit the introduction of foreign forces into Indochina; solve all issues and supervise all settlements through an international control commission; and to hold elections in Vietnam by 1956, in order to unify the country under one government.

Prior to the conference, France announced a withdrawal from Indochina by July 21, 1954. The French withdrawal forced a sense of urgency on the Americans. U.S. policymakers feared that the loss of Southeast Asia would irreparably damage the nation's strategic position in the Far East and that control of "America's first line of defense in the Pacific," the offshore island chain extending from Japan to the Philippines, would be endangered. Air and sea routes between Australia, the Middle East, the United States, and India would be cut, severely hampering military operations in the event of war.[68] The strategic importance of preventing Vietnam from falling to the Communists was further enhanced by the "domino theory," which was first set forth during the Truman administration in 1952. A National Security Council memorandum stated that in Southeast Asia, "the loss of any single country would probably lead to relatively swift submission to or an alignment with communism by the remaining countries of this group." Dominoes would continue to fall because "An alignment with communism of the rest of Southeast Asia and India, and in the longer term, of the Middle East . . . would in all probability progressively follow. Such widespread alignment would endanger the stability and security of Europe."[69]

John F. Kennedy, then a senator, expressed the domino theory vividly two years after the fall of Dien Bien Phu by describing Vietnam as "The cornerstone of the Free World in Southeast Asia, the keystone to the arch, the finger in the dike. Burma, Thailand, India, Japan, and obviously Laos and Cambodia would be threatened if the red tide of communism overflowed into Vietnam."[70] This domino theory was based on a crude assumption that societies and politics in the vast, diverse Asian-Pacific region were essentially all alike. It did not distinguish nationalist independent movements from Communist revolutions.

Under these circumstances, with the withdrawal of the French, the United States had to decide what it would do to stop the next domino from tumbling over. At the Geneva conference, the United States and South Vietnam abstained in signing the final agreement.[71] After the conference, the United States supported a non-elected but non-Communist government in the South under President Ngo Dinh Diem who ruled the country in an authoritarian manner. Thus, American involvement in Vietnam entered the second stage. Diem himself embodied an older generation of Vietnamese nationalists who spoke French, had acquired wealth, and were generally Roman Catholic. His nearly exclusive reliance on the Catholic population for support drove a wedge between his regime and the Buddhist majority. Diem's regime was characterized by "manhunts, political re-education camps, and the regroupment of the population," which "caused spreading discontent and then armed resistance on the countryside."[72] By 1958, the civil violence and insurrection in the south had intensified, as had northern support of the Viet Cong (as Diem called the Communists in the south). A secret decision by the Central Committee of the Lao Dong Party (the Communist Party in the north) in January 1959 launched armed struggle in the south and officially recognized the recently created National Liberation Front (NLF—the political wing of the South Communist insurrectionists). Ho Chi Minh declared that it was time for the liberation of the South from the imperial grip of the United States.[73] By the beginning of 1961, the Viet Cong attacks in the south had become more brazen and successful. This was bad enough in itself, but when added to the fact that Ngo's forces were clearly not trained to fight the war, the prospects for the future were certainly grim.

The Kennedy administration became increasingly frustrated with President Ngo and encouraged a military coup against Ngo on November 1-2, 1963. The coup, which was originally designed to exile Ngo and his brother Nhu, ended up as a shootout that led to the brutal murders of the Ngo brothers in the back of an armored personnel carrier. This coup was planned with "the tacit approval of the US Ambassador, Henry Cabot Lodge, and the CIA."[74] Ironically only three weeks later, President Kennedy also lay dead from an assassin's bullet in Dallas. The climate of the opening phase of America's involvement in Vietnam came with the military coup because "this episode began a period of political chaos in South Vietnam that forced the United States to send its troops into the war."[75]

On August 4, 1964, President Johnson, in a national address, revealed that the US destroyer *Maddox,* on routine patrol in international waters near the Gulf of Tonkin, had been attacked by four North Vietnamese torpedo boats two days earlier. Based on this and an unspecified attack on an unnamed U.S. ship the next day, the president announced that U.S. aircraft from the carrier *USS Ticonderoga* had attacked the patrol boat's bases as well as oil storage depots in the area near the port city of Haiphong. This was the first air attack on the North by American air forces. When the president made his announcement, he asked the congress for special powers to prosecute the conflict in Southeast Asia. Within hours, Congress passed what became known as the Gulf of Tonkin resolutions, allowing the president to "take all necessary measures to repel any armed attack against the forces of the United States and to prevent further aggression." It further allowed the president, without congressional approval, "to take all necessary steps, including the use of forces, to assist any member or protocol state of the Southeast Asian Collective Defense Treaty requesting assistance in defense of its freedom."[76]

As a result, America's commitment to Vietnam escalated into the third stage: the Americanization of the war. The president initiated a series of moves that eventually built up U.S. combat troops to 550,000 by 1968. Hanoi met every U.S. escalation with an escalation of its own. A quick victory was beyond their reach. For the United States, the Vietnam War turned into a "limited war" just as the Korean War was in the early 1950s: "A great power of 200 million people fighting a limited war found itself stalemated by a small Asian nation of 17 million fighting a total war."[77] On January 31, 1968, Hanoi mounted a massive offensive attack, known as the Tet Offensive—a simultaneous attack by 85, 000 troops on five major cities, dozens of military installations, and more than 150 towns and villages. The North Vietnamese Tet offensive was a turning point in the war and underscored disaster for the United States.[78] Americans at home were now able to see that, despite three years of bombing and a commitment of half a million men, the enemy was still able to mount offensives. It now became clear that the United States suffered from the war of attrition more than the enemy did. The North Vietnamese manpower pool was far from depleted and there was always "the possibility of an intervention by Chinese 'volunteers.'"[79] Newly available Chinese sources reveals that the Chinese government indeed secretly sent about 320,000 logistic, engineering, and construction personnel and anti-aircraft artillery troops to Vietnam from June 1965 to August 1973. Chinese involvement started after Ho Chi Minh's secret visit to Beijing meeting with Mao Zedong and Zhou Enlai to request military and material assistance in April-May 1965.[80]

In this situation, President Lyndon Johnson rejected the request for more troops to be sent to Vietnam by General Westmoreland immediately after the Tet Offensive. This was Johnson's first signal that he would begin to de-escalate the fighting in Vietnam. On March 22, 1968, Johnson announced that he was replacing General Westmoreland, the commander of the U.S. troops since 1964 in Vietnam. In his famous speech of March 31, 1968, the president said that he would like to stop all bombing in North Vietnam and cut down on the fighting. But there was to be no light at the end of the tunnel for Johnson to pull out of the war. it was an election year and he made a formal announcement that he would withdraw from the presidential race in his March 31 speech.[81]

The presidency of Richard Nixon brought a painful groping for extrication and "peace with honor." Nixon and Secretary of State Henry Kissinger, his main architect of foreign policy, devised a formula known as "Vietnamization," whereby the war would gradually be turned over to the Vietnamese as American combat troops were withdrawn. The American hope was to leave behind a viable anti-Communist South Vietnam with a friendly government firmly installed in Saigon. The withdrawal of

American ground troops began in June 1969. As withdrawal gathered momentum, a serious weakness became increasingly apparent in the Vietnamization strategy: as American strength was slowly ebbing, Communist forces became better able to attack the South Vietnamese regime. Nixon's response was the destruction of Communist sanctuaries by ground incursions into Laos and Cambodia and increasing reliance on air power through bombing. As American participation in the ground fighting gradually diminished, the air war reached levels of unprecedented ferocity.[82]

In July 1969 the president announced the Nixon Doctrine, which meant that, in the future, the United States would avoid entanglements like Vietnam by limiting its support to economic and military aid rather than active combat participation.[83] Peace negotiations began in earnest in Paris. On January 27, 1973, the Paris Peace Accord was signed by the United States and North Vietnam. The signing came only after last-minute maneuvers by American diplomats in Saigon convinced President Nguyen Van Thieu not to sabotage the treaty. Promises of massive American aid and efforts to gain a peaceful settlement with the North convinced Thieu to go along with the treaty. As it turned out, the South Vietnamese had good reason to fear the results of the Paris Accords. With the final U.S. withdrawals that followed in 1973 and 1974, the South soon found itself all but abandoned. "The Accords, in retrospect, marked not only the final act of the American involvement in the Vietnamese tragedy, but the beginning of the end of the South Vietnam."[84]

The Vietnam War was "the longest war in American history and the most divisive conflict domestically since the civil war."[85] American participation in the Vietnam War was the logical culmination of the containment policy that began under Truman. Successive administrations never questioned the assumption that national interest required the denial of South Vietnam to communism. "The result was the gradual, yet inescapable, intervention in a local civil conflict."[86] At first the United States sought to uphold French control, then to build and maintain South Vietnamese independence, and finally to deny victory to North Vietnam. Five American presidents struggled with the dilemma of Vietnam; none was successful.

The American policy in Vietnam was formulated according to a rigid, anti-Communist ideology.[87] In hindsight, it was ironic that successive administrations justified Washington's Vietnam involvement on the grounds of checking the expansion of Sino-Soviet influence in Asia when the Sino-Soviet relationship was already deteriorating. Gordon Chang's study finds that one of the tragic consequences of the Sino-Soviet split was the "role it played in the Johnson administration's fateful decision in 1964-65 to escalate American intervention in the Vietnamese revolution."[88] It was not so much that the officials of the Johnson administration believed that a divided Communist world made the Vietnamese Communists vulnerable. Rather, Vietnam appeared to American leaders as the test for whether Moscow's seemingly benign policy or Beijing's radical policy would triumph in the international Communist movement. Vietnamese Communist success would dramatically encourage the radical national liberation doctrine espoused by China. Thus, the intensified American involvement in Vietnam paralleled the emerging American perception of China as the most dangerous threat to the Asian regional order. Escalating military commitments were broadly accepted at first not just by leaders in Washington but by the American public until American casualties reached alarming levels.

The American decision-making process in the Vietnam war was fraught with contradictions. On the one hand, U.S. presidents were mindful of the wrath that voters directed against Truman and the Democrats as a result of the Korean War. On the other hand, each succeeding president did not want to lose a country to communism during his term of office. The conservative backlash from the bitter "who lost China" debate suggested the political hazards of being "soft" on communism. The Vietnam scenario seemed ominously familiar: a violent Asian revolutionary movement supported by a powerful Communist neighbor threatened to overthrow a corrupt, but pro-American, government. Soon after taking office in late 1963, Lyndon Johnson said: "I am not going to be the President who saw Southeast Asia go the way China went."[89] Looking back on the Vietnam War, Richard Nixon said that "the siege of Dien Bien Phu was made possible only by the fall of Asia's largest domino—China."[90]

The Vietnam War left several important and, to some extent, ironic legacies in changing East Asian international relations. First, while Washington was preoccupied with the conflict in Vietnam, the Soviets were strengthening their strategic stockpile and the Japanese were building their industrial structure. In this sense, the cost of the Vietnam War for the United States went far beyond the lives that were lost, money that was spent, and political reputations that were compromised. The war sapped the country's economic vitality, eroded its military superiority, and raised doubts about its political judgment. It was described as a "collapse of national will," the breakdown of a foreign-policy consensus, and a "loss of innocence."[91] America's world-leadership position suffered accordingly.

Second, America's combat involvement in Vietnam to roll back the spread of Asian Communism ironically resulted in Sino-American rapprochement. During the mid-1960s, when the United States was becoming increasingly involved in the war in Vietnam, China started the Cultural Revolution, heading steadily for a mortal internal rift that placed all important party organizations in serious disarray, even risking civil war. Under these circumstances, China was in no position to fight the war against the United States. In fact, the Soviets suspected from the beginning that the true intention of the Chinese regarding the war in Vietnam was to bleed both America and Vietnam so that China would later be able to assert its dominance over the area, while reduce the threat of a direct attack from the United States. This was confirmed when Mao Zedong made his comment to Edgar Snow that "it is good thing to have the Americans in South Vietnam," and that "China would fight only against direct attack by the U.S. on her territory."[92] In addition, the escalating Vietnam War in the 1960s exacerbated friction between the two Communist giants, with Moscow counseling Hanoi to pursue the diplomatic track and Beijing advocating the opposite course of militant armed struggle. By the early 1970s, the Chinese and Soviets had fought border skirmishes and amassed troops and armaments along their extensive borders. It was during this tense period that a delicate courtship, through Pakistan intermediaries, was started between the United States and the PRC.[93] The climate of the Sino-American rapprochement improved because Washington and Beijing were both concerned about the danger of Soviet expansionism and sought to use the other country to contain Moscow's influence. Thus the Vietnam War was fought by Washington to contain China but, in the end, China was brought into strategic relationship with Moscow and Washington.

Third, the Vietnam War served the same function in helping the economic takeoff of Taiwan and especially South Korea just as American military spending for the Korean War gave the Japanese economy a much needed boost: "The military sacrifices of the United States in these conflicts contributed in a sense to the rise of its East Asian trade competitors."[94]

A GEOPOLITICAL REVOLUTION

On July 15, 1971, President Richard Nixon astounded the world by announcing that Henry Kissinger, his national security advisor, had undertaken a secret mission to Beijing and conferred with Chinese leaders to arrange for the president's trip to China the following February. In Kissinger's words, it was an "announcement that shocked the world."[95] President Nixon and a delegation of 13 American officials, including Kissinger and Secretary of State William Rogers, arrived in Beijing on February 21, 1972 for a week of talks with Mao Zedong and Zhou Enlai.

Nixon asserted that this was a "week that changed the world"; an effort by the leaders of the world's most populous nation and the most wealthy nation to "bridge a gulf of almost 12,000 miles and 22 years of non-communication and hostility" that had riven the Asian political landscape since the Korean War.[96] Shaking hands with Nixon at Beijing airport, Zhou Enlai told his visitor that "your hands have crossed the widest ocean in the world."[97] Indeed, Nixon's visit caused a geopolitical revolution. Geopolitics was the term used most frequently by both Nixon and Kissinger in explaining the decision to reverse America's long-standing policy to contain the People's Republic. The term implied recognition of the power realities in the world; namely, that China was a power, whether or not one liked the fact. The United States simply could not ignore a huge and politically unified country with nuclear weapons. China was accepted as a world power and as a legitimate player in the East Asian competition.

Common ground for China and America was their desire to counter the Soviet threat. This understanding was embodied in one of the articles of the joint communiqué signed in Shanghai, which provided that "neither should seek hegemony in the Asia-Pacific region and each is opposed to efforts by any other country or group of countries to establish such hegemony."[98] In effect, this was a promise by China not to support Soviet policies against the United States in East Asia and a promise by the United States to use its influence to prevent a Soviet attack on China. In exchange for China's pledge of independence from Moscow, the United States agreed to stop trying to block Chinese efforts to expand its own contacts and influence; namely, the United States agreed to abandon the containment of China. This mutual understanding was significant for both China and America. For China it was vitally important to reduce the cost and danger of a possible "two-front war" by improving relations with the United States, so as to concentrate its resources against the bigger adversary, the Soviet Union.[99] For the United States, it was necessary to reduce the cost of the "two-and-a-half-war strategy" by improving relations with China so as to concentrate its main military resources on deterring the Soviet Union.[100] The two powers also had some other national concerns. It was in China's interest to find a solution to the reunification of Taiwan with the mainland through Sino-American rapprochement.[101] On the American side, the strategic motivation behind the rapprochement included capitalizing on the Sino-Soviet split to gain leverage over both the Soviet Union and China and to head off a Sino-Soviet rapprochement. In Kissinger's words, it was to play "the China card."[102]

The geopolitical revolution started with an awareness by Nixon and Kissinger of the opportunities that the Sino-Soviet conflict presented to the

United States. Moscow's desire for U.S. support against China, or alternatively, Moscow's desire to prevent a Sino-U.S. alignment against the Soviet Union, created important incentives for Moscow to cooperate with Washington. Beijing's desire to dissuade Washington from endorsing Soviet actions against China might induce it to improve relations with the United States and to lessen its opposition to America's Vietnam policy. Most fundamentally, Nixon believed that American interests would not be served by a Chinese military defeat by the Soviet Union. If China was smashed or humiliated in a Sino-Soviet war, Moscow would be able to shift its entire military weight to oppose the Western alliance. Nixon concluded that the United States should support China against Soviet pressure.[103] During a tour of Asian countries in mid-1969, Nixon informed Asian leaders that the United States would not support Soviet proposals for collective security in Asia. Nixon told Pakistan's leader that the United States would not join with the Soviet Union to isolate China but hoped, instead, for better Sino-American relations. During the first meeting of the renewed ambassadorial-level talks in Warsaw in January 1970, the United States informed China that America would not participate in a condominium with the Soviet Union in Asia or elsewhere.[104]

China's leaders certainly took the American assurance with pleasure because they were extremely apprehensive that the United States might join the Soviet Union to preempt China's nuclear threat. China's decision for rapprochement with the United States was also tied to the shift in Washington's Indochina policies. At this time, Beijing concluded from the American withdrawal of ground troops in Vietnam that the United States had changed directions in Vietnam and would eventually withdraw from that country. At a minimum, this would ease American military pressure on China's southern flank. In September 1970, Zhou Enlai sent a message to Nixon via the Pakistani president saying that Nixon's special envoy would be welcome in Beijing to discuss outstanding issues. Mao also sent his own signal by inviting the American writer Edgar Snow, an old friend of his, to stand beside him atop Tiananmen gate during the National Day celebrations on October 1, 1970. The first public bid to the United States came in April 1971. It was an invitation to a U.S. table tennis team competing in Japan to visit China. Kissinger's secret visit and the well-publicized visit by Nixon completed the first episode of the Sino-American rapprochement.[105]

The most dramatic consequence of the Sino-American rapprochement in East Asia was the sudden normalization of Sino-Japanese relations. The announcement of Nixon's visit to Beijing was so unexpected in Japan that it was referred to as a "Nixon Shock."[106] They had to accommodate the new development into their thinking and reorient their approach to China, as did virtually all other countries. For the Japanese, who had not been consulted or forewarned, the effect of the U.S. move was devastating. The high hopes of Japan for the 1970s on account of its steady economic growth and increased international stature were rudely shattered. The "Nixon Shock" was seen as "the most humiliating treatment that Japan had received from the United States since its defeat in World War II . . . It undermined the basic assumptions of its foreign policy during the 1960s."[107] Although Kissinger later admitted that it had been a serious error in manners and a lack of consideration to Japan, the Americans were hardly able to mitigate the psychological blow. Japan had thought of the United States as a mentor and a guarantor of its security. Moreover, the blow was all the more severe as one of the most controversial issues of the 1960s was the policy toward China. Prime Minister Sato withstood persistent public pressure to normalize relations with China and not disrupt the America's policy of containment. The principal casualty was Sato himself. Charges of misgovernment were leveled against the Sato cabinet, not only from the left, but from a wide range of the population.[108] People were now genuinely alarmed by the way in which the government had allowed the Americans to treat Japan and, more importantly, by the fact that America and China would collude to shut Japan out of such an important development in the relationship between them.

The sense of shock at having been kept completely in the dark by its only ally in the world was so deep that Japan determined to go its own way to accommodate the profound transformation in East Asian international relations into their sense of the regional system. Earlier in the history of U.S.–East Asian relations, "favorable American images of China had almost invariably been combined with unfavorable views of Japan, and vice versa. It had been rare for Americans to entertain positive images of both China and Japan."[109] Given the pragmatism that had been a main feature of Japanese foreign relations since the nineteenth century, it is not surprising that Tokyo's leaders soon began preparing for their own rapprochement with Beijing. In Japan, the enthusiasm for normalization with China, long an unofficial national goal, was reinforced now as the only way to restore the nation's self-respect and international standing, both of which had been seriously undermined by the American policies. Liberated at last from the need to defer to the Americans, the government itself was ready to move fast and far, even to outdistance the United States in the subsequent relationship with China: "The scramble within and between Japan's political parties to win the race to Beijing was on, and the pace quickly proved deadly."[110]

This extraordinary China boom would have no room for Sato as either driver or even humble backseat passenger. The winner in the LDP factional stakes was Tanaka Kakuei. The task for Tanaka and the Japanese was now easy, at least mentally and psychologically, in that Chinese-Japanese ties had never been cut off entirely, but, on the contrary were maintained through trade and other types of contact. Even when they belonged to two hostile camps in a divided world, a "separation of politics and economics" in Chinese-Japanese relations was maintained.[111] Moreover, China had not insisted on any modification of the U.S. security arrangements with Japan as a precondition for the Nixon trip.

By mid-1972 the Chinese were obviously as eager as the Japanese for normalization, partially because the visit of President Nixon to Beijing was not as rich in substance as the press coverage suggested. At the end of Nixon's visit, "continuing differences between China and the United States" were "spelled out" at once.[112] In spite of all the talks of détente and a new balance of power, the United States proved a tough negotiator on the principles of the Cold War, including the issue of Taiwan. Beijing suspected that the ideologically less-committed Japanese would prove more amenable to their wishes, if only because of historical and cultural affinities, reinforced by two decades of unofficial, yet active, people to people exchanges. In addition, China must have expected substantial Japanese economic help, which it needed rather urgently in order to proceed with its modernization program. Although there were more complicated issues in Chinese-Japanese relations that might have created obstacles in the way of a speedy rapprochement, especially Japan's historical aggression in China and the atrocities committed against the Chinese, the leaders in China chose not to press on Japan's war guilt question or to demand huge reparation payments. Instead, they judged, it would appear from circumstantial evidence, that these issues could be raised in the future, but that for the moment the crucial thing was to build on the momentum of the Sino-U.S. détente and to consolidate it by adding Japan to the picture.[113]

In light of the existing mood in both sides, "the old wartime slogans on not missing the bus to China were now once again revived with the intent of encouraging all and sundry to make haste to Beijing."[114] Tanaka lost little time before plunging himself into a kind of normalization fever, after replacing Sato as Prime Minister on July 5, 1972. China's leaders, in turn, were quick to extend an invitation to the new prime minister, giving an assurance that even if they could not agree on the actual terms of a joint communiqué, this need not hinder the principles of establishing diplomatic relations. On September 29, 1972, five months after Nixon made his trip to China, a joint communiqué was signed by Prime Minister Tanaka and Premier Zhou in Beijing declaring that Japan and China had established diplomatic relations. It also stated that Japan was aware of its responsibility for causing enormous damages to the Chinese people in the past through war and deeply reproached itself. On the Taiwan issue, Japan agreed with the position of the Chinese government that "Taiwan is an inalienable part of the territory of the People's Republic of China."[115] The Chinese government agreed to give up its claim to war reparations from Japan on the ground that by being generous on this scope, Japan could be induced to offer various types of economic assistance and cooperate with China in promoting regional stability.[116]

The normalization of the Sino-Japanese relations completed the geopolitical revolution that offered China the greatest diplomatic opportunities since 1949 and removed the ideological restraint of the U.S. Cold War policy on Japan. Both China and Japan set their policy toward each other on an independent basis and the Sino-Japanese relations were no longer dictated only by Cold War bipolar politics.

POWER COMPETITION IN THE DÉTENTE SYSTEM

A détente system emerged along with the deterioration of the rigid bipolar system in East Asia. The two superpowers (the United States and the Soviet Union) and the two regional powers (China and Japan) became partners as well as competitors paradoxically, and played equally significant roles in shaping and maintaining peace and order. This power distribution was characterized as a "quadrilateral" system by President Nixon.[117] In view of the traditional military-strategic power hierarchy, Henry Kissinger aptly described the system as "bi-multipolar," that is, "bipolar militarily and multipolar politically."[118] Both the United States and the Soviet Union possessed more than sufficient nuclear capability to devastate China and Japan. China had little power to retaliate and Japan had none. However, Japan, with the third largest industrial economy in the world, had the potential with its advanced technology and broad industrial capacity, to become a major military power. China, with limited nuclear capacity and its strategic position between the two superpowers, had significant political influence over both the United States and the Soviet Union.

Détente was a new form of contest to promote and protect the interests of major powers through peaceful political and diplomatic means. Theoretically détente is "the expression of a certain stability already achieved in the balance of power."[119] In the East Asian détente system, the United States and the Soviet Union both played mixed superpower and regional power roles in response to different situations.

Two characteristics existed in the power competition of the détente system. One was that the United States tended to restrain itself in pursuing its own concept of world order that had such a high cost in American economic and human terms during the period of the Vietnam War. In the wake of the stalemate that American power experienced in Vietnam and the normalization of relations with China, the United States began to restrain itself by reducing its role in Asia. One striking change in American policy was the tendency to degrade its dominant position to one of more or less equal partners with the intention to lessen the risk of involvement in regional conflicts. By withdrawing its defense commitments to Japan, Korea, and Taiwan, and, at the same time, compelling Japan to assume responsibility in defending its own security and regional stability, the Nixon Doctrine represented the U.S. self-constraint policy in the region and was based on a broad understanding of the deterioration of the bipolar system. The primary thrust of the Nixon Doctrine was "disengagement" of American combat forces from Asia. This pattern was different from that during the period of the rigid bipolar Cold War era when the United States, as the principal power aligned against the Sino-Soviet bloc, had assumed the entire burden of defending its allies in the region from Communist threats either through bilateral security treaties or multilateral treaties.

Another important characteristic of power competition in the new era was that the functional role of each state was no longer strictly conditioned by the two superpowers' confrontation as in the rigid bipolar system. Due to the greater number of opportunities for all the major powers, the U.S.-Soviet relationship became a less dominant axis of East Asian international politics and, in particular, China and Japan took on a larger role and acted with greater freedom. The emergence of China as an independent regional power after the Sino-Soviet split in the early 1960s was the most significant event that led to the new era. The emergence of China created a new condition that other major powers had to reckon with and also created a variety of diplomatic options that the major powers might consider in dealing with one another. While China was compelled by its perception of the increased Soviet threat to seek détente or a new alignment with former adversaries such as the United States and Japan, these very same countries were also compelled to act upon the logic of the change in the East Asian power structure by playing the China card and counterweighing the Soviet Union. Therefore, the maintenance of peace and order in East Asia was far beyond the joint capacity of the United States and the Soviet Union. It was, rather, dependent on the quadrilateral Asian power balance. The four powers tended to pursue détente, namely, the preservation of the balance of power through peaceful means, as their common interest in the region although they still endeavored to improve their respective power relative to the others and had conflicting interests in Vietnam, Taiwan, Korea, and Southeast Asian nations and disagreed on many issues.

THE DYNAMICS OF THE STRATEGIC TRIANGLE

Power competitions in East Asia during the last episode of the Cold War were distinguished by a significant degree of strategic interdependence among three nations: the United States, the Soviet Union, and China. The security of each nation was shaped by the relationship between the other two. This state of affairs was known as a strategic triangle. "The triangularity meant that each bilateral relationship was contingent upon each participant's relations with the third. The essence of this relationship was not simply two against one but one playing the other (or two playing the third) in a variety of ways."[1] The three states involved in the relationship were large and powerful, and so geopolitically situated that their interactions necessarily impinged on the interests of many other countries in their mutual vicinity. The strategic relationship among these three states was qualitatively different from and more vital than any other relationships in East Asia during the period of the Sino-American rapprochement in the early 1970s. Other relationships and other nations were important in the power competition, but they were usually deemed as functional dependents of one or another of the three principal power players. For example, the quadrilateral relationship (of the United States, the Soviet Union, China, and Japan), which played an important role in East Asian international relations during this period, could be seen, to a certain extent, in a lens of triangular interactions because Japan had less strategic strength than any of the three principals. Although Japan had a powerful economy and its military prowess should not be underestimated, Japan's lack of nuclear capacity meant it could figure in the strategic calculus only in alliance with the United States and/or China against the Soviet Union. By the same token, given the overwhelming power of the three states, the security of the other East Asian states, no matter how large or small, was significantly determined by interactions among the three powers. This situation compelled each country to carefully assess its respective position in regard to the triangular relationship.

THE CHINA FACTOR
IN THE TRIANGULAR RELATIONSHIP

In the strategic triangular relationship, one of the most notable issues was the asymmetry of national power among the United States, the Soviet Union, and China. Not all powers were created equal, and China during this period was significantly less powerful than the other two. China was not a superpower and was, by far, the most "reactive state" within triangular politics.[2]

Despite the asymmetry among the three powers, there was significant attention paid to the triangular interactions. Both the United States and the Soviet Union took China very seriously and played the China card against each other whenever they could. China also enjoyed its position in the triangular politics, playing one against the other. Although it was the weak pole, China's political leverage in the triangular relationship was certainly not much weaker than the two more powerful poles. As a scholar wrote in the early 1980s, "Neither the Soviet Union nor the United States can hope to achieve its goals in Asia without taking into consideration the legitimate interests and concerns of China. If this was true during the early years of the Cold War when China was relatively weak, it is even more true today when China is one of the significant powers in Asia."[3]

China's leaders were well aware of its weight in the triangular politics. In a 1984 speech, high-level Chinese strategic advisor Huan Xiang stated that "contemporary world politics is largely determined by the dynamics of the 'triangle' between Washington, Moscow, and Beijing."[4] In other comments, Chinese leaders, including Deng Xiaoping, displayed keen appreciation of their country's strategic leverage within the triangle. A Chinese textbook of international relations acknowledges that, during 1970-80, "the triangular relationship of China, the United States, and the Soviet Union in the Asia-Pacific region became favorable to China."[5]

Indeed, for the first time in history, China could befriend a superpower without fear of being its junior partner. China was a fully accredited player in the triangular relationship especially in the 1980s, daring to confront both superpowers simultaneously from a position of economic inferiority. The two superpowers, in turn, indicated at various times that they took China's presumptuous self-estimate seriously. To restore Sino-Soviet relations, the Soviet digest of anti-Chinese articles *Opasnyi kurs* (Dangerous Course), published since 1969, produced its final issue in 1981. Polemics against China in the Soviet press virtually ceased in 1982. In addition, "Moscow sought to portray the Soviet Union as a more reliable partner than either Japan or the United States."[6] Americans also took the China factor seriously in its foreign policy. Richard H. Solomon wrote in the early 1980s that "US-PRC normalization initiated processes of change that . . . can contribute significantly to . . . the building of a new coalition of powers supportive of the basic goals of American foreign policy."[7] Indeed, each superpower deemed it highly advantageous to be aligned with China, each in its turn experienced euphoria, almost a "national love affair" during the early stages of entente; contrariwise, each deemed China's realignment to be a traumatic event severely jeopardizing its international security.[8] It was apparent that policymakers in China, just as in the two superpowers, evaluated the respective policies of the other two and developed its own policy with attention to the triangular implications. China, as "the weak pole" in the triangle was "able to benefit far out of proportion to its real power through triangulation."[9]

China's attention to the United States and the Soviet Union is easily comprehensible. But the American and Soviet attention to China's strategic role was qualitatively different from their attention to the other party. Both the United States and the Soviet Union were clearly superpowers sharing strategic capacities of mass destruction, but China's nuclear power was far more limited, resembling that of France and Britain, although its impact on superpower diplomacy and bargaining surpassed that of the NATO powers.[10] Clearly, its diplomatic importance was not solely a function of its military capabilities. China's importance in the East Asian power competition and its membership in the strategic triangle reflected the combination of three peculiar factors.

First, China's strategic position partially rested on "a combination of nuclear deterrence and the idea of a 'people's war.'"[11] China was unique in the world. Although it was not an industrialized state, it possessed a massive military machine. Although its nuclear weapons capability was modest, it was powerful enough to serve as a deterrent force.[12] China's conventional capacity far surpassed that of any country, with the exception of the superpowers, and was sufficient to pose a significant military threat to either superpower. This capacity was based on the fact that China ranked first in the world in population, second in grain output and in size of standing army, and third in size of navy and air force. It was third also in strategic nuclear forces, space satellites, cotton, raw coal, and steel output. China's foreign and defense policies clearly affected the regions of East Asia as well as Europe. Nearly every Asian state must consider China's military posture.[13] China, for instance, could tilt the military balance between North and South Korea or between Vietnam and its

Southeast Asian neighbors. Thus, as a scholar suggested in the early 1980s, "the size and central location of China make almost every Asian state take note of Beijing's military posture. Similarly, China's military power may affect the European strategic military balance between NATO and the Warsaw Pact countries."[14] In view of China's massive conventional capacity and modest nuclear power, the Soviet Union thought seriously about China's military threat. The Soviet Union deployed 52 divisions in its four Far Eastern military districts (which represented about a quarter of all Soviet ground forces), as well as its most advanced military equipment along the Sino-Soviet border during the 1970s and 1980s.[15] The Soviet-Vietnamese and Soviet-Indian alliances of the period demonstrated the financial and diplomatic costs Soviet leaders sustained to prepare for the prospect of a land war with China.

China's unique military capabilities suggested that, apart from the superpowers, it could risk both superpowers' hostility alone. In the late 1970s, Drew Middleton, the military correspondent for *The New York Times,* was fascinated by "China's passionate independence" in the midst of the triangular relationship. He found one theme that always came to the fore was that the Chinese "depend on self-reliance." Chinese deputy foreign minister, Yu Chang, told Middleton that the United States had blockaded and embargoed China and "thought we could not survive. But we did survive and develop. Later on, the Soviet Union learned from the United States and wanted to take us by the neck. But we survived. And we did develop."[16] Indeed, as early as in the 1960s, China had already reinforced such expectations by pursuing and surviving the self-imposed isolation of its dual-adversary policy in confrontation with intense military pressure from both superpowers. Although costs were high, Chinese policy in the 1960s made credible Beijing's decision to distance itself from Washington in the 1970s and 1980s.

Second, China's membership in the strategic triangle also derived from diplomatic practice: a demonstrated and remarkable flexibility in its alignments vis-à-vis the superpowers. China's military weight alone does not explain the preoccupation of both Moscow and Washington with China's strategic influence. Also contributing to the strategic position was Chinese diplomatic flexibility. The uncertainty surrounding Chinese alignment policy was one important factor underlying China's position in the triangular relationship. According to one scholar's account, China was the only major power to have actually switched sides in the post–1945 East-West confrontation, except Egypt's 1972 break with the Soviet Union. China was also the only major country to have engaged, in seriatim, in military conflict with both superpowers, and the only major country, again excluding Egypt, to have been militarily allied with both. Finally, China was the only major country to have simultaneously opposed both superpowers.[17] Unlike France and Great Britain, whose commitment to NATO eliminated any ambiguity concerning their future policies, China maintained sufficient diplomatic flexibility so that there was only limited confidence in Moscow and Washington that Beijing would maintain its diplomatic posture for the foreseeable future. In the late 1970s, it was not clear to the Soviet Union whether Chinese leaders would further consolidate U.S.-Chinese strategic cooperation, thereby aggravating Soviet security considerations in Asia. Nevertheless, when the Soviet Union explored the option of improving its relations with China in the 1980s, Beijing responded positively because Beijing also sought Sino-Soviet rapprochement to ameliorate Soviet pressure. In the meantime, the United States wanted to see China as a partner or member of an alliance in its East Asian as well as in its global security arrangement. Nevertheless, with ongoing ideological opposition to American "imperialism" and under the pressure of Soviet "encirclement," China distanced itself from the United States to alleviate the Soviet strategic burden, which potentially undermined American interests in Asia. In light of this flexibility, both the United States and the Soviet Union were unsure about China's alignment. This striking fluidity made Moscow and Washington apprehensive about China's future alignments. This, in turn, enhanced Beijing's diplomatic leverage with the two superpowers.

The third factor was heightened superpower tensions during the Cold War. The Soviet Union and the United States did not consider Chinese power independent of bilateral considerations. On the contrary, their attention to China reflected their appreciation for China's ability to either exacerbate or ameliorate the burden of the superpower conflict. In isolation, China could not pose a significant threat to Soviet interests and was of little immediate value to America beyond its ability to contribute to America's effort to offset the Soviet Union's growing global power. But in the context of heightened threat perception on the part of both superpowers, China assumed exaggerated strategic importance. It was the Cold War system that enabled Beijing to exploit superpower rivalry as a fulcrum to gain strategic leverage and global influence. The structural reality of the Cold War system explained "the puzzle as to how China, as a developing country, managed to exert global influence and how it acted as a global power, and was treated as such by the rest of the world, including the two superpowers. China has played the Cold War triangular game well and often to its advantage."[18] Thus, the end of the Cold War ended the era of the strategic triangle.

All three factors were crucial to defining China's position in the strategic triangle. Without Chinese military power, the regional and global balances would have remained purely bilateral affairs. Without the emergence of the Chinese flexibility in the late 1960s and the early 1970s, China's role in world affairs would have been sufficiently predictable so that neither Moscow nor Washington would have been concerned with trying to influence Chinese behavior through either coercive or conciliatory initiatives. And if Chinese flexibility had not emerged during the era of Cold War hostility, it was unlikely that Washington would have been sufficiently interested in negotiating the U.S.-Chinese rapprochement.[19] Thus, when the Cold War finally receded, Washington's patience with China's domestic system and aspects of its foreign policy quickly eroded, reflecting diminished American interest in U.S.-Chinese relations in the years after the Tiananmen Incident of 1989, which coincided with the end of the Cold War. Similarly, Chinese alignment with the United States during the 1970s and 1980s encouraged greater Soviet coercion against China than would have otherwise been the case. When U.S.-Soviet tension diminished, Moscow ceased viewing China's U.S. policy as threatening and did not need to balance China's growing influence in the world affairs.

THE NORMALIZATION OF SINO-U.S. DIPLOMATIC RELATIONS

The beginning of the strategic triangle was officially marked by the historic meeting between President Nixon and Chairman Mao in Beijing in 1972. Nevertheless, its significance in shaping East Asian international relations and global power competition did not fully unfold until the mid-1970s when the Soviet Union took dramatic actions to counterweight the impact of the rapid improvement in Sino-American relations, and Beijing, in turn, called for a "united front" against hegemonism. The result was the normalization of Sino-U.S. relations in 1979.

The geopolitical revolution brought about by the Sino-U.S. rapprochement after Nixon's visit to Beijing in 1972 had a profound impact on Soviet strategic thinking and spurred the Soviet arms buildup in preparation for major war on two dispersed fronts. The Sino-U.S. rapprochement occurred when the Soviet Union's détente with the United States declined to a low level following the Soviet invasion of Czechoslovakia in 1968. At the same time, the Soviets were challenged by Chinese initiatives in Eastern Europe and Northeast Asia that offered resistance to Soviet domination.[20] Under these circumstances, the development in Sino-U.S. relations naturally caused great alarm in the Soviet leadership at the possibility of a coordinated Sino-American strategy of a "two-front war" against the Soviets and at the tendency to "be the isolated side of the emerging triangular relationship."[21] To avoid this, Moscow made advances to Washington by a détente strategy. In May 1972, two arms control accords were signed by the Soviet and American leaders, which were regarded as "the single most significant American-Soviet agreement of the post–war period."[22] Washington evidently concluded that the strategy of increasing the leverage on Moscow through Sino-American rapprochement had worked because Soviet insecurity toward China clearly strengthened the overall position of the United States. The result was what Henry Kissinger desired: "it was always better for us to be closer to either Moscow or Peking than either was to the other."[23] A Chinese scholar admitted that, during the mid-1970s, "Washington enjoyed the pivotal role in its positive relations with both Beijing and Moscow, while the latters were still in a tense relationship."[24]

The Sino-Soviet confrontation reached a crucial moment when the Soviet Union began its massive arms buildup along Sino-Soviet borders in the late 1970s. Having secured détente with the United States and its European borders via the Helsinki Agreement, the Soviet Union now turned eastward, moving into the Asia Pacific, establishing a secure power base to fend off prospective Sino-American-Japanese collusion.[25] The buildup began with a pubic visit by Brezhnev and Defense Minister Ustinov to the commands at Khaborovsk, Novosibirsk, and Vladivostok in April 1978. During his inspections, Brezhnev noted that the greater part of the expanded defense budget in his country was now going to the Soviet Far East. For the first time Soviet defense expenditures for Asia moved ahead of those for Europe.[26] In the meantime, the rise of Jimmy Carter in Washington degraded the Kissingerian realpolitik of the pre-1977 period. In early 1977, the Carter administration announced its decision (later reversed) to withdraw America's ground troops from South Korea. And throughout the second half of the 1970s, the strength of American military forces in East Asia and the West Pacific steadily declined.[27]

This situation obviously caused concern in Beijing. Ever since the early 1970s, the Chinese had never stopped warning the Americans of the consequences of détente with the Soviets. China strongly advocated détente would make the Soviets more aggressive and that only by strengthening American military posture would Soviet expansionism be checked.[28]

China's concern and countermeasures to the Soviet threat that resulted from the U.S.-Soviet détente were clearly conveyed by Chinese Foreign Minister Huan Hua in a report on the world situation in July 1977, which stated that "With American power shrinking and isolationism surging, the revisionist Soviet-imperialists are filling the vacuum left by the U.S. and are taking advantage of U.S. weakness to make expansionist and infiltrative moves . . . We must unite with the Third World, win over the Second World, and take advantage of the splits between the two superpowers to divide them and to undermine their collusive scheme to divide the world behind the scenes. By winning the U.S. over to our side, we can concentrate all our forces to deal with the arch-enemy—Soviet revisionist social-imperialism."[29] The evidence of a major Soviet arms buildup along the Sino-Soviet border engendered a visceral anti-Soviet posture in China. The hitherto fairly complacent Chinese estimate of the Soviet threat gyrated upward. In 1977, a commentator in *Remin Ribao* declared that the Soviet Union had become the most dangerous source of world war in the present time. It accused the Kremlin of trying to encircle and isolate China through its "southward thrusts" into Vietnam and, at the end of 1979, into Afghanistan.[30] Beijing responded to those alarming developments by intensifying its diplomatic efforts to build an "international anti-Soviet united front" against Soviet hegemonism and by identifying China "with the strategic objectives of the United States, Japan, and Western Europe."[31]

The Americans were at first reluctant to convert to China's united front against "hegemonism," holding an interest in pursuing arms control negotiations and otherwise nurturing the dying embers of détente. President Carter and his Secretary of State, Cyrus Vance, sought to pursue an "even-handed" policy, hoping that American interests would be best served by seeking to improve relations with both Moscow and Beijing simultaneously, and that this position in the triangle would provide incentives for the latter two to continue their forward movement with the United States.[32] Yet such a policy was not successful when both China and the Soviet Union were in tension, because both then resented an American approach from which only Washington would benefit. As a result, the level of Beijing-Washington relations actually dropped in 1977, and no significant progress was achieved in Soviet-American relations either.

The failure of the policy resulted in a shift from Secretary of State Cyrus Vance's "evenhandedness" to National Security Advisor Zbigniew Brzezinski's "balance of power."[33] The decisive breakthrough came during a visit to Beijing in May 1978 when Brzezinski, the new national security advisor to President Jimmy Carter, told Chinese leaders that the United States had "made up its mind" to achieve normalization as quickly as possible.[34] After six months of intensive negotiations, the two countries reached an agreement on the establishment of diplomatic relations, under which the United States acceded to "three conditions" that Beijing had demanded since 1975: *Chejun* (withdrawal of all U.S. military forces from Taiwan); *huiyue* (termination of the U.S.-Taiwan Mutual Security Treaty of 1954); and *duanjiao* (severance of diplomatic relations with Taiwan).[35] Beijing also made several important concessions on the Taiwan issue. It agreed to establish formal Sino-U.S. diplomatic relations one year prior to the actual cancellation of the U.S. treaty with Taiwan. It agreed to normalize relations even though Washington said it would continue supplying weapons to Taiwan.[36] To Beijing, these concessions were bitter. It agreed to these terms because it believed that strengthened Sino-American ties were essential to prevent a further shift of the global balance of power in Moscow's favor.

The establishment of diplomatic relations between Beijing and Washington permitted a rapid development of ties between the two countries. Deng Xiaoping traveled to the United States in January 1979, becoming the first high-level Chinese Communist leader to make a state visit to America. Beijing and Washington also began concrete measures of security cooperation. At the time of normalization Beijing agreed to allow the United States to establish electronic listening stations in Xinjiang monitoring Soviet rocket firings in Central Asia to replace the U.S. listening posts in Iran shut down by a revolution in that country.[37] U.S. Secretary of Defense Harold Brown and Chinese Defense Minister Geng Biao visited each other's country in January and May 1980 respectively. The United States authorized the sale of dual use (military and civilian) technology to China, and the sale of nonlethal military equipment. In June 1981, the United States agreed to sell arms to China. Sino-American military relations slowly increased until the Tiananmen Incident in 1989.

The Sino-U.S. normalization put the Soviet Union "in the most negative position in the triangle."[38] It had tense relations with both China and the United States, while being faced with new momentum in Sino-American relations. China's position vis-à-vis the two superpowers in the triangle was noticeably strengthened, and Beijing, for the first time, occupied a pivotal seat in the strategic triangle, which, in Lowell Dittmer's words, had evolved into a "Sinocentric Romantic Triangle."[39]

THE SINO-VIETNAM WAR (1979)

China's pivotal position in the strategic triangle was only momentary and was lost soon after the brief Sino-Vietnam War in February 1979. The Sino-Vietnam War was a major event that affected international relations in East Asia and had significant impacts on the evolution of the triangular relationship: "Despite an occasional glance at the conflict by the Western press, very little attention has been paid to this serious rift."[40] One of the most direct consequence of the war was the shift of China's favorable position in the triangular relationship derived from the Sino-American normalization. Deng Xiaoping's authorization at the punitive attack on Vietnam by the PLA in 1979 embarrassed the Americans and caused Beijing to reopen its dialogue with the Soviet Union.

China and North Vietnam shared a common interest in opposing the American presence in South Vietnam during the U.S.-Vietnam War. Because of the U.S. containment policy and Beijing's fear of possible encirclement from the south, China sent economic aid and military assistance to Vietnam Communists to help set up a buffer zone between China and the United States. According to recently available Chinese sources, China sent about 320,000 military personnel and military and civilian materials valued at about $20 billion from 1965 to 1978.[41]

When the Americans began withdrawing from Vietnam, China eased the tension in the south but began a new confrontation with the Soviet Union in the north. Sino-Vietnamese relations plummeted after the fall of Saigon regime: China ended the last of its economic aid programs in the spring of 1978 and recalled hundreds of Chinese technicians and advisors. Believing that the Soviets had great interests in Southeast Asia and knowing that Vietnam had heavily depended on Soviet Union for aid, possible future threats from strong Soviet influence in the region could easily be a real danger for Beijing. "If Vietnam . . . became protectorate of sorts under the aegis of Moscow as guardian of the socialist camp, China's interests would be menaced."[42] A Chinese senior researcher from Beijing Institute for International Strategic Studies revealed at an international Conference in Beijing that Chinese leaders were convinced that Vietnam, after its victory of the anti-American war, proclaimed itself "the world's third largest military power" by virtue of its military strength that had grown in the war, and "pursued regional hegemonic policy in an attempt to annex Cambodia, control Indochina, and carry out its ambitious plan of setting up the Federation of Greater Indochina."[43]

While Chinese leaders felt apprehensive toward Vietnam's ambition, Vietnam had its own concerns about China. Despite claims that the Sino-

U.S. rapprochement did not surprise Hanoi, outside observers found that the move shocked the Vietnamese, who felt that they had lost the "normalization game." Hanoi worried that the normalization of U.S.-China relations would reinforce Beijing's intention to establish hegemony over Southeast Asia. Vietnam believed that China could now proceed to attack Vietnam and reinforce the military potential of Vietnam's adversary in Cambodia. This was because the new relationship gave China confidence to stand up to Vietnam and to the Soviet Union. Hanoi watchers argued that Vietnam had tried to win the friendship of an old enemy (the United States), but was forced into an unhappy alliance with the Soviet Union.[44]

The final breakdown of Sino-Vietnamese relations came in November 1978 when Vietnam joined the Council for Mutual Economic Assistance (CMEA) and signed the Treaty of Friendship and Cooperation with the Soviet Union, which established a military alliance now aimed at China rather than at the United States. As one scholar indicates, "the Treaty gave the Soviet-Vietnamese relationship the quality of an alliance in anticipation of Vietnam's imminent invasion of Cambodia and was intended as a deterrent against the Chinese intervention in support of its ally."[45] Now with closer ties to the Soviet Union, Vietnam had the opportunity to establish its dominance throughout Indochina as part of the regional balance of power in Southeast Asia. It called for "the formation of a special relationship between the three Indochinese countries in the postwar era."[46] But the Democratic Kampuchea (Khmer Rouge) regime rejected the proposal, describing Hanoi's concept of a special relationship as simply a "new name for the old Indochinese Federation and a fig-leaf for Vietnamese domination over its smaller neighbors."[47]

On Christmas Day, 1978, precipitating a blitzkrieg by some 150,000 troops, Vietnam invaded Cambodia, with the intention of striking a fatal blow to the Khmer Rouge leadership in Cambodia, taking Phnom Penh in a matter of a week or two, and placing their man, Heng Samrin, at the head of the puppet government.[48] The invasion was as successful as the final campaign three years before, which had put a quick end to the Saigon regime. Although meeting unexpected resistance, the Vietnamese still found it relatively easy to gain ground against the weaker Cambodian forces and captured Phnom Penh within a little over a week (on January 7, 1979) and overran most of the country within a month. The Khmer Rouge units were forced to seek refuge in the isolated forests of the northwest or in the rugged mountains near the gulf of Thailand. According to the memoirs of a Chinese diplomat in Cambodia, China was caught by surprise and, upon the request of the Khmer Rouge government, the Chinese embassy in Phnom Penh moved and stayed with the Khmer Rouge in the jungle for 15 days.[49]

China's initial reaction to the Vietnamese invasion was limited to vaguely threatening statements in the press. The Chinese foreign ministry issued a statement on January 14, 1979, condemning the attack as "Vietnamese hegemonism abetted by Soviet-imperialism."[50] Only in February after the return of Deng Xiaoping from his visit to the United States, when it became evident that Vietnam's presence in Cambodia was not a temporary one, did China begin to believe that it would have to "teach Vietnam a lesson." Beijing perceived Vietnam's action as part of the Soviet southward strategy, fearing Vietnam was very near to realizing a Hanoi-dominated Indochina and thus completely encircling China's southern border. To prevent the domination of the peninsula by a single power that might threaten its southern flank, China preferred separate and neutral Indochinese states.

The Chinese invasion of Vietnam occurred on February 14, 1979. Mobilizing some 500,000 troops and 800 aircraft, the Chinese PLA struck in what they hoped would be a quick and devastating blow. The invasion was 15 weeks after the signing of the Vietnamese-Soviet Treaty of Cooperation and Friendship and just six weeks after the Vietnamese invasion of Cambodia. China justified the invasion by referring to the need to counterattack Vietnamese troops that repeatedly crossed into Chinese territory and provoked those living along border areas. The Chinese news agency denied that Vietnam's invasion of Cambodia had anything to do with their attack on Vietnam and held on to the border clashes as reason for China "teaching Vietnam a lesson."[51] Everyone in the outside world knew that Chinese troops were coming to the rescue of the defeated Khmer Rouge government.

Chinese forces moved six miles into Vietnamese territory in four days, 15 miles in six days, and finally 25 miles deep in nine days. The invasion was costly to China. China inflicted heavy casualties on the Vietnamese, but the Chinese suffered an estimated 28,000 killed, 43,000 wounded in less than a month. While executing great harm on the enemy, China lost the aura of invincibility it had gained in the otherwise analogous Indian border conflict 17 years earlier. Financial and opportunity costs were also steep. It was only two weeks into the war before China was suggesting a truce and general cessation of hostilities. Vietnam agreed that peace talks were necessary, but made them contingent on a withdrawal of Chinese forces from Vietnam. On March 4, China announced that it had captured the town of Long Son, and subsequently claimed victory (as did Vietnam) and suggested a pull-out was imminent. The following day China announced a formal troop withdrawal and all Chinese troops left Vietnamese territories on March 16.[52]

During the Sino-Vietnam confrontation, China played the America card by the logic of the strategic triangle. For China, the normalization of relations with the United States was not just an end in itself; it was an additional source of insurance in its confrontation with the Soviet Union and Vietnam. Deng Xiaoping's visit to the United States to celebrate and sign normalization documents coincided with the Vietnam invasion in Cambodia, and he made clear in private talks with the Carter administration that China could not accept Vietnam's "wild ambitions." Carter reserved judgment, and "the Chinese seemed to have construed this as tacit approval."[53] This minor tributary state had been in China's orbit since the second century B.C. and Deng would not tolerate its insolence. En route home, Deng stopped off in Tokyo, where his hosts imparted cautionary counsel upon learning of his plans. The final decision to invade was made the day after Deng's return, at a February 9 meeting of the Central Military Commission, and the invasion took place on February 14.

The proximity in timing of the military thrust to the summit meeting suggests that the Chinese were seeking to bluff the Soviets with a nonexistent U.S. endorsement. Deng secured a joint press communiqué reiterating Sino-American opposition to hegemony during his visit, "helping to convey the impression that China had tacit U.S. support."[54] With that communiqué, as a Chinese scholar suggests, China felt that it had the "implicit support of the United States, and the Soviet Union was reluctant to be engaged in direct conflict with both China and the United States for the sake of Vietnam."[55] A Western scholar put it this way, "the timing of the attack seemed deliberately contrived to take advantage of the successful normalization of relations with the United States and leave the impression of U.S. support or sympathy with China's objectives."[56]

However, the reality was somehow different. Although China and America could agree on the need to contain Soviet qua Vietnamese expansionism, they could not agree on the best way to achieve this. One aspect of disagreement was the Cambodian issue. As Sino-Vietnamese relations soured, Beijing transferred allegiance to the Khmer Rouge who seized power from the pro-American Lon Nol regime in 1975 and never allowed its loyalty to flag. To the United States, any link to the Khmer became politically unpalatable in the wake of the urban resettlement policies of 1975-78, which resulted in the deaths of an estimated 1.5 million Cambodians. Compounding cruelty with political stupidity, the Khmer also initiated a series of border incidents against their more powerful neighbors in early 1977.[57]

In spite of its ambivalence, Washington did use diplomatic relations to help contain the repercussions of the crisis. In late January, Moscow reported to have received a private message from Washington urging the Soviet Union not to become involved in Sino-Vietnamese hostilities. That might explain why the Soviet reaction to the Chinese invasion of Vietnam was subdued. Although the official Soviet press agency called the Chinese aggressive and hegemonic for their incursion into Vietnam, it stated that the Vietnamese people were capable of defending themselves.[58] Hoping to play down the international outcry against the invasion by putting it in perspective, Washington called for "two withdrawals": Vietnam from Cambodia, and China from Vietnam. But the American response paled in comparison to the support rendered to Pakistan during the Indian-Pakistan War in 1971. A State Department spokesman made clear that a Soviet strike on China's northern border (the most logistically feasible military response) "would not be of direct concern to the United States."[59] The United States avoided strategic support for China as Beijing faced increased Soviet pressure in the wake of its incursion. During Soviet military exercises along the Sino-Soviet border in March 1979, American officials avoided comment.

The outcome of the Sino-Vietnam War was a disappointment to both the Chinese and the Americans. To the United States, the unilateral Chinese resort to "pedagogical war" in defense of a morally indefensible client demonstrated that Beijing could act boldly and unilaterally without much concern for American sensibilities. Americans were disconcerted by a Chinese predilection for the role of agent provocateur, similar to that of the Soviets during the Taiwan Strait embroilment in 1958. In addition, the U.S. Defense Department conducted a study in 1979 that concluded that China's armed forces were backward in terms of weaponry, could be modernized only at prodigious expense, and posed no threat to Soviet naval and air bases on the Pacific coast or to Soviet territory in Siberia.[60] To China, American backing for a venture in which China bore the main risk was cowardly. It clouded prospects of further "joint action" and placed extended deterrence of America into question. China's interest in an anti-Soviet "alliance" faded rapidly.[61] China was severely disappointed in its new partner's military and diplomatic passivity during its handling of the Vietnam problem within months of the euphoria of normalization. Both the Chinese and the Americans had to seriously reconsider their strategic relationship.

THE SINO-SOVIET RAPPROCHEMENT
AND THE TRIANGULAR DISENGAGEMENT

Partly as an outcome of reconsideration for the Sino-U.S. relations, China began to adopt a considerably more flexible and conciliatory posture toward the Soviet Union. This shift coincided with the change in the Soviet policy presented by a speech given by Leonid Brezhnev in Tashkent on March 1982, in which the Soviet leader provided a "comprehensive statement of the Kremlin's policy toward China."[62] Brezhnev said that the Soviet Union acknowledged "the existence of a socialist system in China" and denied that Moscow posed any threat to China's security. He pointed out that, unlike the United States, the Soviet Union had consistently supported "the PRC's sovereignty over Taiwan island," accepting Beijing's claim that Taiwan was part of China. He also offered to discuss a resolution of the border dispute between the two countries and to resume economic, scientific, cultural, and political relations across the Sino-Soviet frontier.[63] Brezhnev's appeal for normalization of relations was described by *The Financial Times* as "the most emphatic conciliatory gesture since the dispute over the border between the two nations took them to the brink of war in 1969."[64] The Soviet strategy was hereby shifted from containing and encircling China to moving China "toward a more neutral role in the Sino-Soviet-U.S. triangle."[65]

Although the initial Chinese response was guarded, emphasizing that Beijing considered "deeds, rather than words," to be the true measure of Soviet intentions, General Secretary Hu Yaobang, at the 12th Congress of the CCP in August 1982, announced a change in Chinese foreign policy that was reassuring to Moscow. He declared that China would adopt an "independent foreign policy" and would never "attach itself to any big power or group of powers."[66] This implied that China found it feasible to back away from its quasi-alliance with Washington without risk of Soviet-American collusion and to move away from its previous notion of a united front with the United States against the Soviet Union toward a policy of peaceful coexistence with both superpowers. In October, the two countries resumed the negotiations over bilateral relations that had been suspended after the Soviet invasion of Afghanistan. During the 1982 round of talks, the Chinese side listed three demands that were raised by Hu Yaobang in his earlier speech: one, withdrawal of Soviet troops from Mongolia; two, withdrawal of Soviet troops from Afghanistan; and three, cessation of Soviet support for Vietnam's occupation of Cambodia.[67]

Although the talks ended without success, Brezhnev's death in early November 1982 offered an opportunity for Sino-Soviet contact at the highest level. The "funeral diplomacy" that resulted from rapid succession of Soviet leaders (Yuri Andropov in November 1982, Konstantin Chernenko in February 1984, and Mikhail Gorbachev in March 1985), provided interesting clues to the momentum of Sino-Soviet relations, as discussed by one study of the Sino-Soviet relations in the 1980s. According to the study, at Brezhnev's funeral, Chinese Foreign Minister Huang Hua held talks with his counterpart, Andrei Gromyko. But Vietnam's foreign minister, Nguyen Co Thach, met only Leonid Ilichev, a vice foreign minister. At Andropov's funeral, China was represented by Wan Li, a Politburo member and vice-premier, signaling China's positive assessment of the deceased Soviet leader as well as hopes for better relations in the future. For Chernenko's funeral, Beijing sent vice-premier Li Peng, who was educated in the Soviet Union and spoke Russian. Gorbachev received him twice and reaffirmed the Soviet Union's desire that Sino-Soviet relations improve in a major way. This study finds that, "greater progress was made in the Sino-Soviet rapprochement during these years."[68] This development intensified after Gorbachev's succession: the two sides began referring to each other as comrades, "a word suggesting that no serious ideological difficulty exists between them."[69]

The Sino-Soviet détente was powered by significant strategic considerations and the primary source of the Sino-Soviet détente is the changing strategic perceptions of both sides. A more diversified global power structure was perceived by both Beijing and Moscow and improving Sino-Soviet relations became one of the means for both countries to cope with the new situation.

From Beijing's point of view, the rapid restoration of American military strength after Ronald Reagan's election as president in November 1980 meant that there was less need for China to rally the world's anti-Soviet forces. America had apparently awakened from its slumber and the Soviets were increasingly on the defensive. Under these circumstances, China's position as a junior partner of the United States made the Americans less sensitive to Chinese concerns, especially regarding Taiwan. The Taiwan Relations Acts (TRA) passed by the U.S. Congress in April 1979 greatly angered Chinese leaders. Washington then sold $292 million in military equipment to Taiwan in 1980. When press reports indicated that Washington was considering the sale of advanced fighter aircraft to Taiwan, Beijing was further outraged. It seemed that America's disregard for China's sensitivities on Taiwan was related to China's strate-

gic dependence on the United States. If China positioned itself independently of the United States, thereby threatening to defect from the anti-
Soviet camp, Washington would be more sensitive to Chinese wishes on
the Taiwan issue.[70] In the meantime, Beijing believed that the Soviet
Union had largely spent the international momentum it generated in the
1970s, was increasingly preoccupied with its domestic economic problems, and had been counterbalanced by the growth of American military
power during the Reagan administration. The Chinese also concluded
that the greater internal stability and economic growth that had been
achieved in the post–Mao era made China a much less attractive target for
Soviet pressure. China's attitude toward its security environment was
thus much more relaxed now than before. The Soviet Union was still
viewed as a threat but it was a much weaker threat, and both its words and
deeds seemed to indicate that Moscow was genuinely intent on some conciliation with Beijing. Nevertheless, the United States posed a long-term
potential threat, and Japan could enlarge its influence in Asia. Sino-Soviet
rapprochement was viewed as a necessary condition either for gaining
more maneuvering room vis-à-vis the United States and Japan or for finding acceptable solutions to the Taiwan issue. Therefore, China moved
toward a policy of "equidistance."[71]

From Moscow's point of view, the collapse of Soviet-Western détente
and the deteriorating relationship with the United States in the early years
of the Reagan administration; increased Western European, Japanese,
and U.S. defense spending; China's support for NATO; the conclusion of
the Sino-Japanese "anti-hegemony treaty;" and Sino-American security
cooperation was an ominous combination. To Moscow, the developments
of the late 1970s were a realization of its worst nightmare: a two-front
threat. China, the United States, Japan, and Western Europe seemed to be
drawing together into an anti-Soviet military bloc. In Asia, Japan was
moving toward great political power and the tripartite military alliance of
the United States, Japan, and Korea was strengthening. As one Western
scholar suggests, "at this historical juncture, the principal unsatisfied
power in Asia is the Soviet Union."[72] Because the Asian Pacific region
was growing in power and importance, the Soviet Union wanted to return
to the mainstream of Asian diplomacy in order to strengthen its strategic
position and, in the meantime, be relevant to its future development.

Another major source of Sino-Soviet détente was their parallel economic needs. Both China and the Soviet Union were facing a common
threat—rigid and inefficient economic and political systems—and also a
common challenge—the new technological and industrial revolution. If

they did not accelerate their reform programs, both were likely to be thrown farther behind in national strengths. This awareness was a basic understanding in Deng's and Gorbachev's leadership. The Chinese came to this realization in the early 1980s. When Deng identified the major tasks facing China in the coming decades in 1980, he placed anti-hegemonism first, followed by national reunification and modernization.[73] Yet in 1982 he rearranged the order to place modernization first, followed by reunification and anti-hegemonism, and declared that "our strategy in foreign affairs is to seek a peaceful environment for carrying out four modernization."[74] Beijing wanted a peaceful international environment so that it could devote all available resources to the task of economic development and reform. China thus saw compelling economic grounds for a reduction of tensions with the Soviet Union.

On the Soviet side, perestroika in the Gorbachev years was designed to reinvigorate the Soviet economy through modest domestic reforms and further integration into the world economy. However, during the early years (1985-87), economic practices that smacked of genuine capitalism were viewed with suspicion. In this situation, "China's experience with limited private enterprise in agriculture and industry, and the example of the special economic zones of the southern coast areas, intrigued Moscow's economists."[75] Moscow wanted to learn from China's economic reform. China's special economic zones, for example, were studied and evaluated as potentially valuable strategies for attracting capital investment and advanced technology to the Soviet Union. One of the two Soviet special economic zones first approved by Moscow was to be located in the area around Nakhodka.[76] Gorbachev told the readers of a Chinese magazine, *Liaowang,* that "we take special interest in China's on-going economic and political reforms. Our two countries are now faced with similar problems. This will open a broad horizon for useful mutual exchange of experiences."[77]

The increasing commercial relations also showed one aspect of the mutual economic needs. Sino-Soviet trade and economic cooperation accelerated shortly after Gorbachev came to power in March 1985. In that July, a breakthrough came in the conclusion of a five-year trade agreement for 1986-90 between the two countries worth $14 billion, nearly doubling the level of bilateral trade. The Soviet Union also agreed to provide technical assistance to help China replace 156 large industrial projects imported from the Soviet Union, which played a key role in China's industrialization process in the 1950s.[78] Commerce between the two countries grew steadily through the second half of the 1980s. Total trade turnover almost tripled from $960 million in 1983 to $2.36 billion in 1986 and then to more than $3.2 billion in 1988.[79]

Personnel changes in the two countries also entailed policy changes toward détente. Brezhnev's team of Sinologists were recruited in the middle and late 1960s to help Brezhnev formulate a pressure-oriented policy toward China in 1969 and to refuse to offer concrete concessions in the early 1980s. In July 1985, four months after Gorbachev came to power, he replaced old-guard foreign minister Andrei Gromyko with Eduard Shevardnadze, who had virtually no foreign policy experience and no ties to old policies. On China's side, the appointment of Li Peng, who was educated in the Soviet Union, to the premiership was significant. One-third of his cabinet were composed of Soviet-trained ministers, including Foreign Minister Qian Qichen. Just as Huang Hua and Qiao Guanhua, both Americanists, were made to head the foreign ministry at the time of Sino-U.S. rapprochement, so the "Soviet-trained foreign minister Qian's promotion signaled Beijing's intention in further improving Sino-Soviet relations."[80]

Under these circumstances, Sino-Soviet rapprochement accelerated. After 1983, Beijing held that while resolution of the three obstacles was necessary for a normalization of Sino-Soviet relations, it was no longer a precondition for expanded relations. By the time Gorbarchev came to power in March 1985, Sino-Soviet relations were already the most cordial they had been since the late 1950s. In his highly publicized Vladivostok speech of July 28, 1986, Gorbachev made additional, specific overtures toward China. Gorbachev spoke approvingly of China's reformist objectives, and noted that Chinese and Soviet domestic priorities were similar. Most significantly, he promised concessions on two of China's three obstacles by announcing the imminent withdrawal of six Soviet regiments from Afghanistan and the removal of a significant portion of the Soviet troops in Mongolia and by indicating a willingness to negotiate with China a balanced and mutual reduction of the remaining forces along the Sino-Soviet border.[81] Beijing cautiously welcomed Gorbachev's Vladivostok initiatives. His speech was carried on the front page of *Renmin Ribao,*[82] although Soviet support for Vietnam's occupation of Cambodia continued to be considered the major impediment to further improved relations between the two. On a September 1986 broadcast of the U.S. news program "60 Minutes," Deng Xiaoping offered to meet Gorbachev if the Soviet Union was willing to persuade the Vietnamese to withdraw their forces.

In Spring 1988, the Soviet Union began to withdraw its troops from Afghanistan following a UN-sponsored agreement. Gorbachev quietly signaled to Hanoi that Soviet withdrawal from Afghanistan might provide a model for the Vietnamese to follow in Cambodia. During talks between Chinese Foreign Minister Qian Qichen and Soviet leaders in Moscow in December 1988, agreements were reached regarding Cambodia. The next month, Hanoi announced that it would withdraw all its forces from Cambodia in September 1989. This was adequate to clear the way for a meeting between Deng Xiaoping and Gorbachev. When the first Sino-Soviet summit meeting in 30 years took place in Beijing in May 1989, it was an event of great importance for both sides, hailed as marking the restoration of normal state-to-state relations and party-to-party ties.[83] Unfortunately the student demonstration in Tiananmen Square during Gorbachev's visit deflected attention from this historical event, to the dismay of both leaders.

The normalization of Sino-Soviet relations did not entail the suspension of Sino-American or Soviet-American relations. In the process, China gradually shifted to a more "independent" (or equidistant) stance between the two superpowers. While Sino-Soviet relations were improving, both superpowers in the course of their confrontation began experiencing economic difficulties (most acute in the Soviet case) due to overburdened arms budgets and neglected civilian economies. This situation eventually led to the revival of Soviet-American détente, beginning with the Intermediate-Range Nuclear Force (INF) treaty of December 1987 and continuing through the Strategic Arms Reduction Treaty (START) talks. Meanwhile, Moscow and Washington gradually expanded trade and cultural exchange.

THE TRIANGULAR DYNAMICS OF POWER COMPETITION

A state's position in a particular power relationship creates a particular behavior pattern. In the case of the strategic triangular relationship, a central issue concerns how each state, due to its position vis-à-vis its counterparts, develops a unique response to triangular pressures. The tendency toward a coalition or collusion between two of the three countries and the fear of this tendency in each country constitutes the main dynamics of power competition. Each of the three powers had a low degree of tolerance for an improved relationship between the other two powers in the triangle. In this situation, any improvement of the relations between two powers was perceived as a threat to the security of the third one, and the purpose of improving the relationship of one power with the other one was usually to disadvantage the third, not to coordinate the common interests of the three powers.[84]

The triangular dynamic in East Asian international relations was very clear. The main thrust of Chinese foreign policy during the 1970s was to counterbalance a growing Soviet military threat by improving Chinese relations with the United States. One major motivation for doing this was China's fear of the U.S.-Soviet détente and its perception that America was tending to withdraw from the area around China, particularly from Indochina, thereby reducing the direct threat it had presented. However, the withdrawal of the Americans from Vietnam changed the balance of power in Indochina. With a military alliance with the Soviet Union, the Vietnamese could afford to stand firm in their disagreement with the Chinese in their developing conflict with the Khmer Rouge and over the Sino-Vietnamese border dispute. This development pushed the Chinese to further their strategic cooperation with the United States by seeking diplomatic recognition from the United States in the period of 1977-79. Partly because of the normalization and partly for fear of the strengthened Soviet encirclement as a result of the Vietnamese leaning toward the Soviets, China waged its war against Vietnam. Nevertheless, one of the results of the Sino-Vietnamese war was that both China and the Soviet Union began to explore the possibility of improving their relations with each other. The Soviet Union felt compelled to improve its position by reducing Sino-Soviet tensions because it realized that continued tension with China would only enhance the danger of Sino-American collusion. By improving its relations with China, the Soviet Union might be able to play a China card in its dealing with the United States. China responded positively to the Soviet initiative because it had seen the limitation of its relations with the United States and also needed to play the Soviet card to enhance its position vis-à-vis the United States.

The triangular dynamics reinforced several trends of power competition. One common policy trend in the triangular relationship was that each country tried to avoid isolation from the other two. This structure initiated the triangular negotiation in the 1970s when Washington sought improved American-Chinese relations to compensate for U.S. international passivity. The Soviet Union reflected this impulse in 1982, when deteriorating American-Soviet relations first compelled it to reconsider its China policy.

Another trend was for the three powers to use conciliatory tactics to avoid defection on the part of their strategic partner. This was certainly China's posture toward the United States, particularly in the mid-1970s and the mid-1980s. The Reagan administration adopted similar tactics in the early 1980s, when it was faced with what it perceived as an overbearing Soviet threat.

Finally, each of the three powers recognized the value of the "pivot position" and, when adversarial relations permitted, tried to occupy it. Each power wanted to triangulate itself into a better position and, whenever possible, tried to get and keep the leverage of the pivot, which was based on competitive wooing by the other two mutually conflicting poles.[85] Due to the combination of its power and relationships with China and the Soviet Union, the United States was the only nation that was ever truly a pivot power.[86] But each of the other powers recognized the U.S. advantage and tried to manipulate triangular diplomacy in order to possess the pivot position itself. China's 1982 proclamation of its "independent foreign policy" reflected such an effort, but its strategic weakness compelled Beijing to continue to depend on the United States to enhance Chinese security against the Soviet Union and, increasingly, to expedite the modernization of its economy. Gorbachev's effort in the mid-1980s was Moscow's first effort to defuse the Sino-Soviet conflict in order to improve its position in the strategic triangle. But by the time Gorbachev's China policy matured, the collapse of Soviet power had minimized its strategic significance and the end of the Cold War eventually eliminated the triangular relationship.

·8·

POWER COMPETITION IN THE POST–COLD WAR ERA

The Cold War came to a dramatic conclusion through two critical events in the early 1990s: the fall of the Berlin Wall and the disintegration of the Soviet Union. Because the origins of the Cold War were very heavily related to the division of Europe by the United States and the Soviet Union, it was only fitting that changes in that region led to proclamations of its end. Nevertheless, visible symbols of the end of the Cold War in Europe did not imply the insignificance of East Asian events in opening a new epoch. As a matter of fact, the dramatic scene in Beijing's Tiananmen Square in April-June 1989 was the prelude of the new era, and, in an oblique way, the massive political and economic changes in East Asia during the 1970s and 1980s prepossessed the post–Cold War era. The most profound development was the emergence of a group of East Asian newly industrialized countries (NICs), which achieved international prominence through rapid economic development. The NICs' achievements challenged the centrality of military power and brought nonmilitary dimensions of power competition to world attention.

After the concepts of nation-state and sovereignty were introduced into East Asia at the demise of the Chinese world order, power competition was justified for national security, which meant, by and large, military security. That meaning has increasingly been called into question as the waning tensions of the Cold War coincided with rising concern over a variety of nonmilitary threats to the security of nations. Military strength has by no means vanished as a key element of power competition in the post–Cold War era. Nevertheless, as more and more nations came to recognize both military and nonmilitary threats, the concept of power competition widened. New dimensions, notably economic, moral (cultural), and environmental, were included in the security concerns of national leaders. Cracks started to appear in East Asian international relations.

Although cautious sovereign-states continued to wield substantial military power with care and produce stability through a balance of power, non-military dimensions of power competition became more important in their agenda.

THE PRIMACY OF ECONOMIC DEVELOPMENT

Economics has taken command to an unprecedented extent in East Asia in recent years, although the primacy of economic development was not always true. During the peak of the Cold War, politics was paramount. Revolutionary leaders mobilized their people through ideological appeals. They gave lip service to development, but their priorities were political. Superpowers also competed for position through military buildup and the arms race. Economic development was secondary for both East and West. For example, the United States was much more concerned with the pursuit of military power than of wealth: "Endowed with the world's largest economy, most advanced technologies, and abundant natural resources, Americans took their national wealth for granted."[1] Washington defined national security primarily in terms of the military containment of and ideological competition with communism, rarely considering economic imperatives.

While the superpowers came late to the realization of the primacy of economics and fought for ideological correctness and competed for military supremacy up to the last day of the Cold War, the market economies of East Asia put their emphasis on economic development long before the end of the Cold War. After the 1970s, East Asian leaders came to "the realization that the economic health of their society is critical not only to internal stability but to external influence."[2] Even Leninist states, such as China and Vietnam, launched economic reforms in a modernization effort. The economic performance of many East Asian countries has surprised the world. The East Asian NICs approached and exceeded levels of advanced industrial nations, exhibited an economic dynamism attracting global attention, and set the pace for economic development in the world. A highly publicized 1993 World Bank report on the accomplishments of NICs is entitled *The East Asian Miracle.*[3]

While East Asian countries have not developed at the same time nor at same rate, they all have grown rapidly. A four-tier model, which Japanese economists call the flying-geese pattern, has characterized East Asian economic development.[4] Japan was the first East Asian country to realize economic primacy and led the first tier of economic development. From the ashes of Hiroshima and Nagasaki, Japan in 1988 boasted a higher per capita GNP ($19,566 annually) than did the United States ($18,400). In 1993, Japan's per capita GNP reached $31,490, the second highest after Switzerland (the United States was the fifth at $24,740).[5] While these figures did not necessarily translate into a higher personal income, the Japanese "lived longer than Americans and had reached a higher level of literacy."[6] The four little tigers—Singapore, Hong Kong, Taiwan, and South Korea—formed a second tier of nations that increasingly matched the Japanese pace. From 1960 to 1985, Singapore emerged from bleak poverty into a city state with a per capita GNP of $7,000 a year. By 1993, its per capital GNP had doubled to $19,850. Modern medical techniques reduced infant morality to a lower level than in the United States. South Korea surged from a per capita GNP in 1950 of $100 a year to $7,660 in 1993.[7] Taiwan experienced similar remarkable growth in real income. At the close of World War II, Taiwan's per capita GNP stagnated at $70 a year. By 1994, it surpassed $12,000 annually.[8] The two decades after 1960 were a period of extraordinary growth in East Asian market economies. Singapore, South Korea, Taiwan, and Kong Hong enjoyed average annual gross domestic product (GDP) real increases of 8 to 10 percent throughout these years. The four little tigers formed a cluster of newly industrialized economies (NIEs), a term proposed by the OECD in 1979 to designate certain middle-income developing countries whose per capital GNP in 1978 reached $1,600 or more and whose industrial structure and trading activities seriously began to impact the global economic system.[9]

Malaysia, Thailand, Indonesia, and the Philippines constituted a third tier of nations on the edge of the East Asian explosion, making great strides in the 1970s and 1980s. Their governments often looked to Japanese and the four little tigers' models. The results were extraordinary. From 1970 to 1980, Indonesia expanded its actual GNP by 7.2 percent a year, Malaysia by 7.9 percent, and Thailand by 7.1 percent. In 1980-93, these countries retained high growth rates of 5.8 percent, 6.2 percent, and 8.2 percent, respectively.[10] In contrast to the first two tiers, all of these countries were blessed with major, if largely unexplored resources; all had suffered ethnic tension and civil war; all had different cultures from their East Asian predecessors; and all had experienced direct or indirect colonization. Even the Philippines, wrecked by internal dissension, achieved a growth rate of 6.0 percent annually from 1970-80.[11] The third tier of nations joined the four little tigers and are now known collectively as the East Asian NIEs.

On the fourth tier of development, China, Vietnam, and Russia's Far East were poised to join the East Asian renaissance. Among these countries, China's achievements have been the most impressive. Although coming late in the 1980s, China's record of economic development has been astonishing to the world, with a breakneck pace of 9.6 percent average growth rate from 1980 to 1993.[12] Deng Xiaoping hoped to quadruple the economy from its 1978 level by the year 2000. This goal was advanced at the end of 1995. This output in turn is to be doubled by 2010.[13] The Chinese economy, liberated from past restraints, has galloped ahead, and now has to be reined in to prevent further overheating and serious inflation. Within a generation or so, current optimists predict, a country once dismissed as the "sick man" of Asia could have "the largest economy in the world."[14] The West and its neighbors have been talking about China as the "coming power"[15] and the "next superpower."[16] China is engaged with the outside world successfully enough to become "an economic center of gravity in Asia," "a military mover and shaker," and "a peer of any of the Western powers that once nibbled at China's fringes and brought emperors low."[17] Following China's example, the Leninist states of Vietnam, and, to a certain extent, North Korea, have also embarked upon reform efforts in recent years, spearheaded by a commitment to participate in the international marketplace and in the broader technological revolution.[18]

Naturally, the ascendancy of these economies has colored international politics in East Asia as elsewhere. If one focuses on economic trends and accepts the idea that future global politics will be in the hands of what Richard Rosecrance calls the "trading state,"[19] one is forced to conclude that the brief era of U.S. hegemony is coming to an end in East Asia. It is increasingly clear that economic and technological resources are likely to prove increasingly decisive in the power competitions of states, because ultimately they can be transformed into military clout. Even as America's absolute power continued to rise, its relative share of global capabilities, especially economic capacities, is declining. The U.S. export share of technology-intensive products declined from 27 percent in the 1970s to under 21 percent in 1986, while Japan's rose from under 11 percent to almost 20 percent.[20] Washington's difficulty in reversing economic trends has been the topic of increasingly acrimonious U.S.-Japanese negotiations. In the meantime, the rapid economic growth in the region has enhanced the importance of traditionally small players in international politics. By the turn of the century, for example, South Korea may well have an economic size approaching that of Britain or Italy today. Consequently, even without reunification, Korea's political and strategic significance will increase, as will of that of Taiwan and other East Asian nations.

THE TRADE-OFF BETWEEN GUNS AND BUTTER

The choice between military and economic means to power was not always clearly laid out before states. During the period of the two world wars and the peak of the Cold War, military and territorial concerns were primary concerns to all nations. In the 1970s a group of so-called trading states emerged in world politics. Over time this group has grown, and its success, at least in economic terms, has been greater than that of the great military powers of the United States and the former Soviet Union. According to Kennedy's famous historical study of the rise and fall of the great powers, high defense expenditures in the quest for military power are more likely than not to impair economic performance, and military overextension has typically preceded the decline of great powers such as Spain, the Netherlands, France, Britain, Russia, Austria, and Prussia, and now the United States.[21]

The military overextension as a burden that affects economic performance is still controversial among scholars and politicians. Advocates of the view argue that military spending tends to hurt the savings and investment rates, which in turn are major determinants of future economic growth. In addition, defense spending in advanced industrial countries is often capital- and technology-intensive. Such spending diverts resources from the civilian sector, thus handicapping the latter's international competitiveness.[22] In contrast to the above argument, some analysts indicate that a heavy defense burden can have some positive effects on the economy. The capital investments by the military can improve a country's infrastructure in transportation and communication; government purchases of defense items can stimulate production and encourage fuller utilization of existing facilities; and military training equips recruits with modern skills and attitudes and can, therefore, improve a developing society's human resources for industrialization. These positive effects are seen to offset the negative effects.[23]

The East Asian experiences have provided mixed support to the two competing arguments. On the one hand, while the United States spent about 6 percent of its GNP on arms, Japan devoted 99 percent of its GNP to civilian production during the Cold War years. Concomitantly, the Japanese economy grew at a rate that was more than 2.5 times faster than that of the American economy. Consequently, there is a sense that Japan's relatively light defense burden helped its economic expansion, whereas the relatively heavy defense burden of the United States hampered its economic performance. On the other hand, counter-evidence can also be found in East Asian countries. Relatively heavy defense burdens was borne by Singapore (about 6 percent of its GNP in the mid-1980s), Taiwan (about 6 percent), and South Korea (about 5 percent). During the 1950s and 1960s Taiwan and South Korea devoted an even higher proportion (more than 10 percent) of their GNP to defense, thus putting them among the top military spenders (relative to the size of their economy) in the world. Nevertheless, these East Asian NIEs did not appear to have been severely handicapped by their heavy defense burdens in the drive for economic development. Of course, this evidence could be challenged by the fact that the achievements in Taiwan and South Korea were facilitated in part by massive U.S. economic and military aid, which not only offset the negative effects of their heavy defense burden but also stimulated economic development.[24] As one scholar suggests, "this strong U.S. support enabled the regimes of Syngman Rhee and Chiang Kai-shek not only to maintain basic economic and social order but also to make substantial investments in infrastructure development."[25] Nevertheless, the fact that these East Asian NIEs continued high economic growth rates while maintaining a high defense budget after the U.S. aid stopped in the 1970s shows that the trade-off between military spending and economic performance was not significant.

With respect to the tradeoff between guns and butter, hegemonic stability theory, which describes the high cost of pursuing military power, associates the rising importance of economic power with the perception that East Asian countries have become military free-riders.[26] According to the theory, international security is regarded as public goods with two properties: "jointness of supply and impossibility of exclusion."[27] They are nondivisible in the sense that their consumption by one nation does not reduce their consumption by another nation, and they are nonexcludable in the sense that once these goods are provided to any one nation, it is impossible or very costly to prevent others from enjoying them. The nature of public goods encourages free-riding. If, for example, the United States provided the public goods of deterring Soviet aggression, why should Japan provide for its own defense? The United States provision of the public goods of military security, according to the hegemonic stability theory, dwells on the role of the United States as a hegemonic power, which has both the incentive and the means to initiate and sustain such public goods. The hegemonic power was sufficiently large relative to all others so that it would capture a share of the benefits of the public goods larger than the entire costs of providing it.[28] In the Cold War era, the United States as the dominant power had the heaviest stake in and the greatest means for preserving a military security in the world as well as in East Asia. However, over time, a hegemon is apt to suffer a decline in its power. This decline is in part due to the free-riding behavior of the countries that take advantage of the hegemon's generosity, making the hegemon gradually less willing and/or less able to continue asymmetric security relationships. The high military cost of the United States as a hegemonic state provided a security blanket for East Asian countries to be free-riders in pursuing economic security. As such not only was the United States given a big share of the credit for the security and prosperity of East Asian countries, but likewise East Asian states appeared as ungrateful and selfish free riders.

This criticism was concentrated mostly on Japan. U.S. officials and scholars have repeatedly emphasized the theme that Japan has not paid a fair share of the costs of collective defense. They charge that Tokyo has been a free rider, hitching itself to the military coattails of the United States. In their view, Japan's economic success has been the result of its low defense spending, made possible by the protective shield offered by America's conventional forces stationed in and around Japan and by the U.S. nuclear umbrella.[29] Japan has indeed benefited from low military expenditure. Nevertheless, the charges are not accurate. The Japanese pursuit of economic rather than military power was believed to have resulted largely because of their supposed "military allergy" and "nuclear aversion" derived from their disastrous defeat in the Pacific War. Japanese public opinion would object to high defense expenditures and would certainly oppose any projection of Japanese military influence abroad.[30] In addition, Japan contributed to the collective security of Western countries through the application of nonmilitary instruments. It cannot be denied that Japanese capital, technology, and especially developmental assistance fulfill a strategic purpose. In a very important way, Japan picked up the slack when and where the U.S. military projection was unwise or infeasible. Thus, Tokyo's foreign economic and commercial policies often pursued a track complementary to Washington's political and military measures during the Cold War era.

As a matter of fact, the preference of East Asian nations for economic power during the Cold War era reflected more on their difficulties of pursuing military-political power than the so-called free-rider tendency. In this case, the hegemonic stability theory made some American scholars uncomfortable "because of its overtones of force, threat, pressure."[31] One scholar critically summarized the hegemonic stability theory as "the presence of a single, strongly dominant actor in international politics leads to collectively desirable outcomes for all states in the international system. Conversely, the absence of the hegemon is associated with disorder in the world system and undesirable outcomes for individual states."[32] This has obviously not been the case after the decline of the U.S. hegemony in East Asia in recent years.

COMPREHENSIVE NATIONAL SECURITY AND THE TWO WORLDS OF POWER COMPETITION

In response to the importance of nonmilitary dimensions of power competition, some East Asian countries have adjusted their security policy. The best known is the policy of "comprehensive national security," which combined military with political, economic, and cultural concerns, and was adopted by the Japanese government in the 1980s. The policy was put forth as Japan's "most serious response to the changing international environment" with a report instituted by Prime Minister Ohira Masayoshi in 1980.[33] The report characterized the "termination of clear American supremacy in both military and economic spheres" in the 1970s as a fundamental change and stated that U.S. military power was "no longer able to provide its allies and friends with nearly full security."[34] Comprehensive security was thus defined as a policy to protect Japan against all forms of external threats through a combination of diplomacy, national defense, economic power, and other measures. Particular emphasis was given to the stabilization of Japan's external trade relations and a search for secure sources of foreign raw materials.

The Japanese doctrine of comprehensive national security avoided "overt military means of guaranteeing security and relies instead primarily on economic statecraft."[35] Because of Japan's insular geography and the heavy economic dependency on foreign markets for supplies of energy and foodstuffs, Japan was concerned with securing commercial access to foreign markets and supplies: "Disruption of this access poses a far more probable danger to Japan's national security than an overt military attack on its home islands."[36] Tokyo was keen to assure a stable supply of foreign energy, which constituted the lifeline of the Japanese economy and national security. According to the concept of comprehensive security, Japan tried to diversify its supplies and nurture incentives on the part of suppliers that favored continued provision of oil to Japan. Ohira Massayoshi argued that "economic aid was a valid way of advancing these security interests" and making these countries dependent on Japanese investment and technology.[37] At the same time, Japan was engaged in the stockpiling of strategic reserves, development of alternative energy sources and technologies in order to dampen the shock of any possible supply interruption. The Japanese government stressed the security of their energy supply far more than the monetary cost of this supply, as their energy industry customarily imported foreign energy at prices that were higher than the prevailing international norm. Whereas Americans seem prepared to overpay for their military superiority, the Japanese instead were inclined to pay a premium to ensure reliability in the foreign supply of their energy needs. From this perspective, "the core of comprehensive security has been economic power," and is the "security as defined by trading state."[38]

The adoption of the concept of a comprehensive national security implies that power competition in East Asia was stalemated between economic and military imperatives. Japan largely focused on economic power, keeping their military expenditures limited; while the United States has engaged in arms races, military interventions, and occasional wars. Correspondingly, power competition was conducted in what Richard Rosecrance described as the two worlds of international relations: the trading world and the military-political world.[39]

In the two worlds of power competition, the instruments of international relations are different. According to Rosecrance, in a military-political world, nations range in military power and territory from the greatest to the weakest. States in such a world do not have differentiated objectives or perform a variety of functions. They all seek the same territorial objectives and each, at least among the major powers, strives to be the leading military power in the system. The military-political world involves a constant reliance on war because the powers within it compete for military primacy. But each is afraid that the dominance of one power will undermine its domestic autonomy and perhaps its very existence. Hence the balance of power becomes a means to resist threatened hegemony. The means of constructing a balance ultimately involves a resort to force to discipline an ambitious pretender. In addition, since every state in a political-military world seeks to be self-sufficient, each strives to grow larger in order to achieve full independence. This drive itself is a cause of war.

In contrast, the trading world is composed of nations differentiated in function. According to Rosecrance, because nations supply different services and products, in defense as well as in economics, they come to depend upon one another. While trading states try to improve their position and their own domestic allocation of resources, they do so within a context of accepted interdependence. They recognize that the attempt to

provide every service and fulfill every function of statehood on an independent and autonomous basis is extremely inefficient, and they prefer a
situation that provides for specialization and division of labor among
nations. The incentive to wage war is minimal in such a system, for war
disrupts trade and the interdependence on which trade is based. As the
national objective is exchange and trade with other states, trading countries do not need large and self-sufficient territories and resources. Small
countries, such as Singapore and Hong Kong, are little more than cities.
They manufacture raw materials of other nations into finished com-
modities, but gain a high return in foreign trade. Thus, the reciprocal
exchange and division of labor represented by the trading world can prevent military conflict.

Although Rosecrance sees the economy and the military as two distinct
paths to national power in the contemporary world, these two worlds
cannot be separated as concisely as he indicates. Military forces may be
used to gain economic benefit, as European imperialist powers did in East
Asia during the nineteenth and early twentieth centuries. Economic
strength may also be transformed into military power, as seen in the self-
sufficient defense of many East Asian nations following industrialization
in recent years.[40] Which path a nation chooses to enhance its power is
often shaped by the virtue of necessity rather than free will. The role of
Japan in the trading world is interesting because it represents a reversal of
past policies in both the late nineteenth century and the 1930s. Japan
experimented with foreign trade in the 1960s and 1970s because it was dis-
abused of military expansion by World War II. For a time it was incapable
of fighting a war and its endorsement of the trading system was merely an
adoption of the policy alternative. Deprived of its military capability, the
Japanese worked hard to expand trade capacity. As a result, Japan's huge
economy was fueled by foreign trade.

Chosen primarily out of necessity, Japan and a number of other small
East Asian NIEs benefited from the open economy of the trading world.
China has in recent years followed the footsteps of the NIEs to enhance its
national strength through the development of trade. In the 1980s and the
early 1990s, China's trade expanded more than twice as rapidly as world
trade. According to Chinese official sources, China's ratio of foreign trade
to GNP in 1991 reached the astonishing level of 39.1 percent, with the
ratio for exports alone standing at 19.4 percent.[41] In 1992, China entered
the ranks of the world's top ten exporters. Nicholas R. Lardy believes that
"China's reform strategy was premised on increased participation in the
international economy."[42]

An interesting question is whether or not economic primacy is going to change and if the East Asian NIEs' growing economic strength will sustain a nationalistic and militaristic policy when they achieve a high economic development. Some scholars predict that Japan will become a world power with commensurate political and military interests, and China will become a regional military hegemony after success in economic modernization. Indeed, there is the possibility that trading states will assimilate into the military-political realm. Although it would very unlikely for Japan or China to follow the United States or the former Soviet Union to become world-leading naval or military powers in the foreseeing future, the very possibility brought about by economic success in these two countries has made many of its East Asian neighbors nervous and forced them to turn their wealth into arms. Under these circumstances, most East Asian countries aimed at both high rates of economic growth and defense self-sufficiency. Here the issue was not what Rosecrance wondered: If the American model would ultimately be followed by Japan or the Japanese model might be ultimately be followed by America.[43] Rather, there is an interaction of the economic and military world in post–Cold War East Asia where trading states not only depend upon open trade and commercial routes to market goods but also seek military assurance of domestic stability and security of external markets.

THE MORAL DIMENSION OF POWER COMPETITION

While the economic dimension entered into post–Cold War power competition, most of the East Asian nations held the realist concept of national sovereignty against the demand to include moral issues, particularly human-rights issue, into the international arena. Under pressure from the Western countries, human-rights issues became one of the major disputes in East Asian international relations.

Although the notion of absolute territorial sovereignty came to East Asia relatively late, a state-centric view of international relations took a strong hold in many East Asian nations. Any modification was met with strong resistance. Newly independent countries with different levels of military and economic strength wanted to exercise unchallengeable powers within their boundaries and enjoy uncompromised sovereignty in international relations. For them, the government held absolute authority over the people within its territory (internal sovereignty) and outsiders could not legitimately interfere in a country's domestic affairs (external sovereignty). This view was in contrast to that of the old Chinese world order.

There was no clear delineation between the Middle Kingdom (China) and peripheral nations, so there was no concept of external sovereignty. A Chinese emperor's sway in outer realms was limited by the power and authority of local potentates. As for internal sovereignty, although it could be argued that there were no theoretical curbs on an emperor's authority within the Middle Kingdom, it was widely understood that there were limits beyond which a monarch could not go: "When it came to human rights, the mandate of traditional Confucian culture was ambiguous."[44] Rulers persecuted insubordinate officials and dissident intellectuals, but the public reaction was probably more resignation than approval.

The Chinese world order collapsed after the East Asian nations were victimized by the Western powers in the nineteenth century. Ironically, many East Asian nations embraced the Western sovereignty concept with a vengeance. Japan was determined to become an East Asian empire free of interference by anyone. This goal was largely achieved by the Meiji Restoration. It then went to military expansion, which led to the U.S. occupation after the Pacific War. In China, the goal of national independence was achieved by the Communist victory in 1949. However, the thinking of Chinese Communist leaders could not easily be freed from the dead ways of the past. The principle of state sovereignty was the cornerstone of Chinese foreign policy.[45] For the Chinese, "how each sovereign state mistreats or even make[s] war on its own people and minority nationalities" was absolutely no one else's concern.[46] Coincidentally, the victory of the Communists in China happened the year after the adoption of the Universal Declaration of Human Rights by the United Nations, but the Chinese Communists had not been consulted, and they were disinclined to let human-rights considerations interfere with their reach of power or actions within their countries' boundaries. In the following decades, the international human-rights movement gained popularity and legal standing in other parts of the world.[47] It was as if the principles first clearly articulated in the UN charter and the UN Declaration on Human Rights were now being taken seriously as an integral part of a stable international order. Nevertheless, China did not sign the UN's Universal Declaration of Human Rights, and Chinese leaders took a negative view of the Western concept of human rights. A Chinese article on the issue in 1960 asserted that "imperialism frequently uses the pretext of protecting human rights to intervene in the internal affairs of socialist countries."[48]

Many East Asian countries have accused the human-rights policy of the West as centralist; namely, Western countries "mistakenly view their particular institutions and ideas as universally valid."[49] In contrast, East

Asian countries take a cultural relativist approach toward human-rights issues; namely, in applying international human-rights standards, account must be taken of the diversity of international values, and each government is entitled to make allowances for the nation's historical, social, cultural, and political realities.[50] It is in this context that Roberto R. Romulo, Secretary of Foreign Affairs of the Philippines, says a "state may not interfere in others' internal affairs in the name of human rights."[51] Thus, many East Asian countries came into conflict with Western countries that took liberal views of human rights and insisted that human rights are universal and must be respected regardless of historical, cultural, ethnic, or religious backgrounds. In the liberal view that holds human rights to be universal, violation of human rights in any country is the proper concern of the entire international community, which should "stand for all that is good in the world" and "fight evil wherever it may be found."[52]

The events that took place after the June 4, 1989 crackdown on a pro-democracy demonstration in China provided a case to highlight the confrontation between East Asian and Western countries on the human-rights issue. The tremendous international outpouring of concern after the Tiananmen incident came as quite a shock to Beijing's leaders. Although there were complaints from the United States and other Western countries about repression in China in the Cold War era, they were usually so politicized and tied to anti-Communist hysteria that they had little credibility or impact. The United States and many other Western countries began restoring diplomatic contact with China during the Cultural Revolution, the worst period of human-rights violations. In 1979, the crackdown on the Democracy Wall Movement was followed immediately by Deng Xiaoping's upbeat visit to the United States to celebrate the normalization of diplomatic relations between the two countries. Deeply impressed that Deng was "small, tough, intelligent, frank, courageous, personable, self-assured, friendly," President Jimmy Carter told Deng that the United States "viewed favorably the growing desire of people throughout the world for a better quality of life, for more political participation, for liberation from persecution by their own governments, and for freedom from the domination of any outside power."[53] Deng politely presented his view of China's human-rights problem, saying that Chinese people had been permitted substantial freedom of speech and expression. The U.S. leaders did not push further about human-rights violations. Playing the China card in the triangular politics, the United States adopted a double standard to China's human rights issues before the 1989 Tiananmen crackdown. According to Andrew Nathan, the double standard implied that

U.S. policymakers "think China should be judged by different moral criteria than other countries."[54] In this situation, cautious requests from Chinese dissidents for sympathy from the American government seemed to go unheeded. It was partly because of an absence of strong reaction to human-rights abuses during the decades prior to the 1989 event that Chinese leaders were taken by surprise by the strong international reactions to the massacre.

Indeed, concern about human-rights violations in China became an issue of international confrontation in Chinese leaders' eyes because they found themselves unavoidably locked in an unwelcome struggle with many countries on the issue. Immediately after the events at Tiananmen Square, France froze relations with China at all levels. France cut back on cultural exchanges and also became a haven for refugees from Tiananmen. Australia cut back on aid and loans. Sweden put aid on hold and banned military shipments to China. Switzerland likewise banned military sales. Norway froze credits and new exports to China. West Germany took steps similar to these and even delayed the signing of already completed financial assistance agreement. Although the Bush administration tried to constrain its reaction, the United States still took some important steps to register its uneasiness over China's actions. Specifically announced were suspension of all government-to-government sales and commercial exports of weapons, and exchanges of visits between U.S. and Chinese military leaders. When Bill Clinton came to office, he announced a linkage between China's human-rights record and the renewal of China's Most-Favored Nation (MFN) trade status in May 1993 (which were delinked in 1994).[55] Under international pressures, Japan, although ambiguous in actual responses, imposed some modest economic sanctions. No new aid projects were launched, and the government restrained Japan's eager bankers from making loans to China until 1992.[56]

The struggle over international sanctions against China's human-rights violations was apparently a new development in East Asian international relations. For a century prior to the end of the Cold War, power competition in the region centered on strategic and economic interests without moral concerns. That led one scholar to argue that the nation-state system had such a degree of tolerance for the violations of human rights that these rights could be protected only "if a new system of world order, not based on the nation-state, were established."[57] Although cracks started to appear in the monolith of "domestic jurisdiction" in the mid-1970s when the theoretically untrammeled power of sovereign states within their frontiers was being challenged, marked contrasts have existed among regions of the world with respect to awareness, practice, and protection of human rights. In the West, the European Convention on Human Rights, the Inter-American Commission and the Inter-American Court of Human Rights offered opportunities for individuals to utilize regional complaint mechanisms when human rights are abridged. East Asia appeared to lag behind other continents in the delineation and protection of human rights. Although the need for protection of human rights increased in the region, "the readiness of most governments to bind themselves remained limited prior to the end of the Cold War."[58]

After the end of the Cold War, human-rights issues were no longer as marginal as they once were in East Asia. Pressures for change came primarily from the outside the region. In the case of China, the human-rights dispute with the West changed the landscape of China's international relations since 1989. At the time of the Tiananmen massacre, Beijing stubbornly insisted that the incident was nobody's business and publicly denied all charges of human-rights violations. Subsequently, it was forced to take steps to improve its human-rights conditions in order to maintain normal political and economic relations with Western countries. In June 1990, the Chinese government allowed prominent dissident Fang Lizhi, who had taken refuge in the U.S. Embassy in Beijing after Tiananmen, to leave China. Most prominent political prisoners jailed in Beijing after Tiananmen were released as well. In October 1991 and August 1992, "China for the first time issued a White Paper on Human Rights and a White Paper on Prison Conditions which presented a systematic defense of the regime's human rights policy."[59] Along with many other East Asian nations, China participated in the Asian Regional Preparatory Meeting for the World Conference on Human Rights in Bangkok on March 30, 1993, and then the World Conference on Human Rights in Vienna in June the same year. At these meetings, China still held that "state sovereignty is the basis for the realization of human rights. Only when the state sovereignty is fully respected can the implementation of human rights be fully ensured." Nevertheless, under international pressure, it recognized that Asian countries should, "under the guidance of the UN charter, proceed from the reality and overall interests of raising the standard of enjoyment of human rights and fundamental freedoms by the Asian peoples."[60]

Another instance came in May 1991, when European Community (EC) ministers served notice on their ASEAN counterparts that future ties would "depend upon the observance of human rights."[61] The EC argued that political freedoms should be applied universally to the same standard. ASEAN protested that this amounted to interference and showed no understanding of local conditions. Nevertheless, ASEAN counter-rhetoric did not keep the EC's new doctrine at bay. The 12 nations of the EC ranked third among ASEAN's trading partners behind Japan and the United States, purchasing 15 percent of the group's exports. More than half of ASEAN's exports to the EC were manufactured products, and the EC was the second-largest investor in ASEAN after Japan.[62] The human-rights policy became a dispute between ASEAN leaders and their EC counterparts.

THE CULTURAL DIPLOMACY

The growing concern over moral issues revealed an awareness of the cultural dimension of international relations. Evidence of this was found in Samuel P. Huntington's controversial article "The Clash of Civilization?" which made headlines in 1993.[63] Some East Asians believed that the clash-of-civilization thesis showed that Westerners had difficulties in understanding East Asians and often misunderstood non-Western societies. The overconcern for the issue of human rights reflected a cultural misunderstanding between the East and the West.[64]

Indeed, it is ironic that the closer East Asia and the West have become in political and economic relations, the more serious the gap between their mutual knowledge. There has been an asymmetrical perception gap here. For example, both the Japanese and Chinese believe they know far more about Americans than Americans know about the Chinese and Japanese. It is difficult to evaluate such impressions, but at least it is true that far more American books and movies have been translated into Chinese and Japanese than vice versa, and far more Japanese and Chinese understand English than Americans understand Chinese and Japanese. Because of this asymmetrical perception gap, Bilahari Kausikan, an official of the Singapore foreign ministry, says that "the current triumphalism of Western values grates on East and Southeast Asians."[65] Mahbubani, a Singapore official, found "Western thinkers are having considerable difficulty finding the right paradigm to describe a world where non-Western powers are emerging . . . The difficulty that Western minds face in grasping the arrival of East Asia arises from the fact that we are witnessing an unprecedented historical phenomenon: a fusion of Western and East Asian cultures in the Asia-Pacific region."[66]

According to Mahbubani, it took a long time for China and other East Asian societies to accept Western culture and to learn from the West. It will also take time for Westerners to accept and learn from Eastern cultures. "In the past few years, many Americans have been disconcerted by lectures from East Asians, as have many East Asians by American preaching on democracy and human rights." Nevertheless, in the view of Mahbubani, the learning process in the Pacific will become "a two-way street rather than a one-way street."[67] A Chinese scholar suggests that the Sino-American relations in the post–Cold War era "should be made with a sensitivity to and a more nuanced understanding of the cultural divergence of these two societies."[68] Under these circumstances, by providing generous opportunities for an exchange of minds instead of arms, the "clash of civilizations" could be avoided.

A growing awareness of the importance of the cultural aspects of international relations has given rise to cultural diplomacy to promote national interests in East Asia again. In a way it was symptomatic of the era that Japan's comprehensive national security embraced strategic, economic, and cultural aspects of the country's foreign policy. Japan's security was reasoned as dependent not merely on military arrangements with the United States or China, or on trade and investment abroad, but also on establishing close cultural ties with other countries. In 1972, an initial step was taken under Prime Minister Tanaka to promote cultural diplomacy, most visibly through the establishment of the Japan Foundation, formally called the Foundation for the Promotion of International Cultural Exchange. Its operational funds came from an initial government endowment of 5 billion yen. With additional government allocations in subsequent years, the foundation's endowment grew to about 94.9 billion yen as of August 1993. Cultural exchange activities have been financed by capital gains accrued from the government endowment as well as by contributions and donations from the private sector.[69] The purposes of the foundation are "to efficiently carry on activities for international cultural exchange . . . with a view to deepening other nations' understanding of Japan. . . ."[70] The idea is to promote international cultural understanding through the assistance of Japanese studies programs, language training, artistic exhibits, and the like in other countries.

Following the Japanese example, Taiwan launched the Chiang Ching-kuo Foundation in 1989, in memory of its late President Chiang Ching-kuo (1910-88). With the official title of the Chiang Ching-kuo Foundation for International Exchange, it has similar funding sources and aims as the Japan Foundation. With its headquarters in Taipei, the foundation has set up regional offices in the United States, Canada, and several European countries. An annual budget for funding of approximately $7 million has been distributed under such grant categories as Chinese culture-related institutional enhancement, research grants, conference and seminar grants, and subsidies for publications all over the world.[71] These initiatives indicate the efforts that the Japanese and Taiwanese governments have made in promoting cultural diplomacy. In recent years, some large private business organizations in these countries also became interested in funding East Asian studies programs abroad. Toyota professorships were established in America's universities. Taiwan's Times Cultural Foundation and United Daily Cultural Foundation also are active in providing funding for cultural exchanges in the United States and Europe.

With the stress of these foundations almost wholly on Japanese and Chinese cultures, there was a recognition that the government must begin to take a serious interest in the cultural aspect of international relations. A few years after the establishment of the Japan Foundation, when Japanese Prime Minister Fukuda Takeo visited Southeast Asia, he enunciated the Fukuda doctrine, which read very much like a cultural statement. It stressed the need for cultural, intellectual, and psychological rapport between Japan and other countries in order to create a more solid basis for interrelationship. The idea was termed by Fukuda as "heart-to-heart" diplomacy, which was regarded as "the key to better relations among nations."[72] By the same token, the historical visit of the Japanese emperor to China in October 1992 was also regarded by Shinichiro Asao, president of the Japan Foundation, as "an important basis for the future promotion of cultural exchange" between the two countries.[73]

Cultural diplomacy is not an isolated phenomenon. Promoting cultural exchange to enhance political and economic relations was practiced not only by East Asian nations but also by Western countries. In U.S.-Chinese relations, for example, geopolitical and, lately, economic, calculations have been the key to the two countries' relations of reconciliation and normalization. Nevertheless, there was also a strong interest on both sides in cementing these ties through scholarly, educational, and journalistic connections. The U.S. National Science Foundation established a special office to deal with the exchange of scientific information between the United States and China, and a Committee on Scholarly Communication with China was organized as the framework for promoting student and scholarly exchanges in the 1980s. The large number of publications, in both countries, on Chinese-American relations that appeared after the Nixon trip of 1972 attest to a fascination with the cultural, as well as foreign-policy, implications of new development. It is significant that, while geopolitics provides the basis for their rapprochement, their cultural contact fits into the global scene in which communication across national boundaries on the part of individuals, ethnic and religious groups, and ideological movements has facilitated the existing framework of bilateral relations.

ENVIRONMENTAL THREAT AND COMMON SECURITY

Environmental issues are another important dimension that has been considered with increasing frequency in international relations in recent years, partly because the waning of the Cold War coincided with the growing visibility of environmental problems such as industrial waste, pollution, soil erosion, the hole in the ozone layer, acid rain, global warming, and deforestation, which have threatened the security of many nations and required international solutions. Like the human-rights issue, awareness of environmental issues began in some Western industrialized countries. In 1972, a book published in the West, *Only One Earth,* warned that "the two worlds of man—the biosphere of his inheritance, the technosphere of his creation—are out of balance."[74] Ever since, "environmental security" has been regarded as one of the two fundamental aspects of global security, along with avoidance of nuclear war. According to one research report published in the wake of the end of the Cold War, such threats to the global life-support systems as greenhouse warming, ozone depletion, and the loss of tropical forests and marine habitats are just as important to the future of the earth as insuring against nuclear catastrophe. As the cost of environmental degradation to present and further generations becomes clearer, the links among global environmental, economic, and military security issues have become apparent and environmental concerns are accepted as legitimate national security issues. Before the end of the Cold War, industrial countries began to take measures to clean up rivers, fight smog, and restrict uncontrolled damages to nature and species (some of which are now defined as endangered.)

In East Asia, this process is yet to start. Booming economies have been rightly credited with recording year after year of rapid growth and lifting millions out of the despair of poverty. But "with prosperity has come an explosive increase in industrial pollution, rapid deforestation, loss of natural habitats, and serious degradation."[75] This region is now "paying the price for decades of rapid economic growth that has seen little or no concern for the environment."[76] One urgent environmental problem in the region is the loss of tropical rainforests in Southeast Asia. According to some studies, at current rates of harvesting, timber reserves in Asia will last less than 40 years. In Southeast Asia, forest land was reduced from 32 million ha in 1850 to 175 million ha in 1980, while cropland increased correspondingly from less than 70 million ha in 1850 to more than 200 million ha in 1980.[77] Rates of deforestation are particularly high in timber-exporting countries such as Indonesia and Malaysia and in countries that practice extensive agriculture such as Thailand and Vietnam. There were 2.49 million square kilometers of virgin forest in Southeast Asia outside of Papua New Guinea in 1900, but only 602,222 square kilometers remained in 1989.[78] The degradation of forests threatened nontimber resources such as medicinal herbs and wildlife. Japan was criticized for its ignorance of environmental consequences of its trade and industries in the region. A study found that major Japanese trading companies were involved in logging in the Philippines, Indonesia, Malaysia, and Papua New Guinea and tried to avoid any international interference in the tropical timber trade. The Japanese government was deeply involved in helping those companies: in the two major sources of Japanese timber imports, Malaysia and Papua New Guinea, the government subsidized the construction of roads to be used by logging firms financed by Japanese trading companies.[79]

Nowhere in East Asia are environmental problems more serious than in China. A Chinese melancholic and indignant author, He Baochuan, alarmed the world about escalating environmental problems in China at the waning of the Cold War. His book was banned after Tiananmen in 1989 by the Chinese authorities. But it was read broadly in China and translated into English and published in the United States. He warned that "the relentless progress of desertification" is a serious environmental problem China faces.[80] The ancient city of Tongwan, which was the capital of the Mongol Chief Helian Bobo, has vanished from sight. The famous Silk Route that spiraled across the southern slopes of the Heavenly Mountains and the northern foot of the Kunlun Mountains has faded into sand dunes. One of the recent victims is a 300-kilometer-long green corridor at the lower reaches of the Talimu River in Xinjiang province, which has played an important role in checking the southward expansion of the Taklamakan Desert. He Baoquan explained that this was primarily the result of excessive logging and herding, and the failure to conserve water resources over the last few decades. Lake Luobupo was once the largest water source in Central Asia, but it lies dangerously close to the Taklamakan, China's largest desert (in the local language the name means "you can go in but you won't come out"). By the early 1980s the lake was reduced to a vast waterland strewn with the corpses of dead birds.[81] Industrialization in China caused water, soil and air pollution, and eroded large amount of arable land. The Chinese population is now 21.5 percent or about one-fifth of the total world population, but China has only 7 percent or about one-thirteenth of the world's total arable land. Arable lands are shrinking as the population grows. In 1981, the population of China increased by 14.5 million, while arable land was reduced by 2.5 million acres. Between 1979 and 1984, the country lost a total of 19 million acres of arable land, a yearly average of 3.8 million acres were lost. Between then and 1987, over 4.1 million acres were lost every year.[82] One Chinese official source revealed that "rapid economic expansion and reforms have led to an increase in cities and towns from 223 in 1980 to 570 in 1993. China had an urban population of 334 million in 1993, a rise of more than 10 million over 1980."[83] According to the same official source, poorly developed public facilities such as drainage works, heating systems, and disposal of rubbish have contributed to serious environmental problems in cities and towns. Today, a large number of residents in towns and cities use coal to cook and warm themselves in the winter. There are about 700,000 vehicles in Beijing, merely one-eighth of the figure in Tokyo or Los Angeles. However, emissions of carbon dioxide and carbon monoxide in the city are the same as those in Tokyo or Los Angeles.[84]

These environmental problems have become a serious threat to all nations. It is apparent that the impact of the environmental crisis in China is not confined solely within the boundary of Chinese territory. In an article published in the early 1990s, Barber B. Conable indicated that, China depended on coal for 70 percent of its industrial fuel and power generation and 90 percent of its household energy needs. With an expected real economic growth rate of about 5 percent over the 1990s, China's cooperation would be essential to limit global warming and acid rain in Asia.[85] From this perspective, environmental problems in China and other East Asian countries becomes a legitimate security concern of the region as well as the world. A new approach to international collaboration, which may overcome the constraints of the realist security dilemma, becomes necessary.

In dealing with environmental issues, the concept of "common security" was developed in the 1980s. The concept of common security is based on the principle that no country can increase its security without at the same time increasing the security of other countries. It assumes that "the main threats to international security come not from individual states but from global problems shared by the entire international community: nuclear war, the heavy economic burden of militarism and war, disparities in living standards within and among states, and global environmental degradation."[86] The common security concept views international relations in opposition to what is prescribed by traditional realist concept of military security, which thinks of international relations as a zero-sum game in which one state's gain is the other state's loss and every nation is a potential enemy. In contrast, in the environmental sphere, national security is under common global threats and, therefore, is defined by a common interest. The resolution of the global environmental problems requires international cooperation. Redefining national security to include the environmental dimension offers a fruitful basis for cooperation among nations because it is both a positive and inclusive concept. While military security rests firmly on the competitive strength of individual countries at the direct expense of other nations, environmental common security cannot be achieved unilaterally: It "requires and nurtures more stable and cooperative relations among nations."[87]

Due to the persistence of the neorealist image of international relations, the common security concept is yet to be accepted by many countries in East Asia. Until recently, "environmental 'losses' were treated as simply part of the price of economic success."[88] Nevertheless, the winds of opinion are shifting in East Asia, as they are elsewhere. When the consequences of environmental degradation become evident, and as environmental awareness rises, pressure to take international efforts to achieve environmental security throughout East Asia are increasing. Once again, like in the human-rights issue, East Asia is challenged by initiatives from other parts of the world, especially UN-sponsored international agencies. Among early UN efforts was the UN Conference on the Human Environment held at Stockholm in 1972, which brought environmental problems to the forefront. As a direct result of that conference, the UN Environmental Program (UNEP) was established, which initiated the Global Resources Information Database, located in the Asia Pacific region.[89] In 1973, the UN Economic and Social Commission for Asia and the Pacific (ESCAP) convened a meeting of representatives of countries and intergovernmental bodies active in environmental preservation in the region. To integrate environmental considerations into the commission's activities, the Environmental Coordinating Unit was created in the Secretariat with the assistance of the UNEP in 1978.

Under international pressures, many East Asian countries have taken actions to include environmental issues into their considerations of national security in recent years. Thailand was the first to ban logging nationwide after mudslides in 1988 in southern Thailand, killed hundreds of people. The Philippines banned the export of raw logs in 1986 after log exports declined to less than 20 percent of the peak level of 1971, and it banned exports of raw timber in 1989. Vietnam banned log exports in 1991 and then announced a ban on all timber exports in 1992.[90] Japan and Singapore are trying to develop and make use of environmentally friendly technology. Taiwan and South Korea, two good examples of what can go wrong when economic planners treat the environment as a free and limitless public goods, are spending heavily on urban clean-up and pollution control. China, the largest East Asian country with the most serious environmental problems, has also set up a series of high-level working groups to look into energy, water and air standards, and the trade in wildlife.[91] Although the practical effect of these policy changes is still subject to controversy,[92] positive responses to international pressures reflect the change in the direction of international relations.

A NEW WORLD OF POWER COMPETITION

Cold War politicians and scholars paid far more attention to international politics than to international economics, which were dismissed as "low politics," contrasting it with the "high politics" of sovereignty and military power competition.[93] International politics was perceived almost exclusively in terms of the power competition between the two superpowers. In this rivalry, each side tried to recruit as many allies as possible. The contest between capitalism and communism was seen as a zero-sum game in the sense that any gain by one side necessarily meant a loss for the other side. And the gains and losses were in turn defined primarily in territorial terms, for example the loss of China, North Korea, and South Vietnam. The power competition was delineated according to alliance and territorial boundaries and evaluated according to military capabilities and instruments. For 45 years the United States pursued a national security strategy focused on one goal: containing the Soviet Union. Nevertheless, "with the collapse of the Soviet Union and the Soviet Empire, the doctrine of containment has become a victim of its own success."[94] As the United States searches for a new direction, a host of new threats to national security has been identified: the budget and trade deficits, the stagnation of American wages in the face of global economic competition, and the degradation of the environment.[95]

The territorial and military sense of power competition also characterized East Asia's strategic thinking for many years. One extreme example was Japan's campaign of military conquest to establish the "Great East Asian Co-Prosperity Sphere," as it was called by Tokyo's propagandists in the 1930s and 1940s. This Japanese attempt at asserting physical control over foreign territories turned out to be an utter disaster. Japan was decisively defeated in the Pacific War and was physically occupied by the victorious U.S. forces. However, through trade and economic development after its defeat in the Pacific War, Japan became the second largest industrial economy in the post–Cold War world. Forty years after military defeat, Japan obtained the international status and influence that it was not able to gain by military force. It is, therefore, ironically observed by Rosecrance that "it is possible for relationships among states to be entirely transformed or even reversed by the low politics of trade," instead of military superiority.[96]

The inclusion of nonmilitary dimensions such as economic, moral, and environmental issues into power competition has been a trend in line with the new development in the post–Cold War world. Growing economic, moral, and environmental concerns may prove crucial to the change in the current neorealist image of international relations and may reduce the military tensions among East Asian countries. One positive example is that, while the military buildup is still a major concern of many countries in the region, the member states of ASEAN have managed their disputes in recent years without resort to force despite a previous history of military threat and open conflict. In the early 1990s, a quest for economic opportunities and rapid growth of trade and investment has clearly pushed along a détente between ASEAN and Vietnam. In a similar fashion, burgeoning crossborder trade between Russia and China has accompanied a large force reduction along the border of the two former adversaries.

These developments do not deny that the military dimension is still one of the key elements of power competition. Intensified economic and environmental concerns as well as cultural exchanges may reduce reliance on military force in the region, but it does not exclude the use of unilateral military means to defend national boundaries. Japan's tenacious defense of its claim to four northern territories in the face of Russian threats and blandishments is a striking example of the persistence of territorial principle in the goals of the region's principal trading states. The dispute between China, Vietnam, the Philippines, and Malaysia over the Spratly Islands continued in the 1990s, which makes it clear that old-fashioned territorial disputes linger in the new age of the post–Cold War era.[97] Thus the task before both scholars and policymakers is to not only read correctly the dimensions of power competition, but act to render the states of the region a more serious consideration of nonmilitary dimensions of national strength in the new post–Cold War world of power competition.

THE EMERGING REGIONAL APPROACH
TOWARD POWER COMPETITION

Regionalism is not entirely a new phenomenon of the post–Cold War era. Nevertheless, in sharp contrast to Western Europe and North America, East Asia has until very recently been largely devoid of institutionalized regional cooperation.[1] Although emerging economic and security interdependence brought geographically close nations into a variety of cooperative functions as early as the 1960s, these regional initiatives were operated largely in a decentralized manner. Robert Scalapino, in his 1987 study of East Asian international relations, used "soft regionalism" to characterize the emerging regional cooperation that "lacks a formal structure."[2] The Association of Southeast Asian Nations (ASEAN) used to be a classic example of soft regionalism as its goal was cooperation without integration. The approach of cooperation without formal agreement in many "growth clusters," including the Chinese Economic Area (CEA) of Taiwan, Hong Kong, and the southeast coast of mainland China, is a most recent example of soft regionalism. Japan is also a principal party to the emergence of soft regionalism in the Asia Pacific, with its central role in a growing network of economic ties among the nations of the region without any formal organizational arrangement for Japan to be a leader of an economic bloc. Nevertheless, along with the recent wave of regional integration in Europe (European Union or EU) and North America (North American Free Trade Agreement or NAFTA), structured regionalism has emerged in East Asia with the establishment of the intergovernmental Asia Pacific Economic Cooperation (APEC) in 1989 and its institution-building efforts.

The development of interdependence and consequent regionalism reorganized power relations and compelled East Asian nations to make decisions about their relationships through regional schemes. The realist image of anarchy used to be the only background condition of power competition prior to the end of the Cold War. Now strategic interdependence among sovereign states is at least as fundamental as anarchy in shaping international relations in the post–Cold War era.[3] A regional approach toward power competition occurred gradually.

SOFT VERSUS STRUCTURED REGIONALISM

East Asian regionalism took two major forms: one soft and the other structured. Soft regionalism may be defined as cooperation among geographically close nations or economic units without formal agreement. Structured regionalism is a segment of the world bound together by a common set of objectives based upon geographical, economic, and political ties and also possessing "a formal structure provided for in formal intergovernmental agreement."[4] Structured regionalism thus refers to the mise-en-scène of political and economic communities, which involves certain types of supranational institutions based on geographical proximity as well as legal agreement with the underlying idea of a lasting interrelationship between the countries involved.[5] Soft regionalism can be a starting point of structured regionalism. There is often a gliding transition from soft to structured regionalism. Nevertheless, soft regionalism does not necessarily lead to structured regional integration, because structured regionalism often touches, sometimes in a more palpable way, sometimes in a minor degree, the sensitive point of national sovereignty. A fully developed and structured regional scheme always implies partial transfer of national sovereignties to supranational institutions, although structured regionalism does not necessarily supersede nation-state actors; nor does the establishment of structured regional organizations necessarily mean a decline of nation-states as James Rosenau predicted more than two decades ago.[6] The nature of structured regionalism makes it difficult for East Asian countries to accept due to "the traditional Asian distaste for treaty-defined institutions,"[7] and the problem identified by neorealists as "the effects of structure on cooperation."[8]

In contrast to western European and North American states, East Asian countries represent a wide array of political regimes and philosophies, from Communist to Confucianist, from constitutional monarchies to military dictatorships, from personal dictatorship to bureaucratic governance, from democratically elected governments to single-party systems. Even where governance is accomplished through democratic institutions, political styles vary and are in flux. The political contrasts and ethnic suspicions among East Asian countries have a negative impact upon payoff structures of regional institutions because they increase the motivation of cheating and deception. Robert Axelrod's experimental study demonstrates that the greater the conflict of interest between players, the greater the likelihood that the players would in fact choose to defect.[9] For a period after World War II, East Asia's sheer size and extraordinary diversity, including political and ethnic suspicions, long-standing antipathies and economic disparities, were major barriers to building structured regional institutions.

The history of humiliating experiences of many East Asian countries at the hands of the Great Powers still shadows their perception of the future. Along with other parts of the world, East Asia as a whole has entered the post–Cold War era, but some East Asian countries are still in "the post–colonial era," a fact that "heightens many Asian nations' concerns about ceding sovereignty in the name of regional integration."[10] As Hirono indicates, no nation in East Asia, however willing to compromise in the interest of attaining the common objectives of regional/subregional groupings, "is ready to surrender sovereign rights over its domestic affairs and foreign relations."[11] Small or weak nations are suspicious of what they see as attempts by the Great Powers to reassert influence in new ways. But so too are China and Japan reluctant to abandon elements of sovereignty to regional institutions without strong evidence that there is more to be gained from doing so.

Under these circumstances, structured regional organization, while not impossible, would be difficult to establish, unless, in the neorealist view, there is a hegemonic power to take initiative. Nevertheless, there has never been a single hegemonic power dominating East Asia since the end of World War II, although the United States and the Soviet Union were two superpowers competing for predominance in the region during the Cold War era. When the Soviet Union collapsed at the end of the Cold War, U.S. power also declined. The United States is still a critical actor but an irony is that, while in absolute terms U.S. economic engagement in the region is steadily increasing, it is declining in relative terms. What stands out in the region is a shared unease at perceived trends: a contraction of the central economic and military role played by the United States, simultaneous with the ascendance of China and Japan as multifaceted powers. Nevertheless, neither China nor Japan is close to being a hegemonic power in the region, and neither of them can play the leadership role of peacefully energizing its neighbors.[12] It is from this perspective that pessimistic realist scholars such as Manning and Stern assert that the cherished aspiration of Asia Pacific regional institutions "may prove to be a chimera."[13]

Nevertheless, to the surprise of neorealists, the sheer size and primordial differences among East Asian countries have not stopped regional institution-building in recent years. In contrast to Europe and North America, structured regionalism in East Asia developed during the period of decline of the hegemonic powers in the region.[14] A Singapore scholar indicated that the formation of regional cooperation "is driven not by the major powers but by medium-sized or small powers. None of the recent regional initiatives were either conceived or developed in major capitals. Indeed the leadership has come from the smaller or medium powers."[15]

Interdependence, which has been brought about by extraordinary economic growth, is an important factor that has greatly contributed to the recent emergence of East Asian regionalism. Economic interdependence has changed perceptions of the payoff structure of regional cooperation. A report by the Carnegie Endowment study group indicates that, "the relationships among most East Asian states today probably reflect less a heritage of animosity and more a common participation in the modernization process—a global phenomenon."[16] Economic interdependence has made cooperative solutions more attractive and is breaking down Asian parochialism and encouraging East Asian leaders to think regionally.

Nevertheless, just as "interdependence is not the opposite of anarchy,"[17] interdependence does not necessarily result in a shift in even part of national sovereignty to supranational institutions.[18] As all political exercises of some scope, regional organizations would not be created without legitimacy, derived from favorable perceptions of national leaders involved in changing international environment, maintaining identities, and cost-benefit calculations. The adoption of structured regionalism involves "a calculated, deliberate, and discretionary strategy on the part of political elites."[19] From interdependence to regional cooperation, each step is bound to be a political decision.

In this context, while interdependence signifies mutual dependence, it is a situation in which nation-states are linked but remain sovereign. There are two distinct uses for the concept of interdependence.[20] One refers to a relationship of sensitivity, in which there is simply a co-variance in the behavior of two or more states. The second use refers to a relationship of vulnerability, in which one state depends on another for the provision of a commodity or other valued need and cannot move to another supplier without incurring high costs.[21] The concept of interdependence in the sense of vulnerability is "the most well-accepted definition,"[22] and is helpful in analyzing the dynamic relationships that link sovereign states together in varied schemes of security and economic cooperation. In this sense, interdependence implies a relationship in which "the ability of one participant to gain his ends is dependent to an important degree on the choice or decisions that the other participant will make."[23] In this relationship, nation-states are still sovereign, that is, able to make decisions or choices autonomously, although to realize their goals they must be concerned with the choices that other states make.[24]

This definition of interdependence does not imply that the interests of nation-states are in harmony or that asymmetric relations are not important. Due to the differences in size and economic resources as well as in military capacities, larger or more powerful nations involved in an asymmetric interdependent relationship can manipulate it in order to prompt the smaller or weaker nations to do what they want. That is why sovereignty has been the central concern of many East Asian states as growing interdependence makes cooperation a more and more attractive choice. The lack of a single hegemon to press its vision on the other members implies that institutional outcomes of regional cooperation rely on a complex bargaining process among nationalistic leaders of regional powers and medium- and small-sized nations. Soft regionalism remains important and may not necessarily transform into structured regionalism along with growing interdependence, primarily because the soft nature refrains from potential sovereignty disputes.

GROWING ECONOMIC INTERDEPENDENCE

Growing economic interdependence has been a driving force of East Asian regionalism. As was discussed in the previous chapter, economic development in the region took a four-tiers model, which provided a continuous process of transition through successive transfers of technology, goods, and capital flow from the first tier (Japan) to the second tier (four little tigers), to the third tier (other ASEAN countries), and to the fourth tier (China and Vietnam) of Newly Industrialized Economies (NIEs). Thus, a regional division of labor based on "floor-type" specialization in each tier of nations makes their economies mutually complementary. As each of the East Asian NIEs moves up the ladder of development, it tends to accelerate the growth of those at the next tier of development.

The floor-type specialization produced economic interdependence that began to develop in the 1980s and was largely seen in the rapid growth of intraregional trade, which reached about 45 percent of total trade volume in the early 1990s. A World Bank study indicates that, from the end of World War II to the 1970s, trade within East Asia was relatively unimportant because the region developed stronger connections with North America and other countries. However, the growth of the region's own markets began to outweigh the development of external markets, and internal trade began to increase in the 1980s. East Asia's internal trade was only 29.3 percent of its total trade in the 1960s and rose to 40.7 percent in 1990. The internal trade as a percentage of total world trade increased from 2.9 in 1969 to 7.9 in 1990.[25]

The World Bank report suggests that "East Asia is trading more internally simply because its markets have become so important."[26] East Asian markets have become the most profitable and the fastest growing since the 1980s when access to the U.S. market became uncertain due to the depreciation of the U.S. dollar and its contentious trade policy. The sharp appreciation of the Japanese yen after the so-called Plaza Accord of 1985 made East Asian manufacturers more competitive in a wide range of industries previously controlled by Japan, and also contributed to intraregional trade.[27] The dispersion of manufacturing throughout the Asian Pacific created an "interdependence between the region's more advanced economies and the next tier of industrializing countries."[28] The appreciation of the yen and, later, the currencies of the second-tier NICs, as well as some policy measures, made it easier to transfer inputs and outputs across borders in the region, which resulted in a boom in regional direct investment. Japan, Taiwan, Singapore, and South Korea substantially increased their direct foreign investments in neighboring, less-developed areas such as Indonesia, Malaysia, Thailand, the Philippines, and China. Taiwan became the largest foreign investor in Indonesia and Malaysia, as well as one of the top investors in other ASEAN countries in 1991.[29] In particular, rising costs in Japan and the second-tier NIEs shifted industries to other East Asian countries, increasing the trade in components and machinery. It was not incidental that the boom in intraregional capital flows involved large investments from Japan to other East Asian nations. They were directed at first to ASEAN countries with the most suitable resources. Later, China also became a major destination, and the sources of funds broadened to include Hong Kong, Taiwan, and South Korea. China alone received $111 billion in foreign investment commitment in 1993. According to China's official statistics, during the decade of 1983-93, 70 percent of China's trade volume and 80 percent of foreign investment in China were from advanced Asian Pacific countries.[30]

THE SOFT REGIONALISM OF GROWTH CLUSTERS

Growing economic interdependence fostered by the increasing intraregional trade and capital flow led to the emergence of growth clusters: subregional economic networks formed without regard to, and often despite, national borders. These growth clusters transcended political boundaries but did not involve entire national economies.[31] The most effective examples are the Shenzhen Free Trade Zone, which bridges China's Guangdong Province and Hong Kong; the Singapore-Johor-Riau Growth Triangle linking Singapore, Malaysia, and Indonesia; and the Xiamen Special Economic Zone, which embraces China's Fujian province and Taiwan.[32] The economic linkage among three parts of China, the mainland, Taiwan, and Hong Kong, known as the Chinese Economic Area, is also a large "growth triangle." The development area proposed for the part of northern Southeast Asia where Burma, China, Laos, and Thailand meet is a "growth square."[33] In addition, the Sea of Japan Economic Zone includes the Russian Far East, the three northeast provinces of China, the Korean Peninsula, and Japan's 16 coastal prefectures on the Sea of Japan (Hokkaido, Aomori, Niigata, Toyama, Fukui, and others). The Yellow Sea Economic Zone links China, Japan and South Korea.[34] The Tumen River Delta area involves eastern Russia, China, South and North Korea, Mongolia, and Japan.

The development of these growth clusters has been based on geographic proximity and historical linkages as well as on comparative advantage, especially in labor costs. Growth clusters are a typical form of soft regionalism and fit the region's pragmatic approach to regional cooperation, because they do not require complicated legal agreements and can be implemented across diverse economic and political structures without involving the sensitive sovereignty issue. Soft regionalism of these growth clusters can be a starting point of structured regionalism. Indeed, some of them have been transformed from soft to structured subregional cooperation through intergovernmental agreements. One example is the development of Tumen River Delta area in Northeast Asia. The initial UNDP-sponsored project in 1991 straddles the border region between North Korea, Pacific Russia, and China's Jilin province. South Korea and Japan are potential beneficiaries and sources of the enormous financing that is required. Land-locked Mongolia's interest lies with the possibility of gaining another less congested link with the Pacific.[35] When the project was launched, it could only be soft regionalism in nature because South Korea was not recognized by China, and relations between two Koreas and between Japan and Russia were still tense. The dramatic changes of the recent years have eased political tensions to a point where all six political entities concerned can sit at the same table. Three governments (China, Russia, and North Korea) signed an agreement to establish the Tumen River Area Development Coordinating Council on May 30, 1995. Two other agreements were signed by five governments (China, Russia, Mongolia, South and North Korea) on the same day: one to establish the Tumen River Area Development Consulting Council, and the other to set up guidelines for environmental protection in the subregional development.[36] With these intergovernmental agreements, the soft Tumen River area cooperation was transformed into a structured one.

Nevertheless, soft regionalism of growth clusters does not always lead to a structured one, especially when sovereignty and national security is at stake. The unique development of cooperation without formal agreement represented by the CEA highlights the soft regionalism that has been fostered by the growing economic interdependence but can hardly be transformed into a structured one.

Beginning in the late 1980s, the economies of Hong Kong, Taiwan, and mainland China experienced continued strong growth in spite of the recession in the West and a slowdown of activity in other East Asian NIEs. The boom was driven to a great extent by economic growth in mainland China resulting from economic reform and opening toward the outside world, as well as de facto economic integration between the mainland, Hong Kong, and Taiwan. A growing flood of cross-border investment, trade, tourism, and cultural exchange created strong economic interdependence among the three components of CEA, also known as Greater China.[37] An OECD study asserts that "the CEA is now a major player in world trade."[38] It accumulated $165 billion in reserves in 1992, more than Japan's $70.5 billion.[39] Intratrade in the CEA, which grew from about 10 percent of total trade in 1978 to more than 35 percent in 1990, exceeded that of all free trade arrangements outside the OECD area.[40] Harry Harding indicates that CEA has become a "natural economic territory."[41]

The symbiotic economic interdependence between the constituent parts of CEA is well reflected in their trading position vis-à-vis the United States. Beginning in the mid-1980s China's trade surplus with the United States rose dramatically ($2.8 billion in 1987, $10.4 billion in 1990, $12.7 billion in 1991, and $18.3 in 1992).[42] By contrast, during the same period the large surpluses enjoyed by Hong Kong, and especially Taiwan, declined. These contrary trends reflect the accelerated relocation of Taiwan's and Hong Kong's manufacturing and assembly operations aimed at the U.S. market to the mainland in order to take advantage of lower labor and land costs.[43] A study of the impact of the relocation and associated "outward processing" operations for re-export through Hong Kong indicated that between 1989 and the first half of 1992, 71 to 77 percent of Hong Kong's exports to China were destined for outward processing and related to foreign direct investment ventures.[44] Similar relocation took place in Taiwan's manufacturing industry. A report revealed that the investments of Taiwanese businessmen in the Mainland's Guangdong Province and Shanghai City, approved by the Taiwan government, amounted to 10,764 different projects, with a total investment of $4.55 billion from 1991 to 1994.[45]

The factors that drive economic interdependence and combine to sustain the rapid growth of the CEA are Taiwan's capital and its technical and managerial know-how, Hong Kong's intermediation services, and China's cheap labor and natural resources.[46] From an economic perspective, the CEA is indeed a natural economic territory. China's revealed comparative advantage resembles that of other Asian Pacific countries. China's profile fits most closely with Thailand and Indonesia, with comparative advantage in foods, refined petroleum, and miscellaneous manufacturing. This deviation from the profiles of Hong Kong and Taiwan is due mainly to China's abundance of natural resources. In addition, against the background of high indigenous wage costs and land rents, entrepreneurs in Hong Kong and Taiwan increasingly sought to transfer their labor-intensive operations across the border in order to take advantage of an abundant supply of cheap labor and land. The accelerated appreciation of the Taiwan currency against the U.S. dollar since the mid-1980s was a further contributory factor, promoting many Taiwanese firms to move to the mainland in an attempt to reduce export costs. More stringent government legislation to control pollution, as well as greater self-awareness and even militancy on the part of the labor force, were further reasons for the accelerating trend, especially among Taiwanese entrepreneurs.[47] Reforms in mainland China provided opportunity for relocation, and, in turn, Hong Kong and Taiwan, which have provided three-fourths of the foreign investment on the mainland, played a crucial role in China's economic takeoff. In particular, Hong Kong, as the financier, investor, supplier, and provider of technology for Southern China, helped smooth the transition from a central planning system, in contrast to the difficulties faced in Eastern European countries and the former Soviet Union.[48]

In spite of geographic and cultural proximity and intensified economic interdependence, structured regionalism was not produced. Mutual recognition of sovereignty is a prior condition for structured regionalism. Neither China nor Taiwan grant recognition of sovereignty to the other. The possibility that economic interdependence might spill over into broader political cooperation is hampered by the lack of recognition.[49] Thus the CEA, by definition, is a nonarrangement of soft regionalism without formal agreement among the three constituencies.

The official links between China, Taiwan, and Hong Kong were disrupted by a variety of historical events. For the Chinese government, Hong Kong and Taiwan are painful reminders of humiliation at the hands of foreign powers. Hong Kong was ceded to Britain after the first Opium War in 1841. The Japanese occupied Hong Kong for three and a half years during World War II, after which, it was returned to Britain. Taiwan was ceded to Japan as a result of the Sino-Japanese War in 1895. Japan developed the island as a colony dependent on the homeland for manufactured goods and supplied it with food and raw materials. It was briefly reunited with the mainland after World War II in 1945, but the arrival of the Nationalist Government in 1949 led to a nearly complete severance of ties with the mainland. Between Taiwan and Hong Kong there were no official ties since 1955. Hong Kong's role as entrepot for China was disrupted by the Communist victory in 1949 and the mainland's subsequent isolation.[50]

In an economic reform and peace offensive policy for national reunification,[51] China has expanded its economic links with Hong Kong and Taiwan since 1978. Three of China's five Special Economic Zones (SEZs) (Shenzhen, Zhuhai, and Shanto) were established in Guangdong, which is adjacent to Hong Kong, and another SEZ is located in Xiamen, just a few miles from two coastal islands owned by Taiwan. The earliest and fastest opening areas in China are the southern provinces, which are not only geographically and ethnically close to the influence of Taiwan and Hong Kong but also distant from the central power of Beijing. The official framework of policies is not fully binding.

Hong Kong was the first to jump into the economic integration bandwagon and gained importance as the provider of marketing and financial know-how for low-cost producers of the mainland. Many people thought the deal the British cut in 1984 to hand over Hong Kong to China amounted to a death sentence for the colony. Nevertheless, with the 1997 transfer date approaching, Hong Kong is booming. Western executives, Japanese financiers, and ethnic Chinese from Southeast Asia are all scrambling to Hong Kong. When much of the industrial world slogs through recession, "they see the city as the epicenter of an emerging twenty-first century economic superpower dubbed 'Greater China.' It would combine the capital, technology, and entrepreneurial wizardry of Hong Kong and Taiwan with the 1.2 billion-person market, cheap labor, and natural resources of mainland China."[52] According to China's official figures, trade between Hong Kong and the mainland increased 60 times from 1978 to 1993 and Hong Kong's investment in the mainland counts for 61.7 percent of the total foreign investment that China received by 1994.[53]

Nevertheless, China has never recognized the Hong Kong government and has maintained its claim for Hong Kong's sovereignty and signed agreements about refugee repatriation, water supply, aviation, and other issues, only with the British government rather than with the Hong Kong government. Hong Kong's return to Beijing was a decision made in 1984 between the British and Chinese government rather than a political spillover of the growing economic integration.

Taiwan's government has been very cautious toward economic integration, and its policy initially sought to retard the emerging economic exchanges with the mainland, while later accommodating a gradual opening. The Taiwan government began relaxing restrictions on trade, investment, and travel to the mainland only in 1987. The government liberalized indirect imports of mainland goods into Taiwan in June 1989. The green light for indirect investment and technical cooperation came in October 1990, allowing Taiwan businessmen to register with the government their investment on an approval list.[54] In contrast to some predictions at that time, the 1989 Tiananmen incident did not cut, but accelerated the development of the mainland's economic links with Hong Kong and Taiwan.[55] By 1993, Hong Kong and Taiwan ranked as the top two largest foreign investors in mainland China, which, in turn, became the main outlet for Taiwan's overseas investment, accounting for 65.61 percent of the total in 1993. Investment-driven trade grew from a low of $1.5 billion in 1987 to more than $10 billion by 1992.[56] This development triggered a proposal for a "Greater China Common Market" by a Taiwanese professor of economics in spring 1989. The idea generated excitement and considerable enthusiasm among some businessmen in Taiwan, while being totally consistent with the PRC policy of encouraging Hong Kong and enticing Taiwanese trade and investment in the mainland.[57] Nevertheless, the governments in both Taipei and Beijing never endorsed the idea.

Taiwan's official policy is to "promote people-to-people exchanges" without official contacts, which is systematically expressed in the "Guidelines for National Unification," promulgated by the Taiwan government in 1991. The guidelines divide progress in across-Strait relations into three stages, but no timetable is set. In the first stage, while the government should promote people-to-people exchanges, these exchanges "should not endanger Taiwan's safety and stability" or negate Taiwan's status as a political entity. In the second stage, while official communications should be established, they must be on an equal footing and both sides should "assist each other in taking part in international organizations and activities."[58] As Huang Kun-huei, Chairman of Taiwan's Mainland

Affairs Council, stated in 1993, "at the moment, relations between the two sides of the Taiwan Straits are in the first phase, the phase of people-to-people exchanges, so it is still not possible for the two sides to hold talks of a political nature."[59] With the asymmetrical nature of growing interdependence, political leaders in Taiwan suspect that Beijing's policy is "politically motivated," namely, "designed to deepen economic integration of the two entities and to create bargaining chips that can be used when the Communist leadership decides to push for unification."[60] They fear that an official endorsement of economic interdependence with the mainland will make it vulnerable to economic blackmail.

Beijing has never recognized the legitimacy of the government of Taiwan. It cannot officially endorse the CEA because that would imply an acceptance of Taiwan as a political entity (independent sovereignty) that the Taiwan government has claimed in recent years. Beijing's officials were concerned with the more and more open discussion of independence in Taiwan that followed political democratization and the easing of curbs on the media. At the APEC Seattle Summit in November 1993, Taiwan's Minister of Economic Affairs caused quite a stir with his references to "two sovereign nations across the Taiwan strait."[61] Chinese leaders persistently referred to Taiwan as a "province" of China. Therefore, although they view the growing network of people-to-people links across the strait "as a means of diminishing the risk that Taiwan would drift toward permanent separation from the mainland,"[62] they cannot sit together with Taiwan government as equals to negotiate institutional arrangements of the CEA.

Concerning the sovereignty dispute with Taiwan, Beijing was ambivalent toward any formal institutional arrangement in the CEA. With a soft regionalism of cooperation without formal agreement, Beijing could take advantage of economic interdependence with Taiwan and Hong Kong without triggering the sovereignty issue inherent in forming a structured economic bloc. For Beijing, Hong Kong and Taiwan are subordinate units of China and the CEA is really China. Economic integration came about spontaneously as a result of China's reform policies and fast economic growth. Under these circumstances, although the growing economic interdependence among the three components of the CEA has resulted in a de facto economic integration, the soft nature has been maintained and may not necessarily transform into a structured one.[63] It is an anomaly for the neorealists because in this case economic interdependence is not embodied in a mutually respected security regime and intimate economic ties have developed alongside a fierce contest in the political and diplomatic arena. Also, to the disappointment of neoliberal theorists, economic inter-dependence has so far done little to ameliorate tension and animosity across the Taiwan straits. The organizational form of soft regionalism in the CEA is largely determined by Taiwan's security concerns and the mainland's insistence on sovereignty. This is a case where security and sovereignty concerns outweigh economic interdependence.

THE STRUCTURED OPEN REGIONALISM OF APEC

The structured regionalism of APEC was developed largely in response to the emerging "institutional integration" of Europe and North America,[64] and as a result of conscious calculation of self-interest by large, medium, and small countries in the region. While economic interdependence in the Asian Pacific developed rapidly in the early 1980s, a structured and regionwide APEC did not take place until the end of the 1980s when difficulties in concluding the Uruguay Round GATT negotiation heightened speculation that the global economic system might move further toward regional trade blocs.[65] The renewed European integration encompassed all of Europe, and the Western Hemisphere encompassed both American continents. The development that could be most threatening to the East Asian economies was the emergence of a North American economic regionalism. Several East Asian nations planned to be annexed into NAFTA as associate members if they were invited. But the invitation never arrived.[66] The NAFTA agreement itself may not necessarily threaten East Asian countries, as Canada and Mexico already traded extensively with the United States, but a further enlargement of the agreement on a solely geographic basis could have serious implications. Thus, U.S. assur-ances that NAFTA would not discriminate against East Asia were "viewed with some skepticism."[67] As one observer put it, "Are regional free trade agreements 'building blocs' toward global free trade, or are they strategic economic groupings designed to become more competitive vis-à-vis other blocs? If the latter . . . how should East Asian countries and others not part of a major bloc respond?"[68] In frustration, both large and small countries in the region saw their interests lying in the negotiation of new regional, rather than multilateral, trade and other economic arrangements.[69]

Although the APEC idea started with the fear that the Asian Pacific countries would be left outside of emerging trade blocs, it was not clear if an institutionalized and regionwide organization of cooperation was acceptable to various countries in the region. Originally an Australian initiative by Prime Minister Hawke in 1988, APEC was proposed not as an institutionalized organization but as an intergovernmental forum. It was quickly picked up by the United States and was supported by Japan as well as some other East Asian countries. APEC was officially launched in 1989 with initial members from 12 nations: Australia, Brunei, Canada, Indonesia, Japan, South Korea, Malaysia, New Zealand, the Philippines, Singapore, Thailand, and the United States. In November 1991, APEC admitted China, Hong Kong, and Taiwan. In November 1993, Mexico and Papua New Guinea joined APEC, and Chile was admitted in 1994, bringing its members to 18.[70] APEC thus became an organization across the Pacific that involved all major powers in the Asian Pacific as well as the American Pacific.

A multidimensional undertaking with an extremely diversified membership, the establishment of APEC became a process involving intensive power competition in the region, which was seen clearly in two controversial issues: one is the choice between a loose regional forum and a formal regional institution; and the other is the choice between an inclusive open regionalism and an exclusive regional bloc.[71]

With respect to the first issue, APEC was confronted by two competing views: many East Asian members looked for a loose organization in which members encouraged one another to liberalize their trade and foreign investments without formal negotiations and commitment. They argue that the Asian Pacific region did quite well without formal institutional arrangements. Western powers, namely the United States, Canada, and Australia, advocated a "tougher and more formalistic regionalism."[72] This controversy was described by Singapore's Permanent Secretary of Foreign Ministry, Kishore Mahbubani, as a "tension between the institution-building impulses of the Anglo-Saxon participants and the consensus-building impulses of the Asian participants."[73]

At the second ministerial meeting in Singapore in July 1990, a joint statement referred to APEC as a "non-formal forum for consultation."[74] There were no binding agreements of any sort, no secretariat, no plans for heads of state to get together. APEC was at most a culmination of an "Asian-Pacific Diplomacy," composed of governmental and nongovernmental forces,[75] and provided a forum for discussion on a broad range of economic issues of importance to the region. Given those initial reservations, APEC has moved a very long distance in its short life, under the pressures of Western powers, from an informal dialogue group toward a more formalized institution. By the time the APEC ministers met in Seoul in November 1991, a permanent secretariat was agreed to be set up in Singapore (it was established in September 1992). Ten APEC working groups were established to develop activities that would contribute to its overall goal of expanding economic cooperation among the member countries. An Eminent Persons Group (EPG) was commissioned by APEC in 1992 to provide a vision statement for the 1993 Seattle ministerial meeting. The EPG's statement purported to advance institution-building efforts following President Clinton's proposal for a summit meeting of APEC, in spite of several ASEAN states' "suspicions of some hidden American agenda."[76]

The establishment of the APEC summit meeting system was a significant move toward structured regionalism. President Clinton's proposal for an APEC summit drew U.S. media comparisons to President Harry Truman's role in establishing postwar security and economic structures in Europe. One state department participant in the Seattle Summit was quoted as saying, "you have to think of this as a bit like being at a NATO meeting in 1950."[77] A "vision statement" at the inaugural APEC summit meeting in Blake Island near Seattle on November 20, 1993, looked forward to "deepening our spirit of community,"[78] in spite of the reservations of some East Asian leaders over the term *community.* The Seattle Summit decided to hold annual summits. Indonesia hosted the second APEC Summit on November 16, 1994, which led to the Bogor declaration of APEC leaders, which set the goal of free and open trade and investment in the Asian Pacific by the year 2020.[79] Japan held the third Summit in Osaka in November 1995.[80] Apparently, institutionalizing the summits increased APEC's momentum toward a more structured regionalism. In the words of C. Fred Bergsten, chairman of APEC's Eminent Persons Group, "the leaders in Seattle began the process of converting APEC from a purely consultative body into a substantive international institution."[81]

Institutionalization caused worry of some East Asian nations about being dominated by larger partners if APEC became a negotiating rather than a consultative body. In protesting President Clinton's initiative, the Malaysian government went so far as to boycott the Seattle Summit in 1993. The invocation of "community" in the Seattle vision statement also inspired much pre-summit agonizing behind the scenes, which forced the APEC leaders to make it clear that they did not aim at European federalist structures. In its 1994 report, the EPG explicitly retreated from the community concept in favor of the Chinese formulation of APEC as a "big family."[82]

Another controversial issue that APEC confronted was a global versus regional dilemma, crystallizing in competition between APEC and the East Asian Economic Group (EAEG), which was later recast as the East Asian Economic Caucus (EAEC).

APEC was created amid rising threats of protectionism and emerging international economic blocs. The march toward a single market in Europe and the free-trade agreement in North America gave impetus to a search for Asian alternatives. In the first phase of the APEC proposal, both Japan and some ASEAN countries were eager to create an exclusive East Asian bloc as a counterweight to Europe and North America, although some ASEAN members were equally concerned about Japanese or Chinese dominance in the region. This membership proposal was co-opted by Secretary Baker's midyear tour to Asia, which cast the United States as a catalyst for cooperation. The United States is not an Asian country but has crucial economic and security interests in the region. The sheer volume of Asian Pacific commerce gave rise to a U.S. idea of a Pacific community that encouraged likeminded, liberally oriented states to form a "building block" of worldwide trade liberalization on a nondiscriminatory basis rather than an inefficient trade block. This position was expressed by the U.S. government as "a vision of open regionalism,"[83] namely, a commitment of APEC to accept Asian-Pacific as well as American-Pacific members. A report of the Washington-based Carnegie Endowment for International Peace claimed that the decision to include the United States and Canada ensured that "APEC would not become a Fortress Asia, but a potentially important regional anchor for the global trading system."[84] Thus, open regionalism generally came to reassure the commitment of APEC not to be an exclusive economic bloc and not to follow protectionist policies that by definition discriminated against non-members.

In theory, open regionalism would prevent discrimination by ensuring that agreements at the regional level are extended to any country willing to reciprocate the terms of the agreement. But in practice, there are many questions about how it would work. What advantages would there be in APEC membership if one could enjoy the benefits separately? Would potential APEC regulations regarding internal economic practices such as government procurement and competition policy apply to non-APEC countries seeking agreement? In particular, some East Asian leaders are reluctant to accept the idea of open regionalism due to "the fear that APEC could be a field for power projection by the United States."[85] Kiyoaki Kiteuchi, senior advisor to Matsushita Electric and Japan's former Vice-Foreign Minister for Economic Affairs in the early 1980s, saw APEC as "a second Open Door policy recalling the U.S. attempt to open China to Western trade and investment in the 1890s."[86]

Malaysian leaders were skeptical of America's objectives in regard to open regionalism and expressed concern over the two-faced approach by the United States, which claimed to be an Asian Pacific nation yet formed its own exclusive trading group in the form of NAFTA.[87] In a 1991 speech to the UN, Mahathir said: "In East Asia we are told we may not call ourselves East Asians as Europeans call themselves Europeans and Americans call themselves Americans. We are told that we must call ourselves Pacific people and align ourselves with people who are only partly Pacific, but more American, Atlantic, and European."[88] That concern led Malaysian prime minister, Datuk Seri Mahathir Mohamad, to announce in December 1990 the idea of forming a bloc where only bona fide Asian nations are included and the U.S., and even Australia, are excluded. Mahathir named it the East Asia Economic Grouping (EAEG), and argued that EAEG, including ASEAN members, Hong Kong, Taiwan, Japan, South Korea, and China, would give greater bargaining power to East Asian countries in negotiations with the United States and Western Europe, which he felt were moving precipitously toward exclusive trading blocs.

Prime Minister Mahathir is known as the originator of Malaysia's "Look East" policy, which urges Malaysians to emulate the discipline of the Japanese.[89] Tempted by the opportunity to establish an advantaged position in East Asia's dynamic markets, Japanese leaders, in private, express interest, although publicly are wary of, Mahathir's idea. Former Japanese foreign minister, Saburo Okita who planned the postwar renaissance of the Japanese economy, wrote approvingly of the idea: "The EAEG was clearly formulated within a context of concern that Asia would be the loser as Europe and North America rushed to establish their own economic blocs."[90] Nevertheless, Mahathir's proposal caused much unhappiness in and was sharply criticized by the United States. Washington opposed the proposal with unusual vigor. James Baker, secretary of state in the Bush administration, wrote to Japanese Foreign Minister Michio Watanable and said that the EAEG would "divide the Pacific region in half" and asked Japan not to participate. He also put strong pressure on the government of South Korea to oppose EAEG.[91] Under these circumstances, most East Asian governments became noncommittal because they felt they could not risk alienating the United States.[92] Only China offered some support to Mahathir.[93] Some of Malaysia's ASEAN partners were troubled by Malaysia's confrontational leadership and preferred the large framework of APEC where they could benefit from American trade and investment while playing the United States off against Japan and perhaps China. ASEAN economic ministers met in Kuala Lumpur in October 1991 and agreed to a watered-down version of the Mahathir proposal as the East Asian Economic Caucus that could operate inside APEC.

Membership met on an ad hoc basis, as need arose.[94] In return, to mollify ASEAN's fears of domination by the United States, Japan, or China, APEC agreed to hold alternating annual meetings in a Southeast Asian country.[95]

Although the EAEG proposal was essentially abortive, the idea remained alive in nongovernmental circles, and there appeared to be a growing number of proponents. An EAEG was seen as the most important insurance against the perceived trend toward economic regional blocs in Europe and North America, exactly in the way Mahathir proposed it initially. Some believe that the coming of the Asian Pacific century led to the emergence of an East Asian economic community characterized by a high degree of regional integration, manifested at best by emerging East Asian production structures. Projections show that by the year 2000 or 2010, the combined GDP of East Asia will be as large as that of North America.[96] The controversy over open regionalism is not yet over.

The dispute regarding APEC's institution-building reflects a conflict of interests and careful calculation in choosing structured regionalism. Although the sheer size and diversity of nations in the region failed to prevent structured regionalism from emerging, it made institution-building a very complicated task. Within the group of 18 nations there were democratic, authoritarian, and Leninist regimes; Communist, Socialist, and market economies, and historic and contemporary enemies. APEC was the only such regional organization that included members who did not recognize each others' right to exist. This was most evident in the case of the three Chinas: the PRC, ROC, and Hong Kong. The three states did not recognize one another's legitimacy, therefore special arrangements were made to include the three important economies in APEC operation. Following the Seattle model (in Bogor and Osaka), Taiwan's and Hong Kong's top government leaders were not able to attend the summit meetings because the PRC found their presence unacceptable, so their senior economic and financial officials were sent in their places.[97] In addition, each nation came to the APEC negotiating table with a separate agenda beside regional economic cooperation. For example, in Seattle, China's president Jiang Zemin looked for the first summit meeting between China and the United States after the Tiananmen incident in 1989 and tried to secure its most-favored-nation (MFN) status from the United States, which was linked with its dismal human-rights record; Thailand's prime minister Chuan Leekpai came to Seattle looking for US maintenance of special tariff exemptions and to avoid the threat of U.S.-imposed trade sanctions; South Korea's president, Kim Yong Sam, wanted to confer with the United States, China, and Japan on the developing North Korean nuclear threat; Taiwan's representative, Vincent Siew, the economic minister, sought the opportunity to hobnob with the very leaders who did not recognize his government; and U.S. president Bill Clinton took the opportunity to present himself as an effective world leader to an increasingly skeptical domestic and international audience.[98]

East Asian leaders accepted the APEC idea due to their fear that their countries would be left outside emerging trade blocs in the world. However, unlike the European and North American regional institution-building that came into being at "big bang" conferences, structured regionalism in the Asian Pacific arose by a much more incremental process in which many controversies have had to be settled.

ASEAN AND REGIONAL SECURITY COOPERATION

The development of ASEAN was a success story of regional approach toward power competition in East Asia. Formed during the dark days of the Vietnam War at a meeting in Bangkok among the foreign ministers of Indonesia, the Philippines, Singapore, and Thailand and the deputy prime minister of Malaysia on August 8, 1967, "few observers predicted the political success that lay ahead (for) the five neighbors."[99] However, ASEAN proved to be highly valuable to its members. It enabled them to resolve or shelve contentions that plagued member-states. It raised the weight of each in the world arena and thereby the prestige of leaders in their own countries. The effect was to enable each of the member-states to devote substantially more energy to the problem each considered more pressing—nation-building or, as the leaders like to put it, increasing the nation's "resilience." To that end, the five founding governments hoped in time to attract to their ranks all the states of Southeast Asia. The sultanate of Brunei was admitted into ASEAN in January 1984. Vietnam, Laos, and Burma applied for the membership in 1993. In the first ASEAN Regional Forum (ARF) held in July 1994, Vietnam and Laos were encouraged to take part in ASEAN events as a step toward future membership.[100] Vietnam was officially admitted on July 31, 1995. ASEAN's record of facilitating peace in the region and cooperation among its members has made it "the most successful regional organization of developing countries since World War II."[101]

ASEAN operated in a decentralized organizational setting. Although it worked collectively with a regionalist spirit, being called ASEAN and dealing with many regional issues, leaders of ASEAN consciously avoided moving in the direction of meaningful institutionalization. There was not one transnational structure to which national decision-making authority was transferred. There was no ASEAN equivalent to Brussels. The centerpiece of this multilateral institution has not gone beyond creating a secretariat in Jakarta to bureaucratically support the work of the ASEAN committees and to hold regular top-level meetings, such as the annual ASEAN summits, the ASEAN ministerial meetings, and the ASEAN post-ministerial conferences. It was the limited level and nature of institutionalization that "led to some dissatisfaction with the pace of functional cooperation in the region and mounting criticisms from within non-bureaucratic but still elite ASEAN circles of the inadequacy of the structures created to foster cooperation."[102]

At least three views with respect to organizational choice can be identified in the history of ASEAN: constructionist, limitationist, and integrationist.[103] For constructionists, ASEAN's behavioral boundaries are set by the functionally specific inter-governmental activities covered by the Bangkok Declaration as executed through projects approved by the annual meeting of the ASEAN foreign ministers, ASEAN's managing executive authority. The limitationist view carefully distinguishes between ASEAN-sponsored activity and the other activities of the member states, excluding, for example, military cooperation as an ASEAN function. The limitationists deny any integrative goal. As the 1983 ASEAN Task Force reported: "ASEAN has no supranational objectives. Its aim is cooperation rather than economic integration, as the latter implies a degree of supra-nationality."[104] The integrationists fallaciously look to the European experience and would like to build ASEAN as a budding economic and political community. They are dissatisfied with the pace of functional cooperation in the region and criticize the inadequacy of the institutions created to foster cooperation. ASEAN's Singapore Declaration of 1992 responded to the criticism and pledged "to move toward a higher plane of political and economic cooperation to secure regional peace and prosperity."[105]

The limitationists used to represent ASEAN's official view while the constructionist view set practical boundaries of ASEAN's cooperative activities. Operating upon a combination of the two views, "ASEAN was the manifestation of a kind of regionalism in which the collaborating nations identified common functional areas where intergovernmental cooperation would be more efficacious in economic development and international relations terms than uncoordinated, unilateral state behavior."[106] Nevertheless the scope and nature of the limitationist view led to mounting criticism and the integrationist view gradually gained ground in the post–Cold War world. The progress was most strongly manifested in the evolution of multilateralism in the realm of security cooperation, "a topic long considered too controversial to handle in anything but bilateral fashion" in East Asia.[107]

The objectives of ASEAN, as set forth in the Bangkok Declaration, were to promote regional economic growth through active collaboration and mutual assistance on matters of common interest, but it has been difficult for it to remain devoid of political and security components. As a matter of fact, ASEAN came relatively early to focus its diplomatic efforts on collective bargaining with outside powers and followed a political-economic strategy of subregional cooperation. In the early years, security was uppermost in their minds but not conspicuously addressed. It was contemplated in practical terms as a byproduct of regional reconciliation. Nevertheless, after the end of the Vietnam War, while economic issues were still the organization's raison d'être, "security and political matters" also were on "the agenda of the annual ASEAN summit and the important series of post-summit meetings."[108] East Asia has been generally peaceful since 1975. According to one study, one of the pillars for this regional stability was the emerging regional scheme exemplified by ASEAN.[109] Although ASEAN was careful not to turn itself into a military alliance, it became a "security complex," meaning durable and relatively self-contained patterns of multilateral security cooperation generated by the local states themselves.[110]

ASEAN's goal of security cooperation gradually emerged as an explicit as opposed to an implicit organizational emphasis. The five founding governments were drawn together by a recognition of the self-defeating and wasteful nature of contention among neighboring states of a corresponding conservative political disposition. Although the ostensible purpose of establishing ASEAN was to promote economic, social, and cultural cooperation, regional security was the prime preoccupation of its founders. The relationship among the five states was one that might reasonably be termed "security interdependence, taking the form not of an alliance but of an entente, arising out of perceived mutual vulnerability."[111] In other words, these states were caught up in one web of interdependence, or what may be called regional security net. The most immediate and practical common security goal of the founding governments was to expand and stabilize the process of reconciliation that had paved the way for a political settlement to Indonesia's coercive challenge to the legitimacy of Malaysia between 1963 and 1966.[112] Practical utility was recognized in being able to manage and even overcome regional disputes and more deep-seated contentions through a structure of special relationships. This approach to regional security in its external dimension was joined to the instrumentality of economic development as a way of coping with its internal security.

This approach toward regional cooperation was rationalized by the concept of "collective internal security."[113] The original concept of collective security, identified with the ill-fated League of Nations, was meant to protect member states from acts of aggression by any of their members. It was conceived as an operational device for an intermural structure of security with membership envisaged in universal terms. Collective internal security was intended to do the same and more for ASEAN but not through the medium of sanctions as provided for in the League of Nations Covenant. A process of reconciliation in a regional approach was intended to counter any revival of serious contention between member governments. An attendant ability to address problems of domestic political stability through the mechanisms of economic development was expected to produce corporate as well as individual benefits. External adventurism would be discouraged. The contagion of internal political disorder would be prevented from spreading from an infected state to contaminate the body polities of regional partners, and from providing a point of entry to Southeast Asia for competing external powers.[114]

The founding governments of ASEAN perceived their most pressing international security need to be protection within their local environs from threats that might come from disorder in the region, namely, from invasions or revolutionary influences moving across national borders. "Ideal in the perception of each would be establishment of a zone in Southeast Asia in which all the subregional states would agree to respect one another's independence, give up the use of force to settle disputes with one another, and persuade all external powers not to intervene."[115] At a meeting at Kuala Lumpur in November 1972, the foreign ministers of ASEAN enunciated a declaratory policy for regional security of an extramural scope embodied in a formula to establish a regional "Zone of Peace, Freedom and Neutrality" (ZOPFAN).[116] This formula excluded any prerogative role in Southeast Asia for major powers. Devoid of operational relevance, this vague alternative proved to be an acceptable compromise. Its terms did not impose any practical obligations on member governments. As a statement of general aspiration only, none of those governments had a strong reason to quarrel publicly with the proposition that Southeast Asia should be insulated from the intruding rivalries of external powers and that its political destinies should rest in the charge of its resident states. This concept was consistent with ASEAN's working consensus of collective internal security.

Although ASEAN states saw their primary security problems as internal to each society, external threats attracted "more concern as the Soviet-Vietnam alliance solidified and China associated with the ASEAN position on Cambodia" in the 1970s and 1980s.[117] Vietnam's invasion of Cambodia on December 25, 1978, marked a turning point in ASEAN's attempt to assume a regional security role. The presence in Cambodia and Laos of up to 250,000 Vietnamese troops posed threats of intervention and subversion, most notably to Thailand, which for geopolitical and historical reasons considers the trans-Mekong region crucial for its security. Furthermore, the invasion and the subsequent Vietnamese campaign to wipe out the resistance forces sent droves of refugees overland into Thailand.[118] Nevertheless, the Vietnam invasion was viewed by ASEAN members, particularly on the part of Indonesia and Malaysia, with "mixed feelings."[119] Significant differences could be discerned within ASEAN between the "hawks," who wished to pursue relentlessly a policy of attrition to end Vietnam's dominance over Cambodia, and the "doves," who contended that Vietnam was not an intrinsically hostile state, had legitimate security concerns in Cambodia, and, if truly independent and satisfied, had an indispensable part to play in the containment of China and in the fulfillment of the ZOPFAN ideal.

The Vietnamese incursion into Thailand at Mon Mark Moon in June 1980 was a crucial turning point in that it served to dampen, if not to eliminate, debates and brought about a concerted set of ASEAN responses. The governments of ASEAN demonstrated an ability to speak and act most of the time with one voice over Cambodia. Broadly speaking, ASEAN successfully achieved its threefold objectives during the Cambodian crisis: enhancing Thailand's security against direct and indirect threats from Vietnam; promoting a balance of presence and interests among the Great Powers, seen to entail ultimately a curtailment and reduction of Soviet and Chinese influence in Southeast Asia; and bringing about more order in its relations with Vietnam.[120] During the process, ASEAN forged broad international coalitions to isolate and put pressure on Vietnam, including security coalitions with the United States, China, the Khmer Rouge resistance forces, as well as with Australia, Canada, the EEC, Japan, and New Zealand. In the meantime, the ASEAN countries improved their own armed forces and increased bilateral military cooperation among members. Drawing on regional credentials to deny international legitimacy of the administration carried into Phnom Penh literally in the saddlebags of the Vietnamese army, ASEAN played a crucial role in bringing peace to Cambodia in the 1990s. The ability to make such an impact as a diplomatic community was a product of the development and display of a collegial identity. It shows a dexterity that has allowed it to survive and grow stronger over the past quarter-century.[121]

The end of the Cold War made ASEAN's regional approach to power competition more important. The United States reduced its military presence in East Asia and concentrated on the economic challenge of Japan and other East Asian NIEs. In the meantime, there were opportunities for "confidence-building" among East Asian countries. Long-term prospects for regional peace depended increasingly on the ability of East Asians themselves to cooperate with one another and address contentious issues before they become crises. Under these circumstances, ASEAN's efforts in security cooperation gained a renewed imperative.

In the early 1990s, ASEAN demonstrated its flexibility by extending to its former principal enemy, Vietnam, membership (largely as a counterweight to the PRC in the conflict area of the South China Sea), and showed its independence by inviting Burma to be a guest at its ministerial meeting, over U.S. objections. When foreign ministers of Vietnam, Laos, Cambodia, and Myanmar (Burma) for the first time took part in the two-day ASEAN Ministerial Meeting in Bangkok on July 22-23, 1994, a newspaper report in Singapore suggested that "with Vietnam poised to become an ASEAN member, the grouping's expansion and regional security role have been highlights of its recent development."[122] Vietnam's entry was a prelude for Laos, Cambodia, and Myanmar to join ASEAN, which is now stepping up its efforts to enhance security and promote economic growth through a regional approach. One scholar indicated that "a mark of the institutionalization of the ASEAN security community is that fact that it has devised modalities for the incorporation of the Indochinese states into it without disrupting the basic patterns of ASEAN's broader collaborative activities."[123]

Most innovatively of all, ASEAN took the lead in Asian Pacific multilateralism in the realm of security. ASEAN ministers conducted a groundbreaking security dialogue with the major powers in the inaugural meeting of the ASEAN Regional Forum on July 25, 1994. The 18-member forum, including a range of countries at loggerheads: the United States, China, Russia, Vietnam, Japan, South Korea, and Australia, discussed confidence-building measures that could lead eventually to new security arrangements in the Asia-Pacific region. The historical meeting, chaired by Thailand's Foreign Minister Prasong Soonsiri, agreed to convene the forum annually and endorsed ASEAN's Treaty of Amity and Cooperation as a code of conduct for governing relations between states. According to the forum chairman's statement, the ASEAN treaty would be "a unique diplomatic instrument for regional confidence-building, preventive diplomacy, and political and security cooperation."[124] Major powers in East Asia showed their keen interest in the forum and dialogue. Chinese Vice-Premier and Foreign Minister, Qian Qichen, said in Bangkok, "The establishment of the ASEAN Regional Forum has provided us with a good opportunity. China is ready to work along with the other members and make positive contributions to the fulfillment of this important mission."[125] Japanese Deputy Prime Minister and Foreign Minister Yohei Kono also said, "Today, July 25, 1994, will become a memorable day for the Asia-Pacific as the birthday of the ARF. Let us confirm that we will make steady efforts together in order to rear this child called ARF after a year of gestation to an adult in its own rights."[126]

The establishment of ARF represents the coming together of the ASEAN consultative process and new post–Cold War regional anxieties, particularly in relation to major powers, such as China, Russia, Japan, and the United States. According to ASEAN's interpretation, it is not intended to have military functions, but rather to engage the major powers in a dialogue with each other and with smaller countries in order to build trust and facilitate communication on security matters. The regional approach to security cooperation is undoubtedly difficult, but the development of ARF is certainly a significant step toward a regionwide security cooperation.

THE REORGANIZATION OF EAST ASIA

The case studies of growth clusters, APEC, and ASEAN suggest that a regional approach toward power competition emerged in East Asia, albeit with elements of tentativeness, diffusion, and the coexistence of soft and structured regionalism. The experience to date with East Asian regionalism shows an evolutionary and multifaceted regional approach to power competition. The sheer size and extreme diversity were not daunting barriers for regional cooperation. Economic interdependence broke down Asian parochialism and encouraged East Asians to rethink their neighboring relationships in the terms of soft or structured regionalism although interdependence itself does not lead to structured regionalism. The realist image of anarchy is still the fundamental background condition of regional cooperation and power competition.

Seeking to preserve sovereignty and freedom of action, East Asian nations showed caution and flexibility in developing regional institutions. On the one hand, the movement to institutionalize Asian Pacific economic diplomacy in the form of APEC marked important progress toward structural regionalism, although it is still too early to predict the arrival of an Asian Pacific community. On the other hand, the movement to institutionalize regional cooperation coincided with the flourishing of soft regionalism in a variety of "growth clusters," including "growth triangles," "growth squares," and subregional economic zones. Some of these soft growth clusters made a transition toward structured schemes, such as the Tumen River Area Project. Others did not, largely due to political considerations. The de facto economic integration without formal agreement in the CEA was the most significant example. That development conformed to the basic outline of the neorealist argument that interdependence among sovereign states is as fundamental as anarchy in shaping international relations in the post–Cold War era.[127] The recent development of Asian Pacific regionalism also shows that while soft regionalism is still an important form of cooperation in the region, an institutional base for handling regional economic and security issues in the form of structured regionalism is rapidly emerging. The emergence of ASEAN as a regional security negotiating forum provides a powerful example.

The emergence of regionalism constitutes a significant structural and institutional development that may eventually lead to a substantial change in power competition. Nation-states are still the principal actors in the region and behave on the basis of perceptions of self-interest. Relative capabilities (realism's distribution of power) remain important, and states must rely on economic and political capacities to assure themselves securities and power from international relations. Nevertheless, regionalism has played an important role in changing conceptions of national interests. Each state has to find its proper place in a cooperative relationship with its neighboring state(s) and with regional powers, being structured or soft. In this situation although bilateralism is still pursued by every state, a structured multilateral approach has gradually taken hold. Now the question is whether the still fragile regionalism (in particular, the structured one) and the nationalist leaders of sovereign states can cultivate multilateral relations necessary to continue reorganization toward a prospering Asian Pacific of betterment and peace across a vast and crucial part of the world.

·10·

UNCERTAIN REGIONAL MULTIPOLARITY

Two intellectual fashions in the late 1980s made fascinating predictions about the post–Cold War world. One was Paul Kennedy's analysis in his 1987 book that the overextending of military strength had led to the decline of the Great Powers in world history.[1] Kennedy was perfectly right about the impact of military spending and "imperial overstretch" on the decline of the Soviet Union, so much so that the Soviet empire collapsed for these very reasons in 1990. Although this rapid collapse made less obvious the slow decline of the United States, "this does not mean that the United States is not declining."[2] In contrast to the two superpowers, taking economic development in command, East Asian NICs experienced extraordinary economic growth during the decades prior to the end of the Cold War. Nevertheless, the economic success has not reduced these countries' interest in military power. A study of military acquisitions in East Asia finds that the high rate of economic growth provided "the largesse for the weapons acquisition programs" and "the single best indicator of increase in the defense expenditures throughout the region" in recent years.[3] The arms buildup continued regardless, at the end of the Cold War. Nations of East Asia learned little from Kennedy's historical study and from the negative lessons of the superpower's military spending.

Another intellectual fashion was Francis Fukuyama's 1989 assertion about liberal triumphalism.[4] Fukuyama portrayed the end of the Cold War as a triumph of capitalism and Western liberalism and believed that the end of the Cold War was not just "the passing of a particular period of postwar history, but the end of history: that is, the end point of mankind's ideological evolution and the universalization of Western liberal democracy as the final form of human government."[5] As it turns out, Fukuyama was half-wrong and half-right. The collapse of the Soviet empire has not led all societies to become liberal democracies. More than a half decade after the end of the Cold War, East Asia is marked more by a diversity of political systems and governmental forms than by any unity. Some political scientists in the West argued that a world of liberal democracies would be a world in which war would be far less likely.[6] If this argument stands, it is not promising for the nations of East Asia residing in the democratic zone of peace.

Nevertheless, the collapse of communism in Europe indeed marked the conclusion of the Cold War, an era when power competition between capitalist America and Communist Russia dominated international relations. Although there are many reasons for caution against Fukuyama's argument on the end of history, the decline of ideology, defined in a narrow sense as "a set of cosmic ideas and values that provide a comprehensive guide to thought and action,"[7] indeed has been one of the major trends of recent decades in all East Asian countries, as leaders of these nations grappled with problems pragmatically on a nationalist basis. Economic growth and military security are the ultimate national goals of most East Asian societies. Any ideological appeal, including that of liberal democracies, has to be judged by its utility to the pragmatic goals of nationalist interests. Liberal democracy has been rejected ironically by some pragmatic East Asian leaders on the basis that "democracies can be resistant to change, and, as demonstrated by Russia, even prevent rapid economic development."[8]

Regardless of how scholars have judged and will revise the post–Cold War images of Kennedy and Fukuyama, the changing role of the military and the decline of ideology have been real and have made important revisions on the power competition in the post–Cold War world. The image of East Asian international relations that emerged in the post–Cold War era was largely a neorealism of rational, self-interested states that typically behave in a prudent way. Heightened incentives for international economic involvement increasingly overrode long-standing ideological cleavages and transformed foreign policy rhetoric of state. Nevertheless, economic primacy did not inspire an erosion of the military-territorial state or conventional forms of power competition. While there is a trend toward more dependence on economic instruments, very few East Asian countries reduced or even stopped increasing their military capabilities.[9] As a matter of fact, after the superpower rivalry vanished and increased resources were available from economic growth, East Asia was "rushing to arm itself as never before."[10] Along with the military modernization of regional powers, East Asia moved toward an uncertain regional multipolarity in which the rise of regional (local) powers coincided with the retraction of global (outside) powers from the region. In the new round of power competition, the global dimension of strategic competition became less relevant to regional power competition, and worldwide power distribution did not necessarily govern the *regional* distribution of power. After superpower confrontation vanished in the post–Cold War era, the cost of old alliances to the superpowers was no longer justifiable. Therefore, rigid alliance yielded to flexible alignment. The successful management of alignment was vastly more complex than that of earlier alliance, and will continue to be a serious challenge to the political leaders in the region.

THE DISTRIBUTION OF POWER IN POST-COLD WAR EAST ASIA

The end of the Cold War irrevocably altered the distribution of power in East Asia. Although the new power configuration has not taken its final shape, in strategic terms, the vanished superpower bipolarity and China-America-Soviet triangle gave way, not to unipolarity, but to a regional multipolarity. With the collapse of the Soviet empire and a substantial retraction of American power, regionalized power competition became dominant. This is in line with the general trend of the post–Cold War world observed by Christensen and Snyder that "regional multipolar processes are likely to become a more and more important feature of international politics."[11] In the movement toward regionalized power competition, the regional (local) powers played more and more important roles while the global (outside) powers tended to restrain themselves in pursuing their concepts of world order.

The rise of the Asian Pacific regional powers, particularly China and Japan, attracted world attention in the past decade. China became a key player in the strategic triangular relationship during the 1970s and 1980s. Although the end of the Cold War temporarily eliminated Beijing's immediate strategic importance to both Washington and Moscow, the demise of the strategic triangle has not reduced China's importance in the Asian Pacific power competition.[12] Chinese policy during the years after Tiananmen in 1989 reveals Beijing's continued capacity to act independently of the United States and other powers. In many respects, it scorned America's pressure to accommodate itself to U.S. national interests. Despite Beijing's bellicosity, the United States and other advanced industrial countries lifted their sanctions against China and restored normal diplomatic relations. In spite of repeated threats, the Clinton administration renewed China's MFN status unconditionally in May 1994. In addition, China played an important role in resolving local conflicts, as in Indochina and on the Korean Peninsula. Its immense population, historical self-consciousness and sense of destiny, improved military capability, and rapid economic growth make it a formidable power competitor in Asian Pacific international politics and give Chinese leaders greater confidence in the attainment of China's national defense and Great-Power aspirations.[13] China demonstrated its regional power position in the post–Cold War Asian Pacific. This was evident in the way that it has handled territorial disputes in the South China Sea. Gerald Segal observed that "leaving aside the validity of China's claims, Beijing's regular resort to force in seizing islands appears designed to signal that China will be ruthless in taking what it claims to be rightfully its own." One U.S. Atlantic Council report in 1995 believed that "China is becoming a powerful regional and international player with a rapidly growing economy and a significant military capacity."[14] China's aspirations for Great Power status drew upon strong "nationalist sentiments, traditional cultural ethnocentrism, and a deeply rooted historical sense of injustice at the hands of foreign (especially Western) countries."[15] In view of such aspirations, one Western China-watcher raised the oldest problem in diplomacy: "how the international community can manage the ambitions of a rising power."[16]

Japan is another rising regional power with significant global influence. Cold War bipolarity and triangularity obscured the discrepancies among the country's economic, military, and political weights. After the end of the Cold War, the United States continues to provide the security guarantee, but the reason to do so has steadily become less obvious as time goes on and "the residue of Cold War strategic mentality dissipates."[17] With continuing attenuation of American protection, Japan was pushed toward more normal regional power status. Japan began to sense its destiny and its lopsided economic clout gave it the weight of a hefty Great Power in the regional affairs: "As part of their search for a national identity appropriate for the post–Cold War era, influential (Japanese) intellectuals are increasingly emphasizing Japan's social and cultural affinity with East Asia."[18] This development was known in Japan as New Asianism. Japan's militant effort to use power developed during the Meiji Restoration to force its way to the top of the global hierarchy ended in disaster, but the trauma of that defeat quickly faded. The end of the Cold War moved Japan away from its "moratorium state" status—a state that is passive and reactive diplomatically and minimalist in terms of defense policy.[19] One report by the government-funded RAND Corporation in California found that Japan emerged as a more "normal" country, that wielded "political-military influence more commensurate with its economic power."[20] Its overseas investment and economic assistance programs grew dramatically: "In 1989, with net official development assistance (ODA) disbursements totaling $9 billion, Japan replaced the U.S. as the world's top donor nation for the first time in the history of development aid."[21] Japan's willingness to provide financial support for America's crusade against Saddam Hussein underscored both Tokyo's greater role and America's economic feebleness in international affairs. Japan's 1992 interpretation of its constitution to allow the dispatch of troops to serve the United Nations in Cambodia may open a new era.[22]

Along with the rise of regional powers, global powers either temporarily disappeared from or imposed self-restraints in the Asian Pacific power competition. The former Soviet Union was a casualty of the Cold War and temporarily lost global power status. As its successor, Russia has been preoccupied with internal transformation and troubled Central Asian and European problems. In the long run, if Russia solves its problems, it may return as a strategic heavyweight in the region. But its clout is unlikely to grow as fast as China's and Japan's, at least looking from the perspective of the near future.

The United States is the only global power in post–Cold War East Asia, but it tends to self-restrain when pursuing its own concept of world order, which was costly in economic and human terms during the Cold War, particularly during the Korean and Vietnam wars. Although the United States is still the single richest and strongest nation in the post–Cold War era, the size of America's economic and military leads has diminished as regional powers grew faster and as the United States reduced its armed forces in the region. The end of the Cold War lifted the burden of an ongoing military confrontation with the other superpower. Without the challenge of the Soviet Union to contend with, America's military forces were reduced. The major justification of the American presence, after all, was to deter the Soviet Union. With the decay of Russian military forces, the rationale for the American military presence largely disappeared. In September 1991, President Bush announced a global initiative on nuclear weapons reduction. Such weapons would be removed from South Korea and from surface ships in the Pacific, thus eliminating a source of friction with Japan, which banned port calls for nuclear-armed vessels. The most important military bases in the Southern Pacific–Clark Air Field and the Subic Bay naval facility, both in the Philippines–were closed in 1991 and 1992. In early 1990 Secretary of Defense Richard Cheney announced that 5,000 of the 43,000 American troops in Korea would be withdrawn. The Pentagon's 1992 plan for a global "bases force" called for a 25 percent reduction from Cold War levels in overall military strength in East Asia.[23] With the reductions of the American forces, being the single richest and militarily strongest nation in the post–Cold War Pacific, the U.S. global power no longer translates into "local dominance."[24]

The architecture of America's strategic role in the Asian Pacific after the Cold War was likened by former Secretary of State James Baker to a fan spread wide, with its base in North America and radiating West across the Pacific. The spokes of the fan connect the United States to its regional allies while "connecting these spokes is the fabric of shared economic interests."[25] A 1995 U.S. Department of Defense report confirmed this architecture. The report reaffirmed that East Asia will have a "stable forward-deployed force of about 100,000 United States personnel, backed by the full range of capability at the ready for the United States Pacific Command."[26] The main East Asia outposts are Japan with 47,000 troops and South Korea with 37,000. But how stable this security architecture can remain is uncertain. At every turn in his weeklong trip to Asia in early November 1995, Defense Secretary William Perry confronted the question of whether or not "the Clinton administration could blunt a growing public pressure to force at least [a] token US troop cut."[27] The pressure stemmed particularly from the conviction of three U.S. servicemen for the September 4, 1995, rape of an Okinawan girl. In this case, although America's strategic role for regional stability in the post–Cold War era remains, the United States has been far from a hegemonic power in the region. While Washington felt most comfortable with a traditional bilateral relationship, it recognized the necessity of multilateral approaches to regional security. In practical terms, the United States led, or joined in, ad hoc multilateral efforts of states dealing with particular regional security issues. The UN permanent five negotiations on Cambodia is one case and U.S. coordination of pressure against North Korea on the nuclear issue is another.[28] Richard Solomon, former assistant secretary of state for East Asian affairs in George Bush's administration, properly described the new role of the United States in the region as that of "balancing wheel" and "intercessor," rather than hegemonic security guarantor.[29]

In light of the rise of regional powers and the decline or self-restraint of global powers, East Asia is moving toward regional multipolarity in which the United States, China, and Japan are the leading players, and Russia is a potential major player. In addition, ASEAN has evolved into a major player with the initiative of the ASEAN Regional Forum (ARF) in 1994 in which the ASEAN engaged the major powers in a dialogue with each other (in particular, China, Russia, Japan, Russia, and the United States) and with smaller countries on security matters.[30] There is no single factor contributing to the East Asia regional multipolarity. Rather, there are a number of factors involved, among which are regional defense self-reliance efforts after the retraction of the U.S. forces, military modernization related to economic prosperity, and the rise of pragmatic nationalism.

AMERICAN RETRACTION AND REGIONAL DEFENSE SELF-RELIANCE

The retraction of an American presence and the consequent regional defense self-reliance efforts are two of the most important factors that contributed to the rise of regional multipolarity. Although reductions in U.S. military forces was a logical response to the end of the Cold War, the demand for U.S. military presence remained. Although the American presence became attenuated as the flag came down from Philippine bases, land- and sea-based tactical nuclear weapons were removed, and defense budget cuts trimmed the number of forces regularly stationed in the neighborhood, it by no means implied that America's strategic role in the region was diminished. America's postwar dominance in East Asia, used to being justified as a deterrent to Soviet ambition, had an equally important function of keeping apart the traditional regional rivals: Russia, Japan, and China. The retraction of the United States from the region, to a great extent, triggered off concerns over regional security and stability. Some small- and mid-sized East Asian countries worried that "America's retreat will remove the buffer" that stands between Tokyo and Beijing and that "there is no apparent successor to play this role."[31] An American strategist suggested that "with the end of the Cold War, the case for an American military presence . . . became in some ways even more compelling."[32] There was a pervasive—though probably false—belief within the region that a withdrawal of the United States would leave a "power vacuum" into which aspiring regional powers would seek to move.[33] The departure of the U.S. forces created pressure within each of the Asian Pacific countries to strengthen itself, if only out of fear that if it failed to do so, others would. Each country was tempted to arm itself preemptively, as insurance against threats arising from others doing the same thing.

In this situation, many Asian Pacific countries have determined to enhance their defense self-reliance capacities to deal better with regional contingencies on the basis of their own resources. Several regional powers, such as China, Japan, Indonesia, and Vietnam, adopted policies of self-reliance or national resilience prior to the end of the Cold War and continued their military modernization programs. China and Japan, the two major regional powers, were particularly active in strengthening their military capacities.

China has boosted its defense budget since the late 1980s. Beginning in 1989, China's official defense budget increased annually at a double-digit pace. In its annual budget report to the National People's Congress in March 1994, Chinese Finance Minister Liu Zhongli budgeted 52.04 billion yuan for defense spending in 1994, representing an increase of 22.4 percent from 42.5 billion yuan in 1993. The increase in 1993 was 14.8 percent.[34] Many analysts believe that the official defense budget is not a good indicator of Chinese military spending because "much of military related R.&D. is not included in the defense budget and the Chinese military has a good deal of indigenous funding to support itself."[35] Most analysts believe that China's total defense spending is about two to three times its official budget.[36] One American China-watcher indicated that China's official military expenditures doubled between 1988 and 1993, from $3.8 to $7.3 billion, with double-digit spending hikes in each year of that period.[37] With its increased military budget, China is buying and selling weapons at a fast clip, seeking naval facilities closer to the Malacca Straits, and developing rapid-deployment battalions. It is believed that China has been able to project its capacities to the entire region.

As a matter of policy, Japan's defense spending remained around 1 percent of GNP, but rose from $21.9 billion to $32.6 billion from 1980 to 1990 because of Japan's rapid economic growth.[38] Japan "alone among the rich countries . . . is still increasing its defense spending in real terms."[39] In its five-year plan for defense spending for the first half of the 1990s, announced in December 1990, the Japanese government proposed a growth rate of 2.7 percent per year, although it was only roughly half the previous rate of increase.[40] According to one U.S. government study, at $39.7 billion, Japan's 1993 defense budget was more than three times as large as Korea's, the second-largest regional defense budget at $12.1 billion. At $7.5 billion, China's official defense budget was fourth largest, behind Taiwan's $10.5 billion budget.[41]

The increasing power projection capabilities of Japan and China generate considerable disquiet among their East Asian neighbors. Their concerns about China are based on its increased military capacities as well as its claims to sovereignty over disputed areas. China is a nuclear power and continues to develop its nuclear delivery capacity and expand its military, particularly its naval, capacity. Its potential to shape the international system will be important to the region in the post–Cold War era. China's firm claim of sovereignty over Taiwan, its continued interests in Indochina, and its contested territorial claims in the South China Sea have caused concern among neighboring countries.[42] The region was shocked by China's military exercise in July-August 1995 when Beijing fired six M-9 ballistic missiles, capable of carrying nuclear warheads, to target zones about 60 miles from Taiwan where no effective defense against such a missile system existed.[43] Asian concern about Japan is largely based on its history of militarism and a cultural tendency toward aggression. They are concerned that Japan's defense of its sea lanes out to 1,000 nautical miles from Tokyo might lead to the development of an independent Japanese military capacity. They fear that Japan might add military muscle to its economic domination of the region and "they will not accept a condition where Japan's regional military role becomes commensurate with its economic role."[44]

Some countries, such as Taiwan, South Korea, and several Southeast Asian nations, feel a compelling need to counter regional powers with their own capacities. Many of these countries went through the Cold War dependent upon the United States for their defense against Communist aggression. Defense planning was done in Washington or Honolulu, and operational concepts and doctrines were formulated by the relevant U.S. commands. Now, however, self-reliance dictates military buildup, including the construction of national command centers and joint force headquarters in many East Asian countries. Under these circumstances, in contrast to the reduction of military expending in the United States, the military expenditures of East Asian countries are growing dramatically. According to one study of the U.S. government, between 1987 and 1993 the defense budgets of the global power, the United States, fell by 28 percent (the 1993 U.S. defense budget was $258. 87 billion), while the Asian Pacific regional defense spending rose substantially. Figures for countries vary but are convincing. The defense budgets of Thailand, Singapore, Malaysia, and Indonesia increased in real terms by 34.5, 53.6, 89.6, and 10.6 percent respectively. Taiwan, South Korea, and Japan also showed substantial increases in their defense budgets of 24.1, 35.9, and 16.8 percent, respectively.[45] The dramatic increase in defense expenses enabled regional powers to compete with global powers and made middle and small nations important players, which contributed to the movement toward regional multipolarity.

ECONOMIC PROSPERITY
AND MILITARY MODERNIZATION

The rise of regional powers and movement toward regional multipolarity was propelled by changes in the underlying distribution of material resources in many East Asian nations due to the extraordinary economic growth during the past decade. The sustained high rates of economic growth have not only substantially increased budgetary resources for defense self-reliance efforts but also urged many East Asian countries to modernize military forces to protect economic prosperity from external threats. In addition, military modernization also promoted civilian production capabilities.

With the economic prosperity achieved in recent years, many East Asian countries have been putting their "wealth in military."[46] The high rates of economic growth provide one of the most important indicators of military modernization efforts. In the case of Southeast Asian countries, for example, a series of studies of the relationship between defense expenditure and economic growth from the early 1960s through the late 1980s consistently showed a close and positive correlation between them.[47] Those countries with the highest rates of growth of GNP, such as Singapore and Malaysia, had the highest rates of increase in defense spending, while those with slower economic growth, such as Indonesia and the Philippines, had the slowest increases in defense spending. As a matter of fact, Singapore's defense budget was officially pegged at 6 percent of GNP.

The success of economic prosperity not only provided more resources but also created a necessity to deal with increasingly urgent national security issues in a favorable domestic environment. As a result of economic prosperity and effective counterinsurgency programs, many East Asian countries face diminished internal threats to their security and legitimacy. At the same time, these nations find their economic prosperity increasingly tied to military modernization efforts, especially to high technology equipment of air and navy forces in protection of navigation and the maritime resources contained in their exclusive economic zones. These economic and security interests took on additional importance ever since the implementation of the 1982 UN Law of the Sea Convention, which for the first time defined the concept of an archipelagic state and allowed many regional states to claim 200-nautical mile Exclusive Economic Zones (EEZs) in the regional seas.[48] One *International Defense Review* analysis on the dispute in South China Sea found that the Law of the Sea Convention ironically may be partially responsible for the dispute taking place over the

Spratlys. According to the convention, an EEZ may be established around islands only if these are capable of supporting human habitation. It can be argued that clays and sandbanks, some of which disappear at high tide, and have no fresh water, cannot support a human community, but disputants would claim there is no bar to external support for nationals placed on what they claim to be sovereign territory. Therefore, that study asserts that "in its present form, the Law of the Sea tends to complicate the tangles in the South China Sea."[49]

Indeed, as maritime resources, territories, and sea lanes become more important, East Asian nations seek to protect them from potential threats by air or sea. As a result, they seek to acquire maritime patrol and response capacities needed to intercept intrusions into areas of interests, to help protect offshore territories and resources, and to keep hostile forces away from their territories. Thus, many East Asian countries concluded that the current security concern "requires greater preparation for limited local wars and unanticipated low intensity conflicts, and that these contemporary wars and conflicts require quick-reaction forces structured around high technology arms and equipment."[50] A focus on modern maritime and air forces to support new economic and security interests in the surrounding seas replaced earlier emphasis on ground forces oriented to internal security.[51] In Southeast Asia, defense forces were "restructured from counter-insurgency capabilities to modern, high-technology forces, with increased emphasis on maritime (including land-based air) capabilities."[52] South Korea, where the principal military threat is a land offensive across the Demilitarized Zone (DMZ) by the North Korean Army, plans to allocate some 60 percent of the increasing defense budget in 1993-98 to the Air Force and Navy, rather than "the usual 40 percent."[53]

The military modernization efforts, particularly efforts to acquire advanced military technologies, also played an important economic role of facilitating the development of indigenous civilian production capabilities. As a U.S. government report indicates, military and civilian manufacturing activities in some Asian countries are closely connected. Many recent acquisitions of advanced weapon systems in Asia have a clear technology transfer purpose.[54] A study of Sino-Japanese-U.S. military technology relations found Japanese officials often elected to produce sophisticated U.S. weapon systems in Japan instead of buying them from U.S. sources even though the unit cost of such items produced in Japan is higher because Japan gains more than it loses over time by procuring greater access to U.S. technology and by significantly reducing its research and development (or "learning curve") expenditures in the process.[55] Military modernization has thus been related to technological modernization in many East Asian nations.

Given the military modernization efforts sustained by increasing resources and mandated by economic prosperity, East Asian countries have become major importers of modern weapon systems. In conjunction with declining defense spending in the United States, Europe, and the former Soviet Union since 1989, the Asian Pacific's share of the world military expenditure on arms imports was doubled from 15.5 percent in 1982 to 34 percent in 1991.[56] The arms imports for military modernization have been described by some observers as a regional arms race. One newspaper article says that there is a "new Asian arms race" underway that "bodes ill for a region already racked by ancient animosities and border disputes."[57] Countries in the race may well be caught by the classic security dilemma. Since the requirements for defense self-reliance cannot be defined without some consideration of the capacities possessed by neighbors and potential adversaries further afield, the defense modernization efforts in a few East Asian countries have generated counterprograms in others. Thus, the new East Asian arms race could be profoundly disturbing and come to the detriment of both self-reliance and regional security. It may become worse because the wave of putting wealth in military is proceeding in an atmosphere of uncertainty and lack of trust. Uncertainty and suspicion are fueled by a lack of transparency in the region about long-range objectives and motivations behind the current acquisition programs, as well as particular force elements of these programs.[58] Nevertheless, it seems difficult to control military modernization in East Asia because most of these countries can provide not only the strategic justification but also increasing economic resources for it. In this situation, the interactions between economic prosperity and defense modernization efforts gave rise not only to regional powers but also to the regional insecurity.

THE RISE OF PRAGMATIC NATIONALISM

The decline of conflicting ideologies and the consequent rise of pragmatic nationalism is another factor that contributed to the emergence of regional powers in East Asia. In the Cold War era, the political structure of the state and ideological value attached to it influenced the process by which decisions were reached as well as the content of those decisions. The foremost task for each nation was to resolve or contain conflicts in national interests that were defined largely in ideological terms. The end of the Cold War started a new era of international relations based not essentially on ideological differences but on pragmatic nationalism. The Soviet Union was created by individuals in whose minds the vision of a unified Socialist world burned brightly, but that vision dimmed since the bureaucratic administrator Gorbarchev came to power. For first-generation Chinese revolutionaries, the goal was liberation of the Chinese people and the nation within the framework of the international Socialist movement. Now Maoism has been in decline and Deng's query, "will it work?" dominates the scene. In its foreign relations, Beijing changed from doctrinaire Communist internationalism to a pragmatic emphasis on patriotic and national interests.[59] During the height of the Cold War period, the U.S. containment policy in East Asia was framed mostly on the anti-Communist ideological base. After its withdrawal from Vietnam, the United States showed its suspiciousness to cosmic theories and was prone to pragmatic approaches in its Asian policy. For Japan, the zenith of the ideological era was reached only during the 1930s when a mythological past was built into a rationale for a corporate state and regional dominance. Defeat in war ended old dreams and has brought a new era of pragmatism to Japanese foreign policy.

In certain parts of the world, the decline of secular ideology resulted in the reemergence of religion as a powerful political force. Fundamentalist Islam, Christianity, and Judaism have moved forward to answer the need for a set of values—a faith—that can sustain individuals in a time when old moorings are being swept away.[60] For societies like China and Japan, however, with Confucian backgrounds, religion has always played a lesser political role in their foreign policies. In contrast to many parts of the world, the common denominator that can be most clearly identified in major Asian Pacific states and that shows evidence of being on the ascendancy is not politicized religion but pragmatic nationalism. The rise of Asian nationalism is in part a reflection of the region's diversity, its geographic dispersal, its troubled past, and its lack of the kinds of soothing interconnections that have existed for some time in Western Europe. In this case, the end of the Cold War brought about not only the victory of capitalism and Western liberalism but also the rise of pragmatic nationalism.

Upon reflection, it is not surprising that nationalism became the single most powerful political force in post–Cold War East Asia, notwithstanding growing interdependence among nations. Nationalist tides in East Asia are running swiftly, under the push of pragmatist political leaders. In a sense, nationalism is a reflection of and is strengthened by East Asian pragmatism. For example, East Asia's remaining Socialist leaders have been "downplaying—or completely jettisoning—Marxism-Leninism in favor of resorting to nationalist appeals in an effort to bolster faith in a system in trouble."[61] In China, in particular, the essential foreignness of Marxism-Leninism to Chinese culture was revealed and the Communist government was forced to rely heavily upon nationalism. Deng Xiaoping and his successor, Jiang Zemin, moved quickly to stimulate Chinese nationalism and to channel it toward support of their regime. Imbedded in Chinese nationalism are certain traditional feelings that can be revitalized, including anti-foreign sentiments. When conservative Chinese leaders warned citizens against foreign forces that would subvert Chinese socialism by infiltrating the society using the technique of "peaceful revolution," they hoped to strike a responsive chord among a people that have periodically struck out against those external forces that earlier penetrated China in one form or another. Deng's regime sought to "position itself as the worldwide representative of Chineseness" since the Tiananmen Incident, which resulted in sanctions against China by the Western countries.[62] The clearest example of Deng's success in identifying his regime with Chinese national pride was his bid to become host to the year 2000 summer Olympic Games in Beijing. China failed to get the games, and Chinese popular resentment was directed at foreign countries and human-rights groups whose bullying was blamed for the failure. As much as it can, the Beijing government presents itself as the guardian of pan-Chinese economic interests, including China's entry into the GATT (renamed the World Trade Organization in 1995), and maintenance of the low-tariff treatment on exports to the United States, known as MFN status. In the same fashion, when North Korean leaders speak of socialism under *juche* (self-reliance), with "iron-clad unity around one leader, one party, one nation," they are making a traditional appeal to people that have lived in a country once known as "the hermit Kingdom."[63] These nationalist appeals are ironically more pragmatic than nationalistic.

In Japan, where low-posture politics have been in vogue, a revitalized nationalism can be discerned. Here, as in South Korea, newer generations are imbued with the "can do" spirit, and their essential optimism about the future manifests itself in a variety of ways, including self-confidence that brooks no individual or national slights. The high economic growth has given rise to a renewed pride in Japanese cultural values and promoted a new nationalist mood in the land that was fed by writers urging a more assertive political role in the world since the 1970s.[64] Some pragmatic Japanese political leaders have named the mood "political nationalism," which emerged along with the development of "economic nationalism." Political nationalism argues that Japan should acquire military power commensurate with its new economic strength and should exercise an independent political role in the world. The political nationalists have advocated clear and decisive resolution that touches deep and ambivalent emotions among many Japanese: "Japan had lived for decades under a constitutional order forced on it by occupying military forces. It had abnegated the essential characteristics of a nation-state: military power and the required loyalty of its citizens."[65]

In the face of the pragmatic impulse of nationalism, ideology as a universally applicable theory has declined. The successful insertion of nationalism in the post–Cold War era has made regional powers act more independently in their relationship with each other and with the global powers. When the Cold War subsumed strategic competition in East Asia, although China and Japan could enjoy relatively independent roles, they were never independent of the strategic relationship imposed by the outside superpowers. Now regional powers no longer contend with the prospects of an epochal struggle over which of two universalist value systems would dominate the region as well as the world. They contend solely in their pragmatic and nationalist considerations of an intrinsic interest in the place itself rather than a derivative interests in the place as it affects the worldwide balance of power defined by the relationship between the two superpowers.[66] Regional powers inspired by pragmatic nationalism have grown more easily as major players in the post–Cold War power competition. The leading regional powers, such as China, Japan, and ASEAN, are competing (and collaborating) for the sake of intrinsic national interests. Outside powers such as the United States, remain major players in East Asia not because of a derivative interest in balancing other superpowers or caring about Japan's security, but because of the need to compete with the regional powers for intrinsic interests.

THE MOVEMENT FROM ALLIANCE TO ALIGNMENT

Uncertain as the regional multipolarity is, global military strategies are more or less being decoupled from regional conflicts. The old alliances are no longer assured because the costs of the old alliances to superpowers are no longer justifiable. Although the United States, as the remaining global power, stays as an active Pacific player, it still has to search for a new role and justification. Russia, abandoning its hegemonic aspirations, appears to be in full retreat from previous alliances and forward deployments. As ascending powers, though on different dimensions, China and Japan are still seeking their places and proper roles as regional powers in a changing world, while the two Koreas, the Indochinese nations, and Southeast Asian states have "concentrated on establishing their own autonomous subregional orders."[67]

This development is conducive to a trend of profound significance taking place in East Asian international relations, namely, the movement of international relations from alliance to alignment. At the end of World War II, both the United States and the Soviet Union created alliances that were tightly constructed, with a major power guaranteeing extensive military and economic support and receiving in return pledges of faithful allegiance. These alliances were exclusive, leading to the coinage of such terms as "camps." Increasingly, in recent decades, especially after the end of the Cold War, relations between great powers and the states affiliated with them have been marked by a growing measure of fluidity. The guarantees of military and economic support by the major party, even where required, are less absolute, being generally couched in conditions and limited in nature. On the other side, obedience or allegiance to the "benefactor" has also become more conditional, with the quotient of independent action or separate, even conflicting positions rising.

The movement from alliance to alignment has been clear in the uncertain development of regional multipolarity in post–Cold War East Asia. During the Cold War era, U.S. alliance goals were straightforward: "to create a series of primarily bilateral security agreements that would serve as a *cordon sanitaire* around the Soviet Union and the PRC as well as their allies in North Korea and Indochina."[68] It was hoped that these alliances would deter any expansionist designs on the parts of Moscow, Beijing, Pyongyang, and Hanoi. Where deterrence failed, the United States fought protracted wars in Korea and Vietnam with mixed results for Washington's future alliance commitments. The Cold War era, no matter if it was strictly bipolar, or loosely quadrilateral and triangular, produced something of a division of labor among East Asian states, with individual nations assigned well-defined roles to play. The United States and the former Soviet Union faced each other as adversaries. Japan and Korea were the frontline of a defense against communism, and American troops in the Philippines, Korea, and Japan were there to keep the region stable both from internal and external threats. China, the balancer, could ally with the United States against any growth in Soviet power and ambition. "The loyalties and alliances and relationships were clear and changed only slowly, if at all."[69] In such a context, smaller East Asian nations as well as regional powers, even thought they chafed under their superpower's influence, understood clearly their role in the power politics. With the confrontation between the two superpowers came imposed stability; they stood for mutually understood roles and alliance relationships.

Changes in the alliance relationship took place since the late 1970s. It was caused by changes in the situations of the United States as well as the East Asian nations. President Nixon's 1969 Guam doctrine, formatted to cope with the disappointments and trauma of the Vietnam War, underlay America's changing Asian strategy through the 1980s. It promised military aid to friendly and allied states to assist in the creation of their own capacities to defend against potential Communist aggressors, but it no longer guaranteed direct U.S. military involvement in the event of hostilities. Both the decision to go to war and its prosecution became the responsibility of East Asian leaders, not American leaders.[70] Another change came in the 1980s when America's Asian allies became important economic competitors. In the context of the Cold War competition, the United States subsidized the early industrialization of its Asian allies' economies by providing preferential access for their products in the American market and permitting protectionism against American goods and services in Asian markets. These policies encouraged American, Japanese, and European multinational corporations to establish export industries throughout East Asia whose primary consumers were in the United States. Indeed, during the 1980s, exports to the United States generated by these East Asian countries contributed substantially to the current U.S. balance of payment deficit. This situation complicated the alliance relationships that were established over the Cold War years. As one scholar observes, "the key issue for U.S. strategic planners dealing with Asia" in recent years has become "whether alliances and economic rivalry can coexist."[71]

Since the end of the Cold War, the change continued and became so dramatic that the old alliance rules no longer applied in East Asian international relations. China, Japan, Russia, and America, as well as the two Koreas, Taiwan, Vietnam, and the ASEAN countries, are all trying to make sense of what has taken place, what it augers for them, and are seeking new rules, new order, and new relationships. In the early 1990s, Russia had its attention primarily fixed on Europe and the Atlantic world. "Given the scale of the problems facing the Russians, it will be some time before its Asian policy becomes a priority."[72] China focused on its own economic development and political stability while reaching out to be a regional power with its new economic and military capabilities. The ASEAN states and Vietnam moved toward a new rapprochement as the latter abandoned its plan for Indochinese hegemony and agreed to a UN permanent five plan for resolution of the protracted Cambodian imbroglio. In spite of the crisis caused by the nuclear device in the North, the two Koreas continued in their negotiation of peaceful coexistence. While the United States retained a western Pacific military presence, these forward-deployed forces increasingly depended on financial payments from Japan and South Korea. As the 1995 U.S. Defense Department report claimed, "In the post–Cold War era, the United States began to share responsibility as well as benefits of global and regional security with its friends and allies . . . Japan and the Republic of Korea contributed to regional as well as their own security when they provided generous host-nation support for United States forces."[73] Japanese and Korean subsidies for American forces in their countries permit the U.S. government to make the case to Congress that it costs less to maintain these forward-deployed forces in the western Pacific than to repatriate them.[74]

These changes confirmed Scalapino's observation in the mid-1980s that, in East Asia, "the general trend is from alliance to alignment, and that central fact colors many of the political relationships of the region."[75] The alliance gives way to alignment but not to nonalignment, because, despite rhetoric, nonalignment is invariably a myth and virtually every nation tilts and has a relationship closer with some countries than others. It is no longer necessary, or indeed possible, however, for most states to pledge absolute allegiance to either superpower or to a regional power with which they are aligned, or for that superpower or regional power to guarantee complete protection and support. The dismantling of the alliance structure, nevertheless, does not mean the cessation of power competition and international politics. On the contrary, the transition through which the world now moves may be potentially more unstable than its Cold War predecessor. Clear lines between old allies and enemies are obscured as the former may become commercial competitors and the latter may be new trade, aid, and investment partners.

In light of the uncertainty in the post–Cold War movement toward regional multipolarity, just as exclusive alliances of the earlier type have become more difficult to maintain, so alignments become a more necessary form of relationship, especially among pragmatic national leaders of differing political systems or economic interests. The relationships that dominate international relations of the post–Cold War era are those in which commitments on all sides are conditional, with a premium upon forbearance, concessions, and above all a continuous process of consultation. Within the general context of East Asia, three patterns of political alignments are emerging. First, the pattern of the American-Japanese relationship, which still is as close to an alliance as possible in our times. It is not the old alliance of the Cold War era, however, because, although Japan depends to a certain extent on the United States in security and political terms, it competes fiercely with the United States for its own economic interest. Second, the pattern of the Sino-American and the Sino-Japanese relationships, in which China maintains close relationships with America and Japan in economic and strategic terms while it seeks to ward off the political influences that flow from that fact, and competes for its independent political and economic interests. And finally, the pattern of alignment centering upon the ASEAN, a subregional security arrangement whose members have categorically rejected an alliance option ever since its very first existence. While ASEAN has been expanding to include Indochinese countries after the end of the Cold War, the relationship among member states is more like alignment than alliance.

From this perspective, it is increasingly appropriate to speak of alignments rather than alliance in the uncertain movement toward regional multipolarity of post–Cold War East Asia. The successful management of alignments is vastly more complex than that of earlier alliances. It requires a capacity for compromise, an acceptance of difference, and, above all, a willingness to consult and to develop genuinely collective policies.

TOWARD A REGIONAL MULTIPOLARITY

In Western academic circles on issues of the post–Cold War international relations, "discussion of the impending return to regional multipolarity has this far centered almost exclusively on Europe."[76] Neorealists believe that the end of the Cold War means a return to multipolarity and the beginning of a new era of conflict among major European powers. Neoliberalists foresee rising levels of integration and harmony in Western Europe and, ultimately, in Central and Eastern Europe as well.[77] The study of East Asia regional multipolarity can learn a lot from the literature of the European regional system. There are many similarities as well as differences in the development of regional multipolarity between Europe and East Asia. The classic European multipolar systems preserved peace (when the balance of power was maintained) but also produced wars, sometimes not only small wars for limited ends, but big, system-shattering struggles. Now, there appears to be an abundance of factors at work in Europe that have served to mitigate the troubling tendencies to which multipolar systems have often been prone in the past. Some scholars worry that many of these same soothing forces are either absent or of dubious strength and permanence in East Asia. Friedberg suggests that "while civil wars and ethnic strife will continue for some time to smolder among Europe's peripheries, in the long run, East Asia may be the cockpit of multi-power conflict. The half millennium during which Europe was the world's primary generator of war (as well as of wealth and knowledge) is coming to a close. But, for better and for worse, Europe's past could be Asia's future."[78]

Some East Asian political leaders defy this comparison and believe that "this tendency to extrapolate the future of East Asia and the Pacific from the past of Europe reveals an intellectual blindness: the inability to see that non-Europeans may have reached a stage of development where they can progress without having to repeat Europe's mistake."[79] Indeed, what is true of Europe may not be true of East Asia. The workings of regional multipolarity in East Asia could turn out to be far different from those of its European counterpart. Nevertheless, the destination of the movement toward regional multipolarity in post–Cold War East Asia is still uncertain and not in favor of the neoliberalists. Neoliberal models of international relations suggest that the primacy of economic development should influence the pattern of international politics in the region in predictable ways. One set of predictions that concerns East Asia are models of "trading states" or "civilian powers" that should tilt away from a concern with territorial acquisition and military capacities in favor of national goals defined in terms of economic welfare. Given economic success in many of East Asian countries, one might expect to find lower dependence on military capabilities and decreased concern over issues of territoriality. Nevertheless, in the wave of defense self-reliance and military modernization efforts, "one can find little evidence overall of their increasing 'civilization.'"[80] East Asian countries, especially the regional powers, still seem to cling to the "old" goals of territory and military power to defend their national boundaries. Although each is motivated by self-defense, the defensive objective can be perceived as offensive by its neighbors and they may still be caught by the "old" security dilemma to fall into "the war trap" described by Mesquita.[81]

As a matter of fact, the widely held belief that an era of peace was not only emerging but would be in some sense be self-managing in the post–Cold War era has already given way to more sober judgment, helped not only by the regional arms race but also by emerging East Asian nationalism. Reduced superpower influence and threat have increased the importance of the two great regional powers—Japan and China—both maintain or have resurrected territorial claims in the region, and both are large or growing economic and military powers. Along with the decline of ideological confrontation and the rise of nationalism, these two great regional powers "are becoming more central to the concerns of the smaller countries" in East Asia.[82] There is a fear of the possibility that there could be some form of arms race between China and Japan in the first decade of the twentieth century that would inevitably embroil the rest of the region. Confusion was caused by the lack of common threat perceptions throughout the region. "Some countries are more concerned than others about Japan's power-projection capabilities, some are more concerned about increasing Chinese capabilities, and some are more worried about the plans and intentions of their nearer neighbors."[83] In the mid-1990s, "China is at the center of the post–Cold War security calculations of all East Asian regional actors," because it is a rising power and "there has never been a rising power quite like China that has [a] 1.2 billion population with a nuclear arsenal."[84] The expression of a new "containment" has been applied increasingly to China.[85]

In this situation, while the end of superpower confrontation removed a layer of antagonism from East Asian regional disputes and reduced the likelihood of global war, the development of uncertain regional multipolarity probably increased the likelihood of local wars and conflicts. The shift from alliance to alignment removed the tempering mechanism that often served to keep regional powers under control. Without the constraints of alliance, regional powers are free to use force while still keeping conflict at the local level to settle regional tensions involving competing sovereignty claims, unresolved territorial disputes, and challenges to government legitimacy. The dismantling of the alliance between the superpowers and the regional states has resulted in the search for a new type of alignment relationship in the region. As regional powers develop further, the situation could become more complicated if alignments are fluid. Without stable alliances led by superpowers or regional powers, the balance of power in the regional multipolar system could be very complicated. The vulnerability of the structure to quick realignment could make the regional multipolar system shaky and dangerous. How to manage the flexible alignment relationships has been a major subject of inquiry for political leaders in the region as well as the international relations theorists.

AMERICA AND EAST ASIAN POWER COMPETITION

This chapter focuses on America's involvement in the East Asian power competition during the historical period covered in this book. The long-standing pursuit of cultural, economic, and military policy objectives by the United States highlights the three dimensions of power competition discussed in the first chapter of this book.

Geographically speaking, the United States does not belong to East Asia, but it is a Pacific country. Americans were involved culturally, economically, and militarily in the Asian Pacific region since the eighteenth century. As a 1995 U.S. Department of Defense report indicated, "The United States has been the pre-eminent Pacific power since World War II, but our interests in the region date back more than two centuries."[1] When the United States was only a few years old in 1784, a United States trading ship, the *Empress of China,* inaugurated commercial ties with China. The first American missionary arrived in China in the early 1820s. The United States emerged as an active participant in East Asian economic and security affairs following its victory in the Spanish-American War (1898) and its acquisition of the Philippine Islands. Subsequently the United States involved itself in the settlement of the Russo-Japanese War, in the decade of Japanese aggression leading up to the Pacific War and the consequent Occupation of Japan, in the Korean War, and in the Vietnam War. In the wake of the Cold War, the United States has attempted to redefine its Pacific identity and to remain a partner of East Asian dynamism.

In the process of involvement, the United States policy turned into a long-standing pursuit of three sets of objectives. Winston Lord, assistant secretary for East Asian and Pacific affairs in the Clinton administration, put these objectives into three terms: "*security, prosperity,* and *freedom.*"[2] Robert G. Sutter, senior East Asian policy analyst in the American Congressional Service, elaborates on these three overarching goals: first, in the security arena, the United States has remained concerned with maintaining a balance of power favorable to U.S. interests and opposed to efforts at domination of the region by hostile powers; second, the United States has endeavored to advance its economic interests in the region through involvement in economic development and expanded U.S. trade and investment; and, third, the United States has tried to foster democracy, human rights, and other trends deemed culturally progressive by Americans.[3]

These three policy objectives coincide with the three dimensions of East Asian power competition. Looking at broad trends, we can see that the priority given to each of these dimensions in America's East Asian policy has been changing over time. American leaders varied in their ability to set priorities and organize policy objectives as part of a well-integrated national approach to East Asia. Examining the history of U.S. involvement in the region, we find a pattern of shifting priorities of U.S. objectives from commercial and cultural interactions to military intervention, and to a revival of commercial and cultural competition. In an early period, American policy goals were based upon idealism and priorities were determined largely by commercial and cultural interests. After the breakout of the Pacific War, the United States set aside idealism and its involvement stressed the role of military power and the primacy of strategic and security interests. Since the end of the Cold War, economic interest, and, to a less extent, cultural interest, have returned to be as important as military security in U.S. policy priorities. As Winston Lord stated to a business audience in 1995, "security remains central but economic interests are ascendant and the spread of freedom enhances both."[4]

EARLY INTERESTS DEFINED BY MERCHANTS AND MISSIONARIES

Merchants and missionaries defined U.S. interests in East Asia throughout the eighteenth and the nineteenth centuries. The United States, as a new country seeking rapid economic development, was first lured to East Asia by the region's trade potential. John Adams wrote to John Jay in 1785, "there is no better advice to be given to the merchants of the United States than to push their commerce to the East Indies as fast and as far as it will go."[5] By 1800 American merchants were converging on China from both sides of the Pacific and sought a way to benefit from the existing trade privileges that the European powers had established in China. Because European monopolies there limited American trade, the U.S. government focused on Japan and hoped that the North Pacific Ocean might become "a vast American lake," the bridge to the wealth of the Far

East from trading and whaling.[6] Commodore Matthew C. Perry, who successfully pried open a door to Japan in 1854 that was closed to foreigners for more than 200 years, wrote that "When we look at the possessions in the east of our great maritime rival England . . . we should be admonished of the necessity of prompt measures on our part . . . Fortunately the Japanese and many other islands in the Pacific are still left untouched by this gigantic power; and as some of them lay in a route of commerce which is destined to become of great importance to the United States, no time should be lost in adopting active measures to secure a sufficient number of ports of refuge."[7]

During the early period of interactions with East Asia, the United States, endeavoring to be seen as a nation interested in peaceful and friendly dealings with the world, focused primarily on commercial and cultural affairs, such as trade, tourism, and missionary endeavors. "Military and related diplomatic considerations played only a minor role and were almost always subordinate to commerce and shipping. Economic activities, in turn, were secondary to cultural relations."[8] American trade with Asia never amounted to more than a few percent of total U.S. trade and America's Pacific venture added up to "no more than one-tenth of the nation's maritime enterprises,"[9] whereas thousands of Americans went to Asia as missionaries and in other capacities to bring American civilization to Asia. The U.S. initiatives in this regard were timely in that Japan, China, and Korea were in the midst of the process of modernization—a process that benefited from the presence of American educators, scientists, engineers, travelers, and missionaries who offered East Asian elites and others needed advice and information. Thus, in the first phase in their encounter, which ended with the nineteenth century, although America and East Asia met at three levels: strategic, economic, and cultural, the cultural dimension was clearly the most significant.[10]

Religious fever, called by Tang Tsou as "a humanitarian idealism,"[11] was the major component of the cultural impetus for Americans coming to East Asia. The American missionary community found expansive territory for Christian conversion.[12] The religious and cultural basis of colonial America, the Protestant ethic, was nurtured by the proselytizing of heathen souls. Native American Indians had been earlier candidates for the proselytizing of religious zealots. The thousands of "heathen" souls in China and Japan presented an even more bountiful challenge. But American missionaries were not successful in either China or Japan. Christian conversions never represented more than a fraction of the populations of either country. Yet the missionaries, however distorted their views, were "instrumental as cultural bridges between America and the civilization of East Asia."[13]

In the mid-nineteenth century, the principal foreign-policy goals of the United States were shifted to foster lucrative trade and establish American trade rights. With commercial goals, the United States set out to maintain a trade presence in China and develop political relations with the Japanese that would support U.S. trade interests in China. The United States thereby became a party to the system of "unequal treaties," which the Europeans established in China and other East Asian countries and which these countries' nationalists and communists of future days would resent so bitterly.[14] Yet for years to come Americans assumed self-righteously that East Asians favored them over Europeans because the United States government had not won their privileges by using armed force.[15]

Regardless of the Americans' self-righteous feeling about not using armed force, commercial expansion was regarded by the Chinese and other East Asian nationalists as imperialist because it was backed by the emerging U.S. military capability. The United States emerged as a Pacific power starting from its war in the Philippines in 1898, when America's international behavior and diplomacy departed from the continental boundaries envisioned in Washington's Farewell Address. The Spanish-American War in 1898, in John Hay's words, was transformed from "the splendid little war" to liberate Cuba from Spanish oppression into a war in the Pacific "to civilize and protect not only their close neighbors, the would-be independent Cubans, but the recalcitrant Filipinos, who, it was at last realized, dwelled seven thousand miles away from California on the doorstep of China."[16] As The Washington Post noted, the war meant "an imperial policy, the Republic renascent taking her place with the armed nations."[17] The settlement of the generation-old Samoa problem, the annexation of the Hawaiian Islands, the Philippines, and Guam further asserted America' position as a Pacific power. Thus the United States embarked on her policy of imperialism and became an imperialist power in the region. William H. Seward, stressing U.S. interest in the Pacific, said, "This ocean, its land were fated to become the chief theater of events in the world's great hereafter and that America must command the empire of the sea, which alone is real empire."[18] Observing a more intense competition with Germany, Russia, and Great Britain for the market of the Orient, Commodore Matthew C. Perry urged not only the annexation of Hawaii but that of additional naval stations off the Asiatic coast such as the Ryukyu Islands and Taiwan as a measure of positive necessity for the sustenance of American maritime rights.[19] Increasingly involved in competition for overseas trade, the United States viewed its expansion to the west as essential—a fulfillment of its manifest destiny.

Before the outbreak of the Pacific War in the 1940s, in spite of the imperialist nature, the U.S. interest in East Asia was limited to a desire for economic gain and the cultural expansion. Although the United States had military capabilities to challenge European trade monopolies in East Asia, it did not use them because "the US war in the Philippines created public sentiments that would not support further US military activity in the region."[20] Consequently, the U.S. government faced the task of establishing a policy that protected U.S. trade rights but did not threaten the use of force. The Open Door policy was designed to serve this objective. The architects of the U.S. Open Door policy were John Hay, secretary of state in the William McKinley administration, and William Rockhill, Hay's advisor on Asia. They drafted a series of famous Open Door notes in 1899-1900. Hay's first note, dated September 6, 1899, asked Japan, Russia, Germany, Great Britain, France, and Italy each to sustain a policy of equal trading opportunity for all nations within their spheres. Hay's second Open Door note went out on July 3, 1900, during the Boxer Rebellion amid widespread anti-foreign violence and the prospect that the powers might dismember China in retaliation. This time Hay appealed for China's independence and suggested that the actions of any country should not jeopardize China's sovereignty.[21] Thus, the principles of the Open Door policy notes were twofold: first, the demand for equal opportunity to trade and the opposition to monopoly; and second, the respect for the Chinese territorial integrity.[22] These two principles served as the basis of U.S. actions in East Asia for the next 40 years. The United States thus sought the advantages of a sphere of influence in China through diplomatic notes instead of military force. The other powers, including Russia and Japan, recognized the self-serving nature of the U.S. policy overture in China. None, however, was willing to challenge the new military strength of the United States by rejecting U.S. diplomacy. So although the goal of the Open Door policy was to establish a U.S. sphere of interest in East Asia that excluded the use of force, "it was the perceptions of US military might that facilitated the acceptance of Hay's Open Door Doctrine by the European powers, Russia, and Japan."[23]

American involvement in East Asia without the use of force reached its peak when President Theodore Roosevelt received the Nobel Peace Prize for his effort in achieving a peaceful settlement between Russia and Japan in 1905. The U.S. government and public support was grudgingly with Japan when the Russo-Japanese War broke out in 1904. The United

States had regarded Russian advances in Manchuria as a threat to Chinese sovereignty and to the U.S. Open Door policy. Moreover, U.S.-Russian relations had been considerably strained by the Russian attempts to intrude on the Sino-American commercial treaty. Yet the Japanese represented such a different culture that full U.S. support for the Japanese position was held in check: "For many Americans, the Russians were wrong, but they were white and their culture was easier to relate to than that of the Japanese."[24] Thus, victory by either Russia or Japan could present a threat to U.S. trade interests in China. It was on the basis of this perception that Roosevelt sought to place the United States in the position of mediator between Russia and Japan. To maintain a balance of power in East Asia, neither Japan or Russia could be totally defeated in the war. President Roosevelt's effort resulted in the Treaty of Portsmouth on September 5, 1905. Roosevelt's role in the resolution of the conflict enhanced America's commercial interests by an active participation in the politics of East Asia.

MILITARY INTERVENTION
MANDATED BY STRATEGIC INTERESTS

The priorities of American objectives in East Asia shifted from commercial and cultural activities to strategic and military involvement beginning with America's fight of the Pacific War in 1941-45. Although thousands of American soldiers and sailors experienced warfare in the Philippines and many thousands served during the Boxer uprising in China at the turn of the century, East Asia was never considered crucial to American strategic interest until the late 1930s when growing Japanese hegemony in the region and its southward expansion strategy severely threatened U.S. security and commercial activities. The Pacific War set the priority of military involvement in U.S.–East Asian relations. Militant, postwar fear and hatred of communism led the United States to participate in the Korean and Vietnam wars.

The period between World War I and the Pacific War was a time of transformation, during which the American experience in East Asia gradually became as much military as economic and cultural. Woodrow Wilson pursued an idealist and new isolationist policy after he assumed the presidency in 1913. He was preoccupied with holding together the League of Nations and establishing the American role in peace maintenance in the post–World War I world. In 1917, the United States concluded the Lansing-Ishii agreement, which acknowledged Japan's special interests in China and accepted Japanese predominance in East Asia as long as America's economic interests were not disturbed. From an American standpoint, the Lansing-Ishii agreement promoted the principle of the Open Door policy in China and made sure that China would offer equal and unrestricted access to all foreign powers.[25] However, the Open Door policy at that time, in Akira Iriye's words, was considered "America's confession of its lack of military power in East Asia and its inability and unwillingness to become militarily involved on the Asian continent." Iriye indicates that the United States was trying to "play the role of an Asian power without military backing."[26] Wilson diplomacy in Asia was characterized by one scholar as "moral imperialism."[27] Taking advantage of Wilsonian moral imperialism and, later, the U.S. government policy of avoiding direct military confrontation, Japan launched its Greater East Asian Co-prosperity Sphere in an attempt to establish a Japanese empire. Facing the Rising Sun, U.S. security and commercial interests were seriously threatened.

After the Japanese attack on Pearl Harbor in 1941, the Wilsonian idealist reaction to Japanese militarism gave way to a new realist vision authored by President Franklin D. Roosevelt. The United States became more willing to augment its armed forces and to be involved in East Asia to protect its strategic interest. President Truman's successful strategies to win the war with Japan did not end the U.S. military presence in the region, nor did the defeat of Japan ameliorate the perceived threats to U.S. strategic interests in East Asia. With Japan's defeat in 1945, a power vacuum was created in the region. The result was a surge of nationalism and independence as East Asian nations, previously held as colonies by European powers and Japan, struggled to establish their own independence. This rise in nationalist movements created political and economic instability that should not have represented a serious threat to America's strategic interests. Coupled, however, with the shift in the international balance of power and the emergence of a bipolar Cold War power competition between the United States and the Soviet Union, it created a new perception of threat to U.S. strategic interests in East Asia. The Soviet Union and Communist China would replace Japanese hegemony and threaten U.S. security and economic interests.

For the next two and a half decades, America's East Asian policy was mandated by military-strategic considerations. The "loss of China" set the stage for this strategic interest, the Cold War and the confrontation with China and, indirectly, with the Soviet Union, on the Korean Peninsula provided justification for its continuation. Failure of the policy in Korea encouraged an attempt at its vindication in Vietnam. During the entire period of the Cold War, East Asia became part of a global anti-Soviet coalition led by the United States. American troops and bases were maintained in Japan, Korea, the Philippines, and Taiwan. Japan was encouraged to rearm. The United States became more willing to protect its so-called strategic interest in the region even at the cost of military intervention. President Johnson's statement that America stood ready "to defend an honored cause—whatever price, whatever the burden, whatever the sacrifice that duty may require"[28] expressed America's determination. Mandated by the "honored cause" of strategic interest, thousand of American troops were sent to Vietnam to fight an interventionist war. The Vietnam War pushed U.S. military intervention policy to the extreme and also brought East Asia into focus for American policymakers. American Cold War confrontations with China and Soviet-backed regimes in the region temporarily shifted U.S. foreign policy from a Eurocentric to an East Asian focus. Policymakers were forced to give high priority to the East Asian region where military victory became the central element of policy goals.

During the four decades from the 1940s to the 1970s, the United States fought its three most devastating wars in the twentieth century. Two of them were a result of the military intervention policy mandated by strategic interest. "The defeat of Japan, the Korean War, and the Vietnam War were all inextricably linked in U.S. foreign policy in East Asia."[29] The three wars marked the rise and fall of the military priority in U.S. East Asian policy.

THE REVIVAL OF ECONOMIC PRIORITIES

The defeat of the United States in Vietnam, augmented by the end of the Cold War itself, revived one of the older priorities: commercial exchange and a favorable trade balance. Although economic prowess has not replaced military power in shaping international relations, Japan and other East Asian NIEs' postwar economic miracles have unsettled many Americans by introducing a new, competitive set of circumstances. China's re-emergence as an economic giant and the mounting impact of East Asian regional cooperation also combine to compound America's disquietude.

The end of the Vietnam War experience for the United States represented a turning point in American foreign policy in East Asia. They were forced to rethink the use of direct military intervention as a hedge against Soviet and Chinese Communist expansion. President Johnson's statement about the military readiness for the "honored cause" had to be reassessed against the actual costs of that sacrifice relative to the outcome. Richard Nixon began a new chapter in U.S. policy toward East Asia with rapprochement with China in 1971. The Nixon Doctrine of less direct involvement in political conflicts reduced the U.S. military presence and eventually proclaimed an end to U.S. military intervention in Vietnam as well as in all of East Asia.

The end of the Cold War brought about a new transformation of U.S.–East Asian relations. With the rise of the East Asian NICs and the trade war with Japan, the priorities of the U.S. policy shifted toward a revival of economic interactions and competition. Considerations of economic competitiveness and, to a lesser extent, American values and culture, have once again become as important as, if not more important than, strategic and security interests. In his remarks to a business audience in Indonesia on November 16, 1994, President Bill Clinton said that "for five decades after the Second World War, our presence in Asia was intended to help guarantee security and to allow prosperity to take root." While "the United States will honor its commitments to Asian security, it is also a fact, and a healthy one, that the balance of our relationship with Asia has tilted more and more toward trade."[30]

Just after the Pacific War, many Americans viewed East Asia as a burden to the United States. Poverty and high population densities threatened to turn the region, at best, into a steady drain on American resources, or at worst, into a vast Communist challenge to the West. Nevertheless, after the end of the Cold War, East Asia became, in an American scholar's words, "America's biggest competitor and possibly the engine that could put it and other Western economies from their recent malaise."[31] Indeed, the United States trades more with the East Asia region than with any other region in recent decades. U.S. trans-Pacific trade first surpassed trans-Atlantic trade in 1980. In 1992, U.S. trans-Pacific trade rose to $344 billion, 51 percent more than trans-Atlantic trade of $228 billion.[32] U.S. investment in the East Asia region almost doubled from 1988 to 1993. More than 40 percent of U.S. trade was with Asia, including exports worth $120 billion, in 1992-93, accounting for more than 2.5 million U.S. jobs.[33] Only 25 years ago, total U.S. trade with all of East Asia was less than that with Latin America. In 1992, U.S. trans-Pacific trade was three times as much as U.S.–Latin American trade.[34] At the 1994 APEC summit, President Clinton gave a group of astounding figures to illuminate the importance of the U.S. economic involvement in East Asia. According to him, one-third of the U.S. exports already went to Asia, supporting more than two million American jobs. Over the next decade, Asia could add more than 1.8 million jobs to the American economy—jobs that pay on average 13 percent above non-export-related jobs. In this context, President Clinton called for the United States to "remain ever more committed to deeper, and deeper, and deeper economic, political, and security engagement in Asia."[35]

Vital economic interest compelled American leaders to reiterate America's Pacific identity in recent years. Warren Christopher, Clinton's secretary of state, stressed that "America is a Pacific nation, and our stake in the region is enormous," because he believed that "no region is more important to the United States and its future than Asia and the Pacific."[36] A report to Congress by the Department of Defense in 1992 stated that "by virtue of geography and history, the US is a Pacific power with enduring economic, political and security interests in the Asia-Pacific region."[37] To pursue its economic interest in the Asian Pacific, the United States has been a key participant in APEC. After assuming the APEC chairmanship in 1992, the United States proposed and sponsored the first APEC Summit Meeting in Seattle in November 1993. U.S.–ASEAN dialogue meetings occur about every 18 months and traditionally include participants at the subcabinet level. These meetings provide opportunities for U.S. government officials and private sector representatives to discuss a broad range of economic issues with East Asian partners. In addition, the United States shares a leading position in the Asian Development Bank with Japan and maintains its share of the bank's capital and the Asian Development Fund, which the bank administers.

Nevertheless, there was still a host of policy problems for the United States as it sought to adjust its policy priorities in relation to countries in the region. These problems derived not only from national indebtedness and a perceived decline in U.S. economic competitiveness relative to the dramatic growth of Japan and other East Asian economies, but also from the difficulties of U.S. leaders to approach East Asians in a changed post–Cold War environment. Despite its auspicious promise of reinvigorated engagement, the Clinton administration's approach to East Asia added to East Asian ambivalence about the United States. It set out the economic priority, but tried to pursue multiple, often contradictory, policy objectives at once.[38] As a result, over the course of the Clinton administration's first two years in office, American sensitivities found voice in unusually public economic and political disputes with China (over most-favored-nation trade status, human rights, weapons proliferation, Taiwan issue), Japan (trade), Singapore (the caning of a U.S. citizen), Indonesia (labor rights, trade, and human-rights violation in East Timor), Thailand (drug-trafficking), Myanmar (political legitimacy), and more generally over differing approaches to human-rights, labor rights, and the environment. In practice, "difficulties balancing the pursuit of interests and the imposition of values have robbed U.S. policy of cogency and resolve even when the right decision is made,"[39] as seen dramatically in May 1994, when Clinton boldly reversed his stance on China's human-rights record to grant it MFN status.

The difficulty in re-assigning economic priorities to U.S. objectives in East Asia is not only a result of a "clash of civilizations," but rather a lack of understanding of changing context of power competition in East Asia. Fortunately, as a Singapore scholar official put it, "Americans are an open-hearted and compassionate people."[40] The compelling force of geoeconomics and the exchange of information are creating a new calculus and redefining U.S. interests in East Asia. A clear-eyed pursuit of U.S. interests will lay the best basis for realizing broader economic, security, and cultural objectives in a region that is certain to be one of the decisive voices in twenty-first century international relations.

Notes

Preface

1. Office of International Security Affairs, Department of Defense, *United States Security Strategy for the East Asia-Pacific Region* (Washington, D.C., USDP/ISA/AP, 1995), p. 1.
2. Among many recent books making this argument, see Mark Borthwick, *Pacific Century: The Emergence of Modern Pacific Asia* (Boulder, CO.: Westview Press, 1992); William MaCord, *The Dawn of the Pacific Century: Implications for the Three Worlds of Development* (New Brunswick, N.J.: Transaction Publishers, 1993); Frank Viviano, *Dispatches from the Pacific Century* (Reading, MA.: Addison-Wesley Publishing Company, 1993); and John Naisbitt, *Megatrends Asia: Eight Asian Megatrends That Are Reshaping Our World* (New York: Simon & Schuster, 1996).
3. Among these attempts are Michael Yahuda, *The International Politics of the Asia-Pacific, 1945-1995* (London: Routledge, 1996); Steve Chan, *East Asian Dynamism: Growth, Order and Security in the Pacific Region* (Boulder, CO.: Westview Press, 1993); Gerald Segal, *Rethinking the Pacific* (Oxford, England: Clarendon Press, 1990); Alvin Y. So and Stephen W. K. Chiu, *East Asia and the World Economy* (Thousand Oaks, CA.: Sage Publications, 1995); Robert A. Scalapino, *Major Power Relations in Northeast Asia* (Lanham, MD.: University Press of America, 1987). There are also a few edited, collective efforts that try to integrate some of the security issues in Asia. See, for example, Michael Mandelbaum, ed., *The Strategic Quadrangle: Russia, China, Japan, and the United States in East Asia* (New York: Council on International Relations Press, 1995); Sheldon W. Simon, ed., *East Asian Security in the Post-cold War Era* (Armonk, N.Y.: M. E. Sharpe, 1993); James C. Hsiung, ed., *Asia Pacific in the New World Politics* (Boulder, CO.: Lynne Rienner Publishers, 1993); Yoshikazu Sakamoto, ed., *Asia: Militarization and Regional Conflict* (Tokyo: The United Nations University, 1988); Manwoo Lee and Richard W. Mansbach, eds., *The Changing Order in Northeast Asia and the Korean Peninsula* (Boulder, CO.: Westview Press, 1993); James C. Hsiung, ed., *Asia Pacific in the New World Politics* (Boulder, CO.: Lynne Rienner Publishers, 1993); Robert A. Scalapino, Seizaburo Sato, Jusuf Wanandi, and Sung-Joo Han, eds., *Asia and the Major Powers: Domestic Politics and Foreign Policy* (Berkeley, CA.: Institute of East Asian Studies, University of California, 1988); Stephen P. Gibert, ed., *Security in Northeast Asia: Approaching the Pacific Century* (Boulder, CO.: Westview Press, 1988); Warren I. Cohen, ed., *Pacific Passage* (New York: Columbia University Press,

1996); and Fred Bergsten and Macus Noland, eds., *Pacific Dynamism and the International Economic System* (Washington, D.C.: Institute for International Economics, 1993).

4. Speech by Mr. Lee Kuan Yew at the Twenty-First Century Forum in Beijing on September 4, 1996.

5. Robert A. Manning and Paula Stern, "The Myth of the Pacific Community," *Foreign Affairs,* vol. 73, no. 6 (November/December 1994), p. 81.

6. Among many studies of East Asian economic models, see Stephan Haggard, *Pathways from the Periphery: Politics of Growth in the Newly Industrializing Countries* (Ithaca, N.Y.: Cornell University Press, 1990); Frederic C. Deyo, ed., *The Political Economy of the New Asian Industrialism* (Ithaca, N.Y.: Cornell University Press, 1987); James W. Morley, ed., *Driven by Growth: Political Change in the Asia-Pacific Region* (Armonk, N.Y.: M. E. Sharpe, 1993); Peter L. Berger and Hsin-Huang Michael Hsiao, *In Search of an East Asian Development Model* (New Brunswick, N.J.: Transaction Publishers, 1988); Keun Lee, *New East Asian Economic Development* (Armonk, N.Y.: M. E. Sharpe, 1993); and James Fallows, *Looking at the Sun: The Rise of the New East Asian Economic and Political System* (New York: Vintage Books, 1995).

7. Among them are Harley F. MacNair and Donald F. Lach, *Modern Far Eastern International Relations* (New York: D. Van Nortrand, 1955); Paul Hibbert Clyde, *The Far East: A History of the Impact of the West on Eastern Asia* (Englewood Cliffs, N.J.: Prentice-Hall 1958); John K. Fairbank, ed., *The Chinese World Order* (Cambridge, MA.: Harvard University Press, 1968).

8. This customary assumption may be seen even in some classic works on international relations. See, for example, Hans Morgenthau, *Politics Among Nations* (New York: Knopf, 1955); Charles R. Beitz, *Political Theory and International Relations* (Princeton, N.J.: Princeton University Press, 1979); Robert Gilpin, *War and Change in World Politics* (Cambridge, England: Cambridge University Press, 1981); Kenneth N Waltz, *Theory of International Relations* (Reading, MA.: Addison-Wesley, 1979); Hedley Bull, *The Anarchical Society: A Study of Order in World Politics* (New York: Columbia University Press, 1977).

9. According to some observers, by the second decade of the twenty-first century, East Asia's economic output is likely to exceed that of both North America and the European Community. See Urban C. Lehner, "Belief in an Imminent Asian Century is Gaining Sway," *The Wall Street Journal,* May 17, 1993, p. A12.

10. Kishore Mahbubani, "The Pacific Way," *Foreign Affairs,* vol. 74, no. 1 (January/February 1995), p. 100.

11. For a study of the post–Cold War East Asian power competition that contains a comparative perspective between East Asia and Europe, see Aaron L. Friedberg, "Ripe for Rivalry, Prospects for Peace in a Multipolar Asia," *International Security,* vol. 18, no. 3 (Winter 1993/94), pp. 5-33.

12. Indeed, historically, the Westerners fell into the easy habit of referring to these heterogeneous peoples in East Asia simply as "Orientals" and the varied lands they inhabited as constituting the "Far East."

13. East Asia encompasses two subregions: One, Northeast Asia, including the East Asian mainland, which is principally occupied by the People's Republic of China (PRC) and Korea. Taiwan and the Japanese islands are situated to the northeast of the PRC. They are the most industrialized part of Asia. Further to the north are Siberia and Sakhalin Island, both are territories of Russia. And, two, Southeast Asia, including Indochina and the members of the Association of Southeast Asian Nations (ASEAN) and Papua New Guinea. Indochina is to the south of the PRC, consisting of Vietnam, Laos, and Cambodia. The ASEAN members are Thailand, Malaysia, Singapore, Brunei, Indonesia, and the Philippines, forming a semicircular around the Indochinese countries. After the end of the Cold War, the three Indochinese countries: Vietnam, Cambodia, and Laos, applied to be admitted into ASEAN (Vietnam was officially admitted in July 31, 1995). Once this process is complete, Indochina will be a genuine part of Southeast Asia.

Chapter 1

1. There are many works of East Asian general geography that contain discussions on its political geography. See, for example, Norton S. Sinsburg, ed., *The Pattern of Asia* (Englewood Cliffs, N.J.: Prentice-Hall, 1958); Joseph E. Spencer and William L. Thomas, *Asia, East by South: A Cultural Geography* (New York: John Wiley, 1971); Alfred Kolb, *East Asia* (London: Methuen & Co., 1971); W. Gordon East and O. H. K. Spate, eds., *The Changing Map of Asia: A Political Geography* (London: Methuen & Co., 1966); and Clifton W. Pannell, ed., *East Asia: Geographical and Historical Approaches to Foreign Area Studies* (Dubuque, IA.: Kendall/Hunt Publishing Company, 1983).

2. Shannon McCune, *Islands in Conflict in East Asian Waters* (Hong Kong: Asian Research Service, 1984), p. 24.

3. Huntington suggests that "the world will be shaped in large measure by the interactions among seven or eight major civilizations. These include Western, Confucian, Japanese, Islamic, Hindu, Slavic-Orthodox, Latin American and possibly African civilization." Samuel Huntington, "The Clash of Civilization," *Foreign Affairs*, vol. 72, no. 3 (Summer 1993), p. 25.

4. For a classic study of the China-centered world order, see John King Fairbank, ed., *The Chinese World Order: Traditional China's Foreign Relations* (Cambridge, MA.: Harvard University Press, 1968).

5. World Bank, *World Development Report, 1995* (New York: Oxford University Press, 1994), pp. 162-63.

6. The term *security theater* refers to an area in which "the security of each of a group of nations is vitally affected by the interactions among all." James W. Morley, "The Structure of Regional Security," in James W. Morley, ed., *Security Interdependence in the Asia Pacific Region* (Lexington, MA.: Lexington Books, 1986), p. 10.

7. Among studies of the dispute in South China Sea, see Allen Shepard, "Maritime Tensions in the South China Sea and the Neighborhood: Some Solutions," *Studies of Conflict and Terrorism* (April-June 1994), pp. 181-211; Richael Richardson, "US and ASEAN Tiptoe Round China on Spratlys," *Asia-Pacific Defense Reporter* (May-June 1995), p. 48; Sheng Lijun, "Beijing and the Spratlys," *Issues and Studies,* vol. 31, no. 7 (July 1995), pp. 18-45; and Chen Jie, "China's Spratly Policy, With Special Reference to the Philippines and Malaysia," *Asian Survey,* vol. 32, no. 10 (October 1994), pp. 893-903.

8. On January 30, 1995, Jiang Zemin, the president of the PRC, suggested a high-level negotiation to reach an agreement officially ending the hostility between Beijing and Taipei. For Jiang's suggestions, see *Renmin Ribao* (People's Daily), January 31, 1995, p. 1. If such an agreement can be reached, the possibility of using force to resolve the problems across the Taiwan Straits would be greatly reduced. However, a private visit of the Taiwan president, Lee Teng-hui, to the United States in May 1995 angered the Beijing government. Started on July 21-25, 1995, the People's Liberation Army (PLA) launched a series of surface-to-surface ballistic missile tests in the East China Sea, just 150 km off the tip of northern Taiwan. On August 12-25, 1995, Beijing held a second series of military exercises, including three days of guided-missile, cannon and other military tests in the sea 136 km north of Taiwan. In November PLA marines and tanks made a beach-head landing exercise from amphibious landing craft, backed by jet fighters and naval vessels. In March 1996, before Taiwan's direct presidential election, Beijing conducted a new wave of military exercise. On March 8, the PLA launched three missiles on target areas just 20 nautical miles from Keelung, Taiwan's second busiest seaport, and just offshore from the harbor of Kaochung, the third largest container port in the world. On March 18 to 25, joint ground, naval, and air military exercises were conducted in the Taiwan Strait.

9. United States General Accounting Office, *International Trade, Coordination of US Export Promotion Activities in Pacific Rim Countries* (Washington, D.C.: GAO/GGD-94-192), p. 3.

10. Nicholas R. Lardy, *China in the World Economy* (Washington, D.C.: Institute for International Economics, 1994), p. 35.

11. Robert O. Keohane, "Realism, Neorealism and the Study of World Politics," in Robert O. Keohane, ed., *Neorealism and Its Critics* (New York: Columbia University Press, 1986), pp. 10-11.

12. K. J. Holsti, "Power, Capacity, and Influence," in Charles W. Kegley, Jr. and Eugene R. Wittkopt, eds., *The Global Agenda, Issues and Perspectives* (New York: Random House, Inc. 1988), p. 9.

13. Akira Iriye, *China and Japan in the Global Setting* (Cambridge, MA.: Harvard University Press, 1992), p. 3.

14. Edward Hallett Carr, *The Twenty Years' Crisis, 1919-1939* (New York: Harper Torchbooks, 1964), p. 108.

15. Iriye, *China and Japan in the Global Setting,* pp. 8-9.

16. Carr, *The Twenty Years' Crisis, 1919-1939,* p. 109.

17. Richard Rosecrance, "Force or Trade: The Costs and Benefits of Two Paths to Global Influence," in Charles W. Kegley, Jr. and Eugene R. Wittkopt, eds., *The Global Agenda, Issues and Perspectives,* p. 21.

18. For the division between the hard core and soft power, see Joseph Nye, *Bound to Lead: The Changing Nature of American Power* (New York: Basic Books, 1990), pp. 174-91.

19. Carr, *The Twenty Years' Crisis, 1919-1939,* p. 132.

20. David D. Latin, *Hegemony and Culture: Politics and Religious Change Among the Yoruba* (Chicago, IL.: The University of Chicago Press, 1986), p. 76.

21. Lucian W. Pye, *Asian Power and Politics: The Cultural Dimensions of Authority* (Cambridge, MA.: Harvard University Press, 1985), p. vii.

22. Huntington, "The Clash of Civilization," p. 23.

23. Mahbubani, "The Pacific Way," p. 102.

24. To a large degree, this division encompasses most of the other theoretical variants that have arisen at one time or another. According to one scholar, the debate between these traditions "has permeated the last four centuries." Michael Banks, "The International Relations Discipline: Asset or Liability for Conflict Resolution?" in Edward E. Azar and John W. Burton, eds., *International Conflict Resolution* (Boulder, CO.: Lynne Rienner, 1986), p. 9.

25. Exemplary classical realists include Thucydides, Niccolo Machiavelli, and Thomas Hobbes, and in the twentieth century, E. H. Carr, Hans Morgenthau, Reinhold Niebuhr, Arnold Wolfers; exemplary neorealists include Kenneth Waltz and Robert Gilpin. For a representative selection of realist arguments, see part 2 of Richard K. Betts, ed., *Conflict After the Cold War* (New York: Macmillan, 1994).

26. James W. Morley, "The Structure of Regional Security," in James W. Morley, ed., *Security Interdependence in the Asia Pacific Region* (Lexington, MA.: Lexington Books, 1986), p. 7.

27. Joseph S. Nye, Jr., *Understanding International Conflicts* (New York: Harper Collins, 1993), p. 30.

28. Among the studies of states' behaviors in different types of power distribution, see Edward Vose Gulick, *Europe's Classical Balance of Power: A Case History of the Theory and Practice of One of the Great Concepts of European Statecraft* (New York: Norton, 1976); F. H. Hinsley, *Power and the Pursuit of Peace: Theory and Practice in the History of Relations Between States* (New York: Cambridge University Press, 1963); Albert Sorel, (Francis H. Herrick, trans.), *Europe Under the Old Regime* (New York: Harper Torchbooks, 1964); Ludwig Dehio, *The Precarious Balance* (London: Chatto and Windus, 1962); Geoffrey Blainey, *The Causes of War* (New York: Free Press, 1988); and Samuel P. Huntington, "Why International Primacy Matters," *International Security,* vol. 17, no. 4 (Spring 1993), pp. 68-83.

29. It was because nuclear weapons made the prospect of global war too awful that there was no overall central war in the Cold War bipolar world.

Extrapolating from the destructiveness of thermonuclear weapons, Jonathan Schell argued that nuclear war was so "senseless" that "the choice doesn't include war any longer." Jonathan Schell, *The Fate of the Earth* (New York: Alfred A. Knopf, 1982), p. 193. But Robert J. Art challenged the position that military force had lost its utility in the Cold War bipolar system, and argued for the continuing relevance of military power. See Robert J. Art, "To What Ends Military Power?" *International Security*, vol. 4, no. 4 (Spring 1980), pp. 3-35.

30. Among the most important works of liberalism are Edward Morse, *Modernization and the Transformation of International Relations* (New York: Free Press, 1976); Robert Keohane, and Joseph S. Nye, Jr., *Power and Interdependence* (Boston: Little, Brown, 1977); James Rosenau, *The Study of Global Interdependence* (London: F. Pinter, 1980); Richard Manshach and John Vasques, *In Search of Theory: A New Paradigm for Global Politics* (New York: Columbia University Press, 1981); Andrew M. Scott, *The Dynamics of Interdependence* (Chapel Hill, N.C.: University of North Carolina Press, 1982); and James Rosenau, *Turbulence in World Politics* (Princeton, N.J.: Princeton University Press, 1990). For a collection of major works on the realism-liberalism debate, see Charles W. Kegley, Jr., *Controversies in International Relations Theory: Realism and the Neoliberal Challenge* (New York: St. Martin's Press, 1995).

31. See, for example, John A. Vasquez, *The Power of Power Politics: A Critique* (New Brunswick, N.J.: Rutgers University Press, 1983).

32. Joseph S. Nye, Jr., "The Misleading Metaphor of Decline," in Charles W. Kegley, Jr., and Eugene Wittkopf, eds., *The Global Agenda* (New York: McGraw-Hill, 1992), pp. 309-20.

33. Josef Hoffe, "Entangled Forever," in Charles W. Kegley Jr., and Eugene R. Wittkopf, eds., *The Future of American Foreign Policy* (New York: St. Martin's Press, 1992).

34. For a number of key articles on the debate between neorealism and neoliberalism, see David A. Baldwin, ed., *Neorealism and Neoliberalism: The Contemporary Debate* (New York: Columbia University Press, 1993).

35. Military power has been increased or decreased by all sorts of means. To increase power, China and Japan both chose from a wide range of alternatives—intensifying domestic controls to get more out of their peoples, enlarging their armed forces, strengthening their alliance relations, seeking new alliances, and trying to deter or pacify their adversaries. Conversely, when Japan decided that it was safe to relax its power-building or power-asserting efforts after the Occupation by the Allied Forces, it began to liberalize its political controls at home, put restrictions on military expenses in its peace constitution, and sought to expand normal relations with states formerly perceived to be adversaries.

36. Joseph S. Nye, Jr., *Understanding International Conflicts,* p. 12.

37. Key-hiuk Kim, *The Last Phase of the East Asian World Order* (Berkeley, CA.: University of California Press, 1980), p. 79.

38. Since the publication of Kenneth Waltz's *Theory of International Politics* (Reading, MA.: Addison-Wesley, 1979), neorealism has become a dominant school of thought in international relations theory. His book inspired critical literature, best exemplified in Robert O. Keohane's edited volume, *Neorealism and Its Critics* (New York: Columbia University Press, 1986); and Barry Buzan, Charles Jones, and Richard Little, *The Logic of Anarchy: Neorealism to Structural Realism* (New York: Columbia University Press, 1993). It also gave rise to some interesting attempts at application, including Robert Gilpin, *War and Change in World Politics* (Cambridge, England: Cambridge University Press, 1981); Stephen Walt, *The Origins of Alliances* (Ithaca, N.Y.: Cornell University Press, 1987); Michael Mandelbaum, *The Fate of Nations* (Cambridge, England: Cambridge University Press, 1988); and Barry Posen, *The Sources of Military Doctrine* (Ithaca, N.Y.: Cornell University Press, 1984).

39. Desmond Ball, "Arms and Affluence, Military Acquisitions in the Asia-Pacific Region," *International Security,* vol. 18, no. 3 (Winter 1993/94), p. 82.

40. Jonathan Sikes, "Asia Puts its Wealth in Military," *Washington Times,* February 12, 1990, p. 7. Quoted from Desmond Ball, "Arms and Affluence, Military Acquisitions in the Asia-Pacific Region," p. 78.

41. Steven R. Weisman, "Japan to Share More of US Troop Cost," *New York Times,* December 21, 1990, p. A3, and Karl Schoenber, "Japan to Put Brakes on Military Buildup," *Los Angeles Times,* December 21, 1990, p. A6.

42. According to one observer, China's official military expenditures doubled between 1988 and 1993, from $3.8 to $7.3 billion, with double-digit spending hikes in each year of that period. Chongpin Lin, "The Stealthy Advance of China's People's Liberation Army," *The American Enterprise,* vol. 5, no. 1 (January/February 1994), p. 30.

43. Miles Kahler, "Introduction, Beyond the Cold War in the Pacific," in Miles Kahler, ed., *Beyond the Cold War in the Pacific* (San Diego, CA.: Institute on Global Conflict and Cooperation, University of California, 1991), p. 5.

44. For Rosecrance's argument, see his *The Rise of the Trading State,* p. 26.

45. For the original argument, see John Mearsheimer, "Back to the Future: Instability in Europe After the Cold War," *International Security,* vol. 15, no. 1 (Summer 1990), pp. 5-56. For an application of the argument to post–Cold War East Asia, see Aaron L. Friedberg, "Ripe for Rivalry: Prospects for Peace in a Multipolar Asia," *International Security* vol. 18, no. 3 (Winter 1993-94), pp. 5-33. For a counterargument, see Kishore Mahbubani, "The Pacific Way," *Foreign Affairs,* vol. 74, no. 1 (January/February 1995), pp. 100-111.

Chapter 2

1. There are many studies of the Thirty Years' War and the subsequent international system in Europe. See, for example, C. V. Wedgwood, *The Thirty Years War* (London: J. Cape, 1938); Henrik Tikkanen, *The 30 Years' War,*

translated by George Blecher and Lone Thygesen-Blecher (Lincoln, NB.: University of Nebraska Press, 1987); Hugh Redwald Trevor-Roper, ed., *The Age of Expansion: Europe and the World, 1559-1660* (New York: McGraw-Hill, 1968); John Baptist Wolf, *The Emergence of the Great Powers, 1685-1715* (New York: Harper, 1951); Herbert Langer, *The Thirty Years' War* (Poole, England: Bandford Press, 1978); and Theodore K. Rabb, ed., *The Thirty Years' War* (New York: University Press of America, 1981). For an excellent brief description of the emergence of the great powers in Europe during this period, see Gordon A. Craig and Alexander L. George, *Force and Statecraft* (New York: Oxford University Press, 1983), pp. 3-27.

2. Samuel Kim, "Mainland China and a New World Order," *Issues and Studies,* vol. 27, no. 11 (November 1991), p. 4.

3. For a comparative study of the Westphalian model, see Richard A. Falk, "The Interplay of Westphalia and Charter Conceptions of International Legal Order," in Richard A. Falk and Cyrus E. Black, eds., *The Future of the International Legal Order,* vol. 1 (Princeton, N.J.: Princeton University Press, 1969), pp. 43-48.

4. Donald Kagan, *The Outbreak of the Peloponnesian War* (Ithaca, N.Y.: Cornell University Press, 1969), pp. 31-35, 345-56. For a classic work on the nation-state system in the Western tradition, see Hans J. Morgenthau, *Politics Among Nations: The Struggle for Power and Peace* (New York: McGraw-Hill Inc., 1948).

5. John K. Fairbank, "A Preliminary Framework," in John K. Fairbank, ed., *The Chinese World Order* (Cambridge, MA.: Harvard University Press, 1968), p. 1.

6. The most well-known Chinese classics discussing ancient Chinese war strategy is Sun Zi's *Art of War,* translated into English by S. G. Griffith, (New York: Oxford University Press, 1963). An overview of political thought in general, including the use of coercive power, is provided by Xiao Gong Quan, *A Political History of Chinese Thought: From the Beginning to the Sixth Century AD,* translated by F. W. Mote, Princeton, N.J.: Princeton University Press, 1979). A more recent work of Western scholarship on pre-modern Chinese strategic thought is Alastair I. Johnston, *Cultural Realism: Strategic Culture and Grant Strategy in Chinese History* (Princeton, N.J.: Princeton University Press, 1996).

7. Lien-sheng Yang, "Historical Notes on the Chinese World Order," in John K. Fairbank, ed., *The Chinese World Order,* p. 20.

8. James Legge, translated, *The Chinese Classics,* vol. 5, *The Ch'un Ts'ew with the Tso Chuen* (London: Henry Frowned, 1872; reprinted by Hong Kong University Press, 1961), p. 52.

9. Gerald Segal, *Rethinking the Pacific* (Oxford: Clarendon Press, 1990), pp. 27-28.

10. In a study of East Asian history, Arthur Cotterell indicates, "that Zheng He's intentions were essentially peaceful distinguishes Chinese maritime exploration from the policies of the Portuguese, the first Europeans to sail eastwards." Arthur Cotterell, *East Asia: From Chinese Predominance to the Rise*

of the Pacific Rim (New York: Oxford University Press, 1993), p. 102. Among the books describing the Zheng He Fleet expedition, see Albert Chan, *The Glory and Fall of the Ming Dynasty* (Norman, OK.: University of Oklahoma Press, 1982).

11. Michael H. Hunt, *The Genesis of Chinese Communist Foreign Policy* (New York: Columbia University Press, 1996), p. 5,

12. Lien-sheng Yang, "Historical Notes on the Chinese World Order," in John K. Fairbank, ed., *The Chinese World Order*, p. 20.

13. John K. Fairbank, "A Preliminary Framework," p. 2.

14. Lucian W. Pye, *Asian Power and Politics: The Cultural Dimensions of Authority* (Cambridge, MA.: Harvard University Press, 1985), p. 41.

15. Mark Mancall, "The Persistence of Tradition in Chinese Foreign Policy," *The Annals of American Academy of Political and Social Science*, vol. 349, (September 1963), reprinted in King C. Chen, ed., *The Foreign Policy of China* (South Orange, N.J.: Seton Hall University Press, 1972), p. 31.

16. John K. Fairbank, "A Preliminary Framework," p. 2.

17. Mark Mancall, "The Persistence of Tradition in Chinese Foreign Policy," pp. 31-32.

18. Mark Mancall, "The Ch'ing Tribute System: An Interpretive Essay," in John K. Fairbank, ed., *The Chinese World Order*, p. 66.

19. John K. Fairbank, "A Preliminary Framework," p. 2.

20. For one discussion of the relationship between Sinocentrism and the East Asian international environment, see Hedley Bull and Adam Watson, eds., *The Expansion of International Society* (Oxford: Clarendon Press, 1984).

21. Claude A. Buss, *Asia in the Modern World: A History of China, Japan, South and Southeast Asia* (London: Coller-Macmillan Limited, 1964), pp. 34-35.

22. Lien-sheng Yang, "Historical Notes on the Chinese World Order," in John K. Fairbank, ed., *The Chinese World Order*, pp. 20-33.

23. A bibliography of some 55 studies of aspects of China's tributary relations was published in J. K. Fairbank and S. Y. Teng's, "On the Ch'ing Tributary System," *Harvard Journal of Asiatic Studies*, vol. 6, no. 4 (June 1941), pp. 135-48.

24. Mark Mancall, "The Ch'ing Tribute System: An Interpretive Essay," in John K. Fairbank, ed., *The Chinese World Order*, p. 63.

25. As a matter of fact, there is no Chinese word for it. Perhaps the closest terms in Chinese are *jingong* (pay tribute to the emperor) and *chaogong* (pay respects to a sovereign), but neither of the two terms implies an institutionalized relationship.

26. Wang Gungwu, "Early Ming Relations with Southeast Asia: A Background Essay," in John K. Fairbank, ed., *The Chinese World Order*, pp. 34-62.

27. For the century (1740-1840) immediately before the Opium War, the frequency of tribute visits was as follows: Korea—tribute every year; Ryukyu—ranging from one to nine years; Annam (Vietnam)—once in four years on the average, ranging from one to three years; Burma—once in seven years on the average, ranging from one to twenty four years; Laos—once in three

years on the average, ranging from one to thirteen years; and Nepal—indefinitely (4 missions in 100 years). King C. Chen, "Traditional Chinese Foreign Relations," in King C. Chen, ed., *The Foreign Policy of China,* p. 9.

28. In their classic study of the Qing administration (1644-1911), based on *taqing huidian* (the collected statutes of the great Qing), John K. Fairbank and Shu-yu Teng enumerate the tribute states and the frequency of their missions to Beijing. The earlier description draws mostly from their classical study. See John K. Fairbank and Shu-yu Teng, "On the Ch'ing Tributary System," *Harvard Journal of Asiatic Studies,* vol. 6, no. 4 (June 1941), pp. 135-48.

29. Hae-jong Chun, "Sino-Korean Tributary Relations in the Ch'ing Period," in John K. Fairbank, ed., *The Chinese World Order,* p.109.

30. Ta-tuan Ch'en, "Investiture of Liu-ch'iu Kings in the Ch'ing Period," in John K. Fairbank, ed., *The Chinese World Order,* p. 161.

31. One introduction to the origins and early history of China's foreign trade and tributary relations is Ying-shih Yu, *Trade and Expansion in Han China: A Study in the Structure of Sino-Barbarian Economic Relations* (Berkeley, CA.: University of California Press, 1967).

32. Mark Mancall, "The Persistence of Tradition in Chinese Foreign Policy," p. 30.

33. Benjamin I. Schwartz, "The Chinese Perception of World Order, Past and Present," in John K. Fairbank, ed., *The Chinese World Order,* p. 284.

34. Zhang Yongjin, *China in the International System, 1918-20, The Middle Kingdom at the Periphery* (New York: St. Martin's Press, 1991), p. 16

35. Mark Borthwick, *Pacific Century: The Emergence of Modern Pacific Asia* (Boulder, CO.: Westview Press, 1992), p. 77.

36. There are many works on the history of the European expansion in East Asia. Among them, see, for example, J. T. Pratt, *The European Expansion into the Far East* (London: Macmillan, 1948); Carlo M. Cipolla, *Guns, Sails, and Empires: Technological Innovation and the Early Phases of European Expansion, 1400-1700* (New York: Pantheon, 1960); J. K. Fairbank, E. O. Reischauer, and A. M. Craig, *East Asia—The Modern Transformation* (London: George Allen & Unwin, 1965); and J. B. Crowley, ed., *Modern East Asia: Essays in Interpretation* (New York: Harcout, Brace and World Inc., 1970).

37. Alvin Y. So and Stephen W. K. Chiu, *East Asia and the World Economy,* (Thousand Oaks, CA.: Sage Publications, 1995), p. 34.

38. Hsin-Pao Chang, *Commissioner Lin and the Opium War* (Cambridge, MA.: Harvard University Press, 1964), p. 10. For the early works on the Guangzhou trade, see, for example, Maurice Collis, *Foreign Mud, Being an Account of the Opium Imbroglio at Canton in the 1830's and the Anglo-Chinese War that Followed* (New York: Alfred A. Knopf, 1947); and H. B. Morse, *The Chronicles of the East India Company Trading to China,* 5 volumes (Oxford, England: Oxford University Press, 1926-1929). For some recent works, see, for example, Srasin Viraphol, *Tribute and Profit: Sino-Siamese Trade, 1652-*

1853 (Cambridge, MA.: Harvard University Press, 1977); Lo-shu Fu, *A Documentary Chronicle of Sino-Western Relations, 1644-1820,* two volumes (Tempe, AZ.: University Of Arizona Press, 1966).

39. T. R. Banister, *A History of the External Trade of China, 1834-1881* (Shanghai: Inspector General of Chinese Customs, 1931), p. 99.

40. Peter Ward Fay, *The Opium War, 1840-1842* (Chapel Hill, N.C.: The University of North Carolina Press, 1975), p. 17.

41. John King Fairbank, *The United States and China* (Cambridge, MA.: Harvard University Press, 1983), pp. 161-62.

42. Mark Borthwick, *Pacific Century,* p. 93.

43. Peter Ward Fay, *The Opium War, 1840-1842* (Chapel Hill, N.C.: The University of North Carolina Press, 1975), p. 54.

44. Ibid.

45. Alvin Y. So and Stephen W. K. Chiu, *East Asia and the World Economy,* p. 38.

46. The Compilation Group for the History of Modern China Series, *The Opium War* (Beijing: Foreign Language Press, 1976), p. 19.

47. For an excellent study of Lin Zexu and the Opium War, see Hsin-pao Chang, *Commissioner Lin and the Opium War.*

48. For the Chinese view of the Opium War, see Arthur Waley, *The Opium War Through Chinese Eyes* (New York: Macmillan Company, 1958). For an official view of Communist China, see Hu Sheng, *Cong Yapian Zhanzheng Dao Wusi Yundong* (From the Opium War to the May-Fourth Movement) (Beijing: Renmin Chuban She, 1980).

49. Peter Wesley-Smith, *Unequal Treaty 1898-1997: China, Great Britain and Hong Kong's New Territories* (New York : Oxford University Press, 1983).

50. The Compilation Group for the History of Modern China Series, *The Opium War,* p. 15.

51. John G. Stoessinger, *Nations at Dawn: China, Russia, and America* (New York: McGraw Hill, 1994), p. 12.

52. Quoted in John K. Fairbank and Ssu-yu Teng, eds., *China's Response to the West: A Documentary Survey* (Cambridge: Harvard University Press, 1954), p. 36.

53. Arthur Cotterell, *East Asia: From Chinese Predominance to the Rise of the Pacific Rim* (New York: Oxford University Press, 1993), p. 113.

54. For a bibliography of Chinese sources for the Taiping uprising, see James Chester Cheng, *Chinese Sources for the Taiping Rebellion, 1850-1864* (New York: Oxford University Press, 1963). Among other works are Franz H. Michael and Chung-li Chang, *The Taiping Rebellion: History and Documents,* 3 volumes (Seattle: University of Washington Press, 1966-1971); Yu-wen Chien, *The Taiping Revolutionary Movement* (New Haven, CT.: Yale University Press, 1973); and Prescott Clarke and J. S. Gregory, *Western Reports on the Taiping: A Selection of Documents* Honolulu, HI.: University Press of Hawaii, 1982).

55. According to a study by Skocpol, revolutionary crisis developed when the old regime state became unable to meet the challenges of evolving domestic and international situation. Centrally administrative and coercive control over the potentially rebellions lower classes were disorganized. See Theda Skocpol, *States & Social Revolutions: A Comparative Analysis of France, Russia, and China* (Cambridge, England: Cambridge University Press, 1979).

56. John K. Fairbank, "The Early Treaty System in the Chinese World Order," in John K. Fairbank, ed., *The Chinese World Order,* p. 258.

57. Zhong Shuhe, *Zouxiang Shijie* (Strive toward the World) (Beijing: Zhounghua Shujiu, 1985), p. 78.

58. For details of these two changes, see I. Hsu, *China's Entrance into the Family of Nations, the Diplomatic Phase, 1860-1880* (Cambridge, MA.: Harvard University Press, 1960); and M. Banno, *China and the West, 1858-1861: The Origins of Tsungli Yamen* (Cambridge, MA.: Harvard University Press, 1964).

59. Zhang Yongjin, *China in the International System,* p. 18.

60. Key-hiuk Kim, *The Last Phase of the East Asian World Order,* Berkeley, CA: University of California Press, 1980, p. 36.

61. Zhang Yongjin, *China in the International System,* p. 20.

62. US State Department, *Foreign Relations of the United States, 1899* (Washington D.C.: U.S. Government Printing Office, 1901), pp. 132-33.

63. US State Department, *Foreign Relations of the United States, 1900* (Washington D.C.: U.S. Government Printing Office, 1902), p. 299.

64. The Open Door notes and the emergence of the United States as an actor in the East Asian power competition will be discussed in detail in the conclusion.

Chapter 3

1. Key-hiuk Kim, *The Last Phase of the East Asian World Order: Korea, Japan, and the Chinese Empire, 1860-1882* (Berkeley, CA: University of California Press, 1980), p. vii.

2. Rutherford Alcock, *The Capital of the Tycoon,* 2 vols. (London: Longman, 1863), vol. I, pp. xix-xx.

3. W. G. Beasley, *The Rise of Modern Japan: Political, Economic and Social Change Since 1850* (New York: St. Martin's Press, 1995), p. 2.

4. James Fallows, *Looking at the Sun: The Rise of the New East Asian Economic and Political System* (New York: Vintage Books, 1995), p. 89.

5. W. G. Beasley, *The Meiji Restoration* (Stanford, CA.: Stanford University Press, 1972), pp. 1-2.

6. An overview of Japan's modernization program can be found in Carol Gluck, *Japan's Modern Myths: Ideology in the Late Meiji Period* (Princeton, N.J.: Princeton University Press, 1985). For a recent comprehensive study of Japan's modernization history, see W. G. Beasley, *The Rise of Modern Japan: Political, Economic and Social Change since 1850.*

7. Albert M. Craig, "The Central Government," in Marius B. Jansen and Gilbert Rozman, eds., *Japan in Transition: From Tokugawa to Meiji* (Princeton, N.J.: Princeton University Press, 1986), p. 59.

8. E. Herbert Norman, *Japan's Emergence as a Modern State: Political and Economic Problems of the Meiji Period* (Westport, CT.: Greenwood Press, 1973), p. 102.

9. For the Meiji reform of military organizations, see W. G. Beasley, *The Meiji Restoration,* pp. 350-78.

10. The abolishment of the samurai class has received close scrutiny by scholars. For example, H. D. Harootunia drew on Japanese scholarship for two articles that provided a succinct summary of the process, and W. G. Beasley concluded his study of the restoration with a judicious evaluation of the principal steps in that abolishment. See Harry D. Harootunia, "The Economic Rehabilitation of the Samurai in the Early Meiji Period," *Journal of Asian Studies,* vol. 19, no. 4, (1960), and "The Process of Japan and the Samurai Class, 1868-1882," *Pacific Historical Review,* vol. 28, no. 3, (1959); and W. G. Beasley, *The Meiji Restoration,* pp. 379-90.

11. This is the long-accepted view about the transition of the samurai during the Meiji era, although some studies tried to reject this view. For one study of the opposite view, see Kozo Yamamura, *A Study of Samurai Income and Entrepreneurship: Quantitative Analysis of Economic and Social Aspects of the Samurai in Tokugawa and Meiji Japan* (Cambridge, MA.: Harvard University Press, 1974).

12. For a classic study of the role of the contemporary Japanese government in economic development, see Chalmers Johnson, *MITI and The Japanese Miracle: The Growth of Industrial Policy, 1925-1975* (Stanford, CA.: Stanford University Press, 1982).

13. Johannes Hirschmeier, *The Origins of Enterpreneurship in Meiji Japan* (Cambridge, MA: Harvard University Press, 1964), p. 113.

14. For an excellent study of the government initiatives in the technology transfer during the Meiji era, see Johannes Hirschmeier, *The Origins of Enterpreneurship in Meiji Japan* pp. 111-61.

15. Theodore Friend, *The Blue-Eyed Enemy: Japan Against the West in Java and Luzon, 1942-1945* (Princeton, N.J.: Princeton University Press, 1988), p. 54.

16. Peter Moody, Jr., *Tradition and Modernization in China and Japan* (Belmont, CA.: Wadsworth Publishing Company, 1995), p. 119.

17. Peter Duus, *The Rise of Modern Japan* (Boston: Houghton Mifflin Company, 1976), p. 56.

18. For one study of Japanese resistance to Western powers before the Meiji era, see Bob Tadashi Wakabayashi, *Anti-Foreignism and Western Learning in Early Modern Japan, The New Theses of 1825* (Cambridge, MA.: Council on East Asian Studies, Harvard University and Harvard University Press, 1986).

19. For a study of cultural interaction between Japan and the West, see George B. Sansom, *The Western World and Japan: A Study in the Interaction of European and Asiatic Cultures* (New York: Knopf, 1950).

20. Peter Duus, *The Rise of Modern Japan,* p. 57.

21. For the role of the Britain in the opening of Japan, see William G. Beasley, *Great Britain and the Opening of Japan, 1834-1858* (London: Luzac, 1951).

22. For a classic study of Japan's opening by the Americans, see Samuel Eliot Morison, *"Old Bruin": Commodore Matthew Calbraith Perry* (Boston: Little, Brown, and Co., 1967).

23. Described in Masao Watanable, *The Japanese and Western Science,* translated by Otto Theodor Benfey (Philadelphia: University of Pennsylvania Press, 1990), p. 123.

24. Michio Morishima, *Why Has Japan "Succeeded"?: Western Technology and the Japanese Echos* (Cambridge, England: Cambridge University Press, 1982), p. 135.

25. Claude A. Buss, *Asia in the Modern World: A History of China, Japan, South and Southeast Asia* (London: Coller-Macmillan Limited, 1964), p. 8.

26. Peter Moody, Jr., *Tradition and Modernization in China and Japan,* p. 125.

27. Lafcadio Hearn, *Japan, An Attempt at Interpretation* (New York: Macmillan, 1913), p. 496.

28. For one study of the immobility in Tokugawa Japan, see C. D. Rise, Sheldon, *The Rise of the Merchant Class in Tokugawa Japan* (Locust Valley, N.Y.: Augustin, 1958).

29. Steve Chan, *East Asian Dynamism* (Boulder, CO.: Westview Press, 1993), p. 18.

30. In 1660 the population of China was somewhere around 100 to 150 million, and it rose to 300 million by 1800. Arable land, however, had not increased correspondingly. In 1661 there were 549 million *mou* of land and in 1812 only 791 million. The land increase was less than 50 percent, where the population had increased by more than 100 percent. Immanuel C. Y. Hsu, *The Rise of Modern China* (New York: Oxford University Press, 1995), p. 126.

31. Mikiso Hane, *Modern Japan, A History Survey* (Boulder, CO.: Westview Press, 1992), p. 191.

32. Steve Chan, *East Asian Dynamism,* p. 19.

33. G. C. Allen, *A Short Economic History of Modern Japan, 1867-1937* (London: Macmillan, 1981), p. 10.

34. George Sansom, *The Western World and Japan: A Study in the Interaction of European and Asiatic Cultures* (New York: Knopf, 1950), pp. 327-30.

35. E. Herbert Norman, *Japan's Emergence as a Modern State,* p. 14.

36. According to one classic study, the revolution from below, as exemplified in Russia and China, resulted in communism; and the revolution from above, as in Japan and Germany, culminated in fascism. Barrington Moore, Jr., *Social Origins of Dictatorship and Democracy* (Boston: Beacon Press, 1966).

37. Barrington Moore, Jr., *Social Origins of Dictatorship and Democracy,* pp. 247-48.

38. Quoted in R. H. Myers and M. R. Peattie, eds., *The Japanese Colonial Empire, 1895-1945* (Princeton, NJ: Princeton University Press, 1984), p. 64.

39. Colin Mackerras, *Eastern Asia: An Introductory History* (Sydney, Australia: Longman Cheshire, 1992), p. 179.

40. James Fallows, *Looking at the Sun,* p. 82.

41. Quoted in R. H. Myers and M. R. Peattie, eds., *The Japanese Colonial Empire, 1895-1945* (Princeton, N.J.: Princeton University Press, 1984), p. 64.

42. Colin Mackerras, *Eastern Asia, An Introductory History,* p. 187.

43. Key-hiuk Kim, *The Last Phase of the East Asian World Order,* p. 79.

44. Ibid., p. 81.

45. Ibid., p. 198.

46. Ian Nish, *Japanese Foreign Policy, 1869-1942* (London: Routledge & Kegan Paul, 1977), p. 23.

47. Bonnie B. Oh, "Sino-Japanese Rivalry in Korea, 1876-1885," in Akira Iriye, ed., *The Chinese and the Japanese: Essays in Political and Cultural Interactions* (Princeton, N.J.: Princeton University Press, 1980), p. 37

48. Morinosuke Kajima, *A Brief Diplomatic History of Modern Japan* (Rutland, VT.: Charles E. Tuttle Co., 1965), p. 25.

49. M. Frederick Nelson, *Korea and the Old Orders in Eastern Asia* (Baton Rouge, LA.: Louisiana State University Press, 1945), p. 126.

50. Mark Borthwick, ed., *Pacific Century,* p. 145.

51. Taewongun was the title meaning Prince of the Great Court that was bestowed on Yi Ha-ung, the living father of King Yi Myongbok and the effective ruler of Korea from 1864 to 1873. The Taewongun's son, who was posthumously entitled King Kojong, ascended the throne in 1864 at the age of 12.

52. C. I. Eugene Kim and Han-Kyo Kim, *Korea and the Politics of Imperialism, 1976-1910* (Berkeley, CA.: University of California Press, 1967), p. 75.

53. Takashi Hatada, *A History of Korea,* translated and edited by Warren W. Smith, Jr. and Benjamin H. Hazard (Santa Barbara, CA.: Clio Press, 1969), p. 91.

54. Ibid.

55. M. Frederick Nelson, *Korea and the Old Orders in Eastern Asia,* p. 127.

56. For two different versions of the incident given by the Japanese and the Koreans, see Martina Deuchler, *Confucian Gentleman and Barbarian Envoys: The Opening of Korea, 1875-1885* (Seattle, WA.: University of Washington Press, 1977), pp. 23-24.

57. Key-hiuk Kim, *The Last Phase of the East Asian World Order,* p. 204.

58. K. Hwang, *The Korean Reform Movement of the 1880s: A Study of Transition in Intra-Asian Relations* (Cambridge, MA: Schenkman Publishing Company, 1978), p. 67.

59. Bonnie B. Oh, "Sino-Japanese Rivalry in Korea, 1876-1885," in Akira Iriye, ed., *The Chinese and the Japanese: Essays in Political and Cultural Interactions,* p. 42.

60. Myung Hyun Cho, *Korea and the Major Powers* (Seoul, Korea: Research Center for Peace and Unification of Korea, 1989), p. 66.

61. Ibid.

62. C. I. Eugene Kim and Han-Kyo Kim, *Korea and the Politics of Imperialism, 1976-1910,* p. 33.

63. Myung Hyun Cho, *Korea and the Major Powers,* p. 67.
64. C. I. Eugene Kim and Han-Kyo Kim, *Korea and the Politics of Imperialism, 1976-1910,* p. 40.
65. Fukuzawa Yukichi (1835-1901) was one of the great intellectuals in Japanese history and the most famous exponent of Western civilization in Meiji Japan. Fukuzawa accompanied the first Japanese official mission overseas on the *Kanrin Maru* in 1860 and visited Europe thereafter in 1862. In 1868 he founded a small school for teaching Western learning, Keio Gijuku, in Tokyo. It was the ancestor of Keio University, which Fukuzawa himself brought to university status in 1890. As an educator, his views on the importance of acquiring Western learning inspired several generations of Japanese after him.
66. K. Hwang, *The Korean Reform Movement of the 1880s: A Study of Transition in Intra-Asian Relations,* p. 115.
67. Ibid.
68. C. I. Eugene Kim and Han-Kyo Kim, *Korea and the Politics of Imperialism,* p. 50.
69. Mark Borthwick, ed., *Pacific Century,* p. 148.
70. M. Frederick Nelson, *Korea and the Old Orders in Eastern Asia,* p. 207.
71. Ibid., p. 208.
72. Jeffrey Dorwart, *The Pigtail War: American Involvement in the Sino-Japanese War, 1894-1895* (Amherst, MA.: University of Massachusetts Press, 1975), p. 72.
73. This war was known as Jiawu War because 1895 was the year of Jiawu in the Chinese calendar.
74. Morinosuke Kajima, *A Brief Diplomatic History of Modern Japan,* p. 26.
75. In 1995, one hundred years after the Treaty of Shimonoseki (known in China as the Maguan Treaty), the Chinese Communist government launched an educational campaign to remind the Chinese people about the Chinese humiliation at the hands of the Japanese. For one report, see *Renmin Ribao,* April 18, 1995.
76. Immanual C. Y. Hsu, *The Rise of Modern China,* pp. 407-408.
77. Akira Iriye, *China and Japan in Global Setting* (Cambridge, MA.: Harvard University Press, 1992), pp. 8-9.
78. Jack Gray, *Rebellions and Revolutions: China from the 1800s to the 1980s* (Oxford, England: Oxford University Press, 1990), p. 109.
79. For one study of Zeng Guofan and his army, see William James Hail, *Tseng Kuo-fan and the Taipei Rebellion: With a Short Sketch of His Later Career* (New York: Paragon Book Reprint, 1964).
80. M. I. Sladkovsky, *China and Japan, Past and Present* (Gulf Breeze, FL.: Academic International Press, 1975), p. 47.
81. Harley Farnsworth MacNair, *The Real Conflict Between China and Japan: An Analysis of Opposing Ideologies* (Chicago, IL.: The University of Chicago Press, 1938), p. 63.

82. Theodore de Barry, Wing-tsit Chan, and Chester Tan, eds., *Sources of Chinese Tradition* (New York: Columbia University Press, 1964), p. 45.

83. Akira Iriye, *China and Japan in Global Setting*, p. 13.

84. Peter Duus, *The Rise of Modern Japan*, p. 81.

85. Mikiso Hane, *Modern Japan, A History Survey*, p. 97.

86. For one study of the emergence of Japanese modern state, see E. Herbert Norman, *Japan's Emergence as a Modern State: Political and Economic Problems of the Meiji Period* (Westport, CT.: Greenwood Press, 1973).

87. Akira Iriye, *China and Japan in Global Setting*, p. 19.

88. According to Iriye, Japanese exports to China doubled after the war of 1894-95, tripled after the Russo-Japanese War, and quadrupled during the European war. And Japan's share in Chinese imports increased from less than 3 percent before the Chinese-Japanese War to more 10 percent after the Russo-Japanese war and to around 30 percent during World War I. Japan suffered from a chronic trade deficit until 1914 with regard to the Western nations, the favorable balance of trade vis-à-vis China greatly compensated its deficit with the West. Akira Iriye, *China and Japan in Global Setting*, p. 20.

89. Hosoya Chibiro, "Japan's Policies Toward Russia," in James William Morley, ed., *Japan's Foreign Policy, 1868-1941, A Research Guide* (New York: Columbia University Press, 1974), p. 351.

90. Feodor Dostoievsky (a former Russian diplomat), "Geok-Teppe, What is Asia to Us?" in Robert A. Goldwin, Gerald Stourzh, and Marvin Zetterbaum, eds., *Readings in Russian Foreign Policy* (New York, Columbia University Press, 1959), p. 274.

91. Ibid.

92. Ian Nish, *The Origins of the Russo-Japanese War* (London: Longman, 1985), p. 26.

93. Hosoya Chihiro, "Japan's Policies Toward Russia," in James William Morley, *Japan's Foreign Policy, 1868-1941* (New York: Columbia University Press, 1974), p. 352.

94. Ian Nish, *The Origins of the Russo-Japanese War*, p. 24.

95. The British government's stand was outlined by its Foreign Minister, Lord Kimberley, when he said, "Great Britain has no objection to the Japanese possession of Formosa, but feels that the act of interceding in behalf of Japan would also be regarded as intervention. Furthermore, Britain entertains some doubts as to whether it would be prudent in the interests of Japan's future for her to acquire a toe told on the mainland. Not only would Japan have to increase its military expenditures to maintain such a possession, but she might also incur the potential danger of China and Russia embarking upon a war of revenge. In these circumstances, it might be more judicious for Japan to adopt a conciliatory attitude." Morinosuke Kajima, *A Brief Diplomatic History of Modern Japan*, p. 28.

96. Ian Nish, *The Origins of the Russo-Japanese War*, p. 29.

97. George Akita, "The Meiji Restoration," in Mark Borthwick, ed., *Pacific Century*, p. 149.

98. While the Japanese accepted the advance of triple intervention in returning Liaodong to China, the additional sum of 30 million taels was added to the original indemnity of 200 million taels. The Qing court, with an annual revenue of 89 million taels, was not in the position to meet these obligations except through borrowing.

99. The fact that the Li-Lobanov Treaty was secret and not properly disclosed until 1922 led to infinite speculation in the years that followed. Because it was a secret treaty, all sorts of doubts were created on the part of those who were worried about Sino-Russian relations, notably the country that was the "contemplated enemy," Japan. See Ian Nish, *The Origins of the Russo-Japanese War,* p. 31.

100. Frederick A. McKenzie, *Tragedy of Korea* (London: Holder and Stougton, 1908), pp. 299-300.

101. Myung Hyun Cho, *Korea and the Major Powers,* p. 75.

102. Morinosuke Kajima, *A Brief Diplomatic History of Modern Japan,* p. 29.

103. Ian Nish, *Japanese Foreign Policy, 1869-1942: Kasumigaseki to Miyakezaka* (London: Routledge & Kegan Paul, 1977), p. 67.

104. C. I. Eugene Kim and Hankyo Kim, *Korea and the Politics of Imperialism,* p. 100.

105. For one overview of the Anglo-Japanese alliance, see Ian. H. Hish, *The Anglo-Japanese Alliance: The Diplomacy of Two Island Empire, 1894-1907* (London: Athlone P., 1966).

106. Quoted from Ian Nish, *The Origins of the Russo-Japanese War,* p. 131.

107. Hosoya Chihiro, "Japan's Policies Toward Russia," in James William Morley, ed., *Japan's Foreign Policy, 1868-1941* (New York: Columbia University Press, 1974), p. 364.

108. Hosoya Chihiro, "Japan's Policies Toward Russia," p. 365.

109. Myung Hyun Cho, *Korea and the Major Powers,* p. 77.

110. Morinosuke Kajima, *A Brief Diplomatic History of Modern Japan,* p. 38.

111. For U.S.-Japanese relations during this period, see Akira Iriye, *Pacific Estrangement: Japanese and American Expansion, 1897-1911* (Cambridge, MA.: Harvard University Press, 1972).

112. For a compelling narrative of the disaster at Tsushima by the doomed Russian commander, Vice Admiral Rozhestvensky, see Richard Alexander Hough, *The Fleet That Had to Die* (New York: Viking Press, 1958).

113. Harley F. MacNair and Donald F. Lach, *Modern Far Eastern International Relations* (New York: D. Van Nortrand, 1955), p. 100-101.

114. Jeffrey Dorwart, *The Pigtail War: American Involvement in the Sino-Japanese War, 1894-1895* (Amherst, MA.: University of Massachusetts Press, 1975), pp. 73-90.

115. For a detailed analysis of Japan's expansionist behavior as a rising anti-status quo power in East Asia, see the next two chapters in this book.

116. Peter Duus, "The Takeoff Point of Japanese Imperialism," in Harry Wray and Hilary Conroy, eds., *Japan Examined: Perspectives on Modern Japanese History* (Honolulu, HI.: University of Hawaii Press, 1983), p. 155.

117. Peter Duus, "The Takeoff Point of Japanese Imperialism," p. 154.
118. Key-hiuk Kim, *The Last Phase of the East Asian World Order,* p. 204.
119. Alexander Deconde, *A History of American Foreign Policy* (New York: Charles Scribner's Sons, 1970), p. 368.
120. Myung Hyun Cho, *Korea and the Major Powers,* p. 94.

Chapter 4

1. Akira Iriye, *Across the Pacific: An Inner History of American-East Asian Relations* (Chicago, IL.: Imprint Publications, 1992), p. 56.
2. Myung Hyun Cho, *Korea and the Major Powers* (Seoul, Korea: Research Center for Peace and Unification of Korea, 1989), p. 78.
3. M. I. Sladkovsky, *China & Japan, Past and Present,* edited and translated by Robert F. Price (Gulf Breeze, FL.: Academic International Press, 1975), p. 66.
4. Peter Duus, *The Rise of Modern Japan* (Boston: Houghton Mifflin Company, 1976), p. 190.
5. The immigration dispute between the United States and Japan started during the Russo-Japanese War. A triumphant culmination of the agitation resulted in the Japanese Exclusion Act in 1924. See Akira Iriye, *Across the Pacific: An Inner History of American-East Asian Relations,* p. 151.
6. Myung Hyun Cho, *Korea and the Major Powers,* p. 83.
7. M. I. Sladkovsky, *China & Japan, Past and Present,* pp. 66-67.
8. James E. Sheridan, *China in Disintegration: The Republican Era in Chinese History, 1912-1949* (New York: The Free Press, 1975).
9. Peter Duus, *The Rise of Modern Japan,* p. 196.
10. Shumpei Okamoto, "Ishibashi Tanzan and the Twenty-One Demands," in Akira Iriye, ed., *The Chinese and the Japanese: Essays in Political and Cultural Interactions* (Princeton, N.J.: Princeton University Press, 1980), pp. 184-98.
11. For a detailed analysis of the May Fourth Movement, see Chow Tse-tsung, *The May Fourth Movement: Intellectual Revolution in Modern China* (Stanford, CA.: Stanford University Press,), pp. 77-84.
12. Quoted from Akira Iriye, *Across the Pacific: An Inner History of American-East Asian Relations,* p. 134.
13. Ibid., p. 134.
14. Quoted from Morinosuke Kajima, *A Brief Diplomatic History of Modern Japan* (Rutland, VT.: Charles E. Tuttle Co., 1965), p. 66.
15. Ibid., p. 73.
16. Akira Iriye, *Across the Pacific: An Inner History of American-East Asian Relations,* p. 144.
17. Morinosuke Kajima, *A Brief Diplomatic History of Modern Japan,* p. 74.
18. Claude A. Buss, *Asia in the Modern World* (London: Collier-Macmillan, 1964), p. 308.
19. Michio Morishima, *Why has Japan "Succeeded"?: Western Technology and the Japanese Echos* (Cambridge: Cambridge University Press, 1982), p. 122.

20. Peter Duus, *The Rise of Modern Japan,* p. 199.

21. Donald Macintyre, *Sea Power in the Pacific* (New York: Crane & Russak, 1972), p. 183.

22. Gerald Segal, *Rethinking the Pacific* (Oxford: Clarendon Press, 1990), p. 68.

23. James B. Crowley, "Japan's Military Foreign Policy," in James W. Morley, ed., *Japan's Foreign Policy, 1868-1941* (New York: Columbia University Press, 1974), p. 39.

24. Akira Iriye, *The Origins of the Second World War in Asia and the Pacific* (New York: Longman, 1993), p. 2.

25. Morinosuke Kajima, *A Brief Diplomatic History of Modern Japan,* pp. 77-78.

26. Claude A. Buss, *Asia in the Modern World,* p. 307.

27. Pao-chin Chu, "From the Paris Peace Conference to the Manchurian Incident: The Beginning of China's Diplomacy of Resistance against Japan," in Alvin D. Coox and Hilary Conroy, eds., *China and Japan: A Search for Balance Since World War I* (Santa Barbara, CA.: ABC-Clio, Inc., 1978), pp. 59-82.

28. Donald A. Jordan, *The Northern Expedition: China's National Revolution of 1926-1928* Honolulu, HI.: The University of Hawaii Press, 1976), p. 7.

29. C. Martin Wilbur, *The Nationalist Revolution in China, 1923-1928* (Cambridge, England: Cambridge University Press, 1984), pp. 5-8.

30. Pao-Chin Chu, "From the Paris Conference to the Manchurian Incident: The Beginning of China's Diplomacy of Resistance against Japan," in Alvin D. Coox and Hilary Conroy, eds., *China and Japan: A Search for Balance since World War I,* pp. 59-84.

31. Soon after the outbreak of the Mukden Incident Japan was ostracized by the world, charged with having acted against the Nine Power Treaty, and branded as an aggressor. Nevertheless, a Japanese historian suggests that "it would be unfair to denounce only Japan as being responsible for the events surrounding the Manchurian (Mukden) Incident." According to the Japanese historian, "the fact that China made no serious effort to check civil war and internal chaos and, furthermore, did nothing to create conditions in which various interests could be transferred to her by the powers concerned, was one of the main causes of discord." Morinosuke Kajima, *A Brief Diplomatic History of Modern Japan,* pp. 78-79.

32. Gerald Segal, *Rethinking the Pacific,* p. 68.

33. Morinosuke Kajima, *A Brief Diplomatic History of Modern Japan,* p. 70.

34. Steve Chan, *East Asian Dynamism: Growth, Order and Security in the Pacific Region* (Boulder, CO.: Westview Press, 1993), p. 22.

35. Mark R. Peattie, *Ishiwara Kanji and Japan's Confrontation with the West* (Princeton, N.J.: Princeton University Press, 1975), p. 275.

36. Quoted from Tokutomi Iichiro, "Commentary on the Imperial Rescript Declaring War on the United States and the British Empire," in Theodore de Bary, Ryusaku Tsunoda, and Donald Keene, eds., *Sources of Japanese Tradition,* vol. 2 (New York: Columbia University Press, 1964), p. 293.

37. Claude A. Buss, *Asia in the Modern World,* p. 381.

38. For an overview of the Japanese aggression in this crucial period, see James William Morley, ed., *Japan Erupts: The London Naval Conference and the Manchurian Incident, 1928-1932* (New York: Columbia University Press, 1984).

39. In fact, when war did come in 1937, millions of Chinese died and Chiang's own position within the Chinese political arena was gravely weakened.

40. Lin Han-sheng, "A New Look at Chinese Nationalist 'Appeasers,'" in Alvin D. Coox and Hilary Conroy, eds., *China and Japan: A Search for Balance Since World War I*, pp. 211-242.

41. Parks M. Coble, *Facing Japan: Chinese Politics and Japanese Imperialism, 1931-1937* (Cambridge, MA: Council on East Asian Studies, Harvard University, Distributed by Harvard University Press, 1991), p. 1.

42. Parks M. Coble, *Facing Japan: Chinese Politics and Japanese Imperialism*, p. 2.

43. Joseph S. Nye, Jr., *Understanding International Conflicts* (New York: Harper Collins, 1993), p. 80.

44. Akira Iriye, *The Origins of the Second World War in Asia and the Pacific*, p. 18.

45. For the dilemmas of Britain, see Bradford A. Lee, *Britain and the Sino-Japanese War, 1937-1939* (Stanford, CA.: Stanford University Press, 1973); and Peter Lowe, *Great Britain and the Origins of the Pacific War* (Oxford, England: Clarendon Press, 1977).

46. A. Doak Barnett, *China and the Major Powers in East Asia* (Washington, D.C., The Brookings Institution, 1977), p. 158.

47. Akira Iriye, *Across the Pacific: An Inner History of American-East Asian Relations*, p. 180.

48. U.S. Department of State, *US Relations with China*, pp. 7-8; quoted from A. Doak Barnett, *China and the Major Powers in East Asia*, pp. 158-59.

49. Akira Iriye, *Across the Pacific: An Inner History of American-East Asian Relations*, p. 180.

50. This event is known as Xian Incident and has been studied in great detail by many authors. Among detailed accounts in English are Wu Tien-wei, *The Sian Incident: A Pivotal Point in Modern Chinese History* (Ann Arbor, MI.: Center for Chinese Studies, University of Michigan, 1976); James M. Bertram, *First Act in China: The Story of the Sian Mutiny* (New York: Viking Press, 1938); T. A. Bisson, *Japan in China* (New York: The Macmillan Company, 1938), pp. 154-91; and Edgar Snow, *Red Star Over China* (New York: Random House, 1968), pp. 380-95.

51. Akira Iriye, *The Origins of the Second World War in Asia and the Pacific*, pp. 37-38.

52. Hata Ikuhiko, "The Marco Polo Bridge Incident, 1937," in James W. Morley, ed., *The China Quagmire: Japan's Expansion in the Asian Continent, 1933-1941* (New York: Columbia University Press, 1983), p. 247.

53. For books in English about the Nanjing Massacre, see Shuhsi Hsu, *The War Conduct of the Japanese* (Hankou, China: Kelly and Walsh Ltd., 1938); Lewis Strong Casey Smythe, *War Damage in the Nanking Area, December 1937 to March 1938* (Shanghai, China: Mercury Press, 1938); Harold John

Timperley, *What War Means: The Japanese Terror in China: A Documentary Record* (London: Victor Gollancz Ltd., 1938); Harold John Timperley, *Japanese Terror in China* New York: Modern Age Books, 1938). For books in Japanese about the Nanjing Massacre, see Tomio Hora, *Nankin Daigyakusatsu* (Nanjing Massacre) (Tokyo: Gendaishi Shuppan Kai, 1975); Tomio Hora, *Nitchu Senso Nankin Daizangyaku Jiken Shiryoshu* (Sources on the Nanjing Massacre During the Sino-Japanese Conflict) (Tokyo: Aoki Shoten, 1985); *Nankin Daigyakusatsu: Nihonjin e no Kokuhatsu* (Nanjing Massacre: A Protest to the Japanese) (Osaka: Toho Shuppan, 1992); Yutaka Yoshida, *Tenno No Guntai To Nankin Jiken* (The Japanese Emperor's Army and the Nanjing Incident) (Tokyo: Aoki Shoten, 1985). For books in Chinese about the Nanjing Massacre, see *Nanjing Datusha Tuzheng* (An Illustrated Account of the Nanjing Massacre) (Changchun: Jilin Renmin Chuban She, 1995); *Qinhua Rijun Nanjing Datusha Shiliao* (A True Record of the Nanjing Massacre Committed by the Invading Japanese Army) (Nanjing: Jiangsu Guji Chuban She, 1985); Tianbolie (Harold John Timperley), *Wairen Muduzhong Zhi Rijun Baoxing* (A Foreigner's Eyewitness Account of the Atrocities Committed by the Japanese Army) (Hankou: Guomin Chuban She, 1938); Tianbolie (Harold John Timperley), *Wairen Muduzhong Zhi rijun Baoxing* (A Foreigner's Eyewitness Account of the Atrocities Committed by the Japanese Army) (Nanchang: Jiangxi Renmin Chuban She, 1986); *Xue Ji* (Sacrificial Blood) (Beijing: Zhongguo Renshi Chuban She, 1994).

54. M. I. Sladkovsky, *China and Japan, Past and Present,* p. 118.

55. Nicholas Tarling, *The Fall of Imperial Britain in South-East Asia* (Singapore: Oxford University Press, 1993), pp. 113-14.

56. U.S. State Department, *Papers Relating to the Foreign Relations of the United States, Japan: 1931-1941,* vol. 2 (Washington, D.C.: U.S. Government Printing Office, 1945). Quoted from James Fallows, *Looking at the Sun,* p. 112.

57. Christopher Thorne, *The Limits of Foreign Policy* (London: Hamish Hamilton, 1972), p. 33.

58. Mark Peattie, "Japanese Attitudes Towards Colonialism," in Ramon Myers and Mark Peattie, eds., *The Japanese Colonial Empire, 1895-1945* (Princeton, N.J.: Princeton University Press, 1984), p. 97.

59. These Japanese legacies became the foundation for the subsequent development of an autocratic and strong state in South Korea and Taiwan after World War II. They also facilitated the industrialization efforts of these countries from the 1950s on. For the Japanese colonial policy and legacies, see Ramon Myers and Mark Peattie, eds., *The Japanese Colonial Empire, 1895-1945.*

60. Ian Nish, *Japanese Foreign Policy, 1869-1942* (London: Routledge & Kegan Paul, 1977), pp. 167-72.

61. For one account of U.S. policy toward East Asia during this period, see Dorothy Borg, *The United States and the Far Easter Crisis of 1933-1938: From*

Manchurian Incident Through the Initial Stage of the Undeclared Sino-Japanese War (Cambridge, MA: Harvard University Press, 1964).

62. Much of the enormous popular support the Communists gained during the war years was based on patriotic appeals for national resistance to the Japanese invaders. See Maurise Meisner, *Mao's China, A History of the People's Republic* (New York: The Free Press, 1977), pp. 37-38.

63. For an overview of Japan's southward strategy and its aftermath, see James William Morley, ed., *The Fateful Choice: Japan's Advance into Southeast Asia, 1939-1941* (New York: Columbia University Press, 1980).

64. Nicholas Tarling, *The Fall of Imperial Britain in South-East Asia,* p. 136.

65. Peter Duus, *The Rise of Modern Japan,* pp. 224-25.

66. Quoted in G. R. Hess, *The United States' Emergence as a Southeast Asian Power, 1940-1950* (New York: Columbia University Press, 1987), p. 21.

67. Nicholas Tarling, *The Fall of Imperial Britain in South-East Asia,* p. 138.

68. John Welfield, *An Empire in Eclipse: Japan in the Postwar American Alliance System* (Atlantic Highlands, N.J.: Athlone Press, 1988), p. 15.

69. In 1943 the wartime Japanese government formed the Greater East Asia War Inquiry Commission to look into the causes of the war and said of the ABCD encirclement: "The arrogant Anglo-Saxons, ever covetous of securing world hegemony according to the principles of the white man's burden, thus dared to take resource to measures designed to stifle Nippon to death. It is small wonder that Nippon had to rise in arms." Quoted in John Dower, *War Without Mercy: Race and Power in the Pacific War* (New York: Pantheon books, 1986), pp. 59-60.

70. For one account of the Japanese decision to go to war with the United States, see Louis Morton, "Japan's Decision for War (1941)," in Arnold A. Offner, ed., *America and the Origins of World War II, 1933-1941* (Boston: Houghton Mifflin Co., 1971), pp. 183-211.

71. Statement of Prince Naruhiko Higashikuni, June 9, 1949. Quoted in Louis Morton, "Japan's Decision for War (1941)," in Arnold A. Offner, ed., *America and the Origins of World War II, 1933-1941,* p. 211.

72. Nancy Bernkopf Tucker, "China and America: 1941-1991," *Foreign Affairs* (Winter 1991/1992), p. 76.

73. John Curtis Perry, "Japan and the United States at War," in Mark Borthwick, ed., *Pacific Century, The Emergence of Modern Pacific Asia* (Boulder, CO.: Westview Press, 1992), p. 215.

74. Quoted in Scott Sagan, "The Origins of the Pacific War," in Robert Rotberg and Theodore Rabbs, eds., *The Origin and Prevention of Major Wars* (New York: Cambridge University Press, 1989), pp. 335-36.

75. William A. Renzi and Mark D. Roehrs, *Never Look Back: A History of World War II in the Pacific* (Armonk, N.Y.: M. E. Sharpe, 1991), p. 39

76. Den van der Vat, *The Pacific Campaign: World War II: The US-Japanese Naval War, 1941-1945* (New York: Simon & Schuster, 1991), pp. 140-41.

77. Peter Duus, *The Rise of Modern Japan,* p. 230.

78. Joseph S. Nye, Jr., *Understanding International Conflicts,* p. 93.
79. Tang Tsou, *America's Failure in China, 1941-50* (Chicago, IL.: The University of Chicago Press, 1963), p. ix.
80. Peter Duus, *The Rise of Modern Japan,* p. 228.

Chapter 5

1. For one account on the beginning of the Cold War in Asia, see Marc S. Gallicchio, *The Cold War Begins in Asia: American East Asian Policy and the Fall of the Japanese Empire* (New York: Columbia University Press, 1988).
2. Gordon A. Craig and Alexander L. George, *Force and Statecraft: Diplomatic Problems of Our Time* (New York, Oxford University Press, 1983), p. 115.
3. Joseph Frankel, *International Relations in a Changing World* (New York: Oxford University Press, 1979), p. 161.
4. In the Western scholarship of the Cold War, two views once competed. The traditional approach blamed the Soviet Union for the outbreak of the Cold War. The revisionists in the late 1960s and the 1970s insisted that the United States was not an innocent bystander. By the mid-1980s this controversy was losing its intensity, in a famous article John Lewis Gaddies declared that a post-revisionist consensus was emerging. According to this consensus, the United States had become an imperial nation after World War II. The post–war American empire was a response to the entreaties of governments and peoples who felt threatened by the opportunistic expansion of the Soviet Union. Gaddies article is entitled "The Emerging Post-Revisionist Thesis on the Origins of the Cold War," in *Diplomatic History* no. 7 (Summer 1983), pp. 171-90. For a comprehensive analysis of origins of the Cold War, see Melvyn P. Feffler and David S. Painter, eds., *Origins of the Cold War: An International History* (London: Routledge, 1994).
5. Among the books on the Yalta Conference and its impact on the post–World War II world, see Russell D. Buhite, *Decisions at Yalta: An Appraisal of Summit Diplomacy* (Wilmington, Del.: Scholarly Resources, 1986); J. Joseph P. Morray, *From Yalta to Disarmament; Cold War Debate* (New York: Monthly Review Press, 1961); John L. Snell, *The meaning of Yalta: Big Three Diplomacy and the New Balance of Power* (Baton Rouge, LA.: Louisiana State University Press, 1956); and Edward R. Stettinius, *Roosevelt and the Russians: the Yalta Conference* (Garden City, N.Y.: Doubleday, 1949).
6. Marc S. Gallicchio, *The Cold War Begins in Asia: American East Asian Policy and the Fall of the Japanese Empire* pp. 3-4.
7. Tang Tsou, *America's Failure in China, 1941-50* (Chicago, IL.: The University of Chicago Press, 1963), p. 239.
8. Myung Hyun Cho, *Korea and the Major Powers* (Seoul, Korea: Research Center for Peace and Unification of Korea, 1989), p. 132.
9. John Sbrega, *Anglo-American Relations and Colonialism in East Asia, 1941-45* (New York: Garland, 1983), p. 145.

10. For the position of President Roosevelt, see U.S. Department of State, *The Conferences at Malta and Yalta, 1945* (Washington, D.C.: U.S. Government Printing Office, 1955).

11. George F. Kennan ("X"), "The Sources of Soviet Conduct," *Foreign Affairs,* no. 25 (July 1947), pp. 566-82.

12. Burton I. Kaufman, *The Korean War: Challenges in Crisis, Credibility, and Command* (Philadelphia, PA.: Temple University Press, 1986), p. 17.

13. Harry S Truman, *Years of Trial and Hope,* vol. II, (New York: The New American Library, 1965), pp. 128-29.

14. John W. Garver, *Foreign Relations of the People's Republic of China* (Englewood Cliffs, N.J.: Prentice Hall, 1993), p. 37.

15. When the Chinese Communist forces were gathering on the north bank of the Yangtze River, on January 10, 1949, Stalin forwarded a letter from KMT Foreign Minister Wang Shijie asking the Soviet leader to arbitrate the CCP-KMT dispute. Implying his willingness to do so, Stalin expressed his idea that China be divided along the Yangtze River, with the Communists on the north and the Nationalists on the south. Yu Zhan and Zhang Guanyou, "Did Stalin Ever Persuade Us Not to Cross the Yangtze River?" in Ministry of Foreign Affairs, ed., *Xinzhongguo Waijiao Fengyun* (New China Diplomatic Events) (Beijing: Shijiezheshi Chuban She, 1990), p. 19.

16. Senate Committee on the Judiciary, *Hearings on the Institute of Pacific Relations,* 82d Congress, First and Second Sessions, 1951-52, p. 2839.

17. Akira Iriye, *The Cold War in Asia: A Historical Introduction* (Englewood Cliffs, N.J.: Prentice-Hall, 1974), p. 93.

18. For one detailed study of the decline of the KMT regime, see Lloyd E. Eastman, *Seeds of Destruction: Nationalist China in War and Revolution, 1937-1949* (Stanford, CA.: Stanford University Press, 1984).

19. President Truman to General Marshall, December 15, 1945, in U.S. Department of State, *United States Relations with China* (Washington, D.C., Government Printing Office, 1949), p. 605.

20. Ibid., p. 605.

21. This view was elaborated in great detail by Michael Scholler in his book, *The United States and China in the Twentieth Century* (New York: Oxford University Press, 1979).

22. Tang Tsou, *America's Failure in China, 1941-50* (Chicago, The University of Chicago Press, 1963), p. 378.

23. John Robinson Beal, *Marshall in China* (Toronto: Doubleday Canada Limited, 1970), pp. 348-62.

24. Peter Lowe, *The Origins of the Korean War* (London: Longman, 1986), p. 99.

25. Quoted from John Spanier, *American Foreign Policy Since World War II* (New York: Praeger, 1973), p. 81.

26. Ibid., p. 82.

27. U.S. State Department, *United States Relations With China* (Washington, D.C.: U.S. Government Printing Office, 1949), pp. 14-15.

28. Vladimir Dedjier, *The Battle Stalin Lost: Memoirs of Yugoslavia, 1948-1953* (New York: Viking Press, 1971), p. 68.

29. Gordon H. Chang, *Friends and Enemies: The United States, China, and the Soviet Union, 1948-1972* (Stanford, CA.: Stanford University Press, 1990), p. 28.

30. Shi Zhe, *Zai lishi juren shenbian: Shi Zhe Huiyilu* (Together with the Historical Giants: Shi Zhe's Memoirs) (Beijing: Zhongyang Lishi Wenxian Chuban She, 1992), p. 307-308. In recent years, whether or not Stalin advised Mao is a question that has been widely debated by Chinese diplomatic historians. For example, Yu Zhan and Zhang Guangyou, two former Chinese diplomats, allege that they found no reliable evidence to prove that Stalin had ever offered such advice. Yu and Zhang, "An Exploration of Whether Stalin Advised Our Party Not to Cross the Yangtze River," *Dangde Wenxian* (January 1989), p. 56-58.

31. Tang Tsou, *America's Failure in China, 1941-50,* p. 514.

32. Li Jian, *Tiaoyutai Guoshi Fengyun* (Looking at the Wind and Cloud of Diplomatic Events from Tiaoyutai), vol. 1 (Taiyuan, China: Taibai Wenyi Chuban She, 1995), p. 45. See also Shi Zhe, "Gensui Mao Zhuxi Fangwen Sulian" (With Chairman Mao on a visit to the Soviet Union), *Renwu* (May 1988), pp. 8-10.

33. Mao Zedong, "On the People's Democratic Dictatorship," *Selected Works of Mao Tse-tung,* vol. IV (Beijing: Foreign Language Press, 1969), p. 415.

34. Ibid.

35. For a detailed description of Mao's first Soviet visit from Chinese sources, see Li Jian, *Tiaoyutai Guoshi Fengyun,* vol. 1, pp. 51-98. Also see the memoir of Zhu Zhongli, the wife of Wang Jiaxiang, the first Chinese ambassador to Moscow who personally managed Mao's first visit to the Soviet Union, "Wang Jiaxiang Waijiao Shengyia Zhongyi" (Diplomatic Career of Wang Jiaxiang), in Waijiaobu Waijiaoshi Yanjiushi (Diplomatic History Research Office of Chinese Ministry of Foreign Affairs), ed., *Dangdai Zhongguo Shijie Waijiao Shengyia* (Ambassadors' Diplomatic Lives of Contemporary China) (Beijing: Shijie Zhishi Chuban She, 1995), pp. 1-33.

36. John Spanier, *American Foreign Policy Since World War II,* pp. 84-85.

37. Peter Lowe, *The Origins of the Korean War,* p. 20.

38. John Spanier, *American Foreign Policy Since World War II,* p. 85.

39. Bruce Cumings, *The Origins of the Korean War: Liberation and the Emergence of Separate Regimes, 1945-1947* (Princeton, N.J.: Princeton University Press, 1981), p.179.

40. John Chay, *The Problems and Prospects of American-East Asian Relations* (Boulder, CO.: Westview Press, 1977), p. 208.

41. John Lewis Gaddis, "Korea in American Politics, Strategy and Diplomacy, 1945-1950," in Yonosuke Nagai and Akira Iriye, eds., *The Origins of the Cold War in Asia* (New York: Columbia University Press, 1977), p. 281.

42. Myung Hyun Cho, *Korea and the Major Powers,* p. 192.

43. Ibid., pp. 194-95.

44. Nikita Khrushchev, *Khrushchev Remembers* (Boston: Little, Brown, 1970), pp. 367-69. Although new Chinese, Korean, and Russian sources have emerged in recent years, Khrushchev's memoirs remain the most detailed and authoritative source of describing the roles of Stalin, Kim, and Mao in connection with the Korean War. A new study of the Korean War indicates that "recently released Chinese, Russian, and Korean sources demonstrate that Khrushchev's story about the Korean War . . . is generally consistent with these new sources. Khrushchev's description of Zhou Enlai's secret visit to the Soviet Union after the UN landing at Inchon, for example, is compatible with new Chinese sources even in small details." Chen Jian, *China's Road to the Korean War: The Making of the Sino-American Confrontation* (New York: Columbia University Press, 1994), p. 86.

45. Alexander L. George and Richard Smoke, *Deterrence in American Foreign Policy: Theory and Practice* (New York: Columbia University Press, 1959), p. 164.

46. The Chinese official publication retains an ambiguous attitude toward the outbreak of the Korean War. It recognizes June 25, 1950, as the outbreak of the war, but does not mention that North Korea launched the war against the South. "South Korea's provocation along the 38th parallel" was attributed as the cause of the "Korean civil war." See Junshi Kexueyuan Junshi lishi Yanjiubu (Military History Research Department of the Chinese Military Academy), *Zhongguo Renmin Zhiyuanjun Kangmei Yuanchao Zhanshi* (Battle History of Chinese People's Volunteers in the War Against America and assisting Korea) (Beijing: Junshi Kexue Chuban She, 1992), p. 3.

47. NSC 118/2, "United States Objectives and Courses of Action in Korea," December 20, 1951, quoted from Myung Hyun Cho, *Korea and the Major Powers,* p. 198.

48. Burton I. Kaufman, *The Korean War: Challenges in Crisis, Credibility, and Command,* p. 34.

49. Tang Tsou, *America's Failure in China, 1941-50* (Chicago, IL.: The University of Chicago Press, 1963), p. 558.

50. For one study of Chinese calculation, see Allen S. Whiting, *China Cross the Yalu: The Decision to Enter the Korean War* (Stanford, CA.: Stanford University Press, 1960).

51. Rosemary Foot, *The Wrong War: American Policy and the Dimensions of the Korean Conflict, 1950-1953* (Ithaca, N.Y.: Cornell University Press, 1985), p. 101. According to Chinese sources, at the end of 1950 the UN troops reached 420,000 men. Junshi Kexueyuan Junshi lishi Yanjiubu (Military History Research Department of the Chinese Military Academy), *Zhongguo Renmin Zhiyuanjun Kangmei Yuanchao Zhanshi,* p. 14.

52. John G. Stoessinger, *Nations at Dawn: China, Russia, and America* (New York: McGraw-Hill Inc., 1994), p. 58.

53. Harry S Truman, *Years of Trial and Hope* (Garden City, N.Y.: Doubleday & Co., 1956), pp. 378-80.

54. U.S. Senate Committees on Armed Services and Foreign Relations, *Military Situation in the Far East* (Washington, D.C.,: U.S. Government Printing Office (1951), pp. 731-32.

55. Henry Kissinger, *Nuclear Weapons and Foreign Policy* (New York: Harper, 1957), p. 140.

56. Rosemary Foot, *The Wrong War: American Policy and the Dimensions of the Korean Conflict, 1950-1953*, p. 101.

57. Chen Jian, *China's Road to the Korean War: The Making of the Sino-American Confrontation*, p. 161.

58. Peng Dehuai, *Memoirs of a Chinese Marshal* (Beijing, 1984), pp. 572-573; quoted in John Wilson Lewis and Xue Litai, *China Builds the Bomb* (Stanford, CA.: Stanford University Press, 1988), p. 8.

59. Junshi Kexueyuan Junshi lishi Yanjiubu (Military History Research Department of the Chinese Military Academy), *Zhongguo Renmin Zhiyuanjun Kangmei Yuanchao Zhanshi*, p. 9.

60. For one text of Mao's Order, see Junshi Kexueyuan Junshi lishi Yuanjiubu (Military History Research Department of the Chinese Military Academy), *Zhongguo Renmin Zhiyuanjun Kangmei Yuanchao Zhanshi*, pp. 10-11.

61. Shi Zhe, *Zai Lishi Juren Shenbian: Shi Zhe Huiyilu*, pp. 495-99.

62. Li Jian, *Tiaoyutai Guoshi Fengyun*, vol. 2, pp. 538-39.

63. A Chinese diplomatic history book compiled by a group of Chinese foreign affair officials and specialists (headed by the former Vice-Foreign Minister, Han Nianlong) states that, "in the early days of new China, the major threat came from the United States. In order to safeguard its independence and security, China could not but spearhead its struggle against the United States. 'To resist the United States and aid Korea, to defend the country and protect peoples homes' was the greatest strategic decision made in the struggle against the United States." See Chinese Ministry of Foreign Affairs, *Diplomacy of Contemporary China* (Hong Kong: New Horizon Press, 1990), p. 46.

64. For Chinese leaders' perception about the connection between the U.S. invasion of Korea and the threat to China's security based on the analysis of Japan aggression against China, see Zhou Enlai, "Kangmei Yuanchao, Baowei Heping" (Resisting America, Assisting Korea, and Defending Peace)," *Zhou Enlai Waijiao Wenxuan* (Selected Diplomatic Works of Zhou Enlai) (Beijing: Zhongyang Wenxian Chuban She, 1990), p. 31.

65. A detailed Chinese description of the armistice negotiations is recently available. See Cai Chengwen and Zhao Yongtian, *Banmendian Tanpan* (Panmunjom Negotiations) (Beijing: Jiefengjun Chuban She, 1992).

66. Among many works on MacArthur's role in the occupation of Japan, see, for example, Thomas W. Burkman, ed., *The Occupation of Japan: The International Context* (Norfolk, VA.: The MacArthur Memorial Foundation, 1984); John Gunther, *The Riddle of MacArthur: Japan, Korea and the Far East* (London: H. Hamilton, 1951); William Joseph Sebald, *With MacArthur in*

Japan: A Personal History of the Occupation (New York: W. W. Norton, 1965); and William Louis Neumann, *America Encounters Japan: From Perry to MacArthur* (Baltimore, MD.: Johns Hopkins Press, 1963).

67. Martin E. Weinstein, *Japan's Postwar Defense Policy, 1947-1968* (New York: Columbia University Press, 1971), p. 50.

68. Roger Buckley, *US-Japanese Alliance Diplomacy, 1945-1990* (New York: Cambridge University Press, 1992), p. 27.

69. Peter Lowe, *The Origins of the Korean War,* p. 77.

70. Chae-jin Lee and Hideo Sato, *US Policy Toward Japan and Korea: A Changing Influence Relationship* (New York: Praeger, 1982), p. 17.

71. Roger Buckley, *US-Japanese Alliance Diplomacy, 1945-1990,* p. 33.

72. For the texts of both treaties, see Edwin O. Reischauer, *The United States and Japan* (New York: Viking Press, 1957), pp. 363-80.

73. The People's Republic of China was not present at the San Francisco conference because Secretary of State Acheson rejected Soviet Deputy Foreign Minister Andrei Gromyko's move to invite a delegation from the PRC. Harrison M. Holland, *Japan Challenges America: Managing An Alliance in Crisis* (Boulder, CO.: Westview Press, 1992), p. 149.

74. Akira Iriye, *Across the Pacific,* p. 335.

75. For one study of the impact of the San Francisco system on Japanese politics, see Tetsuya Kataota, *The Price of a Constitution: The Origin of Japan's Postwar Politics* (New York: Crane Russak, 1991).

76. Bradley M. Richardson and Scott C. Flanagan, *Politics in Japan* (Boston, MA.: Little, Brown and Company, 1984), p. 50.

77. Japan's economic situation also compelled the MacArthur administration to modify certain of the original Occupation policies to encourage the Japanese to rebuild their economy. Because of the Occupation policy, in 1946, Japanese industrial production sank to less than one-third of what it had been in 1930 and to one-seventh of the total in 1937. The wrecked state of the Japanese economy was even inadequate to the task of keeping the Japanese from starving. Thus, to the cost of the Occupation, the United States had to support the war-torn Japanese economy. Japan received a larger amount of U.S. aid than either China or Korea during 1945-51. Myung Hyun Cho, *Korea and the Major Powers,* p. 148.

78. Chae-jin Lee and Hideo Sato, *US Policy Toward Japan and Korea: A Changing Influence Relationship,* p. 17.

79. William J. Barnds, "Trends in US Politics and Their Implications for America's Asian Policy," in Robert A. Scalapino, Seizaburo Sato, Jusuf Wanandi, and Sung-joo Han, eds., *Asia and the Major Powers: Domestic Politics and Foreign Policy* (Berkeley, CA.: Institute of East Asian Studies, University of California, 1988), p. 9.

80. Waldo Heinrichs, "Eisenhower and Sino-American Confrontation," in Warren I. Cohen and Akira Iriye, eds., *The Great Powers in East Asia: 1953-1960* (New York: Columbia University Press, 1990), p. 86.

81. William J. Barnds, "Trends in US Politics and Their Implications for America's Asian Policy," in Robert A. Scalapino, Seizaburo Sato, Jusuf Wanandi, and Sung-joo Han, eds., *Asia and the Major Powers: Domestic Politics and Foreign Policy,* p. 12.

82. Ibid.

83. Peter J. Katzenstein and Noburo Okawara, *Japan's National Security: Structures, Norms and Policy Responses in a Changing World* (Ithaca, N.Y.: Cornell University East Asia Program, 1993), pp. 132-33.

84. While the United States was expanding its commitments in much of Asia, it was gradually and successfully adapting to Japanese pressure to reduce its military presence in that country. Many bases were closed or consolidated and U.S. military personnel were reduced. In 1960 a revised security treaty designed to meet some of the objections of Japan's populace as well as many of those of the governing Liberal Democratic Party was signed. Joseph P. Keddell, Jr., *The Politics of Defense in Japan: Managing Internal and External Pressures* (Armonk, N.Y.: M. E. Sharpe, 1993), p. 14.

85. This and the next paragraphs are drawn heavily from National Security Council (NSC) 48/5, "A Report to the National Security Council by the Executive Secretary on United States Objective Policies and Courses of Action in Asia," May 17, 1951, National Archives, Washington DC.

86. Tang Tsou, *America's Failure in China, 1941-50* (Chicago, IL.: The University of Chicago Press, 1963), p. 589.

87. See Johnson's testimony, in the Senate Committee on Armed Services and Committee on Foreign Relations, *Hearings on the Military Situation in the Far East,* 82d Congress, First Session, 1951.

88. For the Chinese text, see *Xinhua Yuebao,* vol. 2, no. 3 (July 1950), p. 525.

89. He Di, "The Evolution of the People's Republic of China's Policy toward the Offshore Islands," in Warren I. Cohen and Akira Iriye, eds., *The Great Powers in East Asia: 1953-1960,* p. 223.

90. Waijiaobu Yuanjiushi (Research Office of Chinese Ministry of Foreign Affairs), *Zhongmei Guanxi Wenjian Huibian* (Collected Documents on Sino-US Relations) (Beijing: Shejie Zhishi Chuban She, 1960), pp. 1942-43.

91. Dwight D. Eisenhower, *Mandate for Change, 1953-1956* (Garden City, N.Y.: Doubleday, 1963), p. 459.

92. Ibid., pp. 476-77.

93. Waijiaobu Yuanjiushi, *Zhongmei Guanxi Wenjian Huibian,* pp. 2250-51.

94. Thomas. E. Stolper, *China, Taiwan, and the Offshore Islands* (Armonk, N.Y.: M. E. Sharpe, 1985), p. 115.

95. Thomas. E. Stolper, *China, Taiwan, and the Offshore Islands,* p. 118.

96. Dwight D. Eisenhower, *Waging Peace, 1956-1961* (Garden City, N.Y.: Doubleday, 1965), p. 300.

97. Li Jian, *Tiaoyutai Guoshi Fenyun,* p. 637.

98. Hoang Van Hoan, Viet Minh Ambassador to Beijing in the 1950s, remembered that the top Chinese leaders "expressed their determination without

any hesitation that China would provide the Vietnamese people all the necessary material assistance, and would be prepared to send troops to fight together with the Vietnamese people when necessary." Quoted from Shuguang Zhang, "Threat Perception and Chinese Communist Foreign Policy," in Melvyn P. Leffler and David S. Painter, eds., *Origins of the Cold War: An International History* (London: Routledge, 1994), p. 286.

99. Shuguang Zhang, "Threat Perception and Chinese Communist Foreign Policy, in Melvyn P. Leffler and David S. Painter, eds., *Origins of the Cold War: An International History,* p. 290.

100. Joseph Frankel, *International Relations in a Changing World,* p. 163.

101. Wang Bingnan, *Review of the Nine-Year-Long Sino-American Ambassadorial Talks* (Beijing: Shijie Zhishi Chuban She, 1985), p. 58.

Chapter 6

1. Ralph N. Clough, *East Asia and US Security* (Washington, D.C.: The Brookings Institute, 1975), p. 46.

2. Most books on the Sino-Soviet dispute were published between the early 1960s and the early 1980s. Among them see Geoffrey Francis Hudson, Richard Lowenthal, and Roderick MacFarquhar, *The Sino-Soviet Dispute* (New York: Praeger, 1961); Donald S. Zagoria, *The Sino-Soviet Conflict, 1956-1961* (Princeton, N.J.: Princeton University Press, 1962); David Floyd, *Mao Against Khrushchev: A Short History of the Sino-Soviet Conflict* (New York: Praeger, 1964); William E. Griffith, *The Sino-Soviet Rift* (Cambridge, MA.: M.I.T. Press, 1964); Dennis J. Doolin, *Territorial Claims in the Sino-Soviet Conflict* (Stanford, CA.: Hoover Institution on War, Revolution, and Peace, Stanford University, 1965); John Gittings, *Survey of the Sino-Soviet Dispute: a Commentary and Extracts From the Recent Polemics, 1963-1967* (London: Oxford University Press, 1968); Drew Middleton, *The Duel of the Giants: China and Russia in Asia* (New York: Charles Scribner's Sons, 1978). Herbert J. Ellison, ed., *The Sino-Soviet Conflict: A Global Perspective* (Seattle, WA.: University of Washington Press, 1982); Richard Wich, *Sino-Soviet Crisis Politics: A Study of Political Change and Communication* (Cambridge, MA.: Council on East Asian Studies, Harvard University, 1980).

3. G. F. Hudson, Richard Lowenthal, and Rodrick MacFarquhur, *The Sino-Soviet Dispute* (New York: Praeger, 1961), p. 1.

4. Alfred D. Low, *The Sino-Soviet Confrontation since Mao Zedong, Dispute, Détente, or Conflict?,* p. 15.

5. In his recent published memoirs, Li Zhisui, Mao Zedong's private doctor from 1954 to Mao's death in 1976, said, "Khrushchev's speech was a watershed in China's domestic politics, too . . . Mao never forgave Khrushchev for attacking Stalin." Dr. Li Zhisui, *The Private Life of Chairman Mao* (New York: Random House, 1994), p. 118.

6. Quoted from an excellent book based on personal interviews of the Chinese leaders in Beijing by Harrison E. Salisbury, *The New Emperors: China in the*

Era of Mao and Deng (New York: Avon Books, 1992), p. 155. This story is confirmed by the Chinese sources, for example, in Li Jian, *Tiaoyutai Guoshi Fengyun* (Looking at the Wind and Cloud of Diplomatic Events from Tiaoyutai), vol. 1 (Taiyuan, China: Taibai Wenyi Chuban She, 1995), pp. 136-46.

7. Li Jian, *Tiaoyutai Guoshi Fengyun*, vol. 1, pp. 138-39.

8. Morton H. Halperin, *Sino-Soviet Relations and Armed Control* (Cambridge, MA.: Harvard University Press, 1967), p. 44.

9. Yu Zhan (former Chinese ambassador to Moscow), "Yici Buxunchang de Shiming: Yi Zhou Zongli Zuihou Yici Fangwen Sulian" (An Unusual Mission: Premier Zhou's Last Visit to the Soviet Union), in Waijiaobu Waijiaoshi Yanjiushi (Diplomatic Research Office of the Foreign Ministry), ed., *Xinzhongguo Waijiao Fengyun: Zhongguo Waijiaoguan Huiyilu* (Diplomatic Winds and Clouds of New China: Memoirs of the Chinese Diplomats) (Beijing: Shijie Zhishi Chuban She, 1994), p. 18.

10. Raymond L. Garthoff, "Sino-Soviet Military Relations, 1945-1966," in Garthoff, ed., *Sino-Soviet Military Relations* (New York: Praeger, 1966), p. 89.

11. For a discussion of China's attack on Soviet policy during the Sino-Indian border conflict, see, Allen W. Whiting, *The Chinese Calculus of Deterrence, India and Indochina* (Ann Arbor, MI.: The University of Michigan Press, 1975), p. 132.

12. Donald S. Zagoria, "Strange Triangle," in Clement J. Zablick, ed., *The Sino-Soviet Rivalry: Implication for United States Policy* (New York: Praeger, 1966), pp. 42-52.

13. Yu Zhan, "Yici Buxunchang de Shiming: Yi Zhou Zongli Zuihou Yici Fangwen Sulian," in Waijiaobu Waijiaoshi Yanjiushi, ed., *Xinzhongguo Waijiao Fengyun: Zhongguo Waijiaoguan Huiyilu*, pp. 18-19.

14. "Lenin Zhuyi Wanshui" (Long Live Leninism), *Hong Qi* (Red Flag) (April 6, 1960). An English translation appeared in Geoffrey Francis Hudson, Richard Lowenthal, and Roderick MacFarquhar, eds., *The Sino-Soviet Dispute* (New York: Praeger, 1961), pp. 82-112.

15. For an English translation of the letters, see Irwin Isenberg, ed., *The Russian-Chinese Rift: Its Impact on World Affairs* (New York: H. W. Wilson Co., 1966). pp. 155-63.

16. For an English translation of the Soviet "Open Letter," see William E. Griffith, *The Sino-Soviet Rift*, pp. 289-325.

17. For an account of the personal antagonism between Mao and Khrushchev, see David Floyd, *Mao against Khrushchev: A Short History of the Sino-Soviet Conflict* (New York: Praeger, 1964).

18. Yu Zhan, "Yici Buxunchang de Shiming: Yi Zhou Zongli Zuihou Yici Fangwen Sulian," in Waijiaobu Waijiaoshi Yanjiushi, ed., *Xinzhongguo Waijiao Fengyun: Zhongguo Waijiaoguan Huiyilu*, p. 19.

19. For a detailed description of Zhou's visit to Moscow, see Yu Zhan, "Yici Buxunchang de Shiming: Yi Zhou Zongli Zuihou Yici Fangwen Sulian," in Waijiaobu Waijiaoshi Yanjiushi, ed., *Xingzhongguo Waijiao Fengyun: Zhongguo Waijiaoguan Huiyilu*, pp. 19-30.

20. *Remin Ribao,* January 27, 1967, p. 1.

21. For the compiled events during the Cultural Revolution period, see Peter Jones and Sian Kevill, *China and the Soviet Union, 1949-84* (New York: Facts on File Publications, 1985), pp. 73-110.

22. Alfred D. Low, *The Sino-Soviet Confrontation Since Mao Zedong: Dispute, Détente, or Conflict?,* p. 2.

23. Later, in 1954, while briefing a new Chinese ambassador about to depart for the Soviet Union, Zhou Enlai, China's premier, said that Soviet actions in 1948 implied a Korea-like division of China between a Communist north and a Nationalist south. Liu Xiao, *Chushi Sulian Banian* (Eight Years as Ambassador to the Soviet Union) (Beijing: Zhonggong Dangshi Ziliao Chuban she, 1986), pp. 4-5.

24. Zhu Zhongli, "Wang Jiaxiang Waijiao Shengya Zongyi" (Reminiscence of Wang Jiaxiang's Diplomatic Career), in Waijiaobu Waijiaoshi Yanjiushi (Diplomatic History Research Office of the Chinese Ministry of Foreign Affairs), *Dangdai Zhongguo Shijie Waijiao Shengya* (Contemporary Chinese Ambassadors' Diplomatic Careers) (Beijing: Shijie Zhishi Chuban She, 1995), pp. 16-17.

25. Alfred D. Low, *The Sino-Soviet Confrontation Since Mao Zedong: Dispute, Détente, or Conflict?,* p. 3.

26. As one Chinese General put it, it was "totally unfair for the PRC to bear all the expenses of the Korean War." New China News Agency, June 18, 1957, quoted in Lowell Dittmer, *Sino-Soviet Normalization and Its International Implications, 1945-1990* (Seattle, WA.: University of Washington Press, 1992), p. 22.

27. James C.F. Wang, *Contemporary Chinese Politics* (Englewood Cliffs, N.J.: Prentice-Hall, 1985), pp. 285-86.

28. For a study of historical origins of the dispute, see Immanuel C. Y. Hsu, *The Ili Crisis: A Study of Sino-Russian Diplomacy, 1871-1881* (Oxford, England: Oxford University Press, 1965).

29. "The Crux of the Sino-Soviet Boundary Question (1)" *Beijing Review,* July 28, 1981, p. 12; "The Crux of the Sino-Soviet Boundary Question (2)" *Beijing Review,* September 14, 1981, pp. 21-23.

30. H. C. Hinton, "Sino-Soviet Relations: Background and Overview," in Douglas T. Stuart and William T. Tow, eds., *China, the Soviet Union and the West* (Boulder, CO.: Westview Press, 1982), pp. 1-16 and 19-21.

31. Alfred D. Low, *The Sino-Soviet Confrontation Since Mao Zedong: Dispute, Détente, or Conflict?,* p. 89.

32. Deng Xiaoping, "An Important Principle for Handling Relations between Fraternal Parties," *Selected Works of Deng Xiaoping* (Beijing: Foreign Language Press, 1983), p. 301.

33. This story was revealed by Mao himself in 1964 when he told a delegation of the Japanese Socialist party that there were too many places occupied by the Soviet Union, and that the Kuriles should be returned to Japan and

Outer-Mongolia to the PRC. *Sekai Shuno,* Tokyo, August 11, 1963, quoted in Alfred D. Low, *The Sino-Soviet Confrontation Since Mao Zedong: Dispute, Détente, or Conflict?,* p. 78.

34. Li Jian, *Tiaoyutai Guoshi Fengyun,* vol. 1, pp. 270-77.

35. "Letter of the Central Committee of the CCP on February 29, 1964, to the Central Committee of CPSU," *Beijing Review,* May 8, 1964, pp. 12-18.

36. For a detailed account of the clash from the Chinese view, see Deng Lifeng, *Jianguohou Junshixingdong Quanlu* (Complete Records of Military Actions Since the Founding of the PRC) (Taiyuan, China: Shanxi Renmin Chuban She, 1994), pp. 398-404.

37. Neville Maxwell, "Why the Russians Lifted the Blockade at Bear Island," *Foreign Affairs,* vol. 57, no. 1, Fall 1978, pp. 138-45; Thomas Robinson, "The Sino-Soviet Dispute," *The American Political Science Review,* vol. xvi, no. 4 (December 1972), pp. 1175-202.

38. For a documentary study of this event, see John Gottings, *Survey of the Sino-Soviet Dispute: A Commentary and Extracts from the Recent Polemics, 1963-1967* (London: Oxford University Press, 1968), pp. 247-53.

39. For a documentary study of Vietnam and Sino-Soviet Relations, see John Gottings, *Survey of the Sino-Soviet Dispute: A Commentary and Extracts from the Recent Polemics, 1963-1967* (London: Oxford University Press, 1968), pp. 254-70.

40. The Chinese Ministry of Foreign Affairs, *Diplomacy of Contemporary China* (Hong Kong: New Horizon Press, 1990), p. 157.

41. Jonathan D. Pollack, "China and the Global Strategic Balance," in Harry Harding, ed., *China's Foreign Relations in the 1980s* (New Haven, CT.: Yale University Press, 1982), p. 150.

42. Quoted from John W. Lewis and Xue Litai, *China Builds the Bomb* (Stanford, CA.:Stanford University Press, 1988), p. 1.

43. Li Haiwen, "Lenyan Xiangyang Kanshijie: Guoji Zhengzhijia Mao Zedong" (Looking the World Through Cool Eyes: Mao Zedong in International Politics), in Hou Shudong, ed., *Yidai Juren Mao Zedong* (A Giant of the Generation: Mao Zedong) (Beijing: Zhongguo Qinglian Chuban She, 1993), p. 271.

44. Danald W. Klein, "China and the Second World," in Samuel Kim, ed., *China and the World: New Directions in Chinese Foreign Policy* (Boulder, CO.: Westview Press, 1989), p. 131.

45. The Chinese Ministry of Foreign Relations, *Diplomacy of Contemporary China,* p. 267.

46. Gordon H. Chang, *Friends and Enemies: The United States, China, and the Soviet Union: 1948-1972* (Stanford, CA.: Stanford University Press, 1990), p. 232.

47. Akira Iriye, *Across the Pacific: An Inner History of American-East Asian Relations* (Chicago, IL.: Imprint Publications, Inc., 1992), p. 308.

48. Ibid., p. 309.

49. For one study of Japan's role in shaping the new power relations, see Herbert J. Ellison, ed., *Japan and the Pacific Quadrille: The Major Powers in East Asia* (Boulder, CO.: Westview Press, 1987).

50. Chalmers Johnson, *MITI and the Japanese Miracle: The Growth of Industrial Policy, 1925-1975* (Stanford, CA.: Stanford University Press, 1982), pp. 7-17.

51. Ardath W. Burks, *Japan, A Postindustrial Power* (Boulder CO.: Westview Press, 1991), p. 130.

52. Article 8 of the IMF's articles of agreement requires the removal of all restrictions on foreign exchange. The status made a floating rather than fixed exchange rate possible in Japan.

53. Reinhard Drifte, *Japan's Foreign Policy* (New York: Council on Foreign Relations Press, 1990), p. 9.

54. Ardath W. Burks, *Japan, A Postindustrial Power,* p. 130.

55. Shibusawa Masahide, *Japan and the Asian Pacific Region* (New York: St. Martin's Press, 1984), p. 41.

56. Agreements were signed with Burma in 1954, with the Philippines in 1956, with Indonesia in 1958, and with South Vietnam in 1959, totaling $1.15 billion. Shibusawa Masahide, *Japan and the Asian Pacific Region,* p. 42.

57. Massashi Nishihara, *The Japanese and Sukarno's Indonesia: Tokyo-Jarkada Relations, 1951-1966* (Honolulu, HI.: The University of Hawaii Press, 1976), pp. 131-36.

58. For a recent overview of Japanese foreign aid, see Toru Yanagihara and Anne Emig, "An Overview of Japan's Foreign Aid," in Shafiqul Islam, ed., *Yen for Development: Japanese Foreign Aid & the Politics of Burden-Sharing* (New York: Council on Foreign Relations Press, 1991), pp. 37-69.

59. Shibusawa Masahide, *Japan and the Asian Pacific Region,* p. 43.

60. Peter J. Katzenstein and Nobuo Okawara, *Japan's National Security: Structures, Norms and Policy Responses in a Changing World* (Ithaca, N.Y.: Cornell University East Asia Program, 1993), p. 131.

61. Peter J. Katzenstein and Nobuo Okawara, *Japan's National Security: Structures, Norms and Policy Responses in a Changing World,* p. 133.

62. Martin E. Weinstein, *Japan's Postwar Defense Policy, 1947-1968* (New York: Columbia University Press, 1971), p. 88.

63. Peter J. Katzenstein and Nobuo Okawara, *Japan's National Security: Structures, Norms and Policy Responses in a Changing World,* p. 133.

64. For Britain's decolonization policy in Southeast Asia, see Nicholas Tarling, *The Fall of Imperial Britain in South-East Asia* (Singapore: Oxford University Press, 1993), pp. 170-203.

65. As Andrew J. Rotter suggests, it was ironic that the American determination to protect Southeast Asia was of such paramount importance to the ultimate success of liberal capitalism that the tactics temporally used to attain these goals might themselves be illiberal. Sending economic aid and military equipment to the French-sponsored government of Vietnam was "support for colonialism," and "represented most starkly the suspension of liberal

capitalism." Rotter, *The Path to Vietnam: Origins of the American Commitment to Southeast Asia* (Ithaca, N.Y.: Cornell University Press, 1987), p. 220.

66. George C. Herring, *America's Longest War: the United States and Vietnam, 1950-1975* (New York: Alfred A. Knopf, 1986), p. 12.

67. For a personal memoirs of the battle in Dien Bien Phu, see Nguyen Giap Vo, *Dien Bien Phu* (Hanoi: Foreign Languages Pub. House, 1964). For the U.S. initial response to Dien Bien Phu, see Melanie Billings-Yun, *Decision Against War: Eisenhower and Dien Bien Phu, 1954* (New York: Columbia University Press, 1988).

68. George C. Herring, *America's Longest War: the United States and Vietnam, 1950-1975,* p. 13.

69. Quoted from Richard Nixon, *No More Vietnams* (New York: Arbor House, 1985), p. 29.

70. Ibid., p. 29.

71. William Head, "Vietnam and Its Wars: A Historical Overview of U.S. Involvement," in William Head and Lawrence E. Grinter, eds., *Looking Back on the Vietnam War* (Westport, CT.: Praeger, 1993), p. 22.

72. Arthur, M. Schlesinger Jr., *The Bitter Heritage: Vietnam and American Democracy, 1941-1966* (Greenwich, CT.: Fawcett, 1967), p. 35.

73. Timothy J. Lomperis, *The War Everyone Lost—and Won: America's Intervention in Viet Nam's Twin Struggles* (Washington, D.C.: CQ Press, 1992), p. 36.

74. William Head, "Vietnam and Its Wars: A Historical Overview of U.S. Involvement," p. 26.

75. Richard Nixon, *No More Vietnams,* p. 62.

76. Quoted in William Head, "Vietnam and Its Wars: A Historical Overview of U.S. Involvement," in William Head and Lawrence E. Grinter, eds., *Looking Back on the Vietnam War,* p. 27.

77. John G. Stoessinger, *Why Nations Go To War* (New York: St. Martin's Press, 1985), p. 103.

78. Among the works on the Tet Offensive and its impact on the war, see Ronald H. Spector, *After Tet: The Bloodiest Year in Vietnam* (New York: The Free Press, 1993); Peter Braestrup, *Big Story: How the American Press and Television Reported and Interpreted the Crisis of Tet 1968 in Vietnam and Washington,* 2 volumes (Boulder, CO.: Westview Press,: 1977); Don Oberdorfer, *Tet: The Turning Point in the Vietnam War* (New York: A Da Capo Paperback, 1984), and Kathleen J. Turner, *Lyndon Johnson's Dual War* (Chicago, IL.: The University of Chicago Press, 1985).

79. John G. Stoessinger, *Why Nations Go To War,* p. 104.

80. The first 80,000 Chinese road-construction troops dressed in Vietnamese army uniforms and crossed the border on July 9, 1965, and the last Chinese military units withdrew from Vietnam in August 1973. For details, see Deng Lifeng, *Jianguohou Junshixingdong quanlu* (Complete Records of Military Actions since the Founding of the PRC) (Taiyuan, China: Shanxi

Renmin Chuban She, 1994), pp. 329-31, and Li Jian, *Tiaoyutan Guoshi Fengyun,* vol. 1, pp. 321-96.

81. Ronald H. Spector, *After Tet: The Bloodiest Year in Vietnam* (New York: The Free Press, 1993), p. 22.

82. Henry J. Kenny, *The American Role in Vietnam and East Asia* (New York: Praeger, 1984), pp. 26-34.

83. For a detailed discussion of the Nixon Doctrine, see Robert Litwak, *Détente and the Nixon Doctrine: American Foreign Policy and the Pursuit of Stability, 1969-1976* (New York: Cambridge University Press, 1984); and Virginia Brodine, ed., *Open Secret: The Kissinger-Nixon Doctrine in Asia* (New York: Harper & Row, 1972).

84. William Head, "Vietnam and Its Wars: A Historical Overview of U.S. Involvement," p. 40.

85. John G. Stoessinger, *Why Nations Go To War,* p. 84.

86. Robert A. Divine, "Forward," in George C. Herring, *America's Longest War: the United States and Vietnam, 1950-1975,* p. vii.

87. A study of U.S. policy in Vietnam finds two viewpoints. One argues that decision makers in the 1950s and early 1960s, operating in the framework of the containment policy, were responding rationally to what they felt was a threat to the United States and the Western world by the Communist movement in Vietnam. The other viewpoint is that each successive administration had as one of its goals not combating communism, or fighting international conspiracy, or defending the Western world, but rather winning the next election, without necessarily anticipating the long-term effect of those decisions on the overall U.S. foreign policy posture. Michael P. Sullivan, *The Vietnam War: A Study in the Making of American Policy* (Lexington, KY.: The University Press of Kentucky, 1985), p. 153.

88. Gordon H. Chang, *Friends and Enemies: The United States, China, and the Soviet Union: 1948-1972,* p. 253.

89. Quoted from Franz Schurmann, *The Logic of World Power: An Inquiry into the Origins, Currents, and Contradictions of World Politics* (New York: Pantheon Books, 1974), p. 460.

90. Richard Nixon, *No More Vietnams,* p. 29.

91. Timothy J. Lomperis, *The War Everyone Lost—and Won: America's Intervention in Viet Nam's Twin Struggles* (Washington, D.C.: CQ Press, 1992), p. 53.

92. Quoted in Shibusawa Masahide, *Japan and the Asian Pacific Region* (New York: St. Martin's Press, 1984), p. 27.

93. For the whole story, see Henry Kissinger, *White House Years* (Boston, MA.: Little, Brown, 1979). pp. 733-87.

94. Steve Chan, *East Asian Dynamism,* p. 34.

95. Henry Kissinger, *White House Years,* p. 755.

96. Richard H. Solomon, "The China Factor in America's Foreign Relations," in Richard, H. Solomon, ed., *The China Factor: Sino-American Relations & The Global Scene* (Englewood Cliffs, N.J.: Prentice-Hall, Inc., 1981), p. 2.

97. Wei Shiyan, "Ni Kesong Zhongtong Fanghua" (The Visit to China by President Nixon), in Waijiaobu Waijiaoshi Yanjiushi (Diplomatic History Research Office, the Ministry of Foreign Affairs), *Xinzhouguo Waijiao Fengyun* (Diplomatic Winds and Clouds of New China) (Beijing: Shijie Zhishi Chuban She, 1994), p. 85.

98. For one text of the communiqué, see appendix 1 in Richard H. Solomon, ed., *The China Factor: Sino-American Relations & The Global Scene,* pp. 296-300.

99. Hongqian Zhu, "China and the Triangular Relationship," in Yufan Hao and Guocang Huan, eds., *The Chinese View of the World* (New York: Pantheon Books, 1989), p. 37.

100. Henry Kissinger, *The White House Years,* p. 765.

101. Wei Shiyan, "Ji Xingge Dierchi Fanghua" (The Second Visit to China by Kissinger), in Waijiaobu Waijiaoshi Yanjiushi (Diplomatic History Research Office, the Ministry of Foreign Affairs), *Xinzhouguo Waijiao Fengyun* (Diplomatic Winds and Clouds of New China) (Beijing: Shijie Zhishi Chuban She, 1994), pp. 69-70.

102. Henry Kissinger, *The White House Years,* p. 763.

103. Richard Nixon, *Memoirs of Richard Nixon,* vol. 1 (New York: Warner Books, 1978), p. 502-11.

104. John W. Garver, *Foreign Relations of the People's Republic of China* (Englewood Cliffs, N.J.: Prentice Hall, 1993), p. 79.

105. The Chinese Ministry of Foreign Affairs, *Diplomacy of Contemporary China,* pp. 269-79.

106. John K. Emmerson and Harrison M. Lolland, *The Eagle and the Rising Sun: America and Japan in the Twentieth Century* (Reading, MA.: Addison-Wesley, 1988), p. 180.

107. Shibusawa Masahide, *Japan and the Asian Pacific Region,* p. 62.

108. Roger Buckley, *US-Japan Alliance Diplomacy, 1945-1990* (Cambridge, England: Cambridge University Press, 1992), p. 131.

109. Akira Iriye, *Across the Pacific,* p. 359.

110. Roger Buckley, *US-Japan Alliance Diplomacy, 1945-1990,* p. 131.

111. Akira Iriye, *China and Japan in Global Setting* (Cambridge, MA.: Harvard University Press, 1992), p. 106.

112. Richard H. Solomon, "The China Factor in America's Foreign Relations," in Richard H. Solomon, ed., *The China Factor: Sino-American Relations & The Global Scene,* p. 2.

113. Lu Weizhao, "Tianzhong Fanghua yu Zhongri Bangjiao Zhengchanghua" (The Visit to China by Tanaka and Normalization of the Sino-Japanese Relations), in Waijiaobu Waijiaoshi Yanjiushi (Diplomatic History Research Office, the Ministry of Foreign Affairs), *Xinzhongguo Waijiao Fengyun* (Diplomatic Winds and Clouds of New China), p. 134.

114. Roger Buckley, *US-Japan Alliance Diplomacy, 1945-1990,* p. 131.

115. R. K. Jain, *China and Japan, 1949-1980* (Oxford: Martin Robertson, 1981), p. 217.

116. Lu Weizhao, "Tianzhong Fanghua yu Zhongri Bangjiao Zhengchanghua" (The Visit to China by Tanaka and Normalization of the Sino-Japanese Relations), in Waijiaobu Waijiaoshi Yanjiushi (Diplomatic History Research Office, the Ministry of Foreign Affairs), *Xinzhongguo Waijiao Fengyun* (Diplomatic Winds and Clouds of New China), pp. 137-38.

117. It was a "pentagonal" system in the world (plus Western Europe). Richard Nixon, *US Foreign Policy for the 1970s—Building for Peace,* report to the Congress, February 25, 1971, Washington, D.C.: U.S. Government Printing Office, 1971.

118. Henry A. Kissinger, *American Foreign Policy: Three Essays* (New York: W. W. Norton, 1969), p. 79.

119. Arthur M. Schlesinger, Jr., "Détente: An American Perspective," in George Schwab and Henry Friendlander, eds., *Détente in Historical Perspective* (New York: Cyrco Press, 1975), p. 129.

Chapter 7

1. Lowell Dittmer, "China and Russia: New Beginnings," in Samuel Kim, ed., *China and the World: Chinese Foreign Relations in the Post-Cold War Era* (Boulder, CO.: Westview Press, 1994), p. 95.

2. Robert S. Ross, "Conclusion: Tripolarity and Policy Making," in Robert S. Ross ed., *China, the United States, and the Soviet Union: Tripolarity and Policy Making in the Cold War World* (Armonk, N.Y.: M. E. Sharpe, 1993), p. 179.

3. Donald Zagoria, "The Soviet Union's Eastern Problem," in Martin E. Weinstein, ed., *Northeast Asian Security after Vietnam* (Urbana: IL.: University of Illinois Press, 1982), pp. 91-92.

4. *Shijie Jingji Daobao* (World Economy Herald), Shanghai, October 13, 1984, pp. 1-3.

5. Du Gong and Ni Liyu, *Zhuanhuanzhong de Shijie Geju* (The World Structure in Transition) (Beijing: Shijie Zhishi Chuban She, 1992), p. 148.

6. Charles E. Ziegler, *Foreign Policy and East Asia: Learning and Adaptation in the Gorbachev Era* (Cambridge, England: Cambridge University Press, 1993), p. 62.

7. Richard H. Solomon, "The China Factor in American Foreign Policy: Perceptions and Policy Choices," in Richard H. Solomon, ed., *The China Factor: Sino-American Relations & the Global Scene* (Englewood Cliffs, N.J.: Prentice Hall, 1981), p. 46.

8. Lowell Dittmer, *Sino-Soviet Normalization and Its International Implications, 1945-1990* (Seattle, WA.: University of Washington Press, 1992), p. 151.

9. Min Chen, *The Strategic Triangle and Regional Conflicts: Lessons from the Indochina Wars* (Boulder, CO: Lynn Rienner Publishers, 1992), p. 3.

10. For a comparative study of the nuclear weapon development in China, Britain, and France, see John C. Hopkins and Weixing Hu, *Strategic Views from the Second Tier: The Nuclear Weapons Policies of France, Great Britain, and China* (New Brunswick, N.J.: Transaction Publishers, 1995).

11. Robert A. Scalapino, "Relations Between the Nations of the Pacific Quadrille: Stability and Fluctuation in East Asian Politics," in Herbert J. Ellison, ed., *Japan and the Pacific Quadrille: The Major Powers in East Asia* (Boulder, CO.: Westview Press, 1987), p. 13.

12. For China's nuclear deterrence, see Chong-Pin Lin, *China's Nuclear Weapons Strategy: Tradition within Evolution* (Lexington, MA.: Lexington Books, 1988), pp. 110-23.

13. For one study of the perception of China by its neighboring Asian countries during this period, see Steven I. Levine, "China in Asia: The PRC as a Regional Power," in Harry Harding, ed., *China's Foreign Relations in the 1980s* (New Haven, CT.: Yale University Press, 1984), pp. 107-145.

14. Raju G. C. Thomas, "Introduction," in Raju G. C. Thomas, ed., *The Great-Power Triangle and Asian Security* (Lexington, MA: D. C. Heath, 1983), p. 13.

15. Robert A. Scalapino, "Relations Between the Nations of the Pacific Quadrille: Stability and Fluctuation in East Asian Politics," in Herbert J. Ellison, ed., *Japan and the Pacific Quadrille: The Major Powers in East Asia,* p. 12.

16. Drew Middleton, *The Duel of the Giants: China and Russia in Asia* (New York: Charles Scribner's Sons, 1978), p. 55.

17. John W. Garver, *Foreign Relations of the People's Republic of China,* pp. 32-33.

18. Suisheng Zhao, "Beijing's Perception of the International System and Foreign Policy Adjustment in the Post-Cold War World," *Journal of Northeast Asian Studies,* vol. XI, no. 3 (Fall 1992), p. 76.

19. Robert S. Ross, "Conclusion: Tripolarity and Policy Making," in Robert S. Ross ed., *China, the United States, and the Soviet Union: Tripolarity and Policy Making in the Cold War World,* p. 182.

20. Herbert J. Ellision, "Soviet-Chinese Relations: The Experience of Two Decades," in Robert S. Ross, ed., *China, the United States, and the Soviet Union: Tripolarity and Policy Making in the Cold War World,* p. 96.

21. Richard W. Stevenson, *The Rise and Fall of Détente: Relaxation of Tension in US-Soviet Relations, 1953-1984* (Champaign. IL.: University of Illinois Press, 1985), p. 156.

22. John Spanier, *American Foreign Policy Since World War II* (New York: Holt, Rinehart and Winston, 1977), p. 278.

23. Henry Kissinger, *Years of Upheaval* (Boston: Little, Brown, 1982), p. 54.

24. Hongqian Zhu, "China and the Triangular Relationship," in Yufan Hao and Guocang Huan, eds., *The Chinese View of the World* (New York: Pantheon Books, 1989), p. 38.

25. Yong Rae Kim, "The Soviet Union's Shifting Policy Toward East Asia: Its Major Determinants and Future Prospect," in J. K. Park and J. M. Ma, eds., *The Soviet Union and East Asia in the 1980s* (Boulder, CO.: Westview Press, 1986), p. 137.

26. Lowell Dittmer, *Sino-Soviet Normalization and Its International Implications, 1945-1990,* p. 209.

27. John W. Garver, "The Reagan Administration's Southeast Asian Policy," in James C. Hsiung, ed., *US-Asian Relations: The National Security Paradox* (New York: Praeger, 1983), p. 96.

28. Hongqian Zhu, "China and the Triangular Relationship," in Yufan Hao and Guocang Huan, eds., *The Chinese View of the World*, p. 39.

29. "Huang Hua's Report on the World Situation," *Issues and Studies*, vol. 14, no. 1 (January 1978), p. 110-11.

30. Harry Harding, *China and Northeast Asia, the Political Dimension* (Lanham, MD.: University Press of America, 1988), p. 20.

31. Kenneth Lieberthal, "Domestic Politics and Foreign Policy," in Harry Harding, ed., *China's Foreign Relations in the 1980s*, p. 59.

32. Regarding Carter's China policy, see Michael Oksenberg (Carter's top China expert), "A Decade of Sino-American Relations," *Foreign Policy*, vol. 61, no. 1 (Fall 1982), pp. 176-95.

33. Michael Oksenberg, "China Policy for the 1980s," *Foreign Policy*, vol. 59, no. 2 (Winter 1980-81), p. 318.

34. Zbigniew Brezinski, *Power and Principle: Memoirs of the National Security Adviser, 1977-1981*, quoted in Harry Harding, *A Fragile Relationship: The United States and China since 1972* (Washington, D.C.: Brookings Institution, 1992), p. 68.

35. According to Harry Harding, the United States had already accepted all three of Beijing's conditions, at least tacitly before the normalization agreement was reached. The Shanghai communiqué had committed the United States to the withdrawal of American military forces and installations from Taiwan; Ford had agreed that the U.S. would maintain only unofficial relations with Taipei after normalization; and Kissinger had concluded that the mutual defense treaty could not be maintained in the absence of formal diplomatic ties with Taiwan. Harry Harding, *A Fragile Relationship: The United States and China since 1972*, p. 71.

36. Li Jian, *Tiaoyutai Guoshi Fengyun*, vol. 1, p. 924.

37. Jeffrey T. Richelson, *Foreign Intelligence Organizations* (Cambridge, MA.: Ballinger, 1988), pp. 291-92.

38. Hongqian Zhu, "China and the Triangular Relationship," in Yufan Hao and Guocang Huan, eds., *The Chinese View of the World*, p. 39.

39. Lowell Dittmer, *Sino-Soviet Normalization and its International Implications, 1945-1990*, p. 217.

40. Steven J. Hood, *Dragons Entangled: Indochina and the China-Vietnam War* (Armonk, N.Y.: M. E. Sharpe, 1992), p. xv.

41. For a detailed description, see Deng Lifeng, *Jianguohou Junshi Xingdong Quanlu*, pp. 324-52.

42. Anne Gilks, *The Breakdown of the Sino-Vietnamese Alliance, 1970-1979*, China Research Monograph, 39 (Berkeley, CA.: Institute of East Asian Studies, University of California, 1992), p. 40.

43. Yu Gang, "The Situation in Kampuchea After Eight Years of Vietnamese Aggression," in International Security Council Conference Proceedings,

The Balance of Power in Asia (New York: International Council, 1987), p. 107.

44. Steven J. Hood, *Dragons Entangled: Indochina and the China-Vietnam War* (Armonk, N.Y.: M. E. Sharpe, 1992), p. 51.

45. Anne Gilks, *The Breakdown of the Sino-Vietnamese Alliance, 1970-1979,* p. 248.

46. William J. Duiker, "China and Vietnam and the Struggle for Indochina," in Joseph J. Zasloff, ed., *Postwar Indochina: Old Enemies and New Allies* (Washington, D.C.: Center for the Study of Foreign Affairs, Foreign Service Institute, U.S. Department of State, 1988), p. 157.

47. Ibid.

48. Yu Gang, "The Situation in Kampuchea After Eight Years of Vietnamese Aggression," in International Security Council Conference Proceedings, *The Balance of Power in Asia,* p. 107.

49. Yun Sui, *Guoji Fengyunzhong de Zhongguo Waijiaoguan* (Chinese diplomats in the International Winds and Clouds) (Beijing: Shijie Zhishi Chuban She, 1992), pp. 85-112.

50. "Chinese Government Statement," *Beijing Review,* January 19, 1979; quoted in Steven J. Hood, *Dragons Entangled: Indochina and the China-Vietnam War,* p. 50.

51. Deng Lifeng, *Jianguohou Junshi Xingdong Quanlu,* pp. 411-14.

52. Ibid., pp. 414-29.

53. Zbigniew Brezinski, *Power and Principle: Memoirs of the National Security Adviser, 1977-1981,* pp. 109-10.

54. Lowell Dittmer, *Sino-Soviet Normalization and Its International Implications, 1945-1990,* p. 214.

55. Min Chen, *The Strategic Triangle and Regional Conflicts: Lessons from the Indochina Wars,* p. 184.

56. William J. Duiker, "China and Vietnam and the Struggle for Indochina," in Joseph J. Zasloff, ed., *Postwar Indochina: Old Enemies and New Allies,* p. 167.

57. For a personal memoir, see Sharon Sloan Fiffer, *Imagining America: Paul Thai's Journey from the Killing Fields of Cambodia to Freedom in the U.S.A.* (New York: Paragon House, 1991).

58. Vietnam News Agency (VNA), February 10, 1979, FBIS Daily Report, East Asia, February 11, 1979.

59. Quoted in Lowell Dittmer, *Sino-Soviet Normalization and Its International Implications, 1945-1990,* p. 215.

60. *The New York Times,* March 15, 1979.

61. Lowell Dittmer, *Sino-Soviet Normalization and Its International Implications, 1945-1990,* p. 215.

62. Harry Harding, *China and Northeast Asia, the Political Dimension,* p. 21.

63. Peter Jones and Sian Kevill, *China and the Soviet Union, 1949-1984* (New York: Facts on File Publications, 1985), p. 176.

64. Ibid., p. 175.

65. Donald Zagoria, "The Soviet Union's Eastern Problem," in Martin E. Weinstein, ed., *Northeast Asian Security after Vietnam*, p. 72.

66. Hu Yaobang, "Create a New Situation in All Fields of Socialist Modernization," in *The Twelfth National Congress of the CPC, September 1982* (Beijing: Foreign Language Press, 1982), p. 59.

67. Hu Yaobang, "Create a New Situation in All Fields of Socialist Modernization," in *The Twelfth National Congress of the CPC*, pp. 58-59

68. Chi Su, "Sino-Soviet Relations of the 1980s: From Confrontation to Conciliation," in Samuel Kim, ed., *China and the World: New Directions in Chinese Foreign Relations* (Boulder, CO.: Westview Press, 1989), p. 112.

69. Guo-cang Huan, *Sino-Soviet Relations to the Year 2000: Implications for U.S. Interests* (Washington, D.C.: The Atlantic Council of The United States, 1986), p. 8.

70. Regarding the Taiwan issue and the 1982 adjustment of China's triangular policy, see John W. Garver, "Arms Sales, the Taiwan Question, and Sino-US relations," *Orbis*, vol. 26, no. 4 (Winter 1983), pp. 999-1104; James C. Hsiung, "Reagan's China Policy and the Sino-Soviet Détente," *Asian Affairs*, vol. 11, no. 2 (Summer 1984), pp. 1-11.

71. Robert Legvold, "Sino-Soviet Relations: The American Factor," in Robert S. Ross, ed., *China, the United States, and the Soviet Union: Tripolarity and Policy Making in the Cold War World*, p. 71.

72. Donald Zagoria, "The Soviet Union's Eastern Problem," in Martin E. Weinstein, ed., *Northeast Asian Security after Vietnam*, p. 72.

73. Deng Xiaoping, "The Present Situation and the Tasks Before US," in *Selected Works of Deng Xiaoping, 1975-1982* (Beijing: Foreign Language Press, 1983), pp. 224-58.

74. Deng Xiaoping, "Opening Speech at the Twelfth National Congress of the Chinese Communist Party," in *Selected Works of Deng Xiaoping, 1975-1982*, p. 396.

75. Charles E. Ziegler, *Foreign Policy and East Asia: Learning and Adaptation in the Gorbachev Era* (Cambridge, England: Cambridge University Press, 1993), p. 63.

76. Ibid., p. 66.

77. Tang Xiuzhe, "Gorbachev Answers Our Correspondent," *Liaowang* (Overseas Edition), January 11, 1988, p. 4.

78. Guo-cang Huan, *Sino-Soviet Relations to the Year 2000: Implications for US Interests*, p. 8.

79. Charles E. Ziegler, *Foreign Policy and East Asia: Learning and Adaptation in the Gorbachev Era* (Cambridge, England: Cambridge University Press, 1993), p. 63.

80. Chi Su, "Sino-Soviet Relations of the 1980s: From Confrontation to Conciliation," in Samuel Kim, ed., *China and the World: New Directions in Chinese Foreign Relations*, p. 123.

81. Harry Harding, *China and Northeast Asia: The Political Dimension*, p. 24.

82. *Renmin Ribao,* July 29, 1986, p. 1.
83. For one analysis of the Deng-Gorbachev summit, see John W. Garver, "The 'New Type' of Sino-Soviet Relations," *Asian Survey,* vol. 29, no. 12 (December 1989), pp. 1136-52.
84. Min Chen, *The Strategic Triangle and Regional Conflicts: Lessons from the Indochina Wars,* p. 174.
85. This tendency was described as the one most important rule by both Lowell Dittmer and Min Chen in their studies of the triangular relations. See Lowell Dittmer, *Sino-Soviet Normalization and Its International Implications, 1945-1990,* p. 154; and Min Chen, *The Strategic Triangle and Regional Conflicts: Lessons from the Indochina Wars,* p. 5.
86. Robert S. Ross, "Conclusion: Tripolarity and Policy Making," in Robert S. Ross, ed., *China, the United States, and the Soviet Union: Tripolarity and Policy Making in the Cold War World,* p. 193.

Chapter 8

1. Steve Chan, *East Asian Dynamism* (Boulder, CO.: Westview Press, 1993), p. 74.
2. Robert A. Scalapino, "The United States and Asia: Future Prospects," *Foreign Affairs,* vol. 70, no. 5 (Winter 1991/92), p. 20.
3. World Bank, *The East Asian Miracle: Economic Growth and Public Policy* (New York: Oxford University Press, 1993).
4. K. Akamatsu is usually credited as the first advocate of the flying-geese theory, see Akamatsu, "A Historical Pattern of Economic Growth in Developing Countries," *The Developing Economies,* no. 1 (March-April, 1962), pp. 3-25. Also see Collin Bradford, Jr., "Trade and Structural Change: NICs and Next Tier of NICs as Transitional Economies," *World Development,* vol. 15, no. 3, pp. 299-316; and Takashi Inoguchi, "The Coming Pacific Century," *Current History,* vol. 93, no. 579 (January 1994), p. 25. For one booklength study of the four-tier model, see William McCord, *The Dawn of the Pacific Century: Implications of the Three Worlds of Development* (New Brunswick, N.J.: Transaction Publishers, 1993).
5. World Bank, *World Development Report 1995* (New York: Oxford University Press, 1995), p. 163.
6. William McCord, *The Dawn of the Pacific Century: Implications of the Three Worlds of Development,* p. 13.
7. World Bank, *World Development Report 1995,* p. 163.
8. Li Teng-Hui (the President of Taiwan), "Always in my Heart," *Free China Review,* vol. 45, no. 8 (August 1995), p. 5.
9. Shinichi Ichimura and James W. Morley, "Introduction: The Varieties of Asian-Pacific Experience," in James W. Morley ed., *Driven by Growth: Political Change in the Asia-Pacific Region* (Armond, N.Y.: M. E. Sharpe, 1993), p. 6.
10. World Bank, *World Development Report 1995,* pp. 164-65.

11. Ibid., p. 164.

12. Ibid.

13. Li Peng, "Guangyu Zhiding Guomin Jingji he Shehui Fazhan jiuwu jihua he 2010 nian yuanjing mubiao jianyi de shuoming" (The Elaboration on Suggestions for the Ninth Five-Year National Economic and Social Development Plan and Long-term Goals), *Remin Ribao,* October 6, 1995, p. 1.

14. An article by Karsten Prager is titled "Waking Up the Next Superpower," see *Times,* March 25, 1996, p. 36-38.

15. Barber B. Conable, Jr. and David Lampton, "China: The Coming Power," *Foreign Affairs,* vol. 72, no. 5 (Winter 1992/93), pp. 133-49.

16. *Times* (International Edition), May, 10, 1993, p. 36.

17. Ibid.

18. For one comprehensive research on reforms in Vietnam, see Study Group on the Economy of Vietnam, *Toward a Market Economy in Vietnam: Economic Reforms and Development Strategies for the Twenty-first Century* (Rockville, MD.: Pacific Basin Research Institute, 1993).

19. Richard N. Rosecrance, *The Rise of the Trading State: Commerce and Conquest in the Modern World* (New York: Basic Books, 1986).

20. Joseph S. Nye, Jr., *Bound to Lead: The Changing Nature of American Power* (New York: Basic Books, 1990), p. 77.

21. Paul Kennedy, *The Rise and Fall of the Great Powers* (New York: Vintage Books, 1987).

22. For an example of the dispute, see Lester R. Brown, "Redefining National Security," in Steven L. Spiegel, ed., *At Issue, Politics in the World Arena* (New York: St. Martin's Press, 1988), pp. 517-30; and Richard Rosecrance, *The Rise of the Trading State: Commerce and Conquest in the Modern World* (New York: Basic Books, 1986).

23. For one example of the argument, see Robert J. Art, "To What Ends Military Power? The Future of Force," *International Security* (Spring 1980), pp. 3-35.

24. Indeed, the average annual inflow of aid to Korea from 1953 through 1958 was $270 million. This aid was nearly 15 percent of per capita Korea GNP. Between 1951 and 1965 Taiwan received U.S. economic aid of about $1.5 billion, averaging about $100 million per year. Ian Little, "An Economic Reconnaissance," in Walter Galenson, ed., *Economic Growth and Structural Change in Taiwan* (Ithaca, N.Y.: Cornell University Press, 1979).

25. Hagen Koo, "The Interplay of State, Social Class, and World System in East Asian Development: the Cases of South Korea and Taiwan," in Frederic C. Deyo, ed., *The Political Economy of the New Asian Industrialism* (Ithaca, N.Y.: Cornell University Press, 1987), p. 168.

26. For one classic book on the hegemonic stability theory, see Robert O. Keohane, *After Hegemony: Cooperation and Disorder in the World Political Economy* (Princeton, N.J.: Princeton University Press, 1984).

27. For two classic works on public goods, see Russel Hardin, *Collective Action* (Baltimore, MD.: Johns Hopkins University Press, 1982), p. 17. For one

classic book on public goods, see Mancur Olson, *Logic of Collective Action: Public Goods and the Theory of Groups* (Cambridge, MA.: Harvard University Press, 1965).

28. Charles Kindleberge, "Systems of International Economic Organization," in David Calleo, ed., *Money and the Coming World Order* (New York: New York University Press, 1974).

29. This argument is summarized by Kenneth B. Pyle in *The Japanese Question* (Washington, D.C.: The AEI Press, 1992), and refuted by Shintaro Ishihara in *The Japan that Can Say No* (New York: Simon & Schuster, 1989).

30. For one excellent study of the low defense expenditure in the context of the postwar Japanese politics, see Tesuta Kataoka, *The Price of a Constitution: The Origin of Japan's Postwar Politics* (New York: Crane Russak, 1991).

31. Charles P. Kindleberger, "Hierarchy Versus Inertial Cooperation," *International Organization,* vol. 40, no. 4 (Autumn 1986), p. 841.

32. Duncan Snidal, "Limits of Hegemonic Stability Theory," *International Organization,* vol. 39, no. 4 (Autumn 1985), p. 579.

33. Reinhard Drifte, *Japan's Foreign Policy* (New York: Council on Foreign Relations Press, 1990), p. 29.

34. Comprehensive National Security Study Group, *Report on Comprehensive National Security,* Tokyo (July 2, 1980), p. 7; quoted in Reinhard Drifte, *Japan's Foreign Policy* (New York: Council on Foreign Relations Press, 1990), p. 29.

35. Steve Chan, *East Asian Dynamism,* p. 75.

36. Ibid.

37. Harrison M. Lolland, *Japan Challenges America: Managing an Alliance in Crisis* (Boulder, CO.: Westview, 1992), p. 171.

38. James Kurth, "East Asia Plus Mitteleuropa: The Return of History and Redefinition of Security," in Miles Kahler, ed., *Beyond the Cold War in the Pacific* (San Diego, CA.: Institute on Global Conflict and Cooperation, University of California, 1991), p. 150.

39. Richard Rosecrance, *The Rise of the Trading State,* pp. 137-41

40. Desmond Ball, "Arms and Affluence, Military Acquisitions in the Asia-Pacific Region," *International Security,* vol. 18, no. 3 (Winter 1993/94), pp. 78-112.

41. Quoted from Nicholas R. Lardy, *China in the World Economy* (Washington, D.C.: Institute for International Economics, 1994), p. 39.

42. Ibid., p. 8.

43. Richard Rosecrance, *The Rise of the Trading State,* p. 26.

44. James D. Seymour, "Human Rights in Chinese Foreign Relations," in Samuel S. Kim, ed., *China and the World: Chinese Foreign Relations in the Post-Cold War Era* (Boulder, CO.: Westview Press, 1994), pp. 202-203.

45. Yi Ding, "Upholding the Five Principles of Peaceful Coexistence," *Beijing Review,* vol. 33, no. 9 (February 26-March 4, 1990), p. 15.

46. Samuel S. Kim, "Mainland China and a New World Order," *Issues and Studies,* vol. 27, no. 11 (November 1991), p. 7.

47. In 1966 the UN adopted two detailed covenants on human-rights. The Helsinki meeting of the Conference on Security and Cooperation in Europe (CSCE) in 1975 adopted a declaration with the ringing endorsement of human rights: freedom of expression, freedom of the press, and so forth.

48. Quoted in Hungdah Chiu, "Chinese Attitudes Toward International Law of Human Rights in the Post-Mao Era," in Victor C. Falkenheim, ed., *Chinese Politics from Mao to Deng* (New York: Paragon House, 1989), p. 239.

49. Zhiyuan Cui, "Particular, Universal, and Infinite: Transcending Western Centralism and Cultural Relativism in the Third World," in Leo Marx and Bruce Mazlish, eds., *Progress: Fact or Fiction* (Ann Arbor, MI.: University of Michigan Press, 1995), p. 141.

50. James D. Seymour, "Human Rights in Chinese Foreign Relations," in Samuel S. Kim, ed., *China and the World: Chinese Foreign Relations in the Post-Cold War Era*, p. 203.

51. Roberto R. Romulo, "We Must Try Harder," *Far Eastern Economic Review,* vol. 156, no. 32 (August 12, 1993), p. 24.

52. Stanley Foundation," *Human Rights and US Foreign Policy: Who Controls the Agenda* (Muscatine, IA.: The Stanley Foundation, 1994), p. 6.

53. Jimmy Carter, *Keeping Faith: A Memoirs of a President* (New York: Bantam Books, 1982), pp. 202-3.

54. Andrew Nathan, *China's Crisis* (New York: Columbia University Press, 1990), p. 82.

55. In May 26, 1994, the Clinton administration delinked the human-rights record with the MFN statues. But the human-rights issue has never stopped being an important dispute in the Sino-U.S. relationship. For the Clinton administration's statement, see U.S. Department of State, *Dispatch,* vol. 5, no. 22 (May 30, 1994), pp. 345-47.

56. Mike M. Mochizuki, "Japan and the Strategic Quadrangle," in Michael Mandelbaum, ed., *The Strategic Quadrangle: Russia, China, Japan, and the United States in East Asia* (New York: Council on Foreign Relations, 1995), p. 132.

57. Stanley Hoffmann, *Duties Beyond Borders: On the Limits and Possibilities of Ethical International Politics* (Syracuse, N.Y.: Syracuse University Press, 1981), p. 139.

58. Claude E. Welch, Jr., "Global Change and Human Rights: Asian Perspectives in Comparative Context, in Claude E. Welch, Jr., and Virginia A. Leary, eds., *Asian Perspectives on Human Rights* (Boulder, CO.: Westview Press, 1990), p. 6.

59. Suisheng Zhao, "Beijing's Perception on the International System and Foreign Policy Adjustment in the Post-Cold War World," *Journal of Northeast Asian Studies,* vol. 11, no. 3 (Fall 1992), p. 80.

60. Ambassador Jin Yongjian (head of the Chinese delegation at the Asian Regional Preparatory Meeting for the World Conference on Human Rights), "Asia's Major Human Rights Concerns," *Beijing Review,* vol. 36, no. 16 (April 19, 1993), p. 11.

61. Michael Vatikiotis, "Trade and Rights," *Far Eastern Economic Review,* vol. 154, no. 47 (November 21, 1991), p. 80.

62. Michael Vatikiotis, "Trade and Rights," *Far Eastern Economic Review,* p. 80.

63. Samuel P. Huntington, "The Clash of Civilization?" *Foreign Affairs,* vol. 72, no. 4, (Summer, 1993), pp. 22-49.

64. Kishore Mahbubani, "The Pacific Way," *Foreign Affairs,* vol. 74, no. 1 (January/February 1995), pp. 100-11.

65. Quoted from Aryeh Neier, "Watching Rights," *The Nation,* vol. 257, no. 10 (October 4, 1993), p. 345.

66. Kishore Mahbubani, "The Pacific War," *Foreign Affairs,* pp. 101-2.

67. Ibid., pp. 107-8.

68. Yong Deng, "Post-Deng China: Sources of Stability," *The Journal of Contemporary China,* no, 7 (Fall 1994), p. 81.

69. The Japan Foundation, *The Japan Foundation Overview of Programs for Fiscal 1993 and Annual Report for Fiscal 1992* (Tokyo: The Japan Foundation, 1993), p. 13.

70. The Japan Foundation, "The Japan Foundation Law," Article 1, in *The Japan Foundation Overview of Programs for Fiscal 1993 and Annual Report for Fiscal 1992,* p. 13.

71. Chiang Ching-kuo Foundation, *1994 Grant Programs of Chiang Ching-kuo Foundation for International Scholarly Exchange* (Taipei: Chiang Ching-kuo Foundation, 1995).

72. Akira Iriye, *Across the Pacific: An Inner History of American-Asian Relations* (Chicago, IL.: Imprint Publications, Inc., 1992), p. 374.

73. Shinichiro Asao, "A Message from the President," *The Japan Foundation Overview of Programs for Fiscal 1993 and Annual Report for Fiscal 1992,* p. 5.

74. Barbara Ward and Rene Dubos, *Only One Earth: The Care and Maintenance of a Small Planet* (New York: W. W. Norton & Company, 1972), p. 12.

75. Adam Schwarz, "Looking Back at Rio," *Far Eastern Economic Review,* vol. 156, no. 43 (October 28, 1993), p. 48.

76. Gareth Porter, "The Environmental Hazards of Asia Pacific Development: The Southeast Asian Rain Forests," *Current History* (December 1994), p. 430.

77. Theodore Panayotou, "The Environment in Southeast Asia: Problems and Policies," *Environmental Science and Technology,* vol. 27, no. 12 (1993), p. 2270.

78. Margaret Scott, "The Disappearing Forests," *Far Eastern Economic Review,* vol. 143, no. 2 (January 12, 1989), p. 34.

79. Francois Nectoux and Yoichi Kuroda, *Timber from the South Seas: An Analysis of Japan's Tropical Timber Trade and Its Environmental Impact* (Gland, Switzerland: World Wildlife Fund, 1989).

80. He Baochuan, *China on the Edge: The Crisis of Ecology and Development* (Berkeley, CA.: Pacific View Press, 1991), p. 22.

81. Ibid., p. 22.

82. Ibid., pp. 32-33.
83. "Environment is Vital to Urban Expansion," *China Daily*, May 11, 1995, p. 4.
84. Ibid.
85. Barber B. Conable, Jr. and David Lampton, "China: the Coming Power," *Foreign Affairs*, p. 142.
86. Gareth Porter and Janet Welsh Brown, *Global Environmental Politics* (Boulder, CO.: Westview Press, 1991), p. 109.
87. Michael Renner, *National Security: The Economic and Environmental Dimensions,* Worldwatch Paper No. 89 (Washington, D.C.: Worldwatch Institute, 1989), p. 63.
88. Adam Schwarz, "Looking Back at Rio," *Far Eastern Economic Review,* vol. 156, no. 43 (October 28, 1993), p. 48.
89. Kazi F. Jalal, "International Agencies and the Asia-Pacific Environment," *Environmental Science and Technology,* vol. 27, no. 12 (November 1993), p. 2277.
90. Gareth Porter, "The Environmental Hazards of Asia Pacific Development: The Southeast Asian Rain forests," *Current History* (December 1994), p. 433.
91. Adam Schwarz, "Looking Back at Rio," *Far Eastern Economic Review,* p. 50.
92. For example, although China has adopted environmental protection policy, it is still very sensitive to any international pressure on its environmental problems. Zhong Shukong, the Chinese delegate to the Second ESCAP Environment and Sustainable Development Conference in Bangkok in October 1994, called for the Asian Pacific countries to resist the "harmful tendency that developed countries use environmental protection to constrain economic and trade development of developing countries." *Renmin Ribao,* October 26, 1994, p. 6.
93. Richard Rosecrance, *The Rise of the Trading State,* p. 22.
94. Joseph J. Romm, *Defining National Security, the Nonmilitary Aspects* (New York: Council on Foreign Relations Press, 1993), p. 1.
95. Ibid.
96. Richard Rosecrance, *The Rise of the Trading State,* p. 22.
97. Miles Kahler, "Introduction," in Miles Kahler, ed., *Beyond the Cold War in the Pacific,* p. 5.

Chapter 9

1. For example, in a comparison, Robert Gilpin finds a "politically motivated and institutionalized movement" toward regional integration in Western Europe, and a "primarily economic and less institutionalized nature" of regional cooperation in East Asia. See Gilpin, "The Debate about the New World Economic Order," in Danny Unger and Paul Blackburn, eds., *Japan's Emerging Global Role* (Boulder, CO.: Lynn Rienner Publishers, 1993), p. 33. For a collection of analysis of institutional-building efforts in Asia-

Pacific, see Andrew Mack and John Ravenhill, eds., *Pacific Cooperation: Building Economic and Security Regimes in Asia-Pacific Region* (Boulder, CO.: Westview Press, 1995).

2. Robert A. Scalapino, *Major Power Relations in Northeast Asia* (Lanham, MD.: University Press of America, 1987), p. 7.

3. In neorealist fashion, Helen Milner suggests that anarchy and interdependence are two key structural features of the international system. See Helen Milner, "The Assumption of Anarchy in International Relations Theory: A Critique," in David A. Baldwin, ed., *Neorealism and Neoliberalism: The Contemporary Debate* (New York: Columbia University Press, 1993), p. 167.

4. A. Le Roy Bennet, *International Organizations, Principles and Issues* (Englewood Cliffs, N.J.: Prentice Hall, 1984), p. 348

5. Economists use "integration" to refer to a movement toward the removal of market barriers across national borders. Structured regionalism is similar to regional integration but emphasizes an institution-building process as a result of government agreements rather than economic interaction. The most successful example of the process of integration is the European Community (now EU). For works on European integration, see, for example, Robert O. Keohane and Stanley Hoffmann, eds., *The European Community: Decision-making and Institutional Change* (Boulder, CO.: Westview, 1991); Leon Hurwitz and Christian Lequesne, eds., *The State of the European Community: Policies, Institutions, and Debates in the Transition Years* (Boulder, CO.: Lynne Rienner, 1991); Brian Nelson, David Roberts, and Walter Veit, eds., *The European Community in the 1990s: Economics, Politics, Defense* (New York: Berg, 1992); and Richard H. Ullman, *Securing Europe* (Princeton, N.J.: Princeton University Press, 1991).

6. Rosenau wrote that "the nation is declining in its importance as a political unit to which allegiances are attached." James Rosenau, "National Interest," *International Encyclopedia of the Social Sciences,* vol. 11, p. 39. For similar views, also see Richard Falk, *A Study of Future Worlds* (New York: The Free Press, 1975) and Richard Rosecrance, *The Rise of the Trading State* (New York: Basic Books, 1986).

7. Jonathan Clarke, "APEC as a Semi-Solution," *Orbis,* vol. 38, no. 1 (Winter 1995), p. 94.

8. Robert Axelrod and Robert Keohane, "Achieving Cooperation Under Anarchy: Strategies and Institutions," in David A. Baldwin, ed., *Neorealism and Neoliberalism: The Contemporary Debate* (New York: Columbia University Press, 1993), p. 87.

9. Robert Axelrod, "Conflict of Interest: An Axiomatic Approach," *Journal of Conflict Resolution,* no. 11 (March 1967), pp. 87-89.

10. The Carnegie Endowment Study Group, *Defining A Pacific Community* (Washington, D.C.: Carnegie Endowment for International Peace, 1994), p. 14.

11. Ryokichi Hirono, "Future Prospects for Economic Cooperation in Asia and the Pacific Region," in Robert A. Scalapino and Masataka Kosaka, eds.,

Peace, Politics & Economics in Asia: The Challenge to Cooperate (Washington, D.C.: Pergamon-Brassey's International Defense Publishers, 1988), p. 101.

12. Scholars have predicted a multipolar strategic quadrangle of the United States, China, Japan, and Russia in the post–Cold War Asian Pacific region. See, for example, Richard H. Solomon, "Who Will Shape the Emerging Structure of East Asia?" in Michael Mandelbaum, ed., *The Strategic Quadrangle: Russia, China, Japan and the United States in East Asia* (New York: Council on Foreign Relations Press, 1995), pp. 196-208.

13. Robert A. Manning and Paula Stern, "The Myth of the Pacific Community," *Foreign Affairs,* vol. 37, no. 6 (November/December 1994), p. 80.

14. Donald Crone, "Does Hegemony Matter? The Reorganization of the Pacific Political Economy," *World Politics,* vol. 45, no. 4 (July 1993), pp. 501-25.

15. Kishore Mahbubani, "The Pacific Way," *Foreign Affairs,* vol. 74, no. 1 (January/February 1995), p. 110.

16. The Carnegie Endowment Study Group, *Defining A Pacific Community,* p. 16.

17. Helen Milner, "The Assumption of Anarchy in International Relations Theory: A Critique," in David A. Baldwin, ed., *Neorealism and Neoliberalism: The Contemporary Debate,* p. 163.

18. According to the definition by Barkin and Cronin, legitimate authority and territoriality are the key concepts in understanding national sovereignty. J. Samuel Barkin and Bruce Cronin, "The State and the Nation: Changing Norms and the Rules of Sovereignty in International Relations," *International Organization,* vol. 48, no. 1 (Winter 1994), pp. 107-30.

19. Peter Smith, "The Politics of Integration, Guidelines for Policy," in Peter Smith, ed., *The Challenge of Integration: Europe and the Americas* (New Brunswick, NJ: Transaction Publishers, 1993), p. 406.

20. The concept of interdependence has come into a precise scholarly usage since the publication of Richard N. Cooper's *The Economics of Interdependence: Economic Policy in the Atlantic Community* (New York: McGraw-Hill, 1968) and Keohane and Joseph S. Nye's *Power and Interdependence: World Politics in Transition* (Boston: Little Brown, 1977).

21. For a critique of the various usage, see David A. Baldwin, "Interdependence and Power: A Conceptual Analysis," *International Organizations,* no. 34 (Autumn 1980), pp. 471-506; also see Richard N. Cooper, "Economic Interdependence and Foreign Policy in the Seventies," *World Politics,* vol. 24, no. 2 (January 1972), p. 159.

22. Helen Milner, "The Assumption of Anarchy in International Relations Theory: A Critique," in David A. Baldwin, ed., *Neorealism and Neoliberalism: The Contemporary Debate* (New York: Columbia University Press, 1993), p. 168, fn. 12.

23. Thomas C. Schelling, *The Strategy of Conflict* (Cambridge, MA.: Harvard University Press, 1960), p. 5.

24. Kenneth Waltz even goes so far as to argue that interdependence reduces systemic stability by increasing the opportunities for conflict because states

in an anarchic, self-help system "worry about securing that which they depend on." Waltz, *Theory of International Politics* (Reading, MA.: Addison-Wesley, 1979), p. 106; also see Waltz, "The Myth of Interdependence," in Charles P. Kindleberger, ed., *The International Corporation* (Cambridge, MA.: The MIT Press, 1970), p. 205.

25. A World Bank Publication, *East Asia's Trade and Investment: Regional and Global Gains from Liberalization* (Washington, D.C.: The World Bank, 1994), p. 25. The official figures for intraregional trade are already impressive, although they are often understated, because many significant relationships, such as China-Taiwan, China-Vietnam, North-South Korea, China-Russia, are not fully reported. Taiwan and Hong Kong account for more than two-thirds of foreign direct investment in China. Taipei, which has been one of the East Asian economies most heavily dependent on U.S. export markets, now has a larger volume of trade with Beijing than with Washington. Robert A. Manning and Paula Stern, "The Myth of the Pacific Community," *Foreign Affairs,* vol. 37, no. 6 (November/December 1994), p. 83.

26. Considerable interest has recently been focused on whether East Asia is changing its economic orientation toward intraregional lingoes. The popular perception of a major shift of this sort, nevertheless, has not been fully supported by empirical evidence. While the share of intraregional trade is increasing, this is due mostly to the rapid economic growth of the region and not to greater preferences for the region's own products. See, for example, A World Bank Publication, *East Asia's Trade and Investment: Regional and Global Gains from Liberalization,* p. 25.

27. Bernard K. Gordon, "Japan: Searching Once Again," in James C. Hsiung, ed., *Asia Pacific in the New World Politics* (Boulder, CO.: Lynne Rienner, 1993), p. 63.

28. Peter A. Petri, "Trading with Dynamos: East Asian Interdependence and American Interests," *Current History* (December 1994), p. 409.

29. Peter C. Y. Chow, "Asia Pacific Economic Integration in Global Perspective," in James C. Hsiung, ed., *Asia Pacific in the New World Politics,* p. 196.

30. *Renmin Ribao* (People's Daily), October 28, 1994, p. 1.

31. Chia Siow Yue and Lee Tsao Yuan, "Subregional Economic Zones: A New Motive Force in Asia-Pacific Development," in C. Fred Bergsten and Marus Noland, eds., *Pacific Dynamism and the International Economic System* (Washington, D.C.: Institute for International Economics, 1993), p. 226.

32. For one study of these subregional economic zones in the from of growth triangles, see Chia Siow Yue and Lee Tsao Yuan, "Subregional Economic Zones: A New Motive Force in Asia-Pacific Development," in C. Fred Bergsten and Marus Noland, eds., *Pacific Dynamism and the International Economic System,* pp. 225-69.

33. Donald K. Emmerson, "Organizing the Rim: Asia Pacific Regionalism," *Current History* (December 1994), p. 437.

34. Lu Zongwei, *Northeast Asian Economic Cooperation in the Post-Cold War Era,* no. 6, (San Diego, CA.: Institute on Global Conflict and Cooperation Policy Papers, October 1993), p. 4.

35. For one systematic study of the Tumen River Area Project, see Andrew Marton, Terry McGee, and Donald G. Paterson, "Northeast Asian Economic Cooperation and the Tumen River Area Development Project," *Pacific Affairs,* vol. 68, no. 1 (Spring 1995), pp. 8-33.

36. *Renmin Ribao* (People's Daily), May 31, 1995.

37. The term, Greater China, is not a precise concept. To some this term refers to all of mainland China, Taiwan, and Hong Kong. Other writers employ the term in a narrower sense to refer to Hong Kong, Taiwan, and the southeast mainland coast from Guangdong and Fujian provinces to Shanghai. Yet other analysts use the term to encompass all ethnic Chinese, including those in Southeast Asia and sometimes in North America and Europe. Therefore, this term is politically sensitive to Southeast Asian countries, particularly to Singapore and Malaysia, because of the potential ethnic implication to the Chinese ancestors in these countries. Among the analyses of Greater China, see Daojiong Zha, "A Greater China: The Political Economy of Chinese National Reunification," *The Journal of Contemporary China,* no. 5 (Spring 1994), pp. 40-63; and Yoichi Funabashi, Michel Oksenberg, Heinrich Weiss, *An Emerging China in A World of Interdependence* (New York: The Trilateral Commission, 1994), ch. 4. *The China Quarterly* had a special issue devoted to the discussion of Greater China. See *The China Quarterly,* no. 136 (December 1993).

38. Randall Jones, Robert King and Michael Klein, *The Chinese Economic Area: Economic Integration without a Free Trade Agreement,* No. 124 (Paris: OECD Working Papers, 1992), p. 5.

39. Stanley Reed, "'Greater China' Could be the Biggest Tiger of All," *Business Week,* September 28, 1992, p. 58.

40. According to the study, about 60 free-trade arrangements were established outside the OECD area since World War II, but none attained major economic importance or led to integration among member countries in the sense that intratrade increased significantly as a share of total trade of the members of the arrangement. Randall Jones, Robert King, and Michael Klein, *The Chinese Economic Area: Economic Integration without a Free Trade Agreement,* pp. 5-6.

41. Harry Harding, "The Emergence of Greater China: How US Policy Will Have to Change," *The American Enterprise,* vol. 3, no. 3 (May-June 1992), p. 47.

42. Nicholas R. Lardy, *China in the World Economy* (Washington, D.C.: Institute for International Economics, 1994), p. 74.

43. Barber B. Conable Jr. and David M. Lampton, "China: The Coming Power," *Foreign Affairs,* vol. 72, no. 5 (Winter 1992/93), p. 145.

44. Robert F. Ash and Y. Y. Kueh, "Economic Integration within Greater China: Trade and Investment Flows between China, Hong Kong and Taiwan," *The China Quarterly,* no. 136 (December 1993), p. 727.

45. The manufacturing industry is especially favored by Taiwanese investors, which took 90 percent of the total investment during four years; and electronic appliances, foodstuffs and beverages, and plastic and rubber industries are on the top of the list. "Taiwanese Capital Flowing into Mainland Manufacturing Industry," *Asia Information China Daily Headline News,* June 8, 1995, reference no: 95060825.

46. Consider the following: in the 1980s, in any department store in the West, toys, dresses, men's wear and shoes all had labels stating "Made in Hong Kong" or "Made in Taiwan." In the 1990s, these same labels all say "Made in China." A more accurate label would read: "Thought of in Taiwan, designed in Hong Kong, and constructed in China." Yoichi Funabashi, Michel Oksenberg, Heinrich Weiss, *An Emerging China in a World of Interdependence,* p. 21.

47. Robert F. Ash and Y. Y. Kueh, "Economic Integration within Greater China: Trade and Investment Flows between China, Hong Kong and Taiwan," p. 737.

48. Hong Kong in effect extended its economic system into southern China, moving outward and fuzzing the "boundary" between Hong Kong and the rest of China. A good example of this interdependence is in the monetary area. The Hong Kong and Shanghai Bank estimates that $2 billion in Hong Kong banknotes, about 30 percent of the total, circulate on the mainland (principally Guangdong), up from 24 percent of the total in 1989. Yoichi Funabashi, Michel Oksenberg, Heinrich Weiss, *An Emerging China in a World of Interdependence,* p. 27.

49. Crane indicates that "the complications of spillover suggest that if deeper integration of China and Taiwan is to occur, it is likely to be as the result of political transformation, not economic intermingling." George T. Crane, "China and Taiwan: Not Yet 'Greater China,'" *International Affairs,* vol. 69, no. 4 (1993), p. 714.

50. For one historical study of the relationship between mainland China and Hong Kong, see Ming K. Chan (with the collaboration of John D. Young), ed. *Precarious Balance: Hong Kong Between China and Britain, 1842-1992* (Armonk, N.Y. : M. E. Sharpe, 1994).

51. For one study of the peaceful offensive policy, see Suisheng Zhao, "Management of Rival Relations across the Taiwan Strait: 1979-1991," *Issues & Studies,* vol. 29, no. 4 (April 1993), pp. 74-76.

52. Stanley Reed, "'Greater China' Could be the Biggest Tiger of All," p. 58.

53. *Renmin Ribao,* January 9, 1995, p. 6.

54. Koong-Lian Kao, *Trade and Investment Across the Taiwan Straits* (Taipei: Mainland Affairs Council, the Executive Yuan, August 1993), p. 2.

55. One 1990 published book on Greater China asserted that "the shift to a conservative regime in Beijing in mid-1989 killed all hope for the best, leaving fear and depression in an expectation of the worst. Fear was the dominant reaction in Hong Kong, depression in Taiwan." Penelope Hartland-Thunberg, *China, Hong Kong, Taiwan and the World Trading System* (New York: MacMillan, 1990), p. 98.

56. Yu-Shan Wu, "Mainland China's Economic Policy Toward Taiwan: Economic Needs or Unification Scheme?" *Issues and Studies,* vol. 30, no. 9 (September 1994), p. 37. This unexpected development after Tiananmen is for several reasons. While the Tiananmen crackdown led to a reduction in foreign investment and lending, the reduced authority of the central government allowed regional governments more latitude to pursue economic reforms. Limits to trade with and investment from Western countries raised the relative importance of the investment from Taiwan and Hong Kong and trade links between Taiwan, Hong Kong, and southern China.

57. Penelope Hartland-Thunberg, *China, Hong Kong, Taiwan and the World Trading System,* p. 97.

58. Mainland Affairs Department of the KMT Central Committee, *Guojia Tonyi Ganglin Ershi Wen* (Twenty Questions and Answers for the Guidelines for National Unification) (Taipei: Mainland Affairs Department of the KMT Central Committee, 1991), 26.

59. Huang Kun-huei, *Bridging the Taiwan Straits: The Republic of China's Mainland Policy,* distributed by Taiwan's Mainland Affairs Council, April 1993, p. 7.

60. Yu-Shan Wu, "Mainland China's Economic Policy Toward Taiwan: Economic Needs or Unification Scheme?" *Issues and Studies,* vol. 30, no. 9 (September 1994), p. 30.

61. Yoichi Funabashi, Michel Oksenberg, Heinrich Weiss, *An Emerging China in a World of Interdependence,* p. 28.

62. Ralph N. Clough, *Reaching Across the Taiwan Strait: People-to-People Diplomacy* (Boulder, CO.: Westview Press, 1993), p. 144.

63. A collection of English translations of Chinese scholars' articles on the CEA is compiled by Joseph Fewsmith, see "The Emergence of Greater China," *Chinese Economic Studies,* vol. 26, no. 6 (Winter 1993-94).

64. Peter Drysdale and Ross Barnaut use *Institutional integration* to refer to the institutional arrangement of the European Community and NAFTA. Peter Drysdale and Ross Barnaut, "The Pacific: An Application of a General Theory of Economic Integration," in C. Fred Bergsten and Marus Noland, eds., *Pacific Dynamism and the International Economic System,* p. 189.

65. There was a nongovernmental effort to formulate a regionwide Pacific Economic Cooperation Council (PECC) in 1980. PECC's membership was tripartite in nature, including government officials, businessmen, and scholars. It organized a number of working groups on issues such as fisheries and the environment, and held an annual Economic Outlook Conference plus workshops. The annual reports contained excellent forecasts of economic conditions for the Asian Pacific economies. These reports have been found to be extremely useful for both governmental and business communities, even when compared with the World Bank reports of similar nature. The ability of the PECC to "facilitate the functions of representation, information, communication, and negotiation" has made it "the central non-governmental element of the regional cooperation movement." Lawrence T. Woods,

Asia-Pacific Diplomacy, Non-governmental Organizations and International Relations (Vancouver, Canada: UBC Press, 1993), p. 89.

66. For example, the prime minister of Singapore, Goh Chok Tong, said at the Seattle Summit that "Singapore would accept readily an offer to join NAFTA to ensure that it could continue selling to the U.S. market." *Straits Times,* November 26, 1993.

67. Hadi Soesasto, "Implications of the Post-Cold War Politico-Security Environment for the Pacific Economy," in C. Fred Bergsten and Marcus Noland, eds., *Pacific Dynamism and the International Economic System,* p. 377.

68. Ernest H. Preeg, "The US Leadership Role in the World Trade: Past, Present, and Future," *The Washington Quarterly,* vol. 15, no. 2 (Spring 1992), p. 88.

69. John Whalley, "The Urugay Round and the GATT: Whither the Global System, in C. Fred Bergsten and Marus Noland, eds., *Pacific Dynamism and the International Economic System,* pp. 96-97.

70. The APEC chair rotates annually among members and is responsible for hosting an annual ministerial meeting. Foreign and economic ministers of the member states first met in Canberra, Australia, in November 1989. Since then, annual ministerial meetings have being held in Singapore, Seoul, South Korea, Bangkok, Thailand, Seattle, the United States, Bali, Indonesia, and Osaka, Japan. The upcoming ministerial meetings are planned for the Philippines in 1996 and Canada in 1997.

71. In a somewhat different fashion, Vinod K. Aggarwal finds four schools of thought with respect to international institution-building in the Asian Pacific: one, pure GATTists; two, the GATT-consistent school of open regionalism; three, skeptics of open regionalism; and four, advocates of an Asian bloc. See Vinod K. Aggarwal, "Building International Institutions in Asia-Pacific," *Asian Survey,* vol. 33, no. 11 (November 1993), pp. 1036-2038.

72. Charles Smith, "The Politics of Economics," *Far Eastern Economic Review,* June 9, 1994, p. 48.

73. Kishore Mahbubani, "The Pacific Way," *Foreign Affairs,* p. 110.

74. The Carnegie Endowment Study Group, *Defining A Pacific Community,* p. 27.

75. The term *Asian-Pacific diplomacy* was used as part of the title of Lawrence T. Woods's book, *Asia-Pacific Diplomacy, Non-governmental Organizations and International Relations.*

76. Robert A. Manning and Paula Stern, "The Myth of the Pacific Community," *Foreign Affairs,* vol. 37, no. 6 (November/December 1994), p. 84.

77. *The New York Times,* November 21, 1994.

78. U.S. Department of State, *Dispatch,* vol. 4, no. 48 (November 29, 1993), pp. 833-34.

79. After intensive negotiation, the declaration stated that "the pace of implementation will take into account the differing levels of economic development among APEC economies, with the industrialized economies achieving

the goal of free and open trade and investment no later than the year 2010 and the developing economies no later than the year 2020." For the text of "APEC Economic Leader's Declaration of Common Resolve," see U.S. State Department, *Dispatch Supplement,* vol. 5, supplement no. 9 (November 1994), pp. 22-24.

80. Japan prepared a full agenda for the summit. See B. Anne Craib, "APEC Summit Transfers Full Agenda to Tokyo for 1995," *JEI Report,* no 45 (Washington, D.C.: Japan Economic Institute, December 2, 1994), p. 4.

81. C. Fred Bergsten, "APEC and World Trade: A Force for Worldwide Liberalization," *Foreign Affairs,* vol. 73, no. 3 (May/June 1994), p. 21.

82. Jonathan Clarke, "APEC as a Semi-Solution," *Orbis,* vol. 39, no. 1 (Winter 1995), p. 85.

83. For one official expression of the U.S. position, see Secretary Warren Christopher's speech at the APEC Ministerial meeting in Jakarta, Indonesia, on November 11, 1994, "Transforming the APEC Vision into Reality," US State Department, *Dispatch Supplement,* vol. 5, supplement no. 9 (November 1994), p. 4.

84. The Carnegie Endowment Study Group, *Defining a Pacific Community,* p. 27.

85. Donald K. Emmerson, "Organizing the Rim: Asia Pacific Regionalism," *Current History,* vol. 93, no. 587 (December 1994), p. 438.

86. Charles Smith, "The Politics of Economics," *Far Eastern Economic Review,* June 9, 1994, p. 50.

87. It is argued that the NAFTA concept has encouraged the creation of a narrow geographically or racially defined Asian regionalism. Hadi Soesasto, "Implications of the Post-Cold War Politico-Security Environment for the Political Economy," in C. Fred Bergsten and Marus Noland, eds., *Pacific Dynamism and the International Economic System,* p. 377.

88. Susumu Awanohara, "Rich Man, Poor Man," *Far Eastern Economic Review,* vol. 154, no. 40 (October 3, 1991), p. 13.

89. John Bresnan, *From Dominoes to Dynamos: The Transformation of Southeast Asia* (Washington, D.C., Council on Foreign Relations Press, 1994), p. 46.

90. *Far Eastern Economic Review,* November 28, 1991, p. 27.

91. Ibid., p. 26.

92. Peter A. Petri, "Trading with the Dynamos: East Asian Interdependence and American Interests," *Current History,* vol. 93, no. 587 (December 1994), p. 410.

93. Personal interview of Chinese government official in Beijing, July 5, 1994.

94. John Bresnan, *From Dominoes to Dynamos: The Transformation of Southeast Asia,* p. 47.

95. Donald K. Emmerson, "Organizing the Rim: Asia Pacific Regionalism," *Current History,* vol. 93, no. 587 (December 1994), p. 438.

96. *The Asian Wall Street Journal Weekly,* June 15, 1992.

97. During the Bogor Summit, China pressed Japan to state clearly that when the city of Osaka hosts the next summit, the current APEC convention of

inviting only financial ministers from Hong Kong and Taiwan would be adopted.

98. Frank Ching, "At APEC Summit, Everyone Won," *Far Eastern Economic Review,* vol. 156 (December 9, 1993), p. 48.

99. Sheldon Simon, *The Future of Asian-Pacific Security Collaboration* (Lexington, MA.: D.C. Heath and Company, 1988), p. 65.

100. *The Straits Times,* July 21, 1994.

101. Donald K. Emmerson, "Organizing the Rim: Asia Pacific Regionalism," p. 437.

102. Donald E. Weatherbee, "ASEAN and Evolving Patterns of Regionalism in Southeast Asia," *Asian Journal of Political Science,* vol. 1. no. 1 (June 1993), p. 31.

103. These three views are discussed in great detail by Donald E. Weatherbee in "ASEAN and Evolving Patterns of Regionalism in Southeast Asia," pp. 29-54.

104. The ASEAN Secretariat, *Report of the ASEAN Task Force to the ASEAN Ministerial Meeting,* Bangkok, June 17, 1983.

105. The ASEAN Secretariat, "Singapore Declaration of 1992," *Thailand Foreign Affairs Newsletter,* February 1992, p. 2.

106. Donald E. Weatherbee, "ASEAN and Evolving Patterns of Regionalism in Southeast Asia," pp. 30-31.

107. Donald K. Emmerson, "Organizing the Rim: Asia Pacific Regionalism," p. 438.

108. David Shambaugh, "Pacific Security in the Pacific Century," *Current History,* vol. 93, no. 587 (December 1994), p. 428.

109. Donald S. Zagoria, "The Changing US Role in Asian Security in the 1990s," in Sheldon W. Simon, ed., *East Asian Security in the Post-Cold War Era* (Armonk, NY: M. E. Sharpe, 1993), p. 48. Zagoria's other four pillars for Asian regional security include: one, a Pax Americana, in which the United States was the central unifying hub of a network of bilateral security relationships; two, the U.S.-Japanese alliance; three, the failure of communism and the increasing preoccupation of China, Vietnam, and other Asian Communist states with modernization and reform at home; and four, the impressive economic performance of the region. See Donald S. Zagoria, "The Changing US Role in Asian Security in the 1990s," in Sheldon W. Simon, ed., *East Asian Security in the Post-Cold War Era,* pp. 45-49.

110. Barry Buzan, "The Southeast Asian Security Complex," *Contemporary Southeast Asia,* vol. 10, no. 1 (June 1988), p. 2.

111. James W. Morley, "The Structure of Regional Security," in James W. Morley, ed., *Security Interdependence in the Asia Pacific Region* (Lexington, MA.: D. C. Heath and Company, 1986), p. 16.

112. Michael Leifer, *ASEAN and the Security of South-East Asia* (London: Routledge, 1989), p. 1.

113. Ibid., p. 3

114. Ibid., p. 5.
115. James W. Morley, "The Structure of Regional Security," in James W. Morley, ed., *Security Interdependence in the Asia Pacific Region*, p. 16.
116. ASEAN Secretariat, *ASEAN Documents Series, 1967-1985* (Jakarta, Indonesia: ASEAN Secretariat, 1985), p. 21.
117. Sheldon Simon, *The Future of Asian-Pacific Security Collaboration*, p. 67.
118. M. R. Sukhumbhand Paribatra, "ASEAN and the Kampuchean Conflict: A Study of a Regional Organization's Responses to External Security Challenges," in Robert A. Scalapino and Masataka Kosaka, eds., *Peace, Politics & Economics in Asia, The Challenge to Cooperate* (Washington, D.C.: Pergamon-Brassey's International Defense Publishers, 1988), pp. 150-151.
119. Michael Leifer, *ASEAN and the Security of South-East Asia*, p. 11.
120. M. R. Sukhumbhand Paribatra, "ASEAN and the Kampuchean Conflict: A Study of a Regional Organization's Responses to External Security Challenges," in Robert A. Scalapino and Masataka Kosaka, eds., *Peace, Politics & Economics in Asia: The Challenge to Cooperate*, p. 153.
121. The Carnegie Endowment Study Group, *Defining A Pacific Community*, p. 25.
122. *The Straits Times*, July 24, 1994.
123. Donald E. Weatherbee, "ASEAN and Evolving Patterns of Regionalism in Southeast Asia," p. 32.
124. *The Straits Times*, July 26, 1994.
125. Ibid.
126. Ibid
127. In neorealist fashion, Helen Milner suggests that anarchy and interdependence are two key structural features of the international system. See Helen Milner, "The Assumption of Anarchy in International Relations Theory: A Critique," in David A. Baldwin, ed., *Neorealism and Neoliberalism: The Contemporary Debate* (New York: Columbia University Press, 1993), p. 167.

Chapter 10

1. Paul Kennedy, *The Rise and Fall of the Great Powers* (New York: Vintage Books, 1987).
2. James Kurth, "East Asia Plus Mitteleuropa: The Return of History and Redefinition of Security," in Miles Kahler, ed., *Beyond the Cold War in the Pacific* (San Diego, CA.: Institute on Global Conflict and Cooperation, University of California, 1991), p. 146.
3. Desmond Ball, "Arms and Affluence, Military Acquisitions in the Asia-Pacific Region," *International Security*, vol. 18, no. 3 (Winter 1993/94), p. 81.
4. Francis Fukuyama, "The End of History," *The National Interest* (Summer 1989), pp. 14-15.
5 Ibid., p. 4.
6. For examples of this school of thought, see Stanley Hoffmann, "Liberalism and International Affairs," in *Janus and Minerva: Essays in the Theory and*

Practice of International Politics (Boulder, CO.: Westview Press, 1987), pp. 394-417; Michael Doyle, "Liberalism and World Politics," *American Political Science Review,* vol. 80, no. 4 (December 1986), and Doyle, "Kant, Liberal Legacies, and Foreign Affairs," Parts I and II, *Philosophy and Public Affairs,* vol. 12, no. 3 (Summer 1984), and ibid., no. 4 (Fall 1983).

7.   Robert A. Scalapino, "The United States and Asia: Future Prospects," *Foreign Affairs,* vol. 70, no. 5 (Winter 1991/92), p. 21.

8.   Kisbore Mahbubani, "The Pacific Way," *Foreign Affairs,* vol. 74, no. 1 (January/February 1995), p. 103.

9.   Miles Kahler, "Introduction, Beyond the Cold War in the Pacific," in Miles Kahler, ed., *Beyond the Cold War in the Pacific,* p. 5.

10.   Jonathan Sikes, "Asia Puts Its Wealth in Military," *Washington Times,* February 12, 1990, p. 7; quoted from Desmond Ball, "Arms and Affluence, Military Acquisitions in the Asia-Pacific Region," *International Security,* vol. 18, no. 3 (Winter 1993/94), p. 78.

11.   Thomas J. Christensen and Jack Snyder, "Predicting Alliance Patterns," *International Organization,* vol. 44, no. 2 (Spring 1990), p. 168.

12.   Robert S. Ross, "Tripolarity and Policy Making," in Robert S. Ross, ed., *China, the United States, and the Soviet Union: Tripolarity and Policy Making in the Cold War* (Armonk, N.Y.: M. E. Sharpe, 1993), p. 194.

13.   Gerald Segal, "Muddle Kingdom? China's Changing Shape," *Foreign Affairs,* vol. 73, no. 3 (May/June 1994), pp. 53-54.

14.   Paul H. B. Godwin and Alfred D. Wilhelm, Jr., "Assessing China's Military Potential: The Importance of Transparency," *The Atlantic Council of the United States Bulletin,* vol. VI, no. 4 (May 1, 1995) p. 1.

15.   Michael D. Swaine, *China: Domestic Change and Foreign Policy* (Santa Monica, CA.: National Defense Research Institute, 1995), p. 84.

16.   Nicolas D. Kristof, "The Real Chinese Threat," *The New York Times Magazine,* August 27, 1995, p. 50.

17.   Richard K. Betts, "Wealth, Power, and Instability: East Asia and the United States after the Cold War," *International Security,* vol. 18, no. 3 (Winter 1993/94), p. 55.

18.   Mike M. Mochizuki, *Japan: Domestic Change and Foreign Policy* (Santa Monica, CA.: National Defense Research Institute, 1995), p. 54.

19.   Kenneth B. Pyle, *The Japanese Question: Power and Purpose in a New Era* (Washington, D.C.: The American Enterprise Institute, 1992), pp. 39-41.

20.   Mike M. Mochizuki, *Japan: Domestic Change and Foreign Policy,* p. 70.

21.   Shafiqul Islam, "Introduction," in Shafiqul Islam, ed., *Yen for Development: Japanese Foreign Aid and the Politics of Burden-sharing* (New York: Council for International Relations, 1991), p. 1.

22.   Sadako Ogata, "The Changing Role of Japan in the United Nations," *Journal of International Affairs,* vol. 37, no. 1 (Summer 1993).

23.   David B. H. Denoon, *Real Reciprocity: Balancing US Economic and Security Policy in the Pacific Basin* (New York: The Council on Foreign Relation, 1993), p. 17.

24. Richard K. Betts, "Wealth, Power, and Instability: East Asia and the United States after the Cold War," p. 42.

25. James A. Baker, "America in Asia: Emerging Architecture for a Pacific Community," *Foreign Affairs,* vol. 70, no. 5 (1991), pp. 3-4.

26. Office of International Security Affairs, Department of Defense, *United States Security Strategy for the East Asia-Pacific Region* (Washington, D.C.: USDP/ISA/AP, 1995), p. 2.

27. Robert Burns, "Asians Question Need for US Troops," Associate Press, November 4, 1995.

28. Andrew Mack, "Key Security Issues in the Asia-Pacific," in Richard Leaver and James L. Richardson, eds., *The Post-Cold War Order: Diagnoses and Prognoses* (Canberra, Australia: Allen & Unwin, 1993), p. 154.

29. Quoted from ibid.

30. According to a Singapore newspaper report, major powers in the Asian Pacific showed their keen interest in the forum and dialogue. Chinese Vice-Premier and Foreign Minister, Qian Qichen, said in Bangkok, "The establishment of the ASEAN Regional Forum has provided us with a good opportunity. China is ready to work along with the other members and make positive contributions to the fulfillment of this important mission." Japanese Deputy Prime Minister and Foreign Minister Yohei Kono also said, "Today, July 25, 1994, will become a memorable day for the Asia-Pacific as the birthday of the ARF. Let us confirm that we will make steady efforts together in order to rear this child called ARF after a year of gestation to an adult in its own rights." *The Straits Times,* July 26, 1994.

31. Richard W. Manscbach, "The New Order in Northeast Asia: A Theoretical Overview," in Manwoo Lee and Richard W. Mansbach, *The Changing Order in Northeast Asia and the Korean Peninsula* (Boulder, CO.: Westview Press, 1993), p. 30.

32. Michael Mandelbaum, "The United States and the Strategic Quadrangle," in Michael Mandelbaum, ed., *The Strategic Quadrangle* (New York: Council on Foreign Relations, 1995), p. 161.

33. Andrew Mack, "Key Security Issues in the Asia-Pacific," in Richard Leaver and James L. Richardson, eds., *The Post-Cold War Order: Diagnoses and Prognoses,* p. 154.

34. "China Boosts Defense Budget but Purchasing Power drops," *Japan Economic Newswire,* March 11, 1994.

35. Weixing Hu, "Beijing's New Thinking on Security Strategy," *The Journal of Contemporary China,* no. 3 (Summer 1993), p. 57.

36. United States General Accounting Office, *Report to Congressional Committee: Impact of China's Military Modernization in the Pacific Region* (Washington, D.C.: GAO/NSIAD-95-84, June 6, 1995), p. 18.

37. Chongpin Lin, "The Stealthy Advance of China's People's Liberation Army," *The American Enterprise,* vol. 5, no. 1 (January/February 1994), p. 30.

38. United States General Accounting Office, *Report to Congressional Committee: Impact of China's Military Modernization in the Pacific Region,* p. 31.

39. "Asia's Arms Race," *The Economist,* February 20, 1993, p. 19.
40. Steven R. Weisman, "Japan to Share More of US Troop Cost," *The New York Times,* December 21, 1990, p. A3, and Karl Schoenber, "Japan to Put Brakes on Military Buildup," *Los Angeles Times,* December 21, 1990, p. A6.
41. United States General Accounting Office, *Report to Congressional Committee: Impact of China's Military Modernization in the Pacific Region,* p. 29.
42. Michael Richardson, "US and ASEAN Tiptoe Round China on Spratlys," *Asia-Pacific Defense Reporter* (May-June 1995), p. 17.
43. Patrick Tyler, "Sound and Fury in East Asia: War Talk Over Taiwan's Status Worries China's Neighbors," *The New York Times,* August 23, 1995.
44. United States General Accounting Office, *Report to Congressional Committee: Impact of China's Military Modernization in the Pacific Region,* p. 38.
45. Ibid., p. 29.
46. Jonathan Sikes, "Asia Puts Its Wealth in Military," *Washington Times,* February 12, 1990, p. 7.
47. See Geoffrey Harris, "The Determinants of Defense Expenditure in the ASEAN Region," *Journal of Peace Research,* vol. 23, no. 1 (March 1986), pp. 41-49; David D. H. Denoon, "Defense Spending in ASEAN: An Overview," in Chin Kin Wah, ed., *Defense Spending in Southeast Asia* (Singapore: Institute of Southeast Asian Studies, 1987); and Andrew L. Ross, "The International Arms Trade, Arms Imports, and Local Defense Production in ASEAN," in Chandran Jeshurun, ed., *Arms and Defense in Southeast Asia,* (Singapore: Institute of Southeast Asian Studies, 1989), pp. 1-41.
48. For a study, see Kenneth R. Simmonds, *U.N. Convention on the Law of the Sea, 1982* (Dobbs Ferry, N.Y. : Oceana Publications, 1983).
49. "No Need for War in South China Sea," *International Defense Review,* no. 6 (1995), p. 25,
50. United States General Accounting Office, *Report to Congressional Committee: Impact of China's Military Modernization in the Pacific Region,* p. 31.
51. Ibid.
52. Desmond Ball, "Arms and Affluence, Military Acquisitions in the Asia-Pacific Region," *International Security,* vol. 18, no. 3 (Winter 1993/94), p. 80.
53. "Bigger Role for Forces," *Jane's Defense Weekly,* August 8, 1992, p. 22.
54. United States General Accounting Office, *Report to Congressional Committee: Asian Aeronautics: Technology Acquisition Drives Industry Development* (Washington, D.C.: GAO/NSIDA-94-140, May 4, 1994).
55. William T. Tow, *Sino-Japanese-US Military Technology Relations* (Malaysia: Institute of Strategic and International Studies, 1988).
56. United States General Accounting Office, *Report to Congressional Committee: Impact of China's Military Modernization in the Pacific Region,* p. 29.
57. James Clad and Patrick Marshall, "Southeast Asia's Quiet Arms Race," *The Chicago Tribune,* May 23, 1992, p. 21; quoted from Desmond Ball, "Arms and Affluence, Military Acquisitions in the Asia-Pacific Region," p. 78.
58. Desmond Ball, "Arms and Affluence, Military Acquisitions in the Asia-Pacific Region," p. 104.

59. Perry Link, "The Old Man's New China," *The New York Review of Books*, vol. XLI, no. 11 (June 9, 1994), p. 32.
60. Francis Fukuyama, "The End of History," pp. 14-15.
61. Robert A. Scalapino, "The United States and Asia: Future Prospects," p. 21.
62. Perry Link, "The Old Man's New China," p. 32.
63. Robert A. Scalapino, "The United States and Asia: Future Prospects," p. 22.
64. See, for example, Ishihara Shintaro, *The Japan that Can Say No* (New York: Simon & Schuster, 1989).
65. Kenneth B. Pyle, *The Japanese Questions, Power and Purpose in a New Era*, p. 61.
66. On intrinsic and derivative interests, see Richard K. Betts, "Southeast Asia and US Global strategy," *Orbis*, vol. 29, no. 2 (Summer 1985), pp. 354-62.
67. Sheldon W. Simon, "Introduction," in Sheldon W. Simon, ed., *East Asian Security in the Post-Cold War Era* (Armonk, N.Y.: M. E. Sharpe, 1993), p. 3.
68. Sheldon W. Simon, "Regional Security Structures in Asia: The Question of Relevance," in Sheldon W. Simon, ed., *East Asian Security in the Post-Cold War Era*, p. 11.
69. Manwoo Lee and Richard W. Mansbach, *The Changing Order in Northeast Asia and the Korean Peninsula* (Boulder, CO.: Westview, 1993), p. 2.
70. For a detailed description of the Nixon Doctrine, see Henry Kissinger, *White House Years* (Boston, MA.: Little, Brown and Company, 1979), pp. 222-25.
71. Sheldon W. Simon, "Regional Security Structures in Asia: The Question of Relevance," in Sheldon W. Simon, ed., *East Asian Security in the Post-Cold War Era*, p. 12.
72. Gerald Segal, "China and the Disintegration of the Soviet Union," *Asian Survey*, vol. 32, no. 9 (September 1992), p. 856.
73. Office of International Security Affairs, Department of Defense, *United States Security Strategy for the East Asia-Pacific Region*, p. 2.
74. In 1992, Tokyo paid almost 50 percent ($3.5 billion) of the maintenance costs of U.S. forces in Japan. By 1995, Japan will cover 75 percent. See Sheldon W. Simon, "Regional Security Structures in Asia: The Question of Relevance," in Sheldon W. Simon, ed., *East Asian Security in the Post-Cold War Era*, p. 14.
75. Robert Scalapino, *Major Power Relations in Northeast Asia* (Lanham, MD.: University Press of America, 1987), pp. 54-55.
76. Aaron L. Friedberg, "Ripe for Rivalry: Prospects for Peace in a Multipolar Asia," *International Security*, vol. 18, no. 3 (Winter 1993/94), p. 6.
77. For a neorealist view, see John Mearsheimer, "Back to the Future: Instability in Europe after the Cold War," *International Security*, vol. 15, No. 1 (Summer 1990), pp. 5-56. For a neoliberalist view, see Stanley Hoffmann and Robert Keohane, "Correspondence: Back to the Future, International Relations Theory and Post-Cold War Europe," *International Security*, vol. 15, no. 2 (Fall 1990), pp. 191-4.
78. Aaron L. Friedberg, "Ripe for Rivalry: Prospects for Peace in a Multipolar Asia," *International Security*, vol. 18, no. 3 (Winter 1993/94), p. 7.

79. Kisbore Mahbubani, "The Pacific Way," *Foreign Affairs,* p. 102.
80. Miles Kahler, "Introduction," in Miles Kahler, ed., *Beyond the Cold War in the Pacific,* p. 5.
81. Bruce Bueno de Mesquita, *The War Trap* (New Haven, CT.: Yale University Press), 1981.
82. Stuart Harris, "The End of the Cold War in Northeast Asia: The Global Implications," in Stuart Harris and James Cotton, eds., *The End of the Cold War in Northeast Asia* (Australia: Longman Cheshire, 1991), p. 259.
83. Desmond Ball, "Arms and Affluence, Military Acquisitions in the Asia-Pacific Region," pp. 104-5.
84. Nicolas D. Kristof, "The Real Chinese Threat," *The New York Times Magazine,* August 27, 1995, pp. 50-51.
85. See for example, "Containing China," *The Economist,* July 29, 1995, pp. 11-12; Karl W. Eikenberry, "Does China Threaten Asia-Pacific Regional Stability," *Parameters,* Spring 1995, p. 82.

Chapter 11

1. Office of International Security Affairs, Department of Defense, *United States Security Strategy for the East Asia-Pacific Region* (Washington, D.C.: USDP/ISA/AP, 1995), p. 1.
2. Winston Lord, "Building a Pacific Community: Statement before the Commonwealth Club, San Francisco, California, January 12, 1995," *U.S .Department of State Dispatch,* vol. 6, no. 3 (January 16, 1995), p. 35.
3. Robert G. Sutter, *East Asia and the Pacific: Challenge for US Policy* (Boulder, CO.: Westview Press, 1992), p. 3.
4. Winston Lord, "Building a Pacific Community: Statement before the Commonwealth Club, San Francisco, California, January 12, 1995," p. 35.
5. Charles Francis Adams, ed., *The Works of John Adams,* vol. 8 (Boston, MS.: Little, Brown, 1853), pp. 343-44.
6. Arthur Power Dudden, *The American Pacific: From the Old China Trade to the Present* (New York: Oxford University Press, 1992), p. 17.
7. Perry to the Secretary of the Navy, dated Madeira, December 14, 1853, originally published in *Senate Executive Documents,* no. 34 of Thirty-third Congress, second session; quoted from Arthur Power Dudden, *The American Pacific: From the Old China Trade to the Present,* p. 3.
8. Robert G. Sutter, *East Asia and the Pacific: Challenge for US Policy,* p. 15.
9. Arthur Power Dudden, *The American Pacific: From the Old China Trade to the Present,* p. 4.
10. The cultural priority during the early period was carefully analyzed by Akira Iriye in *Across the Pacific: An Inner History of American-East Asian Relations* (Chicago, IL.: Imprint Publications, 1992), pp. 3-82.
11. Tang Tsou, *America's Failure in China, 1941-50* (Chicago, IL.: The University of Chicago Press, 1963), p. 4.
12. For an early account of the American missionary in East Asia, see Howard Malcom, *Travels in south-eastern Asia, Embracing Hindustan, Malaya, Siam,*

and China (Boston, MA.: Gould, Kendall, and Lincoln, 1839). Among the studies of American missionaries to East Asia, see James Reed, *The Missionary Mind and American East Asia Policy, 1911-1915* Cambridge, MA.: Council on East Asian Studies, Harvard University, distributed by Harvard University Press, 1983); Thomas A. Breslin, *China, American Catholicism, and the Missionary* (University Park, PA.: Pennsylvania State University Press, 1980); and John King Fairbank, *The Missionary Enterprise in China and America* (Cambridge, MA.: Harvard University Press, 1974).

13. K. Holly Maze Carter, *The Asian Dilemma in US Foreign Policy: National Interest versus Strategic Planning* (Armonk, N.Y.: M. E. Sharpe, 1989), p. 4.

14. For one Chinese Communist account of the policy, see Hu Sheng, *Chong Yapian Zhanzheng Dao Wushi Yundong* (From the Opium War to the May-Fourth Movement) (Beijing: Renmin Chuban She, 1980), pp. 352.

15. Warren I. Cohen, *America's Response to China: A History of Sino-American Relations* (New York: Columbia University Press, 1990), pp. 7-23.

16. Arthur Power Dudden, *The American Pacific: From the Old China Trade to the Present,* p. 86.

17. Ibid., p. 85.

18. Foster R. Dulles, *The Imperial Year* (New York: Thomas Y. Crowell Co., 1966), p. 9.

19. Ibid., p. 10.

20. K. Holly Maze Carter, *The Asian Dilemma in US Foreign Policy: National Interest versus Strategic Planning* (Armonk, N.Y.: M. E. Sharpe, 1989), p. 5.

21. For these Open Door Notes, see U.S. State Department, *Foreign Relations of the United States, 1899, and Foreign Relations of the United States, 1900* (Washington, D.C.: Government Printing Office, 1901 and 1902 respectively).

22. Tang Tsou elaborated these two principles in his book, *America's Failure in China, 1941-50,* pp. 3-30.

23. K. Holly Maze Carter, *The Asian Dilemma in US Foreign Policy: National Interest Versus Strategic Planning* (Armonk, NY: M. E. Sharpe, 1989), p. 6.

24. Ibid., p. 7.

25. U.S. State Department, *Foreign Relations of the United States, 1917* (Washington, D.C.: Government Printing Office, 1926), pp. 264-65.

26. Akira Iriye, *The Cold War in Asia* (Englewood Cliffs, N.J.: Prentice-Hall, Inc., 1974), p. 35.

27. William Appleman William, *The Tragedy of American Diplomacy* (New York: A Delta Book, 1972), p. 70.

28. Quoted from Nicholas Berry, ed., *U.S. Foreign Policy Documents, 1963-1977* (Brunswick, OH.: Kings Court Communications, 1977), p. 36.

29. K. Holly Maze Carter, *The Asian Dilemma in US Foreign Policy: National Interest versus Strategic Planning* (Armonk, N.Y.: M. E. Sharpe, 1989), p. 32.

30. President Clinton, "U.S.-Asia Economic Engagement in the Twenty-first Century" (Remarks to members of the U.S. business community and Pacific

business leaders, Jakarta, Indonesia, November 16, 1994), *U.S. Department of State Dispatch Supplement,* vol. 5, no. 9 (November 1994), p. 12.

31. Peter A. Petri, "Trading with the Dynamos: East Asian Interdependence and American Interests," *Current History* (December 1994), p. 407.

32. "Focus on East Asia and the Pacific, A Periodic Update," *U.S. Department of State Dispatch,* vol. 4, no. 16 (April 19, 1993), p. 274.

33. Warren Christopher, "America and the Asia-Pacific Future," *U.S. Department of State Dispatch,* vol. 5, no. 22 (May 30, 1994), p. 348.

34. *U.S. Department of State Dispatch,* vol. 4, no. 48 (November 17, 1993), p. 835.

35. Bill Clinton, "U.S.-Asia Economic Engagement in the Twenty-first Century" (Remarks to members of the US business community and Pacific business leaders, Jakarta, Indonesia, November 16, 1994), *U.S. Department of State Dispatch Supplement,* vol. 5, no. 9 (November 1994), p. 12.

36. Warren Christopher, "APEC: Changing A Course for Prosperity," *U.S. Department of State Dispatch,* vol. 4, no. 48 (November 29, 1993), p. 822.

37. Department of Defense, *A Strategic Framework for the Asian Pacific Rim: Report to Congress* (Washington, D.C.: Government Printing Office, 1992), p. 2.

38. For example, Winston Lord's list of American policy objectives in East Asia include creating American jobs and freeing political prisoners; gaining military access while gainsaying the caning of an American teenager and the censoring of an American professor; reconciling the U.S.'s bold economic vision with bold demonstrators for freedom; addressing the threat of population explosion and the excesses of population regimentation; and promoting economic development and encouraging human rights. Winston Lord, "Building a Pacific Community: Statement before the Commonwealth Club, San Francisco, California, January 12, 1995," *U.S. Department of State Dispatch,* vol. 6, no. 3 (January 16, 1995), p. 35.

39. Robert A. Manning and Paula Stern, "The Myth of the Pacific Community," *Foreign Affairs,* vol. 73, no. 6 (November/December 1994), p. 86.

40. Kishore Mahbubani, "The Pacific Way," *Foreign Affairs,* vol. 74, no. 1 (January/February 1995), p. 108.

Selected Bibliography

Adams, John. *The Works of John Adams.* Edited by Charles Francis Adams. Vol. 8 Boston: Little, Brown, 1853.

Aggarwal, Vinod K. "Building International Institutions in Asia-Pacific." *Asian Survey,* vol. 33, no. 11 (November 1993), pp. 1029-42.

Akamatsu, K. "A Historical Pattern of Economic Growth in Developing Countries." *The Developing Economies,* no. 1 (March-April, 1962).

Akita, George. "The Meiji Restoration." In Mark Borthwick, ed., *Pacific Century.* Boulder CO.: Westview Press, 1992.

Alcock, Rutherford. *The Capital of the Tycoon,* 2 vols. London: Longman, 1863.

Allen, G. C. *A Short Economic History of Modern Japan, 1867-1937.* London: Macmillan, 1981.

Appleman, William. *The Tragedy of American Diplomacy.* New York: A Delta Book, 1972.

Art, Robert J. "To What Ends Military Power? The Future of Force." *International Security* (Spring 1980).

ASEAN Secretariat, "Singapore Declaration of 1992." *Thailand Foreign Affairs Newsletter* (February 1992).

—— *Report of the ASEAN Task Force to the ASEAN Ministerial Meeting at Bangkok.* June 17, 1983.

—— *ASEAN Documents Series, 1967-1985.* Jakarta: ASEAN Secretariat, 1985.

Asao, Shinichiro. "A Message from the President." The Japan Foundation Overview of Programs for Fiscal 1993 and Annual Report for Fiscal 1992. Tokyo: The Japan Foundation, 1994.

Ash, Robert F. and Kueh, Y. Y. "Economic Integration within Greater China: Trade and Investment Flows between China, Hong Kong and Taiwan." *The China Quarterly,* no. 136 (December 1993), pp. 711-45.

Awanohara, Susumu. "Rich Man, Poor Man." *Far Eastern Economic Review,* vol. 154, no. 40 (October 3, 1991).

Axelrod, Robert and Keohane, Robert. "Achieving Cooperation Under Anarchy: Strategies and Institutions." In David A. Baldwin, ed. *Neorealism and Neoliberalism: The Contemporary Debate.* New York: Columbia University Press, 1993.

Axelrod, Robert. "Conflict of Interest: An Axiomatic Approach." *Journal of Conflict Resolution.* no. 11 (March 1967).

Baker, James A. "America in Asia: Emerging Architecture for a Pacific Community." *Foreign Affairs,* vol. 70, no. 5 (1991).

Baldwin, David A., ed. *Neorealism and Nealiberalism: The Contemporary Debate.* New York: Columbia University Press, 1993.

—— "Interdependence and Power: A Conceptual Analysis." *International Organizations,* no. 34 (Autumn 1980).

Ball, Desmond. "Arms and Affluence, Military Acquisitions in the Asia-Pacific Region." *International Security,* vol. 18, no. 3 (Winter 1993/94), pp. 78-112.

Banister, T. R. *A History of the External Trade of China, 1834-1881.* Shanghai: Inspector General of Chinese Customs, 1931.

Banks, Michael. "The International Relations Discipline: Asset or Liability for Conflict Resolution?" In Edward E. Azar and John W. Burton, eds. *International Conflict Resolution.* Boulder, CO.: Lynne Rienner, 1986.

Banno, M. *China and the West, 1858-1861: The Origins of Tsungli Yamen.* Cambridge, MA.: Harvard University Press, 1964.

Baochuan, He. *China on the Edge, The Crisis of Ecology and Development.* Berkeley, CA.: Pacific View Press, 1991.

Barkin, J. Samuel and Cronin, Bruce. "The State and the Nation: Changing Norms and the Rules of Sovereignty in International Relations." *International Organization.* vol. 48, no. 1 (Winter 1994).

Barnds, William J. "Trends in US Politics and Their Implications for America's Asian Policy." In Robert A. Scalapino, Seizaburo Sato, Jusuf Wanandi, and Sung-joo Han, eds. *Asia and the Major Powers: Domestic Politics and Foreign Policy.* Berkeley, CA.: Institute of East Asian Studies, University of California, 1988.

Barnett, A. Doak. *China and the Major Powers in East Asia.* Washington, D.C.: The Brookings Institution, 1977.

Beal, John Robinson. *Marshall in China.* Toronto: Doubleday Canada Limited, 1970.

Beasley, William G. *The Rise of Modern Japan: Political, Economic and Social Change since 1850.* New York: St. Martin's Press, 1995.

—— *The Meiji Restoration.* Stanford, CA.: Stanford University Press, 1972.

—— *Great Britain and the Opening of Japan, 1834-1858.* London: Luzac, 1951.

Bennet, A. Le Roy. *International Organizations, Principles and Issues.* Englewood Cliffs, N.J.: Prentice Hall, 1984.

Bergsten, C. Fred. "APEC and World Trade: A Force for Worldwide Liberalization." *Foreign Affairs,* vol. 73, no. 3 (May/June 1994).

Berry, Nicholas, ed. *U.S. Foreign Policy Documents, 1963-1977.* Brunswick, OH.: Kings Court Communications, 1977.

Bertram, James M. *First Act in China: The Story of the Sian Mutiny.* New York: Viking Press, 1938.

Betts, Richard K. "Wealth, Power, and Instability: East Asia and the United States After the Cold War." *International Security,* vol. 18, no. 3 (Winter 1993/94).

—— "Southeast Asia and US Global strategy." *Orbis,* vol. 29, no. 2 (Summer 1985).

Billings-Yun, Melanie. *Decision Against War: Eisenhower and Dien Bien Phu, 1954.* New York: Columbia University Press, 1988.

Bingnan, Wang. *Review of the Nine-Year-Long Sino-American Ambassadorial Talks.* Beijing: Shijie Zhishi Chuban She, 1985.

Bisson, T. A. *Japan in China.* New York: The Macmillan Company, 1938.

Borg, Dorothy. *The United States and the Far Easter Crisis of 1933-1938: From Manchurian Incident Through the Initial Stage of the Undeclared Sino-Japanese War.* Cambridge, MA: Harvard University Press, 1964.

—— *American Policy and the Chinese Revolution, 1925-1928.* New York: The Macmillan Co., 1947.

Borthwick, Mark. *Pacific Century: The Emergence of Modern Pacific Asia.* Boulder, CO.: Westview Press, 1992.

Braestrup, Peter. *Big Story: How the American Press and Television Reported and Interpreted the Crisis of Tet 1968 in Vietnam and Washington.* 2 vols. Boulder, CO.: Westview Press, 1977.

Breslin, Thomas A. *China, American Catholicism, and the Missionary.* University Park, PA.: Pennsylvania State University Press, 1980.

Bresnan, John. *From Dominoes to Dynamos: The Transformation of Southeast Asia.* Washington, D.C.: Council on Foreign Relations Press, 1994.

Brezinski, Zbigniew. *Power and Principle: Memoirs of the National Security Adviser, 1977-1981.* New York: Farrar, Straus, Giroux, 1983.

Brodine, Virginia, ed. *Open Secret: the Kissinger-Nixon Doctrine in Asia.* New York: Harper & Row, 1972.

Brown, Lester R. "Redefining National Security." In Steven L. Spiegel, ed. *At Issue, Politics in the World Arena.* New York: St. Martin's Press, 1988.

Buckley, Roger. *U.S.-Japanese Alliance Diplomacy, 1945-1990.* New York: Cambridge University Press, 1992.

Buhite, Russell D. *Decisions at Yalta : An Appraisal of Summit Diplomacy.* Wilmington, Del.: Scholarly Resources, 1986.

Bull, Hedley and Adam Watson, eds. *The Expansion of International Society.* Oxford, U.K.: Clarendon Press, 1984.

Burkman, Thomas W., ed. *The Occupation of Japan: The International Context.* Norfolk, VA.: The MacArthur Memorial Foundation, 1984.

Burks, Ardath W. *Japan, A Postindustrial Power.* Boulder CO.: Westview Press, 1991.

Buss, Claude A. *Asia in the Modern World: A History of China, Japan, South and Southeast Asia.* London: Coller-Macmillan Limited, 1964.

Buzan, Barry. "The Southeast Asian Security Complex." *Contemporary Southeast Asia,* vol. 10, no. 1 (June 1988).

The Carnegie Endowment Study Group. *Defining a Pacific Community.* Washington, D.C.: Carnegie Endowment for International Peace, 1994.

Cai, Chengwen and Zhao Yongtian. *Banmendian Tanpan* (Panmunjom Negotiations). Beijing: Jiefengjun Chuban She (People's Liberation Army Press), 1992.

Carter, Jimmy. *Keeping Faith: Memoirs of a President.* New York: Bantam Books, 1982.

Carter, K. Holly Maze. *The Asian Dilemma in US Foreign Policy: National Interest Versus Strategic Planning.* Armonk, NY: M. E. Sharpe, 1989.

Chan, Albert. *The Glory and Fall of the Ming Dynasty.* Norman, OK.: University of Oklahoma Press, 1982.

Chan, Ming K. (with the collaboration of John D. Young), ed. *Precarious Balance: Hong Kong Between China and Britain, 1842-1992.* Armonk, N.Y.: M. E. Sharpe, 1994.

Chan, Steve. *East Asian Dynamism.* Boulder, CO.: Westview Press, 1993.

Chang, Chung-li. *The Taiping Rebellion: History and Documents.* 3 vols. Seattle, WA.: University of Washington Press, 1966-1971.

Chang, Gordon H. *Friends and Enemies, The United States, China, and the Soviet Union, 1948-1972.* Stanford, CA.: Stanford University Press, 1990.

Chang, Hsin-pao. *Commissioner Lin and the Opium War.* Cambridge, MA.: Harvard University Press, 1964.

Chay, John. *The Problems and Prospects of American-East Asian Relations.* Boulder, CO.: Westview Press, 1977.

Chen, King C. "Traditional Chinese Foreign Relations." In King C. Chen, ed. *The Foreign Policy of China.* South Orange, N.J.: The Seton Hall University Press, 1972.

Chen, Min. *The Strategic Triangle and Regional Conflicts: Lessons from the Indochina Wars.* Boulder, CO.: Lynn Rienner Publishers, 1992.

Ch'en, Ta-tuan. "Investiture of Liu-ch'iu Kings in the Ch'ing Period." In John K. Fairbank, ed. *The Chinese World Order.* Cambridge, MA.: Harvard University Press, 1968.

Cheng, James Chester. *Chinese Sources for the Taiping Rebellion, 1850-1864.* New York: Oxford University Press, 1963

Chiang Ching-kuo Foundation. *1994 Grant Programs of Chiang Ching-kuo Foundation for International Scholarly Exchange.* Taipei: Chiang Ching-kuo Foundation, 1995.

Chibiro, Hosoya. "Japan's Policies Toward Russia." In James William Morley, ed. *Japan's Foreign Policy, 1868-1941, A Research Guide.* New York: Columbia University Press, 1974.

Chien, Yu-wen. *The Taiping Revolutionary Movement.* New Haven, CT.: Yale University Press, 1973.

Chinese Ministry of Foreign Affairs. *Diplomacy of Contemporary China.* Hong Kong: New Horizon Press, 1990.

—— "Chinese Government Statement." *Beijing Review,* January 19, 1979.

Ching, Frank. "At APEC Summit, Everyone Won." *Far Eastern Economic Review,* vol. 156 (December 9, 1993).

Chiu, Hungdah. "Chinese Attitudes Toward International Law of Human Rights in the Post-Mao Era." In Victor C. Falkenheim, ed., *Chinese Politics from Mao to Deng.* New York: Paragon House, 1989.

Cho, Myung Hyun. *Korea and the Major Powers.* Seoul, Korea: Research Center for Peace and Unification of Korea, 1989.

Cotterell, Arthur. *East Asia: From Chinese Predominance to the Rise of the Pacific Rim.* New York: Oxford University Press, 1993.

Chow, Peter C. Y. "Asia Pacific Economic Integration in Global Perspective." In James C. Hsiung, ed., *Asia Pacific in the New World Politics.* Boulder, CO.: Lynne Rienner, 1993.

Chow, Tse-tsung. *The May Fourth Movement: Intellectual Revolution in Modern China.* Stanford, CA.: Stanford University Press, 1960.

Christensen, Thomas J. and Snyder, Jack. "Predicting Alliance Patterns." *International Organization,* vol. 44, no. 2 (Spring 1990).

Christopher, Warren. "America and the Asia-Pacific Future." *U.S. Department of State Dispatch,* vol. 5, no. 22 (May 30, 1994).

—— "APEC: Changing A Course for Prosperity." *U.S. Department of State Dispatch,* vol. 4, no. 48 (November 29, 1993).

Chu, Pao-Chin. "From the Paris Conference to the Manchurian Incident: The beginning of China's diplomacy of Resistance against Japan." In Alvin D. Coox and Hilary Conroy, eds., *China and Japan: Search for Balance since World War I.* Santa Barbara, CA.: ABC-Clio, Inc., 1978.

Chun, Hae-jong. "Sino-Korean Tributary Relations in the Ch'ing Period." In John K. Fairbank, ed., *The Chinese World Order.* Cambridge, MA.: Harvard University Press, 1968.

Cipolla, Carlo M. *Guns, Sails, and Empires: Technological Innovation and the Early Phases of European Expansion, 1400-1700.* New York: Pantheon, 1960.

Clad, James and Marshall, Patrick. "Southeast Asia's Quiet Arms Race." *The Chicago Tribune,* May 23, 1992.

Clarke, Jonathan. "APEC as a Semi-Solution." *Orbis,* vol. 38, no. 1 (Winter 1995), pp. 81-95.

Clarke, Prescott and J.S. Gregory. *Western Reports on the Taiping: A Selection of Documents.* Honolulu, HI.: University Press of Hawaii, 1982.

Clinton, Bill. "U.S.-Asia Economic Engagement in the 21st Century." *U.S. Department of State Dispatch Supplement,* vol. 5, no. 9 (November 1994).

Clough, Ralph N. *Reaching Across the Taiwan Strait: People-to-People Diplomacy.* Boulder, CO.: Westview Press, 1993.

—— *East Asia and US Security.* Washington, D.C.: The Brookings Institute, 1975.

Clyde, Paul Hibbert. *The Far East: A History of the Impact of the West on Eastern Asia.* Englewood Cliffs, N.J.: Prentice-Hall, 1958.

Coble, Parks M. *Facing Japan, Chinese Politics and Japanese Imperialism, 1931-1937.* Cambridge, MA.: Council on East Asian Studies, Harvard University. Distributed by Harvard University Press, 1991

Collis, Maurice. *Foreign Mud, Being an Account of the Opium Imbroglio at Canton in the 1830's and the Anglo-Chinese War that Followed.* New York: Alfred A. Knopf, 1947.

Cohen, Warren I. ed. *Pacific Passage.* New York: Columbia University Press, 1996.

—— *America's Response to China: A History of Sino-American Relations.* New York: Columbia University Press, 1990.

The Compilation Group for the History of Modern China Series. *The Opium War.* Beijing: Foreign Language Press, 1976.

Comprehensive National Security Study Group. *Report on Comprehensive National Security.* Tokyo, July 2, 1980.

Conable, Barber B., Jr. and David Lampton. "China: The Coming Power." *Foreign Affairs,* vol. 72, no. 5 (Winter 1992/93), pp. 133-49.

Cooper, Richard N. "Economic Interdependence and Foreign Policy in the Seventies." *World Politics,* vol. 24, no. 2 (January 1972).

—— *The Economics of Interdependence: Economic Policy in the Atlantic Community.* New York: McGraw-Hill, 1968.

Craib, B. Anne. "APEC Summit Transfers Full Agenda to Tokyo for 1995." *JEI Report,* no. 45, Washington, D.C.: Japan Economic Institute, December 2, 1994.

Craig, Gordon A., and Alexander L. George. *Force and Statecraft: Diplomatic Problems of Our Time.* New York: Oxford University Press, 1983.

Craig, Albert M. "The Central Government." In Marius B. Jansen and Gilbert Rozman, eds., *Japan in Transition: From Tokugawa to Meiji.* Princeton, N.J.: Princeton University Press, 1986.

Crane, George T. "China and Taiwan: Not Yet 'Greater China.'" *International Affairs,* vol. 69, no. 4 (1993).

Crone, Donald. "Does Hegemony Matter? The Reorganization of the Pacific Political Economy." *World Politics,* vol. 45, no. 4 (July 1993).

Crowley, James B. "Japan's Military Foreign Policy." In James W. Morley, ed., *Japan's Foreign Policy, 1868-1941.* New York: Columbia University Press, 1974.

—— ed. *Modern East Asia, Essays in Interpretation.* New York: Harcourt, Brace and World Inc., 1970.

Cui, Zhiyuan "Particular, Universal, and Infinite: Transcending Western Centralism and Cultural Relativism in the Third World." In Leo Marx and Bruce Mazlish, eds., *Progress: Fact or Fiction.* Ann Arbor, MI.: University of Michigan Press, 1995.

Cumings, Bruce. *The Origins of the Korean War: Liberation and the Emergence of Separate Regimes, 1945-1947.* Princeton, N.J.: Princeton University Press, 1981.

de Barry, Theodore, Wing-tsit Chan, and Chester Tan, eds. *Sources of Chinese Tradition.* New York: Columbia University Press, 1964.

Deconde, Alexander. *A History of American Foreign Policy.* New York: Charles Scriber's Sons, 1970.

Dedjier, Vladimir. *The Battle Stalin Lost: Memoirs of Yugoslavia, 1948-1953.* New York: Viking Press, 1971.

de Mesquita, Bruce Bueno. *The War Trap.* New Haven, CT.: Yale University Press, 1981.

Deng, Lifeng. *Jianguohou Junshixingdong Quanlu* (Complete Records of Military Actions Since the Founding of the PRC). Taiyuan, China: Shanxi Renmin Chuban She, 1994.

Deng Xiaoping. "An Important Principle for Handling Relations between Fraternal Parties"; "The Present Situation and the Tasks Before Us"; "Opening Speech at the Twelfth National Congress of the Chinese Communist Party." In *Selected Works of Deng Xiaoping, 1975-1982*. Beijing: Foreign Language Press, 1983.

Deng, Yong. "Post-Deng China: Sources of Stability." *The Journal of Contemporary China*, no, 7 (Fall 1994), pp. 76-81.

Denoon, David D. H. *Real Reciprocity: Balancing US Economic and Security Policy in the Pacific Basin*. New York: The Council on Foreign Relation, 1993.

—— "Defense Spending in ASEAN: An Overview." In Chin Kin Wah, ed., *Defense Spending in Southeast Asia*. Singapore: Institute of Southeast Asian Studies, 1987.

Deuchler, Martina. *Confucian Gentleman and Barbarian Envoys, the Opening of Korea, 1875-1885*. Seattle, WA.: University of Washington Press, 1977.

Ding, Yi. "Upholding the Five Principles of Peaceful Coexistence." *Beijing Review*, vol. 33, no. 9 (February 26–March 4, 1990).

Dittmer, Lowell. "China and Russia: New Beginnings." In Samuel Kim, ed., *China and the World, Chinese Foreign Relations in the Post–Cold War Era*. Boulder, CO.: Westview Press, 1994.

—— *Sino-Soviet Normalization and Its International Implications, 1945-1990*. Seattle, WA.: University of Washington Press, 1992.

Divine, Robert A. "Forward." In George C. Herring, ed., *America's Longest War: The United States and Vietnam, 1950-1975*. New York: Alfred A. Knopf, 1986.

Doolin, Dennis J. *Territorial Claims in the Sino-Soviet Conflict*. Stanford, CA.: Hoover Institution on War, Revolution, and Peace, Stanford University, 1965.

Dorwart, Jeffrey. *The Pigtail War: American Involvement in the Sino-Japanese War, 1894-1895*. Amherst, MA.: University of Massachusetts Press, 1975.

Dostoyevsky, Feodor. "Geok-Teppe, What is Asia to Us?" In Robert A. Goldwin, Gerald Stourzh, and Marvin Zetterbaum, eds., *Readings in Russian Foreign Policy*. New York: Columbia University Press, 1959.

Dower, John. *War Without Mercy: Race and Power in the Pacific War*. New York: Pantheon Books, 1986.

Drifte, Reinhard. *Japan's Foreign Policy*. New York: Council on Foreign Relations Press, 1990.

Drysdale, Peter, and Ross Barnaut. "The Pacific: An Application of a General Theory of Economic Integration." In C. Fred Bergsten and Marus Noland, eds., *Pacific Dynamism and the International Economic System*. Washington, D.C.: Institute for International Economics, 1993.

Du, Gong, and Ni Liyu. *Zhuanhuanzhong de Shijie Geju* (The World Structure in Transition). Beijing: Shijie Zhishi Chuban She, 1992.

Dudden, Arthur Power. *The American Pacific: From the Old China Trade to the Present*. New York: Oxford University Press, 1992.

Duiker, William J. "China and Vietnam and the Struggle for Indochina." In Joseph J. Zasloff, ed., *Postwar Indochina: Old Enemies and New Allies*. Washington,

D.C.: Center for the Study of Foreign Affairs, Foreign Service Institute, U.S. Department of State, 1988.

Dulles, Foster R. *The Imperial Year.* New York: Thomas Y. Crowell Co., 1966.

Duus, Peter. "The Takeoff Point of Japanese Imperialism." In Harry Wray and Hilary Conroy, eds., *Japan Examined: Perspectives on Modern Japanese History.* Honolulu, HI.: University of Hawaii Press, 1983.

—— *The Rise of Modern Japan.* Boston, MA.: Houghton Mifflin Company, 1976.

Eastman, Lloyd E. *Seeds of Destruction: Nationalist China in War and Revolution, 1937-1949.* Stanford, CA.: Stanford University Press, 1984.

Eikenberry, Karl W. "Does China Threaten Asia-Pacific Regional Stability?" *Parameters* (Spring 1995) pp. 82-103.

Eisenhower, Dwight D. *Mandate for Change, 1953-1956.* Garden City, N.Y.: Doubleday, 1963

Ellison, Herbert J. "Soviet-Chinese Relations: The Experience of Two Decades." In Robert Ross, ed., *China, the United States, and the Soviet Union: Tripolarity and Policy Making in the Cold War World.* Armonk, N.Y.: M. E. Sharpe, 1993.

—— ed. *Japan and the Pacific Quadrille: The Major Powers in East Asia.* Boulder, CO.: Westview Press, 1987.

—— ed. *The Sino-Soviet Conflict: A Global Perspective.* Seattle, WA.: University of Washington Press, 1982.

Emmerson, Donald K. "Organizing the Rim: Asia Pacific Regionalism." *Current History,* vol. 93, no. 587 (December 1994) pp. 435-39.

Emmerson, John K., and Harrison M. Lolland. *The Eagle and the Rising Sun: America and Japan in the Twentieth Century.* Reading, MA.: Addison-Wesley, 1988.

Enlai, Zhou. "Kangmei Yuanchao, Baowei Heping" (Resisting America, Assisting Korea, and Defending Peace). *Zhou Enlai Waijiao Wenxuan* (Selected Diplomatic Works of Zhou Enlai). Beijing: Zhongyang Wenxian Chuban She, 1990.

Fairbank, John King. *The United States and China.* Cambridge, MA.: Harvard University Press, 1983.

—— *The Missionary Enterprise in China and America.* Cambridge, MA.: Harvard University Press, 1974.

—— "A Preliminary Framework." In John K. Fairbank, ed., *The Chinese World Order.* Cambridge, MA.: Harvard University Press, 1968.

—— Reischauer, E. O., and Craig, A. M. *East Asia—The Modern Transformation.* London: George Allen & Unwin, 1965.

—— and Shu-yu, eds. *China's Response to the West: A Documentary Survey.* Cambridge, MA.: Harvard University Press, 1954.

—— and Shu-yu Teng. "On the Ch'ing Tributary System." *Harvard Journal of Asiatic Studies.* vol. 6, no. 4 (June 1941).

Falk, Richard A. "The Interplay of Westphalia and Charter Conceptions of International Legal Order." In Richard A. Falk and Cyrus E. Black, eds.,

The Future of the International Legal Order, vol. 1. Princeton, N.J.: Princeton University Press, 1969.

Fallows, James. *Looking at the Sun: The Rise of the New East Asian Economic and Political System.* New York: Vintage Books, 1995.

Fay, Peter Ward. *The Opium War, 1840-1842.* Chapel Hill, NC.: The University of North Carolina Press, 1975.

Feffler, V., and Painter, David S., eds. *Origins of the Cold War: An International History.* London: Routledge, 1994.

Fewsmith, Joseph, ed. "The Emergence of Greater China." *Chinese Economic Studies,* vol. 26, no. 6 (Winter 1993-94).

Fiffer, Sharon Sloan. *Imagining America: Paul Thai's Journey from the Killing Fields of Cambodia to Freedom in the U.S.A.* New York: Paragon House, 1991.

Floyd, David. *Mao Against Khrushchev: A Short History of the Sino-Soviet Conflict.* New York: Praeger, 1964.

Foot, Rosemary. *The Wrong War: American Policy and the Dimensions of the Korean Conflict, 1950-1953.* Ithaca, N.Y.: Cornell University Press, 1985.

Frankel, Joseph. *International Relations in a Changing World.* New York: Oxford University Press, 1979.

Friedberg, Aaron L. "Ripe for Rivalry: Prospects for Peace in a Multipolar Asia." *International Security,* vol. 18, no. 3 (Winter 1993/94), pp. 5-33.

Friend, Theodore. *The Blue-Eyed Enemy: Japan Against the West in Java and Luzon, 1942-1945.* Princeton, N.J.: Princeton University Press, 1988.

Fu, Lo-shu. *A Documentary Chronicle of Sino-Western Relations, 1644-1820.* Tempe, AZ.: University Of Arizona Press, 1966.

Fukuyama, Francis. "The End of History." *The National Interest* (Summer 1989), pp. 3-18.

Funabashi, Yoichi, Michel Oksenberg, and Heinrich Weiss. *An Emerging China in a World of Interdependence.* New York: The Trilateral Commission, 1994.

Gaddies, John Lewis. "The Emerging Post-Revisionist Thesis on the Origins of the Cold War." *Diplomatic History,* no. 7 (Summer 1983).

—— "Korea in American Politics, Strategy and Diplomacy, 1945-1950." In Yonosuke Nagai and Akira Iriye, eds., *The Origins of the Cold War in Asia.* New York: Columbia University Press, 1977.

Gallicchio, Marc S. *The Cold War Begins in Asia: American East Asian Policy and the Fall of the Japanese Empire.* New York: Columbia University Press, 1988.

Gang, Yu. "The Situation in Kampuchea After Eight Years of Vietnamese Aggression." In International Security Council Conference Proceedings, *The Balance of Power in Asia.* New York: International Council, 1987.

Garthoff, Raymond L. "Sino-Soviet Military Relations, 1945-1966." In Garthoff, Raymond L., ed., *Sino-Soviet Military Relations.* New York: Praeger, 1966.

Garver, John W. *Foreign Relations of the People's Republic of China.* Englewood Cliffs, N.J.: Prentice Hall, 1993.

—— "The 'New Type' of Sino-Soviet Relations." *Asian Survey,* vol. 29, no. 12 (December 1989).

—— "The Reagan Administration's Southeast Asian Policy." In James C. Hsiung, ed., *U.S.-Asian Relations: The National Security Paradox.* New York: Praeger, 1983.

George, Alexander L. and Richard Smoke. *Deterrence in American Foreign Policy: Theory and Practice.* New York: Columbia University Press, 1959.

Gibert, Stephen P., ed., *Security in Northeast Asia, Approaching the Pacific Century.* Boulder, CO.: Westview Press, 1988.

Gilks, Anne. *The Breakdown of the Sino-Vietnamese Alliance, 1970-1979.* China Research Monograph, 39. Berkeley, CA.: Institute of East Asian Studies, University of California, 1992.

Gilpin, Robert. "The Debate about the New World Economic Order." In Danny Unger and Paul Blackburn, eds., *Japan's Emerging Global Role.* Boulder, CO.: Lynn Rienner Publishers, 1993.

Gittings, John. *Survey of the Sino-Soviet Dispute: a Commentary and Extracts From the Recent Polemics, 1963-1967.* London: Oxford University Press, 1968.

Gluck, Carol. *Japan's Modern Myths: Ideology in the Late Meiji Period.* Princeton, N.J.: Princeton University Press, 1985.

Godwin, Paul H. B., and Alfred D. Wilhelm, Jr. "Assessing China's Military Potential: The Importance of Transparency." *The Atlantic Council of The United States Bulletin,* vol. VI, no. 4 (May 1, 1995), pp.71-6.

Gordon, Bernard K. "Japan: Searching Once Again." In James C. Hsiung, ed., *Asia Pacific in the New World Politics.* Boulder, CO.: Lynne Rienner, 1993.

Gottings, John. *Survey of the Sino-Soviet Dispute: A Commentary and Extracts from the Recent Polemics, 1963-1967.* London: Oxford University Press, 1968.

Gray, Jack. *Rebellions and Revolutions: China from the 1800s to the 1980s.* Oxford, England: Oxford University Press, 1990.

Griffith, William E. *The Sino-Soviet Rift.* Cambridge, MA.: MIT Press, 1964.

Grimmett, Richard F. *Conventional Arms Transfers to the Third World, 1984-1991.* Washington, D.C.: Congressional Research Service, Library of Congress, 1992.

Gungwu, Wang. "Early Ming Relations with Southeast Asia: A Background Essay." In John K. Fairbank, ed., *The Chinese World Order.* Cambridge, MA.: Harvard University Press, 1968.

Gunther, John. *The Riddle of MacArthur: Japan, Korea and the Far East.* London: H. Hamilton, 1951.

Hail, William James. *Tseng Kuo-fan and the Taipei Rebellion: With a Short Sketch of His Later Career.* New York: Paragon Book Reprint, 1964.

Haiwen, Li. "Lenyan Xiangyang Kanshijie: Guoji Zhengzhijia Mao Zedong" (Looking at the World Through Cool Eyes: Mao Zedong in International Politics). In Hou Shudong, ed., *Yidai Juren Mao Zedong* (A Giant of the Generation: Mao Zedong). Beijing: Zhongguo Qinglian Chuban She, 1993.

Halperin, Morton H. *Sino-Soviet Relations and Armed Control.* Cambridge, MA.: Harvard University Press, 1967.

Hane, Mikiso. *Modern Japan: A Historical Survey.* Boulder, CO.: Westview Press, 1992.

Han-sheng, Lin. "A New Look at Chinese Nationalist 'Appeasers.'" In Alvin D. Coox and Hilary Conroy, eds., *China and Japan: A Search for Balance Since World War I.* Santa Barbara, CA: ABC-Clio, Inc., 1978.

Hardin, Russel. *Collective Action.* Baltimore, MD.: Johns Hopkins University Press, 1982.

Harding, Harry. *A Fragile Relationship: The United States and China since 1972.* Washington, D.C.: Brookings Institution, 1992.

—— "The Emergence of Greater China: How US Policy Will Have to Change." *The American Enterprise,* vol. 3, no. 3 (May-June 1992).

—— *China and Northeast Asia: The Political Dimension.* Lanham, MD.: University Press of America, 1988.

Harootunia, Harry D. "The Economic Rehabilitation of the Samurai in the Early Meiji Period." *Journal of Asian Studies,* vol. 19, no. 4 (1960).

—— "The Process of Japan and the Samurai Class, 1868-1882." *Pacific Historical Review,* vol. 28, no. 3 (1959).

Harris, Geoffrey. "The Determinants of Defense Expenditure in the ASEAN Region." *Journal of Peace Research,* vol. 23, no. 1 (March 1986).

Harris, Stuart. "The End of the Cold War in Northeast Asia: The Global Implications." In Stuart Harris and James Cotton, eds., *The End of the Cold War in Northeast Asia.* Australia: Longman Cheshire, 1991.

Hartland-Thunberg, Penelope. *China, Hong Kong, Taiwan and the World Trading System.* New York: MacMillan, 1990.

Hatada, Takashi. *A History of Korea.* Translated and edited by Warren W. Smith, Jr. and Benjamin H. Hazard. Santa Barbara, CA: Clio Press, 1969.

He, Di. "The Evolution of the People's Republic of China's Policy toward the Offshore Islands." In Warren I. Cohen and Akira Iriye, eds., *The Great Powers in East Asia: 1953-1960.* New York: Columbia University Press, 1990.

Head, William. "Vietnam and Its Wars: A Historical Overview of US Involvement." In William Head and Lawrence E. Grinter, eds., *Looking Back on the Vietnam War.* Westport, CT.: Praeger, 1993.

Hearn, Lafcadio. *Japan: An Attempt at Interpretation.* New York: Macmillan, 1913.

Heinrichs, Waldo. "Eisenhower and Sino-American Confrontation." In Warren I. Cohen and Akira Iriye, eds., *The Great Powers in East Asia: 1953-1960.* New York: Columbia University Press, 1990.

Herring, George C. *America's Longest War: The United States and Vietnam, 1950-1975.* New York: Alfred A. Knopf, 1986.

Hess, G. R. *The United States' Emergence as a Southeast Asian Power, 1940-1950.* New York: Columbia University Press, 1987.

Hinton, H.C. "Sino-Soviet Relations: Background and Overview." In Douglas T. Stuart and William T. Tow, eds., *China, the Soviet Union and the West.* Boulder, CO.: Westview Press, 1982.

Hirono, Ryokichi. "Future Prospects for Economic Cooperation in Asia and the Pacific Region." In Robert A. Scalapino and Masataka Kosaka, eds., *Peace,*

Politics & Economics in Asia: The Challenge to Cooperate. Washington, D.C.: Pergamon-Brassey's International Defense Publishers, 1988.

Hirschmeier, Johannes. *The Origins of Enterpreneurship in Meiji Japan.* Cambridge, MA.: Harvard University Press, 1964.

Hoffe, Josef. "Entangled Forever." In Charles W. Kegley Jr., and Eugene R. Wittkopf, eds., *The Future of American Foreign Policy.* New York: St. Martin's Press, 1992.

Hoffmann, Stanley. "Liberalism and International Affairs." In *Janus and Minerva: Essays in the Theory and Practice of International Politics.* Boulder, CO.: Westview Press, 1987.

—— *Duties Beyond Borders: On the Limits and Possibilities of Ethical International Politics.* Syracuse, NY: Syracuse University Press, 1981.

Hoffmann, Stanley, and Robert Keohane. "Correspondence: Back to the Future, International Relations Theory and Post–Cold War Europe." *International Security,* vol. 15, no. 2 (Fall 1990), pp. 191-94.

Holland, Harrison M. *Japan Challenges America: Managing An Alliance in Crisis.* Boulder, CO.: Westview Press, 1992.

Hood, Steven J. *Dragons Entangled: Indochina and the China-Vietnam War.* Armonk, N.Y.: M. E. Sharpe, 1992.

Hopkins, John C., and Weixing Hu. *Strategic Views from the Second Tier: The Nuclear Weapons Policies of France, Great Britain, and China.* New Brunswick, N.J.: Transaction Publishers, 1995.

Hora, Tomio. *Nankin Daigyakusatsu: Nihonjin e no Kokuhatsu* (Nanjing Massacre: A Protest to the Japanese). Osaka: Toho Shuppan, 1992.

—— *Nitchu Senso Nankin Daizangyaku Jiken Shiryoshu* (Sources on the Nanjing Massacre During the Sino-Japanese Conflict). Tokyo: Aoki shoten, 1985

—— *Nankin Daigyakusatsu* (Nanjing Massacre). Tokyo: Gendaishi Shuppan Kai, 1975.

Hough, Richard Alexander. *The Fleet That Had to Die.* New York: Viking Press, 1958.

Hsiung, James C., ed. *Asia Pacific in the New World Politics.* Boulder, CO.: Lynne Rienner Publishers, 1993;

—— "Reagan's China Policy and the Sino-Soviet Détente." *Asian Affairs,* vol. 11, no. 2 (Summer 1984).

Hsu, Immanuel C. Y., *The Rise of Modern China.* New York: Oxford University Press, 1995.

—— *The Ili Crisis: A Study of Sino-Russian Diplomacy, 1871-1881.* Oxford, England: Oxford University Press, 1965.

—— *China's Entrance into the Family of Nations, the Diplomatic Phase, 1860-1880.* Cambridge, MA.: Harvard University Press, 1960.

Hsu, Shuhsi. *The War Conduct of the Japanese.* Hankou, China: Kelly and Walsh Ltd., 1938.

Hu, Sheng. *Cong Yapian Zhanzheng Dao Wusi Yundong* (From the Opium War to the May-Fourth Movement). Beijing: Renmin Chuban She, 1980.

Hu, Weixing. "Beijing's New Thinking on Security Strategy." *The Journal of Contemporary China,* no. 3 (Summer 1993).

Hu, Yaobang. "Create a New Situation in All Fields of Socialist Modernization." In *The Twelfth National Congress of the CPC* (September 1982). Beijing: Foreign Language Press, 1982.

Huan, Guo-cang. *Sino-Soviet Relations to the Year 2000: Implications for US Interests.* Washington, D.C.: The Atlantic Council of The United States, 1986.

Hudson, G. F., Richard Lowenthal, and Rodrick MacFarquhur. *The Sino-Soviet Dispute.* New York: Praeger, 1961.

Hunt, Michael H., *The Genesis of Chinese Communist Foreign Policy.* New York: Columbia University Press, 1996.

Huntington, Samuel P. "The Clash of Civilization?" *Foreign Affairs,* vol. 72, no. 4 (Summer 1993), pp. 22-49.

—— "Why International Primacy Matters." *International Security,* vol. 17, no. 4 (Spring 1993), pp. 68-83.

Hurwitz, Leon, and Christian Lequesne, eds. *The State of the European Community: Policies, Institutions, and Debates in the Transition Years.* Boulder, CO.: Lynne Rienner, 1991.

Hwang, K. *The Korean Reform Movement of the 1880s: A Study of Transition in Intra-Asian Relations.* Cambridge, MA.: Schenkman Publishing Company, 1978.

Ichimura, Shinichi, and James W. Morley. "Introduction: The Varieties of Asian-Pacific Experience." In James W. Morley, ed., *Driven by Growth: Political Change in the Asia-Pacific Region.* Armonk, N.Y.: M. E. Sharpe, 1993.

Iichiro, Tokutomi. "Commentary on the Imperial Rescript Declaring War on the United States and the British Empire." In Theodore de Bary, Ryusaku Tsunoda, and Donald Keene, eds., *Sources of Japanese Tradition,* vol. 2. New York: Columbia University Press, 1964.

Ikuhiko, Hata. "The Marco Polo Bridge Incident, 1937." In James W. Morley, ed., *The China Quagmire: Japan's Expansion in the Asian Continent, 1933-1941.* New York: Columbia University Press, 1983.

Inoguchi, Takashi. "The Coming Pacific Century." *Current History,* vol. 93, no. 579 (January 1994).

Iriye, Akira. *The Origins of the Second World War in Asia and the Pacific.* New York: Longman, 1993.

—— *Across the Pacific: An Inner History of American-East Asian Relations.* Chicago, IL.: Imprint Publications, Inc., 1992.

—— *China and Japan in Global Setting.* Cambridge, MA.: Harvard University Press, 1992.

—— *The Cold War in Asia: A Historical Introduction.* Englewood Cliffs, N.J.: Prentice-Hall, 1974.

—— *Pacific Estrangement: Japanese and American Expansion, 1897-1911.* Cambridge, MA.: Harvard University Press, 1972.

Isenberg, Irwin, ed. *The Russian-Chinese Rift: Its Impact on World Affairs.* New York: H. W. Wilson Co., 1966.

Ishihara, Shintaro. *The Japan that Can Say No.* New York: Simon & Schuster, 1989.

Islam, Shafiqul. "Introduction." In Shafiqul Islam, ed., *Yen for Development: Japanese Foreign Aid and the Politics of Burden-sharing.* New York: Council for International Relations, 1991.

Jain, R. K. *China and Japan, 1949-1980.* Oxford: Martin Robertson, 1981.

Jalal, Kazi F. "International Agencies and the Asia-Pacific Environment." *Environmental Science and Technology,* vol. 27, no. 12 (November 1993).

The Japan Foundation. *The Japan Foundation Overview of Programs for Fiscal 1993 and Annual Report for Fiscal 1992.* Tokyo, Japan, 1993.

—— "The Japan Foundation Law," Article 1. In *The Japan Foundation Overview of Programs for Fiscal 1993 and Annual Report for Fiscal 1992.* Tokyo, Japan, 1993.

Jian, Chen. *China's Road to the Korean War: The Making of the Sino-American Confrontation.* New York: Columbia University Press, 1994.

Jin, Yongjian. "Asia's Major Human Rights Concerns." *Beijing Review,* vol. 36, no. 16 (April 19, 1993).

Johnson, Chalmers. *MITI and The Japanese Miracle: The Growth of Industrial Policy, 1925-1975.* Stanford, CA.: Stanford University Press, 1982.

Johnston, Alastair I. *Cultural Realism: Strategic Culture and Grant Strategy in Chinese History.* Princeton, N.J.: Princeton University Press, 1996.

Jones, Peter, and Sian Kevill. *China and the Soviet Union, 1949-84.* New York: Facts on File Publications, 1985.

Jones, Randall, Robert King, and Michael Klein. *The Chinese Economic Area: Economic Integration without a Free Trade Agreement.* Paris: OECD Working Papers, No. 124, 1992.

Jordan, Donald A. *The Northern Expedition: China's National Revolution of 1926-1928.* Honolulu, HI.: The University of Hawaii Press, 1976.

Junshi Kexueyuan Junshi lishi Yanjiubu (Military History Research Department of the Chinese Military Academy). *Zhongguo Renmin Zhiyuanjun Kangmei Yuanchao Zhanshi* (Battle History of Chinese People's Volunteers in the War to Resist America and to Assist Korea). Beijing: Junshi Kexue Chuban She, 1992.

Kagan, Donald. *The Outbreak of the Peloponnesian War.* Ithaca, N.Y.: Cornell University Press, 1969.

Kahler, Miles. "Introduction, Beyond the Cold War in the Pacific." In Miles Kahler, ed., *Beyond the Cold War in the Pacific.* San Diego, CA.: Institute on Global Conflict and Cooperation, University of California, 1991.

Kajima, Morinosuke. *A Brief Diplomatic History of Modern Japan.* Rutland, VT.: Charles E. Tuttle Co., 1965.

Kao, Koong-Lian. *Trade and Investment Across the Taiwan Straits.* Taiwan: Mainland Affairs Council, the Executive Yuan, August 1993.

Kataoka, Tesuta. *The Price of a Constitution: The Origin of Japan's Postwar Politics.* New York: Crane Russak, 1991.

Katzenstein, Peter J., and Noburo Okawara. *Japan's National Security: Structures, Norms and Policy Responses in a Changing World.* Ithaca, N.Y.: Cornell University East Asia Program, 1993.

Kaufman, Burton I. *The Korean War: Challenges in Crisis, Credibility, and Command.* Philadelphia, PA.: Temple University Press, 1986.

Keddell, Joseph P., Jr. *The Politics of Defense in Japan: Managing Internal and External Pressures.* Armonk, N.Y.: M. E. Sharpe, 1993.

Kegley, Charles W., Jr. *Controversies in International Relations Theory: Realism and the Neoliberal Challenge.* New York: St. Martin's Press, 1995.

Kennan, George F. ("X"). "The Sources of Soviet Conduct." *Foreign Affairs,* no. 25 (July 1947), pp. 566-82.

Kennedy, Paul. *The Rise and Fall of the Great Powers.* New York: Vintage Books, 1987.

Kenny, Henry J. *The American Role in Vietnam and East Asia.* New York: Praeger, 1984.

Keohane, Robert O. *After Hegemony: Cooperation and Disorder in the World Political Economy.* Princeton, N.J.: Princeton University Press, 1984.

—— and Joseph S. Nye Jr. *Power and Interdependence.* Boston, MA.: Little, Bron, 1977.

—— and Stanley Hoffmann, eds. *The European Community: Decision-making and Institutional Change.* Boulder, CO.: Westview, 1991.

Khrushchev, Nikita. *Khrushchev Remembers.* Boston, MA.: Little, Brown, 1970.

Kim, C. I. Eugene, and Hankyo Kim. *Korea and the Politics of Imperialism, 1876-1910.* Berkeley, CA.: University of California Press, 1967.

Kim, Key-hiuk. *The Last Phase of the East Asian World Order: Korea, Japan, and the Chinese Empire, 1860-1882.* Berkeley, CA.: University of California Press, 1980.

Kim, Samuel."Mainland China and a New World Order." *Issues and Studies,* vol. 27, no. 11 (November 1991).

Kindleberger, Charles. "Hierarchy Versus Inertial Cooperation." *International Organization,* vol. 40, no. 4 (Autumn 1986).

—— "Systems of International Economic Organization." In David Calleo, ed., *Money and the Coming World Order.* New York: New York University Press, 1974.

Kissinger, Henry. *Years of Upheaval.* Boston, MA.: Little, Brown, 1982.

—— *White House Years.* Boston, MA.: Little, Brown and Company, 1979.

—— *American Foreign Policy: Three Essays.* New York: W.W. Norton, 1969.

—— *Nuclear Weapons and Foreign Policy.* New York: Harper, 1957.

Klein, Donald W. "China and the Second World." In Samuel Kim, ed., *China and the World: New Directions in Chinese Foreign Policy.* Boulder, CO.: Westview Press, 1989.

Koo, Hagen. "The Interplay of State, Social Class, and World System in East Asian Development: the Cases of South Korea and Taiwan." In Frederic C. Deyo, ed., *The Political Economy of the New Asian Industrialism.* Ithaca, N.Y.: Cornell University Press, 1987.

Kristof, Nicolas D. "The Real Chinese Threat." *The New York Times Magazine.* August 27, 1995, pp. 50-1.

Kun-huei, Huang. *Bridging the Taiwan Straits: The Republic of China's Mainland Policy.* Taipei: The Mainland Affairs Council, April 1993.

Kurth, James. "East Asia Plus Mitteleuropa: The Return of History and Redefinition of Security." In Miles Kahler, ed., *Beyond the Cold War in the Pacific.* San Diego, CA.: Institute on Global Conflict and Cooperation, University of California, 1991.

Lardy, Nicholas R. *China in the World Economy.* Washington, D.C.: Institute for International Economics, 1994.

Lee, Manwoo and Richard W. Mansbach. *The Changing Order in Northeast Asia and the Korean Peninsula.* Boulder, CO.: Westview Press, 1993.

Lee, Bradford A. *Britain and the Sino-Japanese War, 1937-1939.* Stanford, CA.: Stanford University Press, 1973.

Lee, Chae-jin and Hideo Sato. *U.S. Policy Toward Japan and Korea, A Changing Influence Relationship.* New York: Praeger, 1982.

Legge, James, trans. *The Chinese Classics,* vol. 5. *The Ch'un Ts'ew with the Tso Chuen.* London: Henry Frowde, 1872, reprinted by Hong Kong University Press, 1961.

Legvold, Robert. "Sino-Soviet Relations: The American Factor." In Robert S. Ross, ed., *China, the United States, and the Soviet Union: Tripolarity and Policy Making in the Cold War World.* Armonk, N.Y.: M. E. Sharpe, 1993.

Leifer, Michael. *ASEAN and the Security of South-East Asia.* London: Routledge, 1989.

Levine, Steven I. "China in Asia: The PRC as a Regional Power." In Harry Harding, ed., *China's Foreign Relations in the 1980s.* New Haven, CT.: Yale University Press, 1984.

Lewis, John W. and Xue Litai. *China Builds the Bomb.* Stanford, CA.: Stanford University Press, 1988.

Li, Jian. *Tiaoyutai Guoshi Fengyun* (The Winds and Clouds of Diplomatic Events in Tiaoyutai), 3 vols. Taiyuan, China: Taibai Wenyi Chuban She, 1995.

Li, Peng. "Guangyu Zhiding Guomin Jingji he Shehui Fazhan jiuwu jihua he 2010 nian yuanjing mubiao jianyi de shuoming" (The Elaboration on Suggestions for the Ninth Five-Year National Economic and Social Development Plan and Long-term Goals). *Remin Ribao,* October 6, 1995, p. 1.

Li, Zhisui. *The Private Life of Chairman Mao.* New York: Random House, 1994.

Lieberthal, Kenneth. "Domestic Politics and Foreign Policy." In Harry Harding, *China's Foreign Relations in the 1980s.* New Haven, CT.: Yale University Press, 1982.

Lin, Chongpin. "The Stealthy Advance of China's People's Liberation Army." *The American Enterprise,* vol. 5, no. 1 (January/February 1994).

——— *China's Nuclear Weapons Strategy: Tradition within Evolution.* Lexington, MA.: Lexington Books, 1988.

Little, Ian. "An Economic Reconnaissance." In Walter Galenson, ed., *Economic Growth and Structural Change in Taiwan.* Ithaca, N.Y.: Cornell University Press, 1979.

Litwak, Robert. *Détente and the Nixon Doctrine: American Foreign Policy and the Pursuit of Stability, 1969-1976.* New York: Cambridge University Press, 1984.

Liu, Xiao. *Chushi Sulian Banian* (Eight Years as Ambassador to the Soviet Union). Beijing, Zhonggong Dangshi Ziliao Chuban She, 1986.

Lolland, Harrison M. *Japan Challenges America: Managing an Alliance in Crisis.* Boulder, CO.: Westview, 1992.

Lomperis, Timothy J. *The War Everyone Lost—and Won: America's Intervention in Viet Nam's Twin Struggles.* Washington, D.C.: CQ Press, 1992.

Lord, Winston. "Building a Pacific Community: Statement before the Commonwealth Club, San Francisco, California, January 12, 1995." *U.S. Department of State Dispatch,* vol. 6, no. 3 (January 16, 1995).

Low, Alfred D. *The Sino-Soviet Confrontation Since Mao Zedong: Dispute, Deténte, or Conflict?* New York: Columbia University Press, 1987.

Lowe, Peter. *The Origins of the Korean War.* London: Longman, 1986.

—— *Great Britain and the Origins of the Pacific War.* Oxford: Clarendon Press, 1977.

Lu, Weizhao. "Tianzhong Fanghua yu Zhongri Bangjiao Zhengchanghua" (The Visit to China by Tanaka and Normalization of the Sino-Japanese Relations). In Waijiaobu Waijiaoshi Yanjiushi (Diplomatic History Research Office, the Ministry of Foreign Affairs), *Xinzhongguo Waijiao Fengyun* (Diplomatic Winds and Clouds of New China). Beijing: Shijie Zhishi Chuban She, 1994.

Lu, Zongwei. "Northeast Asian Economic Cooperation in the Post–Cold War Era." *Institute on Global Conflict and Cooperation Policy Paper, #6.* San Diego, CA.: IGCC, University of California, San Diego, October 1993.

McCord, William. *The Dawn of the Pacific Century: Implications of the Three Worlds of Development.* New Brunswick, N.J.: Transaction Publishers, 1993.

McKenzie, Frederick A. *Tragedy of Korea.* London: Holder and Stougton, 1908.

Mack, Andrew. "Key Security Issues in the Asia-Pacific." In Richard Leaver and James L. Richardson, eds., *The Post–Cold War Order: Diagnoses and Prognoses.* Canberra, Australia: Allen & Unwin, 1993.

—— and John Ravenhill, eds. *Pacific Cooperation, Building Economic and Security Regimes in Asia-Pacific Region.* Boulder, CO.: Westview Press, 1995.

Mackerras, Colin. *Eastern Asia: An Introductory History.* Sydney, Australia: Longman Cheshire, 1992.

Macintyre, Donald. *Sea Power in the Pacific.* New York: Crane & Russak, 1972.

MacNair, Harley Farnsworth. *The Real Conflict Between China and Japan, An Analysis of Opposing Ideologies.* Chicago, Il.: The University of Chicago Press, 1938.

—— and Donald F. Lach. *Modern Far Eastern International Relations.* New York: D. Van Norstrand, 1955.

Mahbubani, Kishore. "The Pacific War." *Foreign Affairs,* vol. 74, no. 1 (January/February 1995), pp. 100-11.

Mainland Affairs Department of the KMT Central Committee. *Guojia Tonyi Ganglin Ershi Wen* (Twenty Questions and Answers for the Guidelines for

National Unification), Taipei: Mainland Affairs Department of the KMT Central Committee, 1991.

Malcolm, Howard. *Travels in South-eastern Asia, Embracing Hindustan, Malaya, Siam, and China.* Boston, MA.: Gould, Kendall, and Lincoln, 1839.

Mancall, Mark. "The Persistence of Tradition in Chinese Foreign Policy." *The Annals of American Academy of Political and Social Science,* vol. 349 (September 1963), reprinted in King C. Chen, ed., *The Foreign Policy of China.* South Orange, N.J.: Seton Hall University Press, 1972.

—— "The Ch'ing Tribute System: An Interpretive Essay." In John K. Fairbank, ed., *The Chinese World Order.* Cambridge, MA.: Harvard University Press, 1968.

Mandelbaum, Michael, ed. *The Strategic Quadrangle.* New York: Council on Foreign Relations Press, 1995.

Manning, Robert A. and Paula Stern. "The Myth of the Pacific Community." *Foreign Affairs,* vol. 73, no. 6 (November/December 1994), pp. 79-93.

Manscbach, Richard W. "The New Order in Northeast Asia: A Theoretical Overview." In Manwoo Lee and Richard W. Mansbach, *The Changing Order in Northeast Asia and the Korean Peninsula.* Boulder, CO.: Westview, 1993.

—— and John Vasques. *In Search of Theory: A New Paradigm for Global Politics.* New York: Columbia University Press, 1981

Mao, Zedong. "On the People's Democratic Dictatorship." *Selected Works of Mao Tse-tung,* vol. IV. Beijing: Foreign Language Press, 1969.

Marton, Andrew, Terry McGee, and Donald G. Paterson. "Northeast Asian Economic Cooperation and the Tumen River Area Development Project." *Pacific Affairs,* vol. 68, no. 1 (Spring 1995), pp. 8-33.

Masahide, Shibusawa. *Japan and the Asian Pacific Region.* New York: St. Martin's Press, 1984.

Maxwell, Neville. "Why the Russians Lifted the Blockade at Bear Island." *Foreign Affairs,* vol. 57, no. 1 (Fall 1978).

Mearsheimer, John. "Back to the Future: Instability in Europe after the Cold War." *International Security,* vol. 15, no. 1. (Summer 1990), pp. 5-56.

Meisner, Maurise. *Mao's China: A History of the People's Republic.* New York: The Free Press, 1977.

Michael, Franz H., and Chung-li Chang. *The Taiping Rebellion: History and Documents,* 3 vols. Seattle, WA.: University of Washington Press, 1966-1971.

Middleton, Drew. *The Duel of the Giants: China and Russia in Asia.* New York: Charles Scribner's Sons, 1978.

Milner, Helen. "The Assumption of Anarchy in International Relations Theory: A Critique." In David A. Baldwin, ed., *Neorealism and Neoliberalism: The Contemporary Debate.* New York: Columbia University Press, 1993.

Ministry of Foreign Affairs, ed. *Xinzhongguo Waijiao Fengyun* (New China Diplomatic Events). Beijing: Shijiezheshi Chuban She, 1990.

Mochizuki, Mike M. *Japan: Domestic Change and Foreign Policy.* Santa Monica, CA.: National Defense Research Institute, 1995.

—— "Japan and the Strategic Quadrangle." In Michael Mandelbaum, ed., *The Strategic Quadrangle: Russia, China, Japan, and the United States in East Asia*. New York: Council on Foreign Relations, 1995.

Moody, Peter, Jr. *Tradition and Modernization in China and Japan*. Belmont, CA.: Wadsworth Publishing Company, 1995.

Moore, Barrington, Jr. *Social Origins of Dictatorship and Democracy*. Boston, CA.: Beacon Press, 1966.

Morgenthau, Hans J. *Politics Among Nations: The Struggle for Power and Peace*. New York: McGraw-Hill Inc., 1948.

Morishima, Michio. *Why Has Japan "Succeeded"?: Western Technology and the Japanese Ethos*. Cambridge, U.K.: Cambridge University Press, 1982.

Morison, Samuel Eliot. *"Old Bruin": Commodore Matthew Calbraith Perry*. Boston, MA.: Little, Brown, and Co., 1967.

Morley, James W. "The Structure of Regional Security." In James W. Morley, ed., *Security Interdependence in the Asia Pacific Region*. Lexington, MA.: D. C. Heath and Company, 1986.

—— ed. *Japan Erupts: the London Naval Conference and the Manchurian Incident, 1928-1932*. New York : Columbia University Press, 1984.

—— ed. *The Fateful Choice : Japan's Advance into Southeast Asia, 1939-1941*. New York: Columbia University Press, 1980.

Morray, J. Joseph P. *From Yalta to Disarmament: Cold War Debate*. New York: Monthly Review Press, 1961.

Morse, Edward. *Modernization and the Transformation of International Relations*. New York: Free Press, 1976.

Morse, H. B. *The Chronicles of the East India Company Trading to China*, 5 vols. Oxford, England: Oxford University Press, 1926-1929.

Morton, Louis. "Japan's Decision for War (1941)." In Arnold A. Offner, *America and the Origins of World War II, 1933-1941*. Boston, MA.: Houghton Mifflin Co., 1971.

Myers, R. H., and M. R. Peattie, eds. *The Japanese Colonial Empire, 1895-1945*. Princeton, N.J.: Princeton University Press, 1984.

Naishbitt, John. *Megatrends Asia: Eight Asian Megatrends That Are Reshaping Our World*. New York: Simon & Schuster, 1996.

Nanjing Datusha Tuzheng (An Illustrated Account of the Nanjing Massacre). Changchun: Jilin Renmin Chuban She, 1995.

Nathan, Andrew. *China's Crisis*. New York: Columbia University Press, 1990.

National Security Council (NSC) 48/5. "A Report to the National Security Council by the Executive Secretary on United States Policies and Courses of Action in Asia." Washington, DC.: National Archives, May 17, 1951.

Nectoux, Francois and Yoichi Kuroda. *Timber from the South Seas: An Analysis of Japan's Tropical Timber Trade and Its Environmental Impact*. Gland, Switzerland: World Wildlife Fund, 1989.

Nelson, M. Frederick. *Korea and the Old Orders in Eastern Asia*. Baton Rouge, LA.: Louisiana State University Press, 1945.

Nelson, Brian, David Roberts, and Walter Veit, eds. *The European Community in the 1990s: Economics, Politics, Defense.* New York: Berg, 1992.

Neier, Aryeh. "Watching Rights." *The Nation,* vol. 257, no. 10 (October 4, 1993).

Neumann, William Louis. *America Encounters Japan: From Perry to MacArthur.* Baltimore, MA.: Johns Hopkins Press, 1963.

Nish, Ian H. *The Origins of the Russo-Japanese War.* London: Longman, 1985.

—— *Japanese Foreign Policy, 1869-1942.* London: Routledge & Kegan Paul, 1977.

—— *The Anglo-Japanese Alliance: The Diplomacy of Two Island Empire, 1894-1907.* London: Athlone P., 1966.

Nishihara, Massashi. *The Japanese and Sukarno's Indonesia: Tokyo-Jarkada Relations, 1951-1966.* Honolulu, HI.: The University of Hawaii Press, 1976.

Nixon, Richard. *No More Vietnams.* New York: Arbor House, 1985.

—— *Memoirs of Richard Nixon,* vol. 1. New York: Warner Books, 1978.

—— *U.S. Foreign Policy for the 1970s—Building for Peace.* A report to the Congress, February 25, 1971. Washington, D.C.: Government Printing Office, 1971.

Norman, E. Herbert. *Japan's Emergence as a Modern State: Political and Economic Problems of the Meiji Period.* Westport, CT.: Greenwood Press, 1973.

Nye, Joseph S., Jr. *Understanding International Conflicts.* New York: Harper Collins College Publishers, 1993.

—— "The Misleading Metaphor of Decline." In Charles W. Kegley, Jr., and Eugene Wittkopf, eds., *The Global Agenda.* New York: McGraw-Hill, 1992.

—— *Bound to Lead: The Changing Nature of American Power.* New York: Basic Books, 1990.

Oberdorfer, Don. *Tet: The Turning Point in the Vietnam War.* New York: A Da Capo Paperback, 1984.

Office of International Security Affairs, Department of Defense. *United States Security Strategy for the East Asia-Pacific Region.* Washington, D.C.: USDP/ISA/AP, 1995.

Ogata, Sadako. "The Changing Role of Japan in the United Nations." *Journal of International Affairs,* vol. 37, no. 1 (Summer 1993).

Oh, Bonnie B. "Sino-Japanese Rivalry in Korea, 1876-1885." In Akira Iriye, ed., *The Chinese and the Japanese: Essays in Political and Cultural Interactions.* Princeton, N.J.: Princeton University Press, 1980.

Okamoto, Shumpei. "Ishibashi Tanzan and the Twenty-One Demands." In Akira Iriye, ed., *The Chinese and the Japanese: Essays in Political and Cultural Interactions.* Princeton, N.J.: Princeton University Press, 1980.

Olson, Mancur. *Logic of Collective Action: Public Goods and The Theory of Groups.* Cambridge, MA.: Harvard University Press, 1965.

Oksenberg, Michael. "A Decade of Sino-American Relations." *Foreign Policy,* vol. 61, no. 1 (Fall 1982).

—— "China Policy for the 1980s." *Foreign Policy,* vol. 59, no. 2 (Winter 1980-81).

Panayotou, Theodore. "The Environment in Southeast Asia: Problems and Policies." *Environmental Science and Technology,* vol. 27, no. 12 (1993).

Paribatra, M. R. Sukhumbhand. "ASEAN and the Kampuchean Conflict: A Study of a Regional Organization's Responses to External Security Challenges." In

Robert A. Scalapino and Masataka Kosaka, eds., *Peace, Politics & Economics in Asia: The Challenge to Cooperate*. Washington, D.C.: Pergamon-Brassey's International Defense Publishers, 1988.

Peattie, Mark R. "Japanese Attitudes Towards Colonialism." In Ramon Myers and Mark Peattie, eds., *The Japanese Colonial Empire, 1895-1945*. Princeton, N.J.: Princeton University Press, 1984.

—— *Ishiwara Kanji and Japan's Confrontation with the West*. Princeton, N.J.: Princeton University Press, 1975.

Petri, Peter A. "Trading with the Dynamos: East Asian Interdependence and American Interests. *Current History* (December 1994).

Pollack, Jonathan D. "China and the Global Strategic Balance." In Harry Harding, ed., *China's Foreign Relations in the 1980s*. New Haven, CT.: Yale University Press, 1982.

Porter, Gareth. "The Environmental Hazards of Asia Pacific Development: The Southeast Asian Rainforests." *Current History*, December 1994.

Porter, Gareth, and Janet Welsh Brown. *Global Environmental Politics*. Boulder, CO.: Westview Press, 1991.

Prager, Karsten. "Waking Up the Next Superpower." *Times*, March 25, 1996, p. 36-38.

Pratt, J. T. *The European Expansion into the Far East*. London: Macmillan, 1948.

Preeg, Ernest H. "The US Leadership Role in the World Trade: Past, Present, and Future." *The Washington Quarterly*, vol. 15, no. 2 (Spring 1992).

Pye, Lucian W. *Asian Power and Politics: The Cultural Dimensions of Authority*. Cambridge, MA.: Harvard University Press, 1985.

Pyle, Kenneth B. *The Japanese Question: Power and Purpose in a New Era*. Washington, D.C.: The American Enterprise Institute, 1992.

Rabb, Theodore K., ed. *The Thirty Years' War*. New York: University Press of America, 1981.

Reed, James. *The Missionary Mind and American East Asia Policy, 1911-1915*. Cambridge, MA.: Council on East Asian Studies, Harvard University, Distributed by Harvard University Press, 1983.

Reed, Stanley. "Greater China' Could be the Biggest Tiger of All." *Business Week*, September 28, 1992.

Reischauer, Edwin O. *The United States and Japan*. New York: Viking Press, 1957.

Renner, Michael. *National Security: The Economic and Environmental Dimensions*. Worldwatch Paper No. 89. Washington, D.C.: Worldwatch Institute, 1989.

Renzi, William A., and Mark D. Roehrs. *Never Look Back: A History of World War II in the Pacific*. Armonk, NY: M. E. Sharpe, 1991.

Richardson, Bradley M., and Scott C. Flanagan. *Politics in Japan*. Boston, MA.: Little, Brown and Company, 1984.

Richardson, Richael. "US and ASEAN Tiptoe Round China on Spratlys." *Asia-Pacific Defense Reporter*, (May–June 1995).

Richelson, Jeffrey T. *Foreign Intelligence Organizations*. Cambridge, MA.: Ballinger, 1988.

Rise, C.D., Sheldon. *The Rise of the Merchant Class in Tokugawa Japan.* Locust Valley, N.Y.: Augustin, 1958.

Robinson, Thomas. "The Sino-Soviet Dispute." *The American Political Science Review,* vol. xvi, no. 4 (December 1972).

Romm, Joseph J. *Defining National Security: The Nonmilitary Aspects.* New York: Council on Foreign Relations Press, 1993.

Romulo, Roberto R. "We Must Try Harder." *Far Eastern Economic Review,* vol. 156, no. 32 (August 12, 1993).

Rosecrance, Richard. *The Rise of the Trading State: Commerce and Conquest in the Modern World.* New York: Basic Books, 1986.

Rosenau, James. *Turbulence in World Politics.* Princeton, N.J.: Princeton University Press, 1990.

—— *The Study of Global Interdependence.* London: F. Pinter, 1980

—— "National Interest." *International Encyclopedia of the Social Sciences,* vol. 11, 1968.

Ross, Andrew L. "The International Arms Trade, Arms Imports, and Local Defense Production in ASEAN." In Chandran Jeshurun, ed., *Arms and Defense in Southeast Asia.* Singapore: Institute of Southeast Asian Studies, 1989.

Ross, Robert S. "Conclusion: Tripolarity and Policy Making." In Robert S. Ross, ed., *China, the United States, and the Soviet Union: Tripolarity and Policy Making in the Cold War World.* Armonk, N.Y.: M. E. Sharpe, 1993.

Rotter, Andrew. *The Path to Vietnam: Origins of the American Commitment to Southeast Asia.* Ithaca, N.Y.: Cornell University Press, 1987.

Sagan, Scott. "The Origins of the Pacific War." In Robert Rotberg and Theodore Rabb, eds., *The Origin and Prevention of Major Wars.* New York: Cambridge University Press, 1989.

Sakamoto, Yoshikazu, ed. *Asia: Militarization and Regional Conflict.* Tokyo: The United Nations University, 1988.

Sansom, George. *The Western World and Japan: A Study in the Interaction of European and Asiatic Cultures.* New York: Knopf, 1950.

Sbrega, John. *Anglo-American Relations and Colonialism in East Asia, 1941-45.* New York: Garland, 1983.

Scalapino, Robert A. "The United States and Asia: Future Prospects." *Foreign Affairs,* vol. 70, no. 5 (Winter 1991/92).

—— "Relations Between the Nations of the Pacific Quadrille: Stability and Fluctuation in East Asian Politics." In Herbert J. Ellison, ed., *Japan and the Pacific Quadrille: The Major Powers in East Asia.* Boulder, CO.: Westview Press, 1987.

—— *Major Power Relations in Northeast Asia.* Lanham, MD.: University Press of America, 1987.

Schelling, Thomas C. *The Strategy of Conflict.* Cambridge, MA.: Harvard University Press, 1960.

Schlesinger, Arthur, M., Jr. "Détente: An American Perspective." In George Schwab and Henry Friendlander, eds., *Détente in Historical Perspective.* New York: Cyrco Press, 1975.

—— *The Bitter Heritage: Vietnam and American Democracy, 1941-1966.* Greenwich, CT.: Fawcett, 1967.

Schoenber, Karl. "Japan to Put Brakes on Military Buildup." *Los Angeles Times,* December 21, 1990.

Scholler, Michael. *The United States and China in the Twentieth Century.* New York: Oxford University Press, 1979.

Schurmann, Franz. *The Logic of World Power: An Inquiry into the Origins, Currents, and Contradictions of World Politics.* New York: Pantheon Books, 1974.

Schwarz, Adam. "Looking Back at Rio." *Far Eastern Economic Review,* vol. 156, no. 43 (October 28, 1993), pp. 48-58.

Schwartz, Benjamin I. "The Chinese Perception of World Order, Past and Present." In John K. Fairbank, ed., *The Chinese World Order.* Cambridge, MA.: Harvard University Press, 1968.

Scott, Andrew M. *The Dynamics of Interdependence.* Chapel Hill, NC.: University of North Carolina Press, 1982

Scott, Margaret. "The Disappearing Forests." *Far Eastern Economic Review,* vol. 143, no. 2 (January 12, 1989), pp. 34-8.

Sebald, William Joseph. *With MacArthur in Japan: A Personal History of the Occupation.* New York: W.W. Norton, 1965.

Segal, Gerald. "Muddle Kingdom? China's Changing Shape." *Foreign Affairs,* vol. 73, no. 3 (May/June 1994).

—— "China and the Disintegration of the Soviet Union." *Asian Survey,* vol. 32, no. 9 (September 1992), pp. 848-68.

—— *Rethinking the Pacific.* New York: Oxford University Press, 1990.

Seymour, James D. "Human Rights in Chinese Foreign Relations." In Samuel S. Kim, ed., *China and the World: Chinese Foreign Relations in the Post–Cold War Era.* Boulder, CO.: Westview Press, 1994.

Shambaugh, David. "Pacific Security in the Pacific Century." *Current History,* vol. 93, no. 587 (December 1994), pp. 423-429.

Sheng Lijun. "Beijing and the Spratlys." *Issues and Studies,* vol. 31, no. 7 (July 1995), pp. 18-45.

Sheridan, James E. *China in Disintegration, The Republican Era in Chinese History, 1912-1949.* New York: The Free Press, 1975.

Shi, Zhe, Shi, Ze. *Zai lishi juren shenbian* (Working with the Historical Giant). Beijing: Lishi Wenxian Chuban She, 1991.

—— "Gensui Mao Zhuxi Fangwen Sulian" (With Chairman Mao on a Visit to the Soviet Union). *Renwu,* May 1988.

Shintaro, Ishihara. *The Japan that Can Say No.* New York: Simon & Schuster, 1989.

Sikes, Jonathan. "Asia Puts Its Wealth in Military." *Washington Times,* February 12, 1990.

Simmonds, Kenneth R. *U.N. Convention on the Law of the Sea, 1982.* Dobbs Ferry, N.Y.: Oceana Publications, 1983.

Simon, Sheldon W. "Regional Security Structures in Asia: The Question of Relevance." In Sheldon W. Simon, ed., *East Asian Security in the Post–Cold War Era.* Armonk, N.Y.: M. E. Sharpe, 1993.

—— *The Future of Asian-Pacific Security Collaboration.* Lexington, MA.: D. C. Heath and Company, 1988.

Skocpol, Theda. *States & Social Revolutions: A Comparative Analysis of France, Russia, and China.* Cambridge, England: Cambridge University Press, 1979.

Sladkovsky, M. I. *China and Japan, Past and Present.* Gulf Breeze, FL.: Academic International Press, 1975.

Smith, Peter. "The Politics of Integration, Guidelines for Policy.' In Peter Smith, ed., *The Challenge of Integration: Europe and the Americas.* New Brunswick, N.J.: Transaction Publishers, 1993.

Smythe, Lewis Strong Casey. *War Damage in the Nanking Area, December 1937 to March 1938.* Shanghai, China: Mercury Press, 1938.

Snell, John L. *The Meaning of Yalta: Big Three Diplomacy and the New Balance of Power.* Baton Rouge, LA.: Louisiana State University Press, 1956.

Snidal, Duncan. "Limits of Hegemonic Stability Theory." *International Organization,* vol.39, no. 4 (Autumn 1985).

Snow, Edgar. *Red Star Over China.* New York: Random House, 1968.

So, Alvin Y., and Stephen W. K. Chiu. *East Asia and the World Economy.* Thousand Oaks, CA.: Sage Publications, 1995.

Soesasto, Hadi. "Implications of the Post–Cold War Politico-Security Environment for the Political Economy." In C. Fred Bergsten and Marus Noland, eds., *Pacific Dynamism and the International Economic System.* Washington, D.C.: Institute for International Economics, 1993.

Solomon, Richard H. "Who Will Shape the Emerging Structure of East Asia?" In Michael Mandelbaum, ed., *The Strategic Quadrangle: Russia, China, Japan and the United States in East Asia.* New York: Council on Foreign Relations Press, 1995.

—— "The China Factor in America's Foreign Relations." In Richard H. Solomon, ed., *The China Factor: Sino-American Relations & The Global Scene.* Englewood Cliffs, N.J.: Prentice-Hall, Inc., 1981.

Spanier, John. *American Foreign Policy Since World War II.* New York: Holt, Rinehart and Winston, 1977.

Spector, Ronald H. *After Tet: The Bloodiest Year in Vietnam.* New York: The Free Press, 1993.

Stanley Foundation. *Human Rights and U.S. Foreign Policy: Who Controls the Agenda.* Muscatine, IA.: The Stanley Foundation, 1994.

Stevenson, Richard W. *The Rise and Fall of Détente: Relaxation of Tension in US-Soviet Relations, 1953-1984.* Champaign, IL.: University of Illinois Press, 1985.

Stoessinger, John G. *Nations at Dawn: China, Russia, and America.* New York: McGraw-Hill Inc., 1994.

—— *Why Nations Go To War.* New York: St. Martin's Press, 1985.

Stolper, Thomas. E. *China, Taiwan, and the Offshore Islands.* Armonk, N.Y.: M. E. Sharpe, 1985.

Stettinius, Edward R. *Roosevelt and the Russians: the Yalta Conference.* Garden City, N.Y.: Doubleday, 1949.

Study Group on the Economy of Vietnam. *Toward a Market Economy in Vietnam: Economic Reforms and Development Strategies for the 21st Century.* Rockville, MD.: Pacific Basin Research Institute, 1993.

Su, Chi. "Sino-Soviet Relations of the 1980s: From Confrontation to Conciliation." In Samuel Kim, ed., *China and the World: New Directions in Chinese Foreign Relations.* Boulder, CO.: Westview Press, 1989.

Sullivan, Michael P. *The Vietnam War: A Study in the Making of American Policy.* Lexington, KY.: The University Press of Kentucky, 1985.

Sun, Zi. *Art of War.* Translated into English by S. G. Griffith. New York: Oxford University Press, 1963.

Sutter, Robert G. *East Asia and the Pacific, Challenge for US Policy.* Boulder, CO.: Westview Press, 1992.

Swaine, Michael D. *China: Domestic Change and Foreign Policy.* Santa Monica, CA.: National Defense Research Institute, 1995.

Tang, Xiuzhe. "Gorbachev Answers Our Correspondent." *Liaowang* (Overseas Edition), January 11, 1988.

Tarling, Nicholas. *The Fall of Imperial Britain in South-East Asia.* Singapore: Oxford University Press, 1993.

Thomas, Raju G. C. "Introduction." In Thomas, ed., *The Great-Power Triangle and Asian Security.* Lexington, MA.: D. C. Heath, 1983.

Tianbolie (Harold John Timperley). *Wairen Muduzhong Zhi Rijun Baoxing* (A Foreigner's Eyewitness Account of the Atrocities Committed by the Japanese Army). Hankou, China: Guomin Chuban She, 1938. A new edition was published by Jiangxi Renmin Chuban She, 1986.

Timperley, Harold John. *What War Means: The Japanese Terror in China: A Documentary Record.* London: Victor Gollancz Ltd., 1938.

—— *Japanese Terror in China.* New York: Modern Age Books, 1938.

Tow, William T. *Sino-Japanese-US Military Technology Relations.* Malaysia: Institute of Strategic and International Studies, 1988.

Truman, Harry S. *Years of Trial and Hope,* Vol. 2. New York: The New American Library, 1965.

Tsou, Tang. *America's Failure in China, 1941-50.* Chicago, IL.: The University of Chicago Press, 1963.

Tucker, Nancy Bernkopf. "China and America: 1941-1991." *Foreign Affairs,* (Winter 1991/1992), pp. 75-92.

Turner, Kathleen J. *Lyndon Johnson's Dual War.* Chicago, IL.: The University of Chicago Press, 1985.

Ullman, Richard H. *Securing Europe.* Princeton, N.J.: Princeton University Press, 1991.

United States Senate Committees on Armed Services and Foreign Relations. *Military Situation in the Far East.* Washington, D.C.: U.S. Government Printing Office, 1951.

United States Department of Defense. *A Strategic Framework for the Asian Pacific Rim: Report to Congress.* Washington, D,C.: U.S. Government Printing Office, 1992.

United States State Department.*The Conferences at Malta and Yalta, 1945.* Washington, D.C.: Government Printing Office, 1955.

—— *United States Relations With China.* Washington, D.C.: U.S. Government Printing Office, 1949.

—— *Papers Relating to the Foreign Relations of the United States, Japan: 1931-1941,* vol. 2. Washington, DC: U.S. Government Printing Office, 1945.

—— *Foreign Relations of the United States, 1917.* Washington, D.C.: U.S. Government Printing Office, 1926.

—— *Foreign Relations of the United States, 1900.* Washington, D.C.: U.S. Government Printing Office, 1902.

—— *Foreign Relations of the United States, 1899.* Washington, D.C.: U.S. Government Printing Office, 1901.

United States General Accounting Office. *Report to Congressional Committee: Impact of China's Military Modernization in the Pacific Region.* Washington, D.C.: GAO/NSIAD-95-84, June 6, 1995.

van der Vat, Den. *The Pacific Campaign: World War II: The US-Japanese Naval War, 1941-1945.* New York: Simon & Schuster, 1991.

Vasquez, John A. *The Power of Power Politics: A Critique.* New Brunswick, N.J.: Rutgers University Press, 1983.

Vatikiotis, Michael. "Trade and Rights." *Far Eastern Economic Review,* vol. 154, no. 47 (November 21, 1991).

Viraphol, Srasin. *Tribute and Profit: Sino-Siamese Trade, 1652-1853.* Cambridge, MA.: Harvard University Press, 1977.

Vo, Nguyen Giap. *Dien Bien Phu.* Hanoi: Foreign Languages Pub. House, 1964.

Waijiaobu Yuanjiushi (Research Office of Chinese Ministry of Foreign Affairs). *Zhongmei Guanxi Wenjian Huibian* (Collected Documents on Sino-US Relations). Beijing: Shejie Zhishi Chuban She, 1960.

Wakabayashi, Bob Tadashi. *Anti-Foreignism and Western Learning in Early Modern Japan: The New Theses of 1825.* Cambridge, MA.: Council on East Asian Studies, Harvard University and Harvard University Press, 1986.

Waley, Arthur. *The Opium War Through Chinese Eyes.* New York: Macmillan Company, 1958.

Waltz, Kenneth. *Theory of International Politics.* Reading, MA.: Addison-Wesley, 1979.

—— "The Myth of Interdependence." In Charles P. Kindleberger, ed., *The International Corporation.* Cambridge, MA.: The MIT Press, 1970.

Wang, James C. F. *Contemporary Chinese Politics.* Englewood Cliffs, N.J.: Prentice-Hall, 1985.

Ward, Barbara and Rene Dubos. *Only One Earth: The Care and Maintenance of a Small Planet.* New York: W. W. Norton & Company, 1972.

Watanable, Masao. *The Japanese and Western Science.* Translated by Otto Theodor Benfey. Philadelphia, PA.: University of Pennsylvania Press, 1990.

Wedgwood, C. V. *The Thirty Years War.* London: J. Cape, 1938.

Weatherbee, Donald E. "ASEAN and Evolving Patterns of Regionalism in Southeast Asia." *Asian Journal of Political Science,* vol. 1. no. 1 (June 1993), pp. 29-54.

Wei, Shiyan. "Ji Xingge Dierchi Fanghua" (The Second Visit to China by Kissinger). In Waijiaobu Waijiaoshi Yanjiushi (Diplomatic History Research Office, the Ministry of Foreign Affairs), *Xinzhouguo Waijiao Fengyun* (Diplomatic Winds and Clouds of New China). Beijing: Shijie Zhishi Chuban She, 1994.

Weinstein, Martin E. *Japan's Postwar Defense Policy, 1947-1968.* New York: Columbia University Press, 1971.

Weisman, Steven R. "Japan to Share More of US Troop Cost." *New York Times,* December 21, 1990.

Welch, Claude E., Jr. "Global Change and Human Rights: Asian Perspectives in Comparative Context." In Claude E. Welch, Jr., and Virginia A. Leary, eds., *Asian Perspectives on Human Rights.* Boulder, CO.: Westview Press, 1990.

Welfield, John. *An Empire in Eclipse: Japan in the Postwar American Alliance System.* Atlantic Highlands, N.J. : Athlone Press, 1988.

Wesley-Smith, Peter. *Unequal Treaty 1898-1997: China, Great Britain and Hong Kong's New Territories.* New York: Oxford University Press, 1983.

Whalley, John. "The Urugay Round and the GATT: Whither the Global System?" In C. Fred Bergsten and Marus Noland, eds., *Pacific Dynamism and the International Economic System.* Washington, D.C.: Institute for International Economics, 1993.

Whiting, Allen S. *China Cross the Yalu: The Decision to Enter the Korean War.* Stanford, CA.: Stanford University Press, 1960.

Whiting, Allen W. *The Chinese Calculus of Deterrence, India and Indochina.* Ann Arbor, MI.: The University of Michigan Press, 1975.

Wich, Richard. *Sino-Soviet Crisis Politics: A Study of Political Change and Communication.* Cambridge, MA.: Council on East Asian Studies, Harvard University, 1980.

Wolf, John Baptist. *The Emergence of the Great Powers, 1685-1715.* New York: Harper, 1951.

Woods, Lawrence T. *Asia-Pacific Diplomacy, Non-governmental Organizations and International Relations.* Vancouver, Canada: UBC Press, 1993.

World Bank. *World Development Report, 1995.* New York: Oxford University Press, 1995.

—— *East Asia's Trade and Investment: Regional and Global Gains from Liberalization.* Washington, D.C.: The World Bank, 1994.

—— *The East Asian Miracle: Economic Growth and Public Policy.* New York: Oxford University Press, 1993.

Wu, Tien-wei. *The Sian Incident: A Pivotal Point in Modern Chinese History.* Ann Arbor, MI.: Center for Chinese Studies, University of Michigan, 1976.

Wu, Yu-Shan. "Mainland China's Economic Policy Toward Taiwan: Economic Needs or Unification Scheme?" *Issues and Studies,* vol. 30, no. 9 (September 1994), pp. 29-49.

Xiao, Gong Quan. *A Political History of Chinese Thought: From the Beginning to the Sixth Century A.D.* Translated by F. W. Mote. Princeton, N.J.: Princeton University, 1979.

Yahuda, Michael. *The International Politics of the Asia-Pacific, 1945-1995.* London: Routledge, 1996.

Yamamura, Kozo. *A Study of Samurai Income and Entrepreneurship: Quantitative Analysis of Economic and Social Aspects of the Samurai in Tokugawa and Meiji Japan.* Cambridge, MA.: Harvard University Press, 1974.

Yanagihara, Toru and Anne Emig. "An Overview of Japan's Foreign Aid." In Shafiqul Islam, ed., *Yen for Development: Japanese Foreign Aid & the Politics of Burden-Sharing.* New York: Council on Foreign Relations Press, 1991.

Yang, Lien-sheng. "Historical Notes on the Chinese World Order." In John K. Fairbank, ed., *The Chinese World Order.* Cambridge, MA.: Harvard University Press, 1968.

Yoshida, Yutaka. *Tenno No Guntai To Nankin Jiken* (The Japanese Emperor's Army and the Nanjing Incident). Tokyo: Aoki Shoten, 1985.

Yu, Ying-shih. *Trade and Expansion in Han China: A Study in the Structure of Sino-Barbarian Economic Relations.* Berkeley, CA.: University of California Press, 1967.

Yu, Zhan. "Yici Buxunchang de Shiming: Yi Zhou Zongli Zuihou Yici Fangwen Sulian (An Unusual Mission: Premier Zhou's Last Visit to the Soviet Union). Iin Waijiaobu Waijiaoshi Yanjiushi (Diplomatic Research Office of the Foreign Ministry), ed., *Xinzhongguo Waijiao Fengyun: Zhongguo Waijiaoguan Huiyilu* (Diplomatic Winds and Clouds of New China: Memoirs of the Chinese Diplomats). Beijing: Shijie Zhishi Chuban She, 1994.

Yue, Chia Siow, and Lee Tsao Yuan. "Subregional Economic Zones: A New Motive Force in Asia-Pacific Development." In C. Fred Bergsten and Marus Noland, eds., *Pacific Dynamism and the International Economic System.* Washington, D.C.: Institute for International Economics, 1993.

Yun, Sui. *Guoji Fengyun Zhong de Zhongguo Waijiaoguan* (Chinese diplomats in the International Winds and Clouds). Beijing: Shijie Zhishi Chuban She, 1992.

Zagoria, Donald S. "The Soviet Union's Eastern Problem." In Martin E. Weinstein, ed., *Northeast Asian Security after Vietnam.* Urbana, IL.: University of Illinois Press, 1982.

—— "Strange Triangle." In Clement J. Zablick, ed., *The Sino-Soviet Rivalry: Implication for United States Policy.* New York: Praeger, 1966.

—— *The Sino-Soviet Conflict, 1956-1961.* Princeton, N.J.: Princeton University Press, 1962.

Zha, Daojiong. "A Greater China: The Political Economy of Chinese National Reunification." *The Journal of Contemporary China,* no. 5 (Spring 1994), pp. 40-63.

Zhang, Shuguang. "Threat Perception and Chinese Communist Foreign Policy." In Melvyn P. Leffler and David S. Painter, eds., *Origins of the Cold War: An International History.* London: Routledge, 1994.

Zhang, Yongjin. *China in the International System, 1918-20: The Middle Kingdom at the Periphery.* New York: St. Martin's Press, 1991.

Zhao, Suisheng. "Management of Rival Relations across the Taiwan Strait: 1979-1991." *Issues & Studies,* vol. 29, no. 4 (April 1993), pp.72-94.

—— "Beijing's Perception on the International System and Foreign Policy Adjustment in the Post–Cold War World." *Journal of Northeast Asian Studies,* vol. 11, no. 3 (Fall 1992), pp.70-83.

Zhong, Shuhe. *Zouxiang Shijie* (Strive toward the world). Beijing: Zhounghua Shujiu, 1985.

Zhu, Hongqian. "China and the Triangular Relationship." In Yufan Hao and Guocang Huan, eds., *The Chinese View of the World.* New York: Pantheon Books, 1989.

Zhu, Zhongli. "Wang Jiaxiang Waijiao Shengyia Zhongyi" (Diplomatic Career of Wang Jiaxiang). In Waijiaobu Waijiaoshi Yanjiushi (Diplomatic History Research Office of Chinese Ministry of Foreign Affairs), ed., *Dangdai Zhongguo Shijie Waijiao Shengyia* (Ambassadors' Diplomatic Lives of Contemporary China). Beijing: Shijie Zhishi Chuban She, 1995.

Ziegler, Charles E. *Foreign Policy and East Asia: Learning and Adaptation in the Gorbachev Era.* Cambridge, England: Cambridge University Press, 1993.

Index

About the Author

SUISHENG ZHAO is Assistant Professor of Government and East Asian Politics at Colby College, Maine, and the founder and editor of the *Journal of Contemporary China* (published by Journals Oxford Ltd. in England). He received a Ph.D. degree in political science from the University of California, San Diego, and a Master's degree in economics from Beijing University. Before joining the Colby faculty in 1993, he was visiting assistant professor at the Graduate School of International Relations and Pacific Studies, the University of California, San Diego (1992-93). Formerly a research fellow in the Economic Research Center, State Council of China, and an assistant professor in Beijing University before coming to the United States in 1985, he is the author of *Power by Design: Constitution-Making in Nationalist China* (the University of Hawaii Press, 1996) and co-editor (with Carol Lee Hamrin) of *Decision-Making in Deng's China* (M. E. Sharpe, 1995). He has published widely on Chinese politics and foreign policy and East Asian international relations in both Chinese and English languages. His English articles have appeared in *World Affairs, Asian Survey, Journal of Northeast Asian Studies, Asian Affairs, Issues and Studies, Journal of Contemporary China,* and elsewhere.